Samuel Charters Macpherson, William Macpherson

Memorials of Service in India

Samuel Charters Macpherson, William Macpherson

Memorials of Service in India

ISBN/EAN: 9783337061548

Printed in Europe, USA, Canada, Australia, Japan

Cover: Foto ©ninafisch / pixelio.de

More available books at **www.hansebooks.com**

MEMORIALS

OF

SERVICE IN INDIA.

FROM THE CORRESPONDENCE OF THE LATE

MAJOR SAMUEL CHARTERS MACPHERSON, C.B.

POLITICAL AGENT AT GWALIOR DURING THE MUTINY, AND
FORMERLY EMPLOYED IN THE SUPPRESSION OF
HUMAN SACRIFICES IN ORISSA.

EDITED BY HIS BROTHER

WILLIAM MACPHERSON.

'Is genus ynopoile, ac disporti,u rigncibus, altis
Composuit, legasque deuit.' VIRG.

WITH PORTRAIT AND ILLUSTRATIONS.

LONDON:
JOHN MURRAY, ALBEMARLE STREET.
1865.

TO

THE REV. ALEXANDER DUFF, D.D.

LATE OF CALCUTTA,

IN REMEMBRANCE OF THE FRIENDSHIP WHICH

SUBSISTED BETWEEN HIM AND MAJOR MACPHERSON,

.

THESE PAGES ARE, BY PERMISSION,

RESPECTFULLY DEDICATED.

.

CONTENTS.

—⋯⊶⋅—

CHAPTER I.

PAGE

FIRST YEARS OF INDIAN SERVICE—JALNAH—SECUNDERABAD—THE
NILGHERRY HILLS 1

CHAPTER II.

SERVICE IN THE SURVEY DEPARTMENT—THE DECCAN—THE NIL-
GHERRY HILLS—NELLORE (1831-1386) . . . 22

CHAPTER III.

THE GOOMSUR WAR (1836) 35

CHAPTER IV.

FIRST VISIT TO THE HILLS (1837) 51

CHAPTER V.

DESCRIPTION OF THE KHONDS 60

CHAPTER VI.

THE KHOND RELIGION—HUMAN SACRIFICE AND FEMALE INFANTI-
CIDE 84

CHAPTER VII.

PAGE

RETURN TO NELLORE AND VISIT TO THE CAPE OF GOOD HOPE
(from January 1838 to January 1841) 137

CHAPTER VIII.

MEASURES FOR THE ABOLITION OF HUMAN SACRIFICE AMONG THE
KHONDS (from 1837 to 1842) 146

CHAPTER IX.

APPOINTMENT AS ASSISTANT TO THE AGENT IN GANGAM—RETURN
TO GOOMSUR (1841) 158

CHAPTER X.

SECOND VISIT TO THE HILLS (1841–42) . . . 165

CHAPTER XI.

FIRST STEPS TOWARDS THE ABOLITION OF HUMAN SACRIFICE (1842) 173

CHAPTER XII.

THIRD VISIT TO THE HILLS—OPPOSITION AND REMOVAL OF SAM
BISSYE (1842, 1843) 184

CHAPTER XIII.

FOURTH VISIT TO THE HILLS—ABOLITION OF HUMAN SACRIFICE IN
GOOMSUR (January to May 1844) 197

CHAPTER XIV.

RESULTS OF CAPTAIN MACPHERSON'S MANAGEMENT OF THE SACRI-
FICING KHONDS (1842–1844) 212

CHAPTER XV.

PAGE

MEASURES FOR THE ABOLITION OF INFANTICIDE (1842–1844) . 218

CHAPTER XVI.

MR. CADENHEAD'S MANAGEMENT OF THE KHONDS (1844–1845) . 226

CHAPTER XVII.

THE HILL AGENCY—FIFTH VISIT TO THE HILLS (November 1845
—May 1846) 241

CHAPTER XVIII.

RETURN FROM THE HILLS—RUIN OF THE INFANTICIDE WORK—
NEGOTIATIONS WITH THE BOAD RAJAH—GENERAL WORSHIP
OF THE GOD OF LIGHT—REFUSAL OF ESCORTS (April—
October 1846)   256

CHAPTER XIX.

SIXTH VISIT TO THE HILLS—DISTURBANCES—THEIR SUPPRESSION
(November 1846—March 1847)   267

CHAPTER XX.

DISMISSAL AND VINDICATION OF THE HILL AGENCY—RETURN TO
GREAT BRITAIN   277

CHAPTER XXI.

MR. CADENHEAD AND MAJOR PINKNEY   284

CHAPTER XXII.

RETURN TO INDIA—BENARES—BHOPAL—GWALIOR (1853–1857) . 292

CHAPTER XXIII.

PAGE

THE MUTINY—THE GWALIOR CONTINGENT KEPT OUT OF THE
FIELD (1857) 310

CHAPTER XXIV.

SCINDIA'S OVERTHROW AND RESTORATION—ILLNESS AND DEATH OF
MAJOR MACPHERSON 329

APPENDIX A. 353

APPENDIX B. 371

APPENDIX C. 379

APPENDIX D. 382

APPENDIX E. 384

APPENDIX F. 392

ILLUSTRATIONS.

PORTRAIT OF MAJOR S. CHARTERS MACPHERSON, C.B.   *to face title-page*

KHOND VILLAGE, WITH SACRED HILL AND MERIAH
    GROVE . . . .   *to face page* 61

KHONDS DRESSED FOR BATTLE . . . .   „   79

KONOBAGRI, NEAR COURMINGHIA, IN THE GOOMSUR
    KHOND COUNTRY . . . . . .   „   185

VIEW IN THE GOOMSUR KHOND COUNTRY . .   „   197

FORT OF GWALIOR . . . . . .   „   298

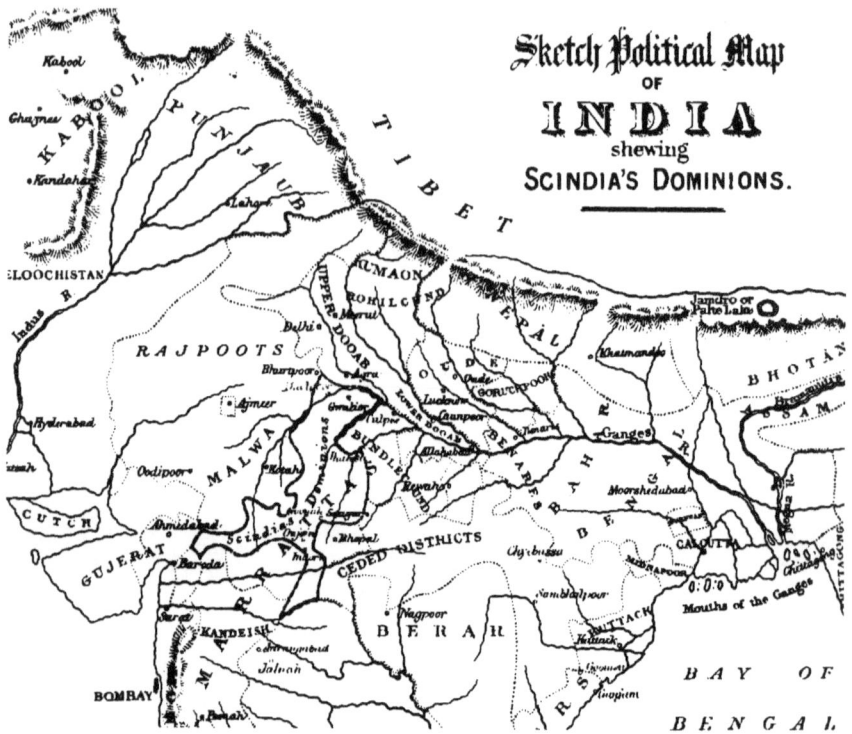

Sketch Political Map
OF
INDIA
shewing
SCINDIA'S DOMINIONS.

MEMORIALS

OF

SERVICE IN INDIA.

———o•:◉:•o———

CHAPTER I.

FIRST YEARS OF INDIAN SERVICE—JALNAH—SECUNDERABAD
—THE NILGHERRY HILLS.

THESE Memorials tell of a barbarous race won over
from dark and cruel rites; and of an important Indian
State rendered in the hour of need a mainstay of the
Empire, when its defection would have involved that of
every Native Power. They show how these objects were
attained through the benevolence, the sagacity, and the
firmness of an officer whose name is almost unknown to
the British public, but whose earnest desire was that good
men should think well of him. They may also serve
to convey to the reader some idea of the labours and
anxieties of Indian Political life.

SAMUEL CHARTERS MACPHERSON, the second son of Dr.
Hugh Macpherson, Professor of Greek in the University
of Aberdeen, and of his first wife Anne Maria Charters,
was born on the 7th January 1806, at King's College,
Old Aberdeen. In consequence of delicate health in child-
hood, the years which most boys pass at school were spent

B

by him at home under private tuition, but he eventually
grew up tall and strong. He studied at King's College,
and afterwards at the College of Edinburgh. His classical
training was carefully attended to, but his favourite studies
were botany, chemistry, and geology. His mind made
a great advance during the winter of 1822–23, when
he studied moral philosophy at Edinburgh, under the
celebrated John Wilson; whose lectures, or rather ora-
tions, reverentially listened to by day, were discussed in
the evening with his tutor, the Rev. Dr. George Tulloch,
who informs the Editor that upon these occasions he was
catechised, puzzled, cross-questioned, and debated with as
he never had the pleasure of being questioned and worked
by a pupil, before or since. Dr. Tulloch adds: 'He unconsciously showed great ability; his talents and capacity
were very far superior to those of his contemporaries;
and I count it great honour to have aided slightly in de-
veloping his reasoning powers, and his love of doing good
for its own sake without the least alloy of vanity or self.'

He spent his two next years at Trinity College, Cambridge. That place of learning has ever contained some
of England's best minds, and at the period referred to
it was perhaps more than usually rich in intellectual
ability and pleasant companionship. Macaulay's voice
had but lately ceased—that of Praed had not ceased—
to be heard at the 'Union' Debating Society; Peacock,
Whewell, and Julius Charles Hare were among the
younger tutors of Trinity College, and many gifted and
active spirits were to be found among the undergra-
duates. The intelligence and genial disposition of the
subject of these Memorials gained him many friends, and
he profited much by his residence at Cambridge. Like
many others, he learnt quite as much from the free collision
of thought which takes place among young men at college,
as from the regular studies of the place.

A near relative, with whom he now formed a close
and intimate friendship, gives the following account of

his Cambridge life : ' He had a quiet dignity of appearance which was very striking. His intellectual powers were of a high order, but he was disabled from cultivating them in the manner prescribed by the University authorities, by the increasing delicacy of his eyes, which rendered him unfit for prolonged study.   Had it not been for this, there was nothing which seemed beyond his grasp.   The result was that he formed a habit of independent and somewhat desultory reading, chiefly upon scientific and abstract subjects, which added largely to the vast mass of miscellaneous information which he possessed. He was honest, upright, and true—too honest perhaps and too plain for his interests.   His vigour of character and firmness of purpose were remarkable.   He was social and joyous, and at the college symposia he was the life and soul of the party ; yet he had entire self-control, and never carried festivity to excess.   Kind and wholly unselfish, he commanded the esteem as well as the love of a small knot of attached friends by whom he was encircled.'

At the end of two years he returned, as had always been intended, to read for the Scottish bar, at which it is usual to commence practice at an earlier age than in England.   At Edinburgh, however, he devoted himself somewhat too eagerly to his new subjects, particularly Political Economy and the Civil Law ; and his eyes, already weak, became subject to an affection which interfered seriously with his studies.   After anxious consultation with the best surgeons of the day, who gave him very little encouragement to hope that his eyes would ever be able to meet the demands of a laborious profession, he became desirous to provide himself with an occupation in which they might be less severely tasked. A cadetship in the East India Company's service was obtained for him, and he sailed in the ship ' Waterloo ' for Madras early in 1827. He had secured the luxury of a large and airy cabin on board the ' Waterloo,' but, with the genuine kindness of heart which characterised him through life, he gave it up to a young cadet, whom he nursed through a long and fatal illness, putting up with very bad quarters himself. In June he arrived at Madras. He was soon after posted to a regiment at Wallajahbad, but his destination was changed at his own request to the 8th Regiment of Native Infantry, which he joined at Jalnah.

The following extracts from letters, addressed to various members of his family, contain the early impressions of a subaltern whom Cambridge had (as he afterwards said himself) somewhat spoiled for his place at the bottom of the Madras Army List:—

'Jalnah, 25th December 1827.

' I have at length arrived at our head-quarters upon the very eve of changing their locality, and shall ever look back with pleasure on my late fine stretch nearly across the peninsula. The continuation of our route from Hyderabad was the pleasantest portion of the march. No longer cumbered with the plodding tread of our recruits, lightly and well, by extended marches, we reached Jalnah, by many spots great in old renown and now magnificent in the gradations of decay. The regions of the Northern Deccan are usually spread in immense plains, portions of which are richly cultivated, while other parts present the aspect of boundless wastes. The climate in the latter portion of the march, although in mean temperature nearly approaching to the European, was not grateful. The cold of the night and morning was extreme, while nothing was abated of midday heat. In this spot the extremes are not at present severely felt. The air is delightful, save during the meridian hours. The thermometer before sunrise from 60° to 65°, in the heat of the day from 74° to 78°. During the march it was often 100° in the coolest tent.'

' I will endeavour to give you a brief account of a late excursion of mine. I left Jalnah with two friends, to visit, in a route of 130 miles, some of the most interesting spots that India now presents, in memory of her civil and religious greatness. On the first evening we rode after sunset eighteen miles, and by ten o'clock found our tent pitched under the wall of a considerable village; for in those territories which have not been long familiar with the English sway the villages are universally fortified. The walls are of mud, and bold and strong; and although, since the final suppression of the great predatory powers, the torrents of heaven have been their sole assailants, their repair is still in general most religiously cared for. We started next morning by two, and, as the sun had just broken fully forth, found ourselves in command of the prospect of the city of Aurungabad. It lay before us on the plain, partly seeming to rest on the broad slope of a hill, which afforded it the most noble and picturesque relief. Its turreted and bastioned wall, waving beneath us in a course of fifteen miles, defined the circling outline of the city. Without, the domes and minarets of the tombs rose profusely from amid the gardens of the dead. The most beautiful is sacred to the peerless daughter of Aurungzebe, whose appellation on earth was " the gem of heaven." Our tent was pitched at its outer gate, itself a structure worthy of any site, with minarets and battlements and gates of brass. The monumental edifice occupies the centre of a garden of fifty acres, spread forth in all the luxuriance of Eastern taste. The building is in shape nearly square. Four principal towers compose the angles, the great dome encircled with glittering minarets the centre. Of this pile, the tomb itself occupies only a single secondary dome. Its form is an octagon, converging in a dome 70 feet overhead. Over a tombstone, very slightly elevated, a

---

* The military station attached to Hyderabad in the Deccan.

coverlet of silk and gold is laid, strewed with the freshest
flowers and constantly perfumed by censers. This is
surrounded by a double fence of rich open palisade
work in white marble. The sides of the octagon are
clothed with the same material to the height of 20 feet,
broken only by niches wrought with exquisite labour.
There a gallery of lattice-work, in which the marbles
vary in every compartment to all the light and beautiful
shades, is carried completely round.

'The next march, along the base of a range of hills,
brought us to Dowlatabad. It rises from the plain as
a bold rock from the sea, and with the perpendicularity of
a house-wall gains the height of about 800 feet. It is
further insulated by a broad ditch cut close round the
base to the depth of 40 or 50 feet. The city lies at the
foot and rises on one side of the hill. The wall enclosing
it joins the fortifications of the rock, which surmount it
as a coronet. On all sides the hills rise beautifully, and
the city is encircled with vineyards and the valley filled
with wild peacocks. In the next succeeding march we
ascended a steep hill and attained an extensive plain at a
new elevation, supported by a circle of hills. We halted
at Rosa in a tomb, after passing through exquisite
scenery. The site of Rosa surpasses in loveliness anything I have seen. From the plain of Rosa we descended
to Ellora, on the old level of Dowlatabad; and in one
of the supporting façades of that elevated plateau we
perceived the dark mouths of the excavations or caves of
Ellora studding the face of the steep for about a mile. The
detail of these most wonderful works of men's hands I
cannot give; but in the solid mountain are nearly twenty
distinct excavated cathedrals of some hundred feet in every
direction. They are pillared and supported by ranges of
columns approaching every architectural style. The walls
are crowded with colossal figures of the gods or men of
the Hindu heroic or deific age. The figures vary from
the colossal to the pigmy scale, and are hewn in the rock

with every variety of relief. They are in some cases
detached, and the excavations often reach the surface and
admit copious light.   Sometimes chapels sculptured outside and excavated with sculpture within ;—and gods and
elephants, and men in loves, in battles, and in triumphs, rise
in tiers composing rich pyramidal spires. For the last month
the wind has been blowing a regular sirocco at 96° of
the thermometer. The rains are just beginning to threaten
and we gasp for relief; however, we are still alive, and
should the thermometer fall to 80°, we should be thankful. The soil here is granitic, and the dust rises in such
columnar clouds as to blind the very sun.'

   Next comes a sketch of regimental life, not meant,
perhaps, to be quite seriously taken.   The truth is, he
very early wearied of what General Wolfe, when still
a young officer, termed ' the barren battalion conversation ' :—

' Secunderabad, 15th July 1828.

   ' On march every tent is struck and every man at
his post by 2 a.m.   The officers are allowed to mount,
and on we plod for the next four or five hours, half
in darkness; and as the sun grows hot take up ground
near a village and a tank, the *apparatus et commeatus*
moving upon elephants, camels, and bullocks innumerable. Breakfast is prepared in advance, and while we
eat in weariness, each man's domicile is rearing.   The
sepoys' pretty tents stand in three rows in front; second,
the moving bazaar or market; the line of subalterns
succeeds, then the staff and superior officers ; and lastly,
in pre-eminence, the commandant environed by a guard.
We have mess-tiffin at two o'clock.   The day is passed
in dozing, or in shooting in the sun; each morrow the
type of the future and the reflection of the past, and
the average advance ten miles per diem.   At length we
reach cantonment, that is,—besides a congregation of laby-
rinthine huts for the sepoys,—some ranges of barracks
serving only as storehouses, &c., and a number of bunga-

lows of all descriptions, generally mixed with trees or
gardens. In the most suitable of these we post ourselves,
paying heavy rents.   I shall write on at random con-
cerning my daily routine.   First, then,—and I write
it not in bile,—as to the " luxury of the East." I believe
1 have seen it in the most attractive guise, and must
pronounce its existence fabulous, unless it is to be discovered among the Himalayas, as it is fully expected the
unicorn will be, for the good reason that it is to be found
nowhere else.   If the allusion be not simply to curry
and rice, the origin of that expression, " luxury of the
East," is to me an enigma.   Before 5 a.m. every morning
I am wakened by my clothes-boy's bawl that the first
bugle-blast is gone.   A pony is at the door with the
complement of keepers for a royal tiger.   The second
trumpet sounds; no other hint is needed by the animal,
and in one minute I am on parade.   There are a dozen
fellows lounging on their bending legs and rapiers, or
dozing against the adjutant's charger, or probing each
other's livers, which they declare to be in a rapid
course of enlargement cr evanescence.   The colonel
comes on the ground, and we are requested to fall in
smartly.   We get in motion, march and countermarch,
under every condition of time, quantity, and place for the
next two hours, and various and frequent may be the
miseries of the morning.   The colonel forgets " what
the book said next," and asks the adjutant, " who had
not read so far," who applies to the major, who protests
" he would tell him if he knew."   Then a luckless
ensign trots wrong in the face of the sun, and is plainly
told he is leading the corps to the lower world of horror ;
and if true misery on earth may be laughed at, I think it
is the misery of a bothered corps of sepoys.   The gaping
of the rank-and-file, the staring fright of the native
officers, and the polyglot jabbering of the European, the
terrific Saracen-like visage of the colonel, the major's
grin, and the adjutant's gallop in dismay—these are

amusing matters in my craft. At length we are dismissed with burning visages, and cantering home (for the art of trotting is here unknown), subject ourselves to a waterfall for half an hour, and replacing our accoutrements by the lightest conceivable vestures, apply to breakfast, consisting of tea and toast, with the addition of some fruit. The thermometer now stands at 96° in your coolest corner, and you dare scarce look upon the glare of the earth. Aching with the fatigue of drill, I assure you that some strength of will is requisite to resist the desire of rest, or to lend the energies of the spirit to exertion. But at twelve o'clock is sword-exercise, and you battle for an hour accordingly. Two is the hour of tiffin ; it is generally the best time to dine, and the mess-house is near a mile off. There you sit till four. At five, in all probability, comes the bugle for evening drill ; there you fag till half-past six ; you mount for a short ride ; get home in time to sleep, and waken with the bugle-blast. I study the languages, and could make myself master of them at a very brief notice ; but in the absence of an immediate motive, it is not very easy to be enamoured of the most graceless tongues in the universe. However late I may see fortune, I do not despair. Friends may arise, but you know how bad a hand I am at making them where soothing and suing are required.'

The health of the writer gave way about this time, and he set out upon a course of travels which lasted for upwards of two years. The remainder of this chapter is made up of letters which he wrote in the course of his wanderings : —

'Secunderabad, 17th September 1828.

'Having been of late annoyed by slight feverish attacks, which are here endemic, I am advised to go to the coast for a few months, where the ailment will speedily and inevitably disappear. I run down to Masuli-

patam, a distance of 200 miles, and it being the depth of
the rains, I am obliged to use precautions, to me rather
expensive. The country is so deluged that, were there
no other reason, its geological traversing must be deferred until my returning march, when I bring to execution the vigour of a sea-lion.

' We had a little expectation here lately which has sadly
evaporated. The Nizam or monarch of the Deccan, who
still exists at Hyderabad amid the forms of power, was
the other day expected to retire to the abodes of the faithful
departed. A younger son, hostile to English interests,
prepared, with considerable force, to maintain his succession to the throne in opposition to the elder, whom the
Company supports. All was warlike; the troops were in
breathless readiness, and I on the point of throwing myself off the sick-list, when lo! the Nizam swallowed an
elixiric bolus, composed of pearls and gold, and all
manner of invaluables; averted fate, and still sticks to
his earthly sovereignty in spite of the prayers of all,
good, bad, or indifferent, in our force. I can, indeed,
give you no idea of the relief which the remotest prospect of having anything to do administers to us in these
quiet times. In a couple of days I am once more on
march, and on a new route, though on this side of the
peninsula; in these latitudes I do not look for much
society; I have four months' leave.'

' Masulipatam, 1st November 1828.

' Here I arrived ten days ago, my health improved by
march, and with the prospect of its early restoration. So
much in truth did my ailing leave me, that by the
time I shall have completed my march, I shall be in
possession of a very complete geological section of the
country in my route (which, by the way, presents not a
geological fragment, but a completed primary series), and
shall have besides a satisfactory collection of illustrative
specimens. I have not yet determined what scientific

annals my memoir shall adorn, but it, with the minerals,
shall be transmitted to you when opportunity can be made
to arrive.   I have visited and explored, with all the toil
within my physical power, the most interesting tract of
old Golconda, including the diamond mines which produced the Regent diamond, &c., and hope to give you a
better account of that country than I have been able to
discover elsewhere.   In truth, if I have nothing better to
do, I believe I shall make an effort some time hence to be
turned loose on this peninsula until I shall have completed
five or six transverse sections of the whole, to the supersession of all paltry and limited observations ; for even to
take a hammer where hammer never was before is something.'

At Masulipatam his medical adviser ordered him
to the cool climate of the Nilgherry Hills, which had
recently been discovered, in the southern part of the
peninsula.

' Nellore, 18th February 1829.

' If in place of your quiet mode of life you can conceive
yourself to have been so long a daily and nightly wan-
derer among these Indian wilds, driving before you your
own tent and provisions, and halting on the grassiest spot
and beneath the freshest tree, then you will imagine the
delight, upon occasionally emerging from the jungles in
one of our by-stations, to find accounts fresh from our
own hearth and household.   And in this life of solitary
travel, though intolerable to many, there is to me perhaps
more pleasure of a certain cast than I can well express.
Starting at two a.m. there is not a dawn-blush till near
six, but a moon brighter than your noontide, and a
firmament which I can only say suggests no comparison,
and beneath these a bright show of nature, which to me,
even in its sameness, brings no pall ; and I assure you
that the fruits, the bowers, the flowers, and the fragrance
of the East owe nothing to fiction.   Moving utterly alone
in the quiet of these scenes, I leave you to imagine

whither my thoughts wander, or rather where they rest. When my breakfast is concluded by seven, and my book-trunks are opened and writing-desk upon the table, I enjoy the day as largely as a day may be enjoyed that passes in calm and solitude, and with employments of abundant interest. Of course when devoted to geologising, the uniformity as well as the silence of my movements is a little interrupted, but the daily addition of a small table of specimens is indeed bread in the wilderness. It may be curious to you that, in the character of a disciple of Thor, I am uniformly reputed among the natives mad, and that as the character of insanity is held by them in superstitious reverence, from the belief that natural reason is never taken away without preternatural endowment being added, the attribute is convenient on the whole. You will probably be aware, ere this reaches you, that my present march has for its object seeing our friend Mr. M., with his family, at Madras, and going from thence nearly to Cape Comorin, to some salubrious hills, for the sake of health and novelty.'

'Ootacamund, Nilgherry Hills, 25th June 1829.

'My route from Madras hither was interesting and beautiful, and rendered pleasant by agreeable halts. I slept for two nights in the palace of Tippoo in Seringapatam. It is not a military station, but I went on pilgrimage, and visited the breach, the death-spot of the sultan, &c., &c., with a religious interest. These hills are encircled by a wide zone of ravenous and pestilential jungles filled with wild elephants, tigers, bears, hogs, leopards, deer, monkeys, &c., but presenting to the eye a wildered paradise. Of the animals, the elephants are almost alone dangerous, and they have played sad pranks at the expense of invalids seeking the hills. The great bucks are met singly on the road whisking the flies with half a tree for a fan, and a poor lady having thus encountered one the other day, took refuge with all her attendants in the thickets. The beast went up to her palanquin and twirled it by one pole over his head with much glee, then by the other pole till it gave way, and then danced upon it with much delight, and capered into the jungle, as she said, with a horse laugh. The top of the hills presents a table-land, if a surface of hill and dale may be so designated. The elevation is 8,000 feet above the sea, the surface varied and beautiful, and the climate like a constant spring in England, the temperature being for three months of the year 59° to 63°, for a short time a little above, and for four months considerably below these points, when there is ice every morning. You cannot easily conceive the luxury of such a retreat at a season when the thermometer at Madras and Hyderabad ranges from 86° to 100°. The inhabitants are of three races of men, entirely distinct in features, language, and observances both from the natives of the plains and from each other. The villages of these tribes are built after distinct fashions, and they do not intermingle in the same districts. The men of the different castes appear to come in contact only for the general purposes to which their distinctive habits direct them, one class being nomadic, another agriculturists, and the third craftsmen and labourers at mean works. Of their religion little is known, but they have one or two neglected buildings of a religious character. The population is very scanty, and the labouring tribe, till within the last few years, uniformly destroyed nine female children out of ten, the surviving ladies enjoying an unlimited plurality of husbands. The figures and features of these people are the finest I have seen, or have ever seen represented. The fine apostle of a painter approaches nearer to their mould of countenance than any other manner of head, their black hair and beards flowing over their necks and breasts in antique ringlets. They have an extreme aversion to the natives of the plain, but are delighted with Englishmen, and receive us with pleasure to inspect their houses, &c., but quite on the footing

of equals. Very little is known of this curious people, but
from Roman coins being found abundantly among their
women's ornaments, it appears plain to some of our anti-
quarians that they are of Italian stock! There are in the
season abundance of woodcock that migrate as in England,
no one knows whither. There are large numbers of a
magnificent species of deer, of bison, of ibex, and of
tigers and leopards, the two last being almost inoffensive
in this climate. There are, besides, a lake without
fish, beds of richly-flavoured wild white strawberries,
and ditto red, very beautiful, but devoid of taste—a
kind of fruit something like a gooseberry; abundance
of potatoes and English vegetables, but neither the gooseberry nor the currant ripens here. There are beautiful white Ayrshire roses and the small deep damask
rose; and I think I have run over the most striking features, animate and inanimate, of the spot, not to omit a
" Cluny " built by a Captain Macpherson, and a chilblain
that one lady had the delight to find.'

' 13th August 1829.

'I have pitched my tent on a lower and somewhat
warmer quarter of these hills than that on which I at first
resided, my thermometer ranging from 62° to 70°, and
the weather being very delightful. What a luxury to
look from this cool height of 8,000 feet upon the Car-
natic that glows beneath with its woods, and lakes, and
plains outspread as smooth as a bowling-green, with a
horizon 100 miles distant! An hour's ride down the
beautiful ghaut * raises my glass to 90°. I cannot picture
the delights of this climate: in a garden close by me is a
geranium hedge as high and thick and long as the hedge
in Colonel F.'s avenue, and absolutely clothed in flowers.
A gentleman on the hills commissioned from England 100
guineas' worth of plants, of which a currant-bush and a

---

* The word ' Ghaut ' is used indiscriminately, for the hills which support
the table-land, and for the passes which connect it with the plains below.

pear-tree alone arrived alive; and these two receive in consequence a species of worship, but don't even promise anything in return.—I have noticed our army reductions, by which I am thrown back from senior ensign to third, and I believe also a later regulation, by which the number of staff officers in each corps is to be equalised. There are to be three or four from every regiment, and mine already furnishes the maximum. The Bengal Army is in a most violent state. Lord W. Bentinck treats them with extreme good-temper, and allows the vent of all feelings in the public prints. He has refused permission to the surgeons of the army to resign, but under a new name has kept up their allowances nearly to the old mark. I should fear much from military commotion in Bengal. Sepoys are a *genus irritabile*, with which poets may not be compared, and of which an adequate idea can only be formed by contact. Would you believe that I have known a company absolutely stirred to mutiny by an officer, who, from ignorance of the language, called their head-dresses caps, when they choose them to be considered turbans?—the head-dress bearing the while as strong similitude to a turban as to a whale!'

'Cannanore, 25th October 1829.

'I have unwillingly sojourned here for nearly twenty days, wasting upon the ocean's brink the time which I hoped to have spent upon its bosom, and encroaching upon the valuable period destined for the prosecution of my geological plan. There is a vicious description of native coasting grab—an harmonic combination of the Cambridge barge and the Roman antique smack (*vide* Adam), in which I expect, through the alternations of land and sea breezes, to edge up to Goa within six days of my embarkation; the said Argo-like craft having, by the way, gone a little to the southward for a somewhat unclassical half cargo of cocoa-nuts, and perhaps, as I begin to dread from her delay, made a diversion in favour of deep-sea coral and seed-pearls.'

At Kuladghee he again became ill, and was sent back to the hills, whence he wrote :—

'26th June 1830.

'I assure you that either as a matter of taste or of advantage I could not have passed my three first Indian years more agreeably or more profitably. than I have done, having travelled nearly 4,000 miles, with my eyes (such as they are) open, and with nothing lacking save an old friend, new books, and now and then a rupee. As to ulterior views, now that I hope well of my health, I have expectations for which I can indeed offer you no base. None of our reductions have been rescinded ; a surveyorship within the next two years is the only thing in sight, as I am not ambitious of appointments on the regimental staff, which would only take up my time without affording any means of coming into notice. I cannot read at present with satisfaction ; yet I study history and India and my health, and hope on.

'I made a pleasant descent lately into the plains to an elephant hunt, which I enjoyed especially from having been myself so much hunted in some of my late marches by these mountainous mammalia. I was not long ago, in treading a deep wild, arrested by the fearful bass of a tiger in a bush close upon our narrow pathway. My guide passed to my astonishment, and I followed as in honour bound. The Hindu stood for a moment as if transfixed, a few feet beyond the tiger's lair, and went on. You may imagine my horror upon finding the savage roaring exactly upon my right, to see a heap of reeking elephant's dung (the reason for the pause) lying immediately upon the left. We were safe in the mutual terrors of the beasts. I should not be so much horrified another time, but I almost plucked a hair to see if it had not turned grey.'

'Nilgherry Hills, 31st August 1830.

'You have often required of me some notice of Hyderabad, which must have become with you almost a household word. This letter must go to-day, so here goes the account of an empire at score. Hyderabad is the capital city of the territory of the Nizam, lying in the centre of the Indian peninsula, and containing a population of twelve millions. The restoration of conquered dynasties not being the policy of the house of Timour, sovereignties were assigned from the subdued provinces to those generals whose power and ambition raised them above obedience; and upon the tenure suited to such circumstances the Nizam has held this kingdom from the Mogul. After the final struggle for British supremacy the Hyderabad state emerged with its independence less impaired than that of any of the greater native powers, weak from the constant flux and reflux of population and devastation which had accrued from collision with the predatory powers, but not inferior in capacity for social advancement to the most favoured of the Asiatic provinces. A native court now subsists in the old Eastern fashion in the vast metropolis. A large subsidiary force is given—in consideration of the provinces ceded to us—to uphold the authorities of the land, and the state maintains an army besides of 20,000 men disciplined in the European style, and commanded by European officers; partly adventurers, partly lent by the Company. The argument of persons will, I think, afford you the best insight into the Hyderabad order of things. First is the Nizam, who, though of illegitimate birth, is the legitimate sovereign on the throne, whilst his occupancy sears the eyeballs of all the remaining scions of royalty who have escaped the gouge. Next is the British Resident, whose duties are those of undefined supervision, assistance, and control, to be exercised according to what Coke calls 'the crooked end of discretion' toward a state that is nominally free. And to omit the multiplicity of bright consolers of royalty, who,

though in these climes of no cerulean hue, yet mingle as
they may, to make—perchance to mar—lady-like interests
in the persons and affairs of state, his highness has, after
the manner of his ancestors, that essential *levamen*, a grand
vizier ; while, on the other hand, to render interference
practicable to him, the British Resident has his " man ;"
and amid these conflicting elements and ministers of
grace and power, while the sovereign attributes remain in
plenary independence to the prince, and his Mahomedan
vizier enjoys every Oriental sublimity of office, the
ruling functions are committed in executive trust to the
Hindu of the Resident.   Such is the cast in theory of
directing powers.   The actual drama has ever been after
the most approved fashion of—

> ' " Power into will, will into appetite,
> And appetite an universal wolf !" '

' The probable elements of political evil may be deemed
yet undiscovered, if they are not realised under a system
of things ruled conjointly by a Nizam, a Resident, a Harem,
a Vizier, and a Hindu.'

' Nilgherry Hills, November 1830.

'I start hence in two or three days for Hyderabad, in
the first instance, and ultimately, I believe for Viziana-
gram, which, if you take the trouble to note my progress
upon the map, you may observe by Vizagapatam above
Masulipatam on the coast.   It is a cheap and healthy
place, twelve miles from the surf, but I shall have
neither society nor books, and our corps will be
solitary and without ladies.   Hog hunting is to be had,
however, which is our solace, as also fish, and I have
an unquiet pleasure in the long lone marches.

'I hope in this favourable season of the year to make
out my new march of 1,000 miles without reserve on the
score of health, and to add to the chances of my so
doing, I have flung my hammer into a tank.   I go in a
right line hence to Hyderabad, the whole way on one
old horse—having sent my charger before.   I have a

small set of minerals to send home very far surpassing in every respect those I sent before.'

'Hyderabad, 9th January 1831.

'I completed my long march hither about a fortnight ago. It was a most pleasant journey in our fine season, and my health has proved so well confirmed that I trust I shall have no more interesting exercitations in the bulletin department. I do not, however, rest here. In three days we commence a 500 miles march to Chicacole, a station of two corps on the east coast, nearly approaching the southern provinces of Bengal. It being a corner of the country yet new to me, I am delighted by this new movement. It is pleasant, too, to be on the coast, where I have always had the best health; and when opportunity shall permit, I have no mind to leave the seas unploughed.

'I write this in extreme haste to catch an unexpected ship, and immediately after some four hours, baking in the sun for the pleasure of His Immensity the Nizam, whose royal caprice it was to inspect our brigade this morning in all his pomp. I have no time for description. The elephants were innumerable; the trappings gorgeous; the rabble incalculable; the heat ineffable; the nuisance intense. We had 8,000 troops of all arms under arms. His highness gave us a splendid breakfast after grill, and sat at meat with us himself. After food attar of roses was distributed to all the officers, and I wish I could send my two bottles to A. Chicacole is the best place for shells in India next to Ceylon.

'Were it not for better hopes in the *long long* run, this system of life would be intolerable. I am not a little jaded by standing *at ease*, &c., &c., in our cloudless atmosphere from seven to eleven a.m.'

'Near Masulipatam, 10th February 1831.

'We have been a month under canvas, on march to Chicacole, since I wrote to you last, and I send this from

my tent to say that all things go with me fairly and well.
We have hitherto been merely upon the track which I
geologised some years ago, but are about to turn to a new
country to the northward, having still about an eight
weeks' march to perform. Though comforts produced
by regimental arrangement vastly surpass those which
may be commanded by a lone way-faring sub, formal procedure with a corps by no means suits my taste so well as
the starving freedom of which I have hitherto enjoyed so
liberal a share. There is a pleasure in pitching one's tent
upon the patch of sward, or under the green tree, or by
the hill or the lake that fancy may fix upon for the day's
rest, which the superior coction of a curry does not
counterbalance even with the added zest of the socialities
of a marching battalion. I reach our encamping ground
a little after sunrise, pass the day in something closely
resembling idleness, for our tent heats are intense till three
o'clock, when we dine; thereafter we sally as our humours
may suggest, the majority to shoot, some to fish, some to
find a fox or hare, in which sport I rather delight to participate. We are in camp by nightfall; the mess assembles
to supper. I drink tea at my tent door, alone with the
stars, or with W., or some other friend, as the case may
be, and "to-morrow, and to-morrow, and to-morrow," are
as the days that went before and those that shall come
after. I hope, however, on my settlement at Chicacole
to be able to notice a less barren scheme of existence.
Our commander-in-chief has determined, in accordance
with some malarian notion of Dr. MacCulloch's, that
marching in the heat of the sun preserves from cholera,
and from his refrigerated office at Madras has issued
orders that corps shall not quit their sleeping ground till
half-an-hour after sunrise. The sufferings of European
troops under this system may be conceived, but as our
officers, almost without exception, spend the complete day
among jungle and snipe grounds, the ordinance is not so
terrible to them as might be imagined, while I am per-

mitted to evade it entirely by marching on when I please. I feel slight inclination to tempt a heat beyond that now indicated on my table in a cool hour of 97°. You will admit this to be pretty decided for two months of the year. A fine river within fifty yards of me is such an alligator-pond, that having no supernumerary legs or arms, I do not think of courting its cool delights; so I hope you will make some allowance for my languid gossip.'

CHAPTER II.

1831–1836.

SERVICE IN THE SURVEY DEPARTMENT — THE DECCAN — NELLORE.

THE summer of 1831 brought with it the grade of lieutenant, and also, by the good offices of friends and the
assent of the governor (who waived on this occasion the
objections which he was alleged to entertain to the employment of Scotchmen in general and of Macs in particular), a staff appointment, the nature of which will
appear from the following letters:—

'Vizagapatam, 4th July 1831.

'I have "stopped the press for you," in the hope now
realised of being at length able to report to you that I
have been appointed to the staff as assistant surveyor-
general, being nominated within a week of the time
when, from my standing in the service, it was first possible for me to be removed from regimental duty. You
may observe on the map the fine extent of the Hyderabad
country, over which I shall move quite unfettered and
unquestioned. It approaches the western sea within 100,
the eastern within 50 miles. It contains the two rivers
of India next in importance to the Ganges (not including
the Indus), and in its limits, 500 miles in length and 500
in breadth, presents as many and as varied objects of
moral and physical interest as are bounded by similar
lines in any portion of Hindostan. The six fine months
of the year I shall pass in the country with the survey
establishment in my tents; the remaining portion given

to rain and heat I spend in Hyderabad with the best society and the best library that Southern India affords. All now depends upon health, which you will believe I shall spare neither pains nor expense to cherish, my new allowances being perfectly adequate to such views. In the last three months, in fact, my pay has risen from 180 rupees per mensem, an ensign's allowance, to nearly 500 rupees a month, being about double my lieutenant's pay. I have, however, to keep up a large marching establishment of tents, palanquin-bearers, servants, horses, and bullocks, at very heavy pay, from my being perpetually on the move in by far the most expensive province of all India. In the seasons of vacation I hope, by accommodating my march to the lines of the different monsoons, to carry on my geological plans, reporting progress to the Bengal Asiatic Society. The trying portion of my new business will consist in taking eternally recurring angles with an instrument in the afternoon while the sun is clear, being sad work for my eyes.'

'Secunderabad, 22nd October 1831.

'If you know anything at Cambridge, you must know of Colonel Lambton and his operations in measuring the arc of a meridian in India. I am employed in completing his work. Not with his view, to ascertain the form of this planet, which you are old enough to know is round, but with the geographical and highly patriotic object of putting everything in India for once in its right place, by means of triangles subordinate to those measured by the great geodest above named. There is but one way of conducting a trigonometrical survey with completeness, and that we pursue. I frame a geological map as we proceed over the land, and in the general memoir of each district which is required of us the matter which we record in all the departments of physical geography and general statistics is limited only by our powers of research. Marching being now my business for the six least hot months of the year, my establishment is of course in

such condition as is most propitious to desultory movements ; and though our survey work is more than sufficient
to occupy all our time, I think I shall contrive to do something printable before my return to summer quarters if
I should trench upon the hot season.   But all depends on
the state of my sight, about which I am now sadly dispirited, though by the way I have got hold of a fellow
who will, I think, save me much optical labour in the
department of flowers, which I mean now to cultivate a
little.   The use of the theodolite, the bother of logarithms
and minute map drawing, in which my duty consists, are
enough to eliminate the eyes of a lynx.   I am, however,
a fluent Hindostani scholar, and not ignorant of Persian,
and can bear creditably the scholastic recommendations
given me.   The temple of written knowledge has been
inexorably shut against me since I was of the age you
now are.   I catch but passing and desultory glimpses of
what goes on within, but I am a worshipper without the
gate, and improve my uncommon opportunities of study-
ing this strange race, and the land which it inhabits,
and so keep my mind active and enlarged in physical and
moral views, and ready for any march that fortune may
assign to it.'

' Near Hyderabad, 21st November 1831.

' I have now been a month in the field, chiefly beating
about for stones and flowers, and pretty villages, and cool
tanks and green ruins, and, in short, in all sorts of idleness.
But I am about to repair to my post, of my success at
which I shall be anxious to give you notice, as from the
illness of my superior and only colleague I expect the
entire duty of the year to fall on my shoulders.   I may
not have mentioned to you, that to each survey are attached two officers, one in charge, the other assistant,
and besides, eight or ten half-castes generally well educated for that class, and all educated on purpose for
the survey, but desperate blunderers the best of them,

and, I am sorry to say, least of all to be trusted in taking angles delicately with the theodolite from the hill tops ; but from this month's seasoning at light work, and from the weather now approaching being the coldest, I really hope to get through all without a pause.

' We are not without our changes in this hemisphere. The Mysore state, the masterpiece of Indian policy, the one bright page in the *retributive* history of our rise, has completed its course in thirty years, and ceased to have a distinct existence, and all the other provinces which we have endeavoured to maintain at once in a substantive and an adjective state of being are tottering rapidly to their fall. The state of Oude passes description, and that of Hyderabad is not much better.'

' Secunderabad, 26th June 1832.

' In the neighbourhood of my regiment a serious revolt is spreading.   There is in the Orissa and Cuttack country a numerous tribe of hill people never at rest, to whom vast numbers of weavers thrown out of employment by the withdrawal of our factories and cloth investments and large bands of irregular troops discharged in these times of reduction have joined themselves.   Through causes of dissatisfaction which no one seems to comprehend, but which are vexing the whole eastern line of country from the Godavery to the Ganges, these people have taken arms, and are plundering and sacking in every direction.[1] It is expected that my regiment will take the field against them as soon as reinforced by a light infantry corps, which is joining it with great speed ; when, on the respectable appearances which the war may assume, depends my going back for a while to the head of a company, or my remaining to extinguish my sight thanklessly through theodolites.'

[1] The Kole war is alluded to.

' My immediate superior, of the upper provinces,[1]
writes as highly gratified with my geological work, which
he enjoins our whole establishment to combine in aiding
me to extend, says that I have now many claims upon his
attention, and promises to have me removed to Bengal to.
afford him my immediate aid in the execution of our
grand and delicate work, the measurement of a base when
it shall next be required in the great survey; for you
must note that there are two distinct surveys now going
on in the land, one the geographical, in which I am engaged, the other that above noticed, the grand trigonometrical, the object of which is to ascertain the length of
a degree of the meridian.

' My own defects form the point of difficulty. By a
curious infelicity of fortune, after having quitted one
hemisphere on account of visual incapacity, I find everything conspire to assign mere optical power as the best
of my faculties in another. For with Everest I shall
have terrestrial observations by day and celestial by
night, while earth and stars abide in his department, and
shall be thought nothing of if I am not a very Chaldean,
and a speller of micrometers to millionth parts.'

' The public prints will probably have noticed, in
Europe, the somewhat alarming conspiracy of a portion
of our troops with Mysore natives to destroy the Europeans
of the force of Bangalore, &c. Taken in connexion with a
number of rows which have recently occurred elsewhere,
it is regarded by the thinking public as an omen of serious
import. Gerard[2] has gone with an engineer officer upon
a very important and perilous expedition through Caubul
and the Indian Caucasus, north towards the Caspian, to
explore the possible routes of an army of invasion from

[1] Major, now Colonel Sir George Everest, C.B.
[2] Dr. Gerard, the companion of Burnes, an Aberdonian neighbour.

that quarter, as well as to collect all the floating views of the tribes with regard to Russian domination upon the border over which it is rolling. There have been late accounts of them, and they are considered now beyond the limit where personal danger is to be feared.'

'Sattara, 25th February 1833.

' I have described a path westward hither to the capital of the Sattara state, just under the great line of Ghauts which bounds as a rampart the western flank of our peninsula. Although the main object of my proceeding hitherward[1] is removed, you will easily believe that my curiosity suffices to carry me onward to take a glimpse of Bombay, particularly as some fine hills, like the Nil-gherries, but lower, some beautiful country, and some delightful sea and river boating, vary the march.'

'Bombay, 3rd June 1833.

'I am, in fact, exactly as you have lately heard, linger-ing here after M.'s departure, until I may hope to find something besides truth in the dried-up tanks and wells betwixt this and Hyderabad; pursuing my translation of a somewhat large but interesting Persian volume of manuscript history, by the Nizam's premier, during the wars with Tippoo, and amending a long geological story, for what fate I do not distinctly know. General reflec-tions or dozing, lounging in a large and well-ordered library, which this place boasts, an occasional visit, a canter in the evening's dust, fill up my passing existence on shore, while I sometimes take a boat and cruise amongst the great fleet here, or beat about Elephanta and its caves. While living upon the other shores of India I have been accustomed *to take to water* in despite of sharks and surf, but in this muddy bay the ocean stream is so extremely hot, that while it scarcely bears either foam or fish of prey, it is a most unrefreshing bath.'

[1] To meet friends who had failed him.

'Madras, 23rd February 1834.

'A small war is getting up with an old dependent rajahship of the Mysore state. The country is a difficult and pestilential jungle; the chief is well supplied with money and men, and somewhat insane. Eight or ten thousand men will be taken into the field against him, but if he resists, as he may, his arms and the climate may do much before we can effect a complete conquest. The name of the district is Coorg, at the base of the Western Ghauts, and the commander-in-chief and the general staff will be near the scene of action. The business in which my regiment has been lately engaged is now at an end. I believe I told you that I had offered to join for the service, but that I was told I was not required. One of our officers was killed, and another died of jungle fever, the best men, of course, in the regiment; one gave me the place of fifth lieutenant; and when I say that an officer who came in the "Waterloo" with me is now fifth ensign, you will at least appreciate my luck.'

'Hyderabad Jungle, 25th December 1834.

'On my way hither I visited an inland salt water lake, one of the most remarkable objects in this country. It is contained in an extraordinary bowl, about 500 feet below the general level, and without any outlet, there being in the rains 10 or 12 feet of water in the centre, in the dry weather only two or three, when the salt, principally a carbonate of potass, is dug out. This deep basin occurs in the centre of a great basaltic district. The circumference of its upper lip is about six miles, that of the green dead lake below about three. Its sides are very steep, and are clothed in the densest jungle, which abounds with bears, tigers, panthers, and such pet animals. From one side a rill of fresh water, over whose source a temple is built, finds its way into the dark hollow, watering some excellent vegetable gardens formed in its ravine. The place recalled to my memory Coruisk, in the Isle of Skye, but, saving that in both cases there is a lake in a mountain basin, no two spots in the world bear fewer points of resemblance. And the barren magnificence of our highland scene, with its black façades of rock, its cascades, its violent stream, its clouds and its eagles, certainly leaves impressions on the ·mind of a much higher order than those which any one but a dervish might derive from the sullen solitudes of this Indian jungle lake.' [1]

'Hyderabad Jungle, 30th January 1835.

'I write this from my tent pitched under a shadowy mango-tree by a village of the Deccan, as in former years; and it being my natal month, I may add that I am certainly in the enjoyment of much better health than has ever yet been my lot. We are this season engaged in the survey of one of the most beautiful districts of India, being not further off than fifty or sixty miles on an average from a provincial cantonment; the good people of which supply me in abundance with newspapers from all parts of India, and books of all descriptions, I should add, except those which I particularly wish to see. Bodily comforts, too, of all sorts, they communicate in great abundance; and my friends the ryots, gardeners, farmers, headmen of villages, &c., besides the higher classes of govern·ment officers, are so much friends indeed, that the Governor-General could not be more abundantly supplied with the best produce of the land, and certainly would not have it tendered after so gratifying a fashion as it is every day at my tent door, totally devoid as all know me to be, of claims to dignity, or distinction, or the power of making return. Poor —— indeed complains to me that he meets with nothing but insolence, and suffers comparative starvation. You would be indeed

---

[1] The name of the lake is Lonar: it is described in a paper by the late Dr. John Malcolmson, in vol. v. of the Transactions of the Geological Society of London.

richly amused by our modes of procedure here, indicating a state of society very unlike any contemplated by
European minds not thoroughly conversant with oriental
subjects.   I, for instance, the other day despatched a servant to plant a flag upon a hill ten miles off; the flag was
to be procured at the village at the foot of the hill, and
was to consist of a branch of a tree, rolled round with thick
bundles of grass, and bearing on its point the largest and
roundest earthen pot to be found in the village, well daubed
over with whitewash.   The potail, or head man, who was
an insolent pale-faced Brahmin lad, declared that this was
some new proceeding of the Feringees (Franks), to which
he had received no order to conform, and ordered my man
to depart from his village bounds without delay.   I believe
that I am not the most patient of mortals under obstruc-
tion, but I could not bring myself to run the risk of
bringing ruin on the family of a foolish boy by reporting the
circumstance to the government through our Resident; yet
it was necessary that this flag should be set up, and that
such insolence should be repressed in such a manner as to
obviate all chance of its recurrence.   The man knew well
that he was disobeying a public order of his government ;
and next day he sent notice to my people to come and
put up their flag, which they did.   In the meantime I
had sent notice of the circumstance to the zemindar, some
sixty miles off, believing that from his knowledge of me,
though we had never met, he would attend to any wish
of mine.   Within an hour from the receipt of my note a
party of horse were on their way to the recusant village,
and a civil personage of great importance despatched to
me to express from the zemindar what was due.   In three
days the potail, with every other village authority, was
laid by the heels, and brought to await their doom at my
tent door, from whence they were of course liberated to
celebrate my mercy, and declare their own sorrow and
repentance.   I have out with me the whole body of
evidence taken on the Renewal of the Charter, for quiet

digestion, and I daily reap knowledge in these village fields which is not to be obtained from books; from the farmers, who give me in the gloamings the history of their leases, and advantages, and exactions; the story of their maize crop, and sugar crop, and tobacco crop, and true and anxious statements of their cattle, including those which died in the drought, and those which have since had calves, and those best for the plough, and those whose feet are too tender for stony ground. I obtain the most curious insight into the manners and condition of the men of this portion of India.'

'Hyderabad Jungle, 20th February 1835. ·

' We are engaged in the survey of a beautiful table-land, which is itself surrounded by tablets of secondary extent. The soil is the richest black loam on the surface of the earth, arising from the decay of rocks of the trap series, and bears the most luxuriant and wide-spreading crops of wheat, maize, cotton, sugar cane, pulse, and oil plants, besides occasional patches of poppies grown for opium. The plains are clothed in fine grasses, unbroken even by brushwood for thousands of square miles, and alive with herds of antelope. The villages are frequent and beautifully placed for the most part, each with its " stern round tower of other days " wasting under the monsoons of these peaceful years. Mango, and tamarind, and peepul trees of extraordinary size and the densest foliage generally surround the villages in groups, or, as it often happens, placed singly, just shunning each other's shades; and amongst them, of course, my canvas dwelling is pitched. My plan is to march in the morning, and I have generally concluded my canter of eight or ten miles before eight o'clock, when the sun becomes powerful. I halt at the village nearest the point at which I intend to make observations; and in the afternoon, between three and four o'clock, sally forth in my palanquin, which bears me whither I may desire. On my descending from this vehicle, a servant bears over my head an umbrella, one of the largest which English prudence ever opposed to an Indian sun. It is of folds reduplicated as the shield of Ajax, and its handle may only be compared to that of the spear borne by that hero. Under this maximum parasol I stand and enjoy the contemplative amusement of angling until the shadows of evening come on. I then mount my horse, and I find my solitary dinner ready in my tent, or if there be light enough remaining, under my tree, where I feel less alone, for there are in general as many bird as leaves, and no voice is *obligato*. The crows caw from the very depth of their soul; the paroquets scream at f, and the flying foxes skirl as if the whole harmony of the thing depended upon their exertions, with notes anomalous as the other accidents of their physiology, and in shrillness rivalling (to my ungallant memory) those shrillest of symphonists, the maiden psalmodists of St. Machar's[1] themselves. The rural population of this part of India, with which I am intimately acquainted, finds great favour in my sight. The people are simple, temperate, and moral, and exceedingly intelligent when rightly estimated by comparison with the peasantry of Europe. But they groan under a despotism[2] the most inevitable and minute in its incidence which was ever inflicted upon any portion of the human race. Amongst the various schemes which enter my imagination for palliating my endless absence from you and it, I often think of J. or W.'s extending, some of these summers, their steam-boat movements to meet me on the shores of the Mediterranean, at Smyrna, or some such point, which will soon be within easy distance of our shores.'

' Hyderabad, 3rd June 1835.

' One of our three Madras surveys having become vacant, I am appointed to the charge of it, which makes

---

[1] The parish church of Old Aberdeen.   [2] That of the Nizam.

me, in point of fact, in my department (as in my regiment) very fortunate ; as since I entered it I have only served *de facto* as a subordinate for a few months.

'My new ground is in the Company's country, in the Nellore district, immediately to the north of Madras, betwixt the sea and the Eastern Ghauts. It is a very hot and a very healthy, and rather favourite country. I have many griefs in quitting this delightful Deccan. My health is so good and the society here is so large and pleasant ; while I am much interested in its inhabitants, its institutions, and its hills, its morale and physique.

'Nellore is a small station, purely civil, with not a dozen people in it, but then it is within 100 miles of Madras.'

'Nellore, 1st January 1836.

'I have never heard from —— since he went to England. I find that people who return home from hence have their minds so completely overlaid with new feelings and associations as almost to supersede all recollections of India, or of those who dwell therein ; and happy they. It is a very singular fact too, bearing a physical analogy to this, that many people after a period of residence in the Nilgherries completely forget the character of the sensations which they have suffered in the tropical plains below. This reminds me that in four or five days hence I shall be again under canvas in these plains of Nellore. No two tracts of country can exhibit a greater contrast in their superficial characters than this and the Hyderabad country. Here we have a vast littoral plain lying betwixt a long line of mountains and the sea ; many rivers flow down from the hills, forming in some cases deltas, in others giving rise to estuaries; they are vast torrents of water in the rains, and when these have subsided, broad sand beds, with here and there a pool connected by barely living rills ; here and there low granite crusts spring up. There are large forests of palmyra and cocoa-nut trees, and most villages are adorned by groves ;

but the whole is flat, stale,—profitable only in rice fields
fed from tanks, and in a fine breed of cattle which over-
spreads the land. However, to make up for all deficiencies
in interest in my subject matter, I shall have my camp
joined this year by at least one fair lady friend, and
in your old land you cannot imagine the difference that
such a happy incident makes in the life of a poor
bachelor. Under my window they are performing an
operation that would surprise you. The collector of the
district is out in the country betwixt 50 and 100 miles
from hence, and they are filling a dozen great pots of
water from my well, the favourite one, which are transmitted daily by relays of men from hence to him!

'I shall be in Madras in the course of the next fortnight
to see a friend or two there, and to buy a strong Burmese
pony for clambering about the country, such ponies as
those the world cannot show. They are exactly Shetland
ponies, on a rather larger scale, never tire, are never sick,
and never die. Besides this, I shall have my fine Arab
charger, one of the most beautiful in the world, and a
horse that does either for my buggy or for the saddle,
and when I am out I keep them all in work.'

CHAPTER III.

THE GOOMSUR WAR, 1836.

Lieutenant Macpherson was now acquiring much information, and the invaluable art—possessed by so few
—of easy intercourse with all classes of the natives of
India, when he was summoned to join his regiment, the
8th Native Infantry, which had been engaged for some
time in operations against a native chief, the rajah or
zemindar of Goomsur in Orissa. In the course of
this service he became acquainted with the aboriginal
tribes, upon whom, at a grievous cost to himself, he
was destined to exercise the happiest influences. The
rajah and the aborigines must now be introduced to the
reader.[1]

The Hindus had in ancient times driven the primitive
races of Orissa—the Khonds,[2] the Koles, and the Sourahs—
to the forest or the hill;[3] and had established a kingdom

---

[1] The next five pages are abridged from the Introduction to the 'Account
of the Religion of the Khonds of Orissa, by Captain S. Charters Macpherson,' read before the Royal Asiatic Society of London in 1852.

[2] N.B. The *o* in Khond is long.

[3] 'The physical conditions most favourable to the preservation of the
aboriginal races were combined in high perfection and on a great scale in
the portion of the north-eastern quarter of the peninsula nearly comprised
between the Vindhya range on the north, the eastern chain of Ghauts, and
a line connecting these drawn from the mouth of the Godavery to the centre
of the valley of the Nerbudda;—a region composed of lofty and rugged
mountains, impenetrable forests, swampy woodlands, and arid wastes, interspersed with extensive tracts of open and productive plain, and possessing a
climate in many districts highly pestilential, while, for strangers, it is salu-

great in arts and arms, extending from the Ganges to the Godavery, and possessing a mighty hierarchy and a body of territorial nobles who bore the title of rajah, and held great estates, mainly wielding the great distinctive institution of Orissa—its Paiks, or hereditary landed militia.

The breadth of the Orissan territory was about three degrees of longitude, and the eastern chain of Ghauts, at an average distance of seventy miles from the coast of Coromandel, traversed its whole length, sending down innumerable buttresses and offshoots to within a few miles of the sea. Upon the west, the range is generally supported by compact plateaux, broad ridges, and expanses of elevated plain.

The maritime division extends along the whole seaboard, nearly 400 miles in length, with an average breadth of fifteen miles. It is an open, salubrious, well-peopled, and highly productive expanse, with the exception of several groups of barren hills, and a tract of marshy and wooded deltas intersected by lagunes. The open and fertile parts of this territory formed the state domain of Orissa, and included a large portion of the lands dedicated to religious purposes. The wilder districts were partitioned into estates, or zemindaries, of very various value and extent. The primitive races were expelled from the whole of this seaward territory, save

brious in the open country alone. In that territory, large remnants of no fewer than five peoples who claimed to be children of the soil—the Khonds, the Koles, the Sourahs, the Goands, and the Bheels,—have preserved, with various degrees of purity and distinctness, their race, their institutions, their language, and their superstitions. Wholly or in part within it, kingdoms were established by the Oriyah, the Telugu, the Mahratta, and the Rajpoot divisions of the Brahminical people; and between the ancient races and each of those kingdoms, strikingly contrasted in their genius and institutions, connexions have sprung up, the most diversified in their origins and their forms, but having one common tendency—towards the supersession and obliteration of the ancient and ruder by the more civilised people—worked out, consciously and unconsciously, through the gradual assimilation of manners, through proselytism to the Hindu or the Mahomedan faith, and through the fusion of races, notwithstanding every barrier of caste and custom.'

where they were permitted to linger in its sequestered and unhealthy tracts, occupying lands on half-servile tenures.

The middle region comprised above one half of the entire area of the kingdom. It forms a vast expanse of hilly wastes, entangled forests, and rugged watercourses, exceedingly unhealthy, but interspersed with beautiful and fertile valleys, and occasionally broken by broad and productive plains. This region was divided into a large number of zemindaries of various sizes. The more important of them are possessed by families which trace their descent from the royal houses of Orissa, or from the principal stocks of Rajputana.

The zemindars were bound by tenure to maintain, and bring into the field, large contingents of the national landed soldiery; to pay tribute, in some cases heavy, in some nominal; to perform special services, both public and personal, to the sovereign; and to receive at his hands investiture with their honours and domains.

The rivalries of the zemindars, and the terms of their tenures under the state, obliged them to maintain, and often to increase, the soldiery even where the necessity in which it had originated ceased to exist. The zemindars stood to it simply in the relation of military patrons; while its chief officers, on whom they depended for the execution of every measure of defence or aggression, greatly influenced and often controlled their councils.

The aboriginal peoples have existed within the zemindaries in two distinct positions.

In the more open tracts they were generally reduced, as in the state domain, to a semi-servile condition; the Khonds, for example, dwelling in petty hamlets, their services appropriated by the rajah to supply himself and his officers with jungle produce, or assigned by him to particular villages or temples, and bearing the appellation of 'Vettiah,' or 'labouring without hire.'

Amongst the rugged bases of the mountain chain, the

aboriginal tribes, on their subjugation, did not fall into servitude, but became free subjects of the zemindars, cultivating the soil on the usual rent tenure, or living by military service, or enrolled amongst the landed militia. They have everywhere tended—and the process goes on daily by the most curious steps—to become assimilated to their conquerors in manners and religion; and the Khonds, in particular, have formed, by intermixture with the latter, new castes, many of which hold a respectable place within the pale of Hindu society.

Lastly—beyond the *proper* limits of the zemindaries— in the mountainous region, comprising the central ridges, the lofty plateaux, and the inner valleys of the chain of Ghauts, large portions of the primitive races remain imperfectly subdued, while some have maintained their independence against the utmost efforts of the Hindus. The zemindaries being interposed between this wild population and the state-domain, the zemindars have had relations with it to the almost complete exclusion of the successive governments of Orissa, and have formed connexions with its several divisions, generally upon equal terms. In the quarter of the Khond people for example —the zemindars having been ever at feud with one another and prone to resistance to the state, while the mountain tribes were exposed to attack by every adventurer who might hope to seize their lands—there have arisen between each zemindar and the cluster of unsubdued tribes bordering on his domain alliances for mutual defence, in which, while the tribes have a part and rank distinctly subordinate, their independence is recognised and equal advantages are stipulated.

Since the extinction of the native monarchy, the zemindar rajahs have acknowledged, in succession, the supremacy of Delhi, of the Mahratta power, and of our empire; but, secure in their mountain strongholds and pestilential climate, they have generally yielded to these governments a precarious and unfruitful allegiance.

The rajah of Goomsur was one of these zemindar rajahs. The zemindary which belonged to him is included within the lines of 19° 36′ 3″ and 20° 20′ north latitude, and those of 84° 14′ and 85° 1′ east longitude, and has an area of 1,350 square miles. Its hill tracts (called Maliahs) are possessed by the Khonds,[1] while the lower or sub-alpine region constitutes the khalisah, or domain. The domain (or Goomsur proper) is divided into eighteen mootahs, which contain 464 villages. Its population, which is estimated at 61,000 souls, is exclusively Hindu, except in a limited tract in its south-western angle, and where families of the ancient people exist in hamlets thinly scattered amongst its least productive wilds.

The area of the domain is 840, that of the Khond districts about 500 square miles. The former, situated beneath the eastern face of the great mountain range, occupies the upper portion of the valley of the Russagorla, a considerable stream which, rising from many widely-spread sources amongst the Ghauts, reaches the sea at Ganjam by a winding course of about 150 miles. The western division of the domain, lying immediately at the base of the mountain plateau, is principally composed

[1] 'Of the primitive peoples, the Koles prevail in the northern division of Orissa, the Khonds in the middle portion, and the Sourahs in the south. The Khonds are now seen within the following ill-defined limits. Upon the eastern side they appear in the wilder tracts of the Ganjam district bordering upon the Chilka lake, and touch in that quarter the coast of the Bay of Bengal. On the north-west, they are found on the boundaries of Gondwana, in long. 83°; while on the west, they extend to an unknown distance within the unsurveyed frontier of the Nagpore state. They are found as far south as Bustar in lat. 9° 43″, while the zemindary of Palconda, in the Vizagapatam district, is possessed by a Khond chief. On the south, the Khonds are replaced in the zemindary of Pedda Kimedy, in the Ganjam district, by the Sourah race, which is said thenceforward generally to occupy the eastern acclivities of the Ghauts to the Godavery. To the north, fifty miles beyond the Mahanuddee, in the meridian of Boad, the Khonds are succeeded by the Kole people. On the north-east, they are found high in Cuttack; while Sourahs (not identified with the Sourahs of the south) inhabit there the inferior ridges of the Ghauts.'

of the narrow and rugged glens amongst which the feeders of this river rise. It is included within the great forest of Orissa, which is here interspersed with open glades of great beauty, and frequently varied by lightly wooded tracts, in which, by the streams, villages flourish amongst rich corn fields, gardens, and orchards. These glens becoming gradually less densely wooded, and less insalubrious as they recede from the mountains, expand into open and highly productive valleys upon the eastern frontier of the zemindary; but of the whole khalisah or domain of Goomsur, little more than a fourth part is cultivated.

Of the Khond districts of Goomsur, three are situated upon the table-land above the Ghauts; the fourth (called Chokapaud) lies at the base of the hills, and within the vast forest of Orissa, which forms a zone from fifteen to thirty miles in depth along the eastern face of the Ghauts. The Khonds below the Ghauts consist chiefly of scattered families of the class already described as 'Vettiah Khonds,'[1] or of the free subjects of the zemindary, partially assimilated to their conquerors, and known as 'Benniah Khonds.'

On this subject Lieutenant Macpherson, in his report of 1841 (to be mentioned hereafter), writes as follows :—

'It is most important to understand distinctly the two following points, upon which facts and forms are diametrically opposed. 1st. The military aids to the zemindar, which are given or withheld with perfect freedom by the Khonds, bear much of the external character of " service," while they receive that designation exclusively from the Hindus. 2nd. The tribes recognise the superior social and personal *rank* of the Hindu chiefs in contradistinction to their *authority*, by forms which are nearly identical with those by which the latter acknowledge the political superiority of their paramount sovereign, and these forms

---

[1] See above, p. 37.

nearly resemble those which attached in feudal usage to the incidents of "homage" and "investiture." Hence the distinct and independent Khond tribes of Goomsur and Boad have been regarded as forming an integral part of the population of each zemindary, their territories are habitually styled "included;" they have been considered vassals, not allies, and have been supposed to hold their free lands upon some species of tenure analogous to the feudal.

'A late event established unequivocally the true nature of this relation. The Khond district, or rather half district of Hodzoghoro, lately transferred its attachment from Boad to Goomsur. This affair was the subject of frequent discussion while I was at Boad between the chief servants of the Boad rajah, and the Khond chiefs who visited me. The right of any Khond community to dissolve old and enter into new relations was not disputed on the part of the zemindar. He complained only of the loss, through the arts of Sam Bissye, of an old subordinate ally whom he had never injured. The idea of the defection of a subject society, far less of the departure of a fief from its allegiance, was not for a moment contemplated. The rajah had, however, put forward very different pretensions before I had an opportunity to institute exact inquiry.'

The practical method by which the zemindars availed themselves of the military aid of their mountain friends was this:[1]—The rajah communicated his desire to the federal patriarch of the cluster of tribes connected with him, that patriarch being the Bissye (or hereditary agent of the zemindar for Khond affairs), and styled 'Dora Bissye.' If there was no doubt as to the propriety of compliance with the demand, the Khond patriarch at once sent his 'arrow of summons' through the mountain valleys, and as it circulated like the Celtic fiery cross, each house

[1] See the Report of 1841.

afforded a fighting man. Should the requisition, however, require consideration, the patriarch summoned a council of heads of tribes, or of the whole people, as usage might prescribe, to determine the course to be pursued.

The two forms by which the Khond chiefs significantly recognised the high rank and social superiority of the rajahs are those which have been alluded to as resembling those which were associated with the feudal incidents of 'homage' and 'investiture.' The patriarch of each tribe attended annually, or once in two years, at the Hindu capital, to make a small offering of rural produce, and to perform his simple obeisance to the rajah, this act of ceremony being repaid by equal courtesy and by a gift of superior value, and the heads of tribes all accepted (although the usage is said to have originated at a period comparatively recent) " saris," that is, Orissan dresses of honour and investiture from the zemindar. These they received at any convenient period after their induction into their hereditary offices according to their own ancient forms, and they considered the ceremony to import simply the acknowledgment of their official position by the rajah, from whom, however, they were pleased at all times to receive the slightest mark of honour, such as a dress, a gift, or a rarely-bestowed title. In a word, they regarded this form as adding some degree of ornament, but no manner of sanction, to their ancient dignities.

The Khond tribes sent in their turn to the rajahs, upon their accession, a similar silken sari of investiture. The true signification of this form is of course differently interpreted according to the conflicting pretensions of the parties; but its acceptance is essential to the recognition of the rajah by the Khonds. The rajahs, on the other hand, guard their nominally-included territories and their own proper domains with equal and jealous pride from every aggression by rival communities.

From the time when Southern Orissa fell under the

British sway, in the last century, the Goomsur zemindary had been in a very unsettled state ;[1] each successive zemindar had been in rebellion against us, the public revenue uncertain, and never collected without difficulty; the actual state of the country and its management so little known, that it was governed for more than two years in the name of a boy who was dead, and was personated by a girl; and the endeavours made at different times to establish our power by military force had been attended with a great sacrifice of treasure, life, and character. The sceptre, if it may be so termed, had been swayed for 800 years by a noble Rajput family, whose surname was Bunje. They were now unworthily represented by a father and son, each of whom had been by turns in possession of the zemindary, or living upon a pension in exile—sometimes in confinement.

In 1835 the son (a man of doubtful sanity) was in power. His tribute fell a little into arrear, and as his previous conduct entitled him to no favour, he was pressed very hard by the collector of Ganjam. That officer, under orders from the Madras government, moved forward some troops and summoned him to appear. Having come part of the way, he found himself under constraint, made his escape by a sudden *ruse*, and was at once in rebellion.

The collector, Mr. Stevenson, suggested to the Madras government that another member of the family—perhaps even the old father under proper limitations—should be appointed rajah in his place, as all parties, even our own public servants, desired a rajah, and were adverse to the downfall of the house of Bunje. ' The conquest of the country,' he wrote, ' is attended by many more difficulties than may appear ; so long as there remains a popular, or even any, claimant of the rajah of Goomsur's

_____

[1] See Mr. Russell's Reports on Goomsur, in the ' Selections from Records of Madras Government, published by authority,' No. xxiv., Madras, 1856.

family, the district must be subject to constant disturbance and be held by a military force. Detachments can and do march to any part of the country, but when they arrive at their point, they find nothing but a few deserted thatched huts in some place of difficult access; the post, from the nature of the country, the difficulty of supply, and the climate, cannot be retained there even if there was an object in so doing, and the detachment returns under a heavy and constant fire from an invisible enemy, who consider that they have obliged the troops to retreat. Government is not perhaps aware that its authority is, and has, I believe, ever been little more than a shadow in these districts. It is not in the least acknowledged beyond Koladah, or the limits of the fertile plains; and in the Amanyas, and, indeed, generally, the rajah is all in all. The extensive mountain portions of Goomsur join on to endless tracts of mountain and forest, of which we have no knowledge, and with the independent chiefs of which we are not acquainted by name.'

But the troops had now come into actual collision with the inhabitants, and the Madras government refused to allow the appointment of a rajah.

The policy of annexation was uncompromisingly carried out under the direction of a very able civil commissioner, Mr. Russell, a member of council at Madras, who had been employed a short time before in quelling a revolt in the neighbouring territory of Purla Kimedy, and was now deputed upon this special service at the request of Mr. Stevenson, whose authority was thereby superseded for the time.

The rajah having taken refuge in the hills, we were soon at war with the mountain tribes who sheltered him. Mr. Russell resorted to operations very similar to those which he had pursued in Purla Kimedy, and of which he had given the following account [1] :—

---

[1] P. 75 of Mr. Russell's Report on the Disturbances in the Zemindary of Purla Kimedy, 1st Nov. 1834.

'The only way any impression can be made upon these chiefs (supposing the other Bissyes, &c. to be in league with them, and their aid therefore unattainable) is to destroy their villages and grain. This may appear a harsh proceeding, but it is no more than daily occurs in European warfare, and how else can we hope to subdue an enemy whose jungles render it impossible to close with them, or even to see them? To bring away their grain is impossible; to leave it, is to give them the means of persevering in their rebellion. . . . In cases in which it may be intended to establish outposts, it is absolutely necessary to burn or unroof part of the houses, or the troops would be burnt out the first night.' Mr. Russell further remarks, in his first report on the Goomsur operations,[1] that in the low country the destruction of a village involves the punishment of the innocent with the guilty, but above the Ghauts every man bears arms, and joins the common cause.

By these measures, and by the infliction of capital punishment, of transportation—more dreaded than even capital punishment,—and of imprisonment, opposition was at length crushed. The events of the war are summed up by Lieutenant Macpherson as follows, in his report of 1841 :—

'The barrier by which the Khond tribes were separated from our immediate provinces was suddenly removed by our assumption of the zemindary of Goomsur for arrears of tribute, which was followed by the rebellion of its rajah in the end of the year 1835. That chief retired before a force which advanced to apprehend him, and to take possession of his estates, into the Khond districts above the Ghauts, which were most anciently attached to Goomsur, and there he soon after died. A small body of troops then penetrated the great mountain chain for the first time to endeavour to obtain possession of his heir, of the remaining members of his family, and of his

[1] P. 51.

treasures.   The region into which it advanced was entirely unexplored.   Of the Khond people we knew nothing
save the name.   We were ignorant of the nature of the
connexions which subsisted between them and Goomsur,
or the neighbouring zemindaries.   We knew nothing of
their social organisation, of their feelings towards the late
zemindar or towards ourselves, of their numbers, their
language, or their manners : while they could have formed
no idea of the character of our power, of our views, of
any of our objects.   A part of the mountain population
was already combined against us, without any suspicion
on our part, in anticipation of the course which we pursued ; and was arrayed in the name of every authority
which they regarded as legitimate, confirmed by the most
binding religious solemnities, and in the sacred name of
hospitality.   The dying rajah had obtained a pledge from
several of the tribes of the plateau, given before their great
divinity, to prevent, in any event, *the capture* of his
family, which had suffered treatment in the last degree
dishonourable at our hands upon a former occasion.   The
disposition of the Khonds, at first considered amicable,
was observed to tend towards hostility upon the apprehension of these distinguished guests; but the existence of
their pledge first appeared from a bold, startling, and
partially successful attempt to fulfil it.   They rose and
overwhelmed a small detachment which (contrary to the
intentions of the commissioner) was employed to escort a
portion of the family of the zemindar by a difficult pass
from the plateau to the low country, putting to death, to
prevent their dishonour, seven ladies of his Zenana.

'The tribes which were chiefly implicated in this movement immediately felt the weight of our vengeance ; but
the extreme sickliness of the advancing season soon after
compelled us to suspend active operations.   At the end
of the rains a large and nearly fresh force of every arm
was assembled to compel the unconditional submission of
the Khonds, involving the surrender of their patriarchs,

and of some officers of the late rajah who had taken refuge with them, and a promise for the future to yield to us the obedience and the services which had been given to Goomsur, that obedience being supposed to comprehend submission to the authority of a " Bissye " of our appointment.   No opposition was offered to our advance. But the Khonds refused, with the most admirable constancy, to bring their natural heads, or their guests, bound to our scaffolds.   The country was laid utterly desolate ; the population was unceasingly pursued by the troops. At the end of about two months the rajah's Hindu officers were given up for a reward in the Maliahs of *Boad.*   The patriarchs of the offending district of Goomsur were betrayed one by one through the Naicks of the border, and the *Hindu* inhabitants of the hills ; with the exception of the chief, Dora Bissye, who, favoured or feared by all, escaped to the Patna zemindary, from whence, having obtained the promise of his life from the commissioner for Cuttack, he sometime after came in.   The Khond chiefs of Bara Mootah were condemned and executed almost without exception.[1]   Sunnuds,[2] of the exact terms of which I am not informed, were given generally to their supposed heirs.

'Sam Bissye, the *Hindu* employé of the *Khonds* of Hodzoghoro, a district recently connected with *Boad,* was invested with the authority supposed to belong to the office of the chief Bissye[3] of the rajah of *Goomsur,* and with a title, in the room of the federal *Khond* patriarch Dora Bissye.'

The following letters will now be intelligible :—

' Goomsur, 10th November 1836.

' You know that I came up here to assist in establishing the imperial authority over a fair wide mountain district,

---

[1] Lieutenant Macpherson notices elsewhere the singular courage and dignity with which they met their death.

[2] Charters granting or confirming the possession of lands or office.

[3] See above, p. 41.

which, not being ruled in a manner at all suitable to its
stage of civilisation, its system of manners, or order of
society, rebelled, if this may be said of a community
whose subjugation and allegiance were rather theoretical
than real and practical.   Well, first a small number of
troops was sent to reduce it.   They effected nothing.
Then a large force was sent; but by this time the circle
of the war had also extended, so they were insufficient too.
But although too few for the work, and too few for the
climate, the troops were too many for the food, for the
medicine, and for the carriage; and starved, fevered, and
outwearied, the work was left by them unaccomplished.
Now a new campaign with fresh troops is to begin, and
if there be no very great mismanagement, perhaps all may
be concluded soon, for I am ashamed to tell you, our
poor enemies, a mere wild hill tribe, are not far enough
advanced in civilisation to use gunpowder.   They fight
valorously with battle-axes of the most trenchant shapes,
and only learnt the use of fire-arms from acquiring the
arms of a party of our sepoys, whom they cut off to a
man in a mountain defile.   Well, my regiment having
stood the brunt of all this " war," as it is facetiously called,
is at last allowed to go into quarters.   I joined it some
months ago before the rains, which are now over.   I had
then to build a house, as our tents can scarcely keep out
the torrents of these regions in the monsoon.   It was a
splendid house of jungle trees, bamboo, and grass.   First,
of course, I built my stable, a very fine, large, distinguished
looking shed as one can imagine.   Then, my house consisted of one large room about 20 feet square; four posts
like pillars supporting a bamboo roof warmly thatched.
My walls were what we call wattle and dab, which means
a wattling of bamboos finely split and well dabbled over
and overlaid inside and out with mud.   Inside I made
several divisions, and whitewashed the whole, built
outhouses for my servants, and was most comfortably
established: when, before I had lived in it a week, I

was sent off with my company to take charge of an outpost. It cost me 8*l.*, which the pleasure I had in building it was well worth. Much tabasheer [1], too, did I collect for your cabinet from the splitting bamboos.'

' Camp, Goomsur, 28th December 1830.

'The war still drags out its weary length. It is a war in which there has been no enemy, and it has long been reduced to a mere personal contest of speed, skill, and endurance, betwixt a mountain chief [2] who darts through the jungles of this forest-laden and difficult country with from ten to fifty fugitive followers, and one of our oldest civilians, backed by eight regiments of the Madras army, horse, foot, and artillery. When my corps, knocked up in the last campaign, was permitted to retire to its cantonment in the rear of the scene, I was ordered to proceed to survey a portion of the assumed zemindary.[3] In this task I have since been employed. The whole country is now occupied by our dispersed troops.'

The following letter appears to have been written about the same time.

'I am employed in surveying the portion of country which has just been assumed. A fair portion of the earth is this; mountain, valley, and stream most richly adorned. In certain seasons it is pestilential beyond all measure. Last year the number of sick amongst our troops amounted to 400 per cent. in six months; that is to say, every man in the force was four times under medical treatment. Even now my servants, who are much exposed to the night dews, are suffering dreadfully. My head servant and second servant have been long sick, the latter dying, I grieve to say, after serving me most faith-

---

[1] A kind of silex that forms in the bamboo.

[2] Dora Bissye.

[3] *i. e.*, of the proper territory of the rajah of Goomsur in the plains and lower hills, *not* the country of the mountain Khonds.

E

fully for eight years. My tailor sick, and, as became the
fraction of a man, absconded through fear. The man
who keeps my milk-goats sick, and six or eight other
menials; amongst them my important cook, frightened
and bolted with the tailor. My food for many days has
been the curry of my guard of sepoys, a serjeant's party
of twelve, and all perfect *gentlemen.* I climb the rugged
hills which I am obliged to ascend, after a fashion which
would surprise the men of Eigg, but absolutely necessary
here. I form a swathe of a piece of cloth, and fixing
ropes to either end place it round my waist. Now my
bearers, making a team of six, take these traces and pull
me up the hill. Receiving from them the least assistance
in the world, I reach the summits of the steepest hills
little fatigued and ready at once to begin my work. I
expect to get from hence back to Nellore in a month or
two, but yet know nothing certainly. I think my eyes
are vastly improved lately. I can now, and do every
day, write, read, and work all day, and then am still able,
as at this moment, to write off a light letter by candle-
light. My tent has been nearly pulled down about my
ears while I have been writing. A great herd of cattle
has been careering round and round me like a whirlwind,
now and then darting amongst my tent ropes; the shouting and yelling of my people to keep them off only making
them madder. However, they have not interrupted me;
now they are gone, and the foxes and jackals are howling
prodigiously. We mind them no more than you do a
caterwauling in your garden.'

CHAPTER IV.

1837.

FIRST VISIT TO THE HILLS.

Mr. Russell, after quelling the insurrection, departed for Madras, where his services received the warmest thanks of the government. Mr. Stevenson then resumed his authority, and he immediately despatched Lieutenant Macpherson upon a mission, of which the latter has given the following account [1] :—

‘ On the very day on which authority was restored to him, Stevenson asked me to undertake a mission of survey and inquiry into the unexplored country with respect to which it was of the last consequence that correct information should be obtained, saying “ that he thought me alone capable of such service.” The unhealthy season had set in, and all had fled or were flying from the scene. The general demurred to the exposure of the troops necessary for my support, to that deadly climate. Stevenson said, “ the information which you will procure will be of more consequence than the health of an army.” The day of my departure into that country was amongst the happiest of my life. I succeeded in my objects beyond expectation, but was struck down by fever and blindness, for I was worn out by the hard exertions of three preceding months. But the idea that I had at length achieved some small amount of good, that I had made the first step towards the redemption of my

[1] In a letter dated 24th February 1840.

E 2

time, and the first blessed step towards home, made suffering lighter than I have known many pleasures.   I
thought I had accomplished what in the common course
of things the government could not possibly entirely
overlook, and I expected such recognition of my hard,
dangerous, and most difficult service as would lead to employment, were it in that den of pestilence itself—but employment on which I might raise so much character as
would bear me home ; for my view since I left England
had been this, that I had no right to return thither until
I could say that I had done something, until I had done
what would secure my employment out of the ranks of a
regiment on my return.   For the attainment of this object
I did not hesitate to risk health, nor did I grudge it when
it was gone.   Now poor Stevenson died, who could alone,
with the exception of Russell, have appreciated my work ;
and it then appeared that my overstrained frame refused,
as it still refuses, to enable me to realise the fruits of my
toil.   Whether wisely or not, I acted with my eyes open,
remaining in India until I had put my work roughly
together.'

The survey undertaken at Mr. Stevenson's request comprised the northern part of the Khond country, from
Goomsur to the Mahanuddee.

Having been accustomed during the whole of his Indian
life to hold the freest communication with the natives,
discussing with them every subject that was nearest to
their hearts, Lieutenant Macpherson had peculiar facili-
ties for opening an intercourse with the Khonds ; and as
he saw them not, as others had done, in the character
of enemies, it is not surprising that he became ere long
the depositary of much information which no other
person possessed. The people are half savages, and
generally sacrificers of men ; and most of the officers
who were compelled to enter the country got out of it
as soon as they could, and cared not how little information they brought away with them ; but he was of

a different spirit, and among those barbarians he contracted friendships, if they may be so called, which neither
he nor they forgot. For instance, a fierce old chief, the
patriarch of Baramullick, called Bagwan Sow,[1] commonly
known as 'the Great Sow,' came to his tent to pay him a
visit of mere curiosity, full of ill-will and disaffection, and
believing himself and believed by all his followers to be
one of the most important of living men. He was to call
his new-born son after Dora Bissye the chief (not yet captured) of the insurrection, 'the greatest and wisest man he
knew.' His host jokingly said, 'You had better call your
next son after me, and then you will have friends on both
sides,' a proposal which was received with a snort of indignation. But after passing a week in camp, using his
eyes and ears, and enjoying the hospitality of his new
acquaintance, the Great Sow was quite another being;
and at last he spoke out, saying 'You are a great and
wise people, and know everything, and we are poor jungle
beasts, and know nothing.' So he ended by learning with
much pains the name of 'Maak' to call his next son by,
a promise which he faithfully kept, adding the name of
some Hindu god; and many years afterwards, on hearing
that his friend's authority was opposed, he raised his men
and marched to his assistance.

While Lieutenant Macpherson was in the hills,—

'The rajah of Boad,' he says,[2] 'was required by the authorities on the south-western frontier of Bengal, but in
terms which are not precisely known to me, to announce
to the tribes of his zemindary the abhorrence of the government of the Meriah rite, and to exert his authority for
its suppression. He represented to me, then at Boad, that,
as I knew, it was in his power to yield even a formal obedience to this order in the case of many of the Khond districts, only if his messengers were allowed the protection of
my camp, and that protection I very willingly gave, as the
occasion promised to afford me valuable opportunities of

---

[1] 'Sow' is a title of honour.   [2] Report of 1841.

observation. A considerable degree of alarm followed the receipt above the Ghauts of the communications of the rajah, which were, I believe, made in very vague and various terms to the different chief patriarchs. Councils met everywhere. The whole population was deeply agitated, and all friendly intercourse with me ceased. In the remote and sequestered district of Ruttabarri it was believed that I was come to enforce compliance with the mandates, and on arriving there, I found that active preparations had commenced for resistance. Very serious results threatened, when the opportune appearance upon the scene of the great Khonro of Boad, whose friendship I had previously made, removed every difficulty. The Khonds could arrive at no distinct conclusion respecting the real meaning of the intimations which were thus made to them ; and, under all the circumstances, it was exceedingly difficult for me to give any explanation of them. But the tribes having made out that no coercive measures were then intended, and that I, at least, was there with views purely friendly, they gradually became at ease, and laid their minds bare to me on the whole subject.

' In the end they consented, without much difficulty, to deliver up their victim-children to me as other tribes have done to other officers, and not as signifying the slightest intention to relinquish the rite, but as a peace offering, or a mark of deference for our power. But to this surrender they assented only on the express condition that the tribes of Goomsur should also be required to give up their victims. The Meriah children they looked upon merely as property of a certain value, and as victims which could be immediately replaced. Their real and deepest anxiety was, lest they should even seem to submit to a necessity which was not acknowledged by all the tribes within their social sphere. As the authorities on either side of the Mahanuddee did not on this occasion act in concert,.the necessary requisition could not at the moment be effectually made in Goomsur for the fulfilment of the condition stipulated, and so the victims were not liberated, and the tribes were left bewildered between the apparently discrepant counsels of the two governments.[1]

'I may remark here what I should have supposed to be self-evident, but for much proof to the contrary, that nothing can be effected, in any case, either by the simple liberation of victims which can be replaced, or by the prevention of sacrifices at any particular time, or in any single district, when they can be performed, at some sacrifice of convenience, elsewhere and at another season. Had these victims in the Boad Maliahs been liberated, I was afterwards distinctly informed that a larger number must have suffered in their stead.'

The expedition was stopped by sickness, and he was compelled to return to the low country before he had spent a month in the hills. He remained for about a year at Ganjam, by the sea-side, engaged—as far as his broken health would permit—in completing his survey reports, in preserving and arranging the miscellaneous information which he had collected, and in obtaining from personal conversation with Khond prisoners (of whom there was a very large number in the gaol of Ganjam), and from every available source, as much intelligence as possible regarding the hill tribes.

'Ganjam, 1st June 1837.

'I have not been able, in perfect safety, until now to follow up my blind scrawl despatched to you above a month ago. My sight and health are perfectly restored. The affection of the former was merely an effect of the Goomsur malaria upon my constitution, which has thrown it off entirely. I would, however, have preferred to suffer more than to have omitted the labours which produced this ailment. I was at the close of the military opera-

---

[1] This was the first exemplification of the inconvenience, so much felt throughout, of the Bengal Government acting separately from that of Madras.

tions—I should say military forms—employed in exploring
a perfectly new and unvisited tract of country in the
valley of the Mahanuddee river; and could I have spent
two months instead of one in those scenes of absorbing
interest, I should have been able to exhibit a new and
clearly-written page of the history of rude nature. The
people amongst whom my routes chiefly lay were the
Khond tribes, the highlanders of the Eastern Ghauts,
whom, at the expense of several of our best regiments
and of nearly all our public credit, the government
was compelled, after a two years' struggle, to acknowledge to be at least *morally* invincible. But so profitable a sojourn my lot forbade. The season was too far
advanced. The detachment kept in the field to support me if necessary, went into hospital to a man, and I
was compelled to return to prevent its entire sacrifice.
Still, as it is, I shall have an interesting report to make,
and one which, from the novelty of the matter at least,
will attract *some* notice. I have been afraid yet to plunge
into the labour of its preparation. I cannot easily, *in
paucis*, give you distinct ideas of my field, or of what I
have gleaned. You can imagine a people, distributed
into clans, occupying the mountain valleys and plateaux
of this chain, and existing, from the beginning of time,
undisturbed by the political and religious revolutions of
Hindostan. This people we discovered, by accident, two
years ago. I found my way through the territories of a
number of these fine clans, and so conciliated their good
will as to get all their chiefs to meet me in confidential
intercourse. From them I learnt a good many—all that
my time permitted—of the most important facts relative
to a large portion of this new country and people, and
executed a very extensive survey. The religion[1] of these
Khonds is an original system. Its base is a weak, incoherent theism, with a subordinate demonology, the re-

[1] See Chapter VI.

flection of the wants and fears and predominant sentiments of a rude society. It acknowledges, 1. A supreme power; 2. An earth god, analogous to Pan in his province and functions; 3. A god of limits; and 4. Lares without end. Local divinities besides abound. You will be astonished to hear that the main feature, and, in effect, the animating principle of this system of superstition, is the rite of human sacrifice. This rite is solemnly perpetrated in every district every month of the year! The Governor-General has vowed to put an end to the horrible practice. *How* is the question. Our troops can exist in the country but during three months in the year. The language, manners, and institutions of the people, and nine-tenths of the country itself, are utterly unknown. The country of the Khonds is beautiful and often very rich, and their agricultural industry is of the best sort. Every man has his farm, a perfect freehold; I should say, held in fee simple, and subject to no form of impost whatever. The people are a very fine race.'

'Ganjam, 9th October 1837.

'Besides this story of Orissa and the Khonds, I have been so exceedingly fortunate as here, sitting by the sea, to have been able to get in the most satisfactory shape an account of a probably cognate aboriginal people of the same part of India called the Souras. Will you credit that until I made the discovery no one suspected that a mountain group within three miles of one of our oldest stations here [1] was exclusively inhabited by Khonds, of whom no one had ever heard till the Goomsur war led us above the Ghauts; and can you believe that we have been mixed up with these Souras in the relations of war and peace for nearly 100 years, while no one has ever made a vocabulary of their language? Is it not strange, too, that these two primitive races should have been in the habit of carrying off our subjects in large numbers

---

[1] Berhampore is the station referred to.

annually for human sacrifices to the earth god, their
great divinity—and that this should have become known
last year? The principles of the institutions of these
rude societies are strongly contrasted.   The Khond
community is ruled by an hereditary aristocracy, jeal-
ously limited by democratic councils; the Souras are
ruled by a theocracy.   But for my stumbling, under circumstances peculiarly favourable, upon these Souras, I
should have been ere now at Madras. My report will still
take me a long time to digest. Without my good friend
Cadenhead, who occasionally lends me his hand when
writing would hurt my eyes, I could not get on at all.'

Although the report which cost him so much labour
was not completed till a later period, it may be convenient
to introduce in this place the description which it contains of some of the chief characteristics of this strange
hill people, of whom he alone has up to this day given
any connected and systematic account. The fifth chapter
of the present work is accordingly taken, with some
alteration of the arrangement, from that report; but
many interesting passages are omitted, as they would take
up too much room.

In answer to some criticisms upon the report he observes, ' When you talk of zoology, geology, and other
ologies, you surely forget that I was among the mountain
Khonds only a few weeks, in which time I executed
a most laborious survey, besides obtaining the great mass
of my information.   Had I been there five or six months,
I should have doubtless collected matter enough for a
complete account and a good book.   Then as to statistics,
properly so called, you might as well have expected from
Captain Cook the statistics of the land which he described
as " either an island or a peninsula; very hazy; passed at
night under double-reefed topsails."   My statistics include
the name of every district, subdivision, and village, with
number of houses (whence population) in each, and names

of chiefs of every grade, besides, of course, area; all, you know, of vast importance. But what I wish to impress on you is that the whole thing amounts only to a sketch, not a complete picture with all its incidents.'

The most important part of the report is the account of the Khond religion; but though correct as a description of the religion of the tribes which he visited in the beginning of 1837, a visit several years later to the southern tracts convinced him that it was incomplete. He made full reports to government of all the additional knowledge which he had obtained, and finally, after many years of close observation, he combined the whole in a single paper, which, as already mentioned, was read before the Royal Asiatic Society of London in the year 1852.[1] This paper forms the sixth chapter of these Memorials.

---

[1] An abstract of the religious chapter of the report of 1841 had been read before the same Society.

CHAPTER V.

DESCRIPTION OF THE KHONDS.

The Khonds are fitted by physical constitution to undergo the severest exertions and to endure every form of privation. Their height is of about the average standard of Hindus of the peninsula. Their forms are characterised by strength and symmetry. The muscles of the limbs and body are clean and boldly developed. The skin is clear and glossy, its colour ranging from a light bamboo to a deep copper shade; the heel is in a line with the back of the leg, the foot is somewhat larger than that of the Hindu, and the instep not highly arched, although the Khond, nevertheless, has extraordinary speed of foot. The forehead is full and expanded. The cheek bones are high and rather prominent; the nose is seldom, though occasionally, arched, and is generally broad at the point. The lips are full but not thick; the mouth is rather large. The whole physiognomy is generally indicative of intelligence and determination, blended with good humour.

Their clothing consists of a single piece of coarse cloth, either white or chequered, from twelve to twenty cubits in length, which is in some districts girt round the loins with its extremities flowing loose behind, and in others wrapped round the waist, and thrown across the chest something in the Hindu fashion. The women wear cloths of the same material, wound round the waist, and brought over the shoulders. They in some districts wear brass

KHOND VILLAGE, WITH SACRED HILL AND MERIAH GROVE.

armlets and anklets, and small nose and ear ornaments of
gold and silver.

The villages are in general beautifully situated, either
by a clump of trees, or at the bases of the wooded hills,
or on the knolls of the valleys, slightly raised above the
level of irrigation.   In the southern districts they consist
of two rows of houses, slightly curved so as to form
a broad street, which is closed at each end by a strong
wooden barrier gate.   In the northern tracts they are
built, like Hindu villages, after no regular plan.   In
founding a village, the first act is to plant a great
cotton tree, consecrated to the village deity, in the centre
of the site, where the house of the patriarch, or abbaya
(called the Mullicko by the Hindus), is placed. The Panwa,
or weaver, lives at either end of the village, his dwelling
being marked by the pegs used for weaving before the
door.   The site of a village is determined by the priest
after carefully consulting the will of the god.   Each man
builds his own house, and in the southern districts the
walls are formed exclusively of planks placed edgewise as
in a ship, the roofs being thatched. When a village begins
to decay it is not repaired, but a new one is built on a
different site, and none of the old materials are used.   A
Khond village lasts on an average about fourteen years, but
its locality is readily changed on account of other causes
besides decay; upon the slightest suspicion that the site has
become unlucky from the occurrence of an unusual number of deaths, or from the loss of stock, &c., the priest is
put in requisition and a new hamlet is constructed.

The Khonds use no medicine of any sort.   To wounds
they apply the earth of an ant-hill made into a warm
mud, or a poultice of millet.   They also apply in extreme
cases the actual cautery to the belly, using a hot sickle
over a wetted cloth.   They are very subject to fever, and
apparently to inflammation of the bowels from excessive
drinking.   They are often swept off in numbers by smallpox, and many are blind.   The women suffer little or

nothing in child-bearing, and nurse their children only six months.

The pursuit of agriculture, varied by war and the chase, is exclusively held in honour, the only exception being in the southern districts, and in favour of the arts of working in iron and in clay; there are no renters of land or labourers for hire, and each petty freehold consists of a portion of the irrigated soil of the valley, which is minutely subdivided, and of a tract of the upland, which is held in much larger portions. The paternal authority is absolute, and the son cannot possess property of any kind before his father's death. Upon that event landed property and agricultural stock descend exclusively in the male line, females being incapable of holding land. In most districts the eldest son receives an additional share of both of these species of property; in a few, they are equally divided. In case of failure of issue, brothers inherit equally, and then the brothers of the father. Daughters divide equally personal ornaments, household furniture, money, and movables, while their brothers are obliged to maintain them and to contribute equally to the expense of their marriages. On the failure of heirs male, land becomes the property of the village, and is divided among its members.

The right of possession of land is simply founded in the case of tribes upon priority of appropriation, and in the case of individuals upon priority of culture. The usages of different districts in respect to waste land vary much.

In some quarters the waste land is partitioned amongst the villages, but in others not. The exclusive use of unreclaimed land, for pasturage or for jungle produce, was, however, in no case asserted, and generally few practical restrictions existed as to the occupation of waste by individuals within the boundaries of their tribe.

Agriculture is practised by the Khonds with a degree of skill and energy which is perhaps nowhere surpassed in India, and which has produced a degree of rural affluence

rarely paralleled.   At the season of labour the Khond
rises at daybreak.   Before quitting his cottage he eats a
full meal, consisting of moong, raggi, or tuar,[1] boiled with
a portion of jungle herbs, and flavoured with a piece of
goat's or swine's flesh.   Then yoking his team, or shoulder-
ing his axe, he goes out for the day.   When employed in
ordinary work, as at the plough, he labours without intermission until three o'clock in the afternoon, when he
bathes in the nearest stream.   But when his toil is more
severe, as in felling wood, he rests to eat a mid-day mess,
which is brought to him in the field.   At evening he returns home to a meal similar to that of the morning, with
the addition of liquor or tobacco.   At harvest and seed
time the women share in every form of field labour, and
where there is no Hindu cowherd, those of each family
watch the village cattle by turns.

The Maliah [Mountain] Khonds are extremely rich in
every species of agricultural stock.   They have large herds
of bullocks of a small breed, and of buffaloes, numerous
flocks of fine goats and abundance of swine, and every
hamlet teems with poultry.   Rice of several sorts, various
oils, millets, pulse, and fruits, with tobacco, turmeric, and
mustard of superior quality, are the most important
species of hill produce ; and these the Khonds exchange
with resident Hindu merchants, principally of the Soodoo
caste, or at the fairs of Koladah and Codundah (where
the Khonds are aided in their bargain-making by the
Panwas), for salt, cloth, brass vessels and ornaments, and
a few other necessaries.

Transfers of land by sale constantly take place in these
districts, and the value of a piece of ground at Borogootza,
which required four bullocks for its cultivation, and sufficed
for the support of a family of four persons, was estimated
by some intelligent Khonds at from forty to fifty pairs of
bullocks, while Lieutenant Macpherson was told by an
inhabitant of Borapall in Nowsagur, that it would fetch at

---

[1] Raggi is a small grain like millet. Moong and tuar are kinds of pulse.

least as much if situated in that district. This being with reference to the rent of land in Boad, as nearly as could be judged, about ten or twelve years' purchase; and a village of Bulscoopa, which was sold by its abbaya and inhabitants, as having become unlucky, to a rich Khond from Chokapaud, brought a price which was in keeping with this estimate.

The forms observed in the transfer of land by sale are these: The selling party intimates his purpose to the abbaya of the section, not to obtain his sanction, but to give publicity to his intentions. He then goes with the intending purchaser to the village in which the property is situated, and summons five respectable inhabitants to bear witness to the act of sale. When assembled on the land to be transferred, the seller calls upon those witnesses, and at the same time solemnly invokes the village deity to bear testimony that a portion of land specified is alienated by him for ever to a certain person for a certain consideration. He then delivers a handful of soil to the purchaser, who in return makes over part of the purchase-money, when the transaction is complete. The close similarity between the forms which obtain among this people and those which are employed by the nations of Europe and of Western Asia, to give publicity and certainty to transfers of real property, is sufficiently striking.

The use of money, with the exception of cowries, was until recently nearly unknown to the Maliah Khonds, and the value of all property is estimated by them in 'lives,' a measure which requires some adjustment every time that it is applied, a bullock, a buffalo, goat, a pig or fowl, a bag of grain, or a set of brass pots being each, with anything else that may be agreed upon, a 'life.' A hundred lives, on an average, may be taken to consist of ten bullocks, ten buffaloes, ten sacks of corn, ten sets of brass pots, twenty sheep, ten pigs, and thirty fowls.

The practice of the art of agriculture exclusively by

the mountain Khonds, with the partial exception above
noticed, is rendered possible by the settlement in these
districts of families of the following Pariah or Hindu castes,
who manufacture first necessaries, and perform other indispensable services.

1. The Panwa, or weaver.
2. The Lohara, or ironsmith.
3. The Komaroo, or potter.
4. The Gouro, or herdsman.
5. The Soondi, or distiller (in the eastern districts).

Of these, the Panwa is proverbially indispensable to
every Khond hamlet. His duties are to provide human
victims, an occupation which is, however, restricted to
certain families in which it is hereditary ; to carry messages, such as summonses to council or to the field; to act
as musician at ceremonies, and to supply the village with
cloth, of which the Khond allowance is a yearly garment.

These castes which have been settled in the Khond country
from time immemorial, all partake of food which has been
prepared by the Khonds, who will not, however, eat from
their hands. They use both the Khond and the Oriyah
languages. They appear to have their own gods, to whom
they sacrifice, but they generally participate in the worship
of the Khonds. By these they are treated, particularly the
Panwas, with great kindness, but as an inferior and protected, perhaps as a servile race. They are never neglected
at a feast ; and any injury done to them is promptly
resented. But they are never allowed to bear themselves
as equals; and they in few cases hold land. They generally maintain their blood pure.

Hospitality is regarded as one of the first duties. It is
equally imperative upon all. ' For the safety of a guest,'
say the Khonds, ' life and honour are pledged; he is to be
considered before a child.' Every stranger is an invited
guest, and any person may acquire, under any circumstances, the privileges of the character by claiming them.

No person, whether Khond or Hindu, can appear at a
Khond village without being invited to enter, and the
burden of public hospitality does not fall more upon the
abbaya (patriarch) than upon any one else.   There is no
limit to the period to which hospitality may be claimed; a
guest can never be turned away, and his treatment must
be that of a member of the family.   Fugitives upon any
account whatever from other tribes must be received and
protected.   Meriahs, however, cannot claim refuge as
guests: they are given up as property amongst friendly
tribes; in unfriendly ones they generally find an asylum;
a person who has sought refuge is supported until he can
make up his mind to return to his tribe, or to seek
adoption into that of his host, and in the latter case he
generally labours on the land of his protector until he can
procure a share for himself.

If a man can make his way by any means into the house
of his enemy it is considered a case of refuge, and he cannot be touched, even although his life has been forfeited
to his involuntary host by the law of blood-revenge.   A
Panwa, having killed the son of the abbaya of his village, fled and escaped vengeance.   Two years after he
returned, and in the middle of the night rushed into the
house of the abbaya.   A council of the tribe, any one of
whom would have previously destroyed the murderer,
determined that he must be regarded as a guest, and he
was accordingly permitted to remain unharmed.   Sometimes, however, when an enemy thus makes himself a
guest, the house may be vacated and food may be refused
to him, and he may be killed if he comes out.   But this
proceeding is very rarely considered justifiable.

One tribe must receive another if it become fugitive.
Two branches of a tribe having fallen out at a feast, fought
until one was driven from its lands, of which, with the
villages, the other part took possession; the expelled
branch sought refuge with another tribe, and was supported by it for a year; in the end, an abbaya of the
victorious portion relented, and secretly became a party

to a scheme for the re-admission of the others. He sent them notice, when the watch which was kept for their exclusion was somewhat relaxed. The people rushed into one of their old villages, from which as guests it became impossible to expel them, and they at last obtained possession of their lands.

The family of the rajah of Goomsur were considered by the Khonds, to whose care he confided them, in the light of guests, in the most sacred sense, and this was in a great measure the origin of our first quarrel with these people.

The genuine instinctive spirit of savage freedom still occasionally shows itself in the preference of death to the endurance of the least restraint. A Khond, captured by our troops in Baramootah, immediately tore out his tongue by the roots and died ; another, made prisoner after maintaining a long and gallant conflict with a horseman, until he was stabbed by another assailant from behind, sternly refused food, and perished on the fourth day.

The Khond patriarchs are very proud of their race ; even when they most affect Hindu customs, they delight to assert their superiority to the more civilised people. Their most common boasts are, that they reverence their fathers and mothers, while the Hindus treat theirs with contempt ; that they are men of one word, whilst Hindus are false and uncertain ; that the Khonds are one as a race, while the Hindus are endlessly subdivided. They have the easy bearing of men who are unconscious of inferiority, and they rarely employ expressions of courtesy. In salutation they raise the hand perpendicularly above the head. In meeting on the road the younger person says, 'I am on my way,' the elder replies 'Go on.'

In the districts which have enjoyed most intercourse with the low country, the chiefs readily embrace any opportunity to acquire all that is learnt by the Hindus. ' In the small valley of Borogootza, for example (says the Report), three abbayas read the shasters with considerable

case.   An intelligent Sunnyasi, who resides there, in-
structs a good many Khond children with his own in
letters, and ascribes to them a capacity quite equal to
that of Hindu children of any caste.   The manjee of
Nowsagur in Duspullah has learnt all that is generally
taught in that zemindary; and the patriarch of Punchora,
who entertains a number of Soodoo priests at his chief
village, is said to be well informed in the doctrines and
strictly observant of the ceremonies of the Hindu religion.   I first met Madwa Khonro at Raneegunge, seated
at his door engaged in teaching his child to read.

'Dora Bissye, chief patriarch in Goomsur, commands to
a great extent the admiration both of the Hindu and
the Khond population of the districts which lie between
Kimedy and the Mahanuddee, and he is well known
beyond that river.   He is the object of feelings of the
deepest veneration to his own race in Goomsur, Duspullah, and a great part of Boad; and having had opportunities of observation, I may state that my estimate of his
character justifies the opinion of those before whom his
life has been spent.

'In person he is somewhat below the middle size,
according to the Hindu standard; of spare habit, and by
no means robustly formed.   His physiognomy is spirited,
and when excited intellectual, but with a predominating
expression of benevolence. His features are regular, sufficiently bold for expression, but by no means striking,
and not strongly marked by the peculiarities of his race
His manner is animated, perfectly self-possessed, and very
pleasing. He might pass for a well-bred Brahmin of Orissa.

'His views upon every subject on which he is informed
are clear and discriminating; and he perceives new facts
and their relations with remarkable facility.   His habits
not being military (as is also the case with Nowbhun
Khonro, chief patriarch of Boad), cowardice was vulgarly
imputed to him in our camp, as if a people ever lavished
its affections upon a poltroon.

'Having passed his time by turns amongst the Khond valleys of the Ghauts and the petty courts of the zemindars, he is as well informed of all that relates to the Hindu population of a considerable portion of Orissa as of the usages and interests of his own people.   He is well read in the Puranas, and forgot his prison in enquiring of the present state of the jewelled palace of Lunka.   His personal habits are those of an Orissan Bramin, and he is attended exclusively by persons of this caste.'

Women, among the Khonds, appear to enjoy a degree of social influence at least equal to that which has been attributed to them in the patriarchal communities of Western Asia.   They are uniformly treated with respect ; the mothers of families generally with much honour. Nothing is done either in public or in private affairs without consulting them, and they generally exert upon the councils of their tribes a powerful influence favourable to humanity.

' Our women are not deficient in intelligence,' said the fierce old Bagwan Sow of Baramullick,[1] ' but they have this fault, that when we are at feud with our next neighbours we never dare intrust to them a purpose of war. It would be strongly opposed, and inevitably revealed to some relative or friend whom it might endanger.'   But, added the Sow, with an expression of deep thankfulness, ' we can impart such designs without risk of betrayal to the youngest stripling who can bear an axe.'

Marriage can take place only betwixt members of different tribes, and not even with strangers who have been long adopted into or domesticated with a tribe ; and a state of war or peace appears to make little difference as to the practice of intermarriage betwixt tribes.   The people of Baramootah and of Burra Des in Goomsur have been at war time out of mind, and annually engage in fierce conflicts, but they intermarry every day.   The

[1] See above, p. 53.

women of each tribe after a fight visit each other to condole on the loss of their nearest common relatives.

Reversing the usage which prevails amongst other people, boys of from ten to twelve years of age amongst some of the Khonds are very frequently married to girls of fifteen or sixteen. The arrangement is of course completed by the parents of the parties. The father of the bridegroom pays twenty or thirty lives to the father of the bride,[1] and the marriage is at once thus solemnised. The father of the boy, with his family and friends, bear a quantity of rice and liquor in procession to the house of the parents of the girl. The priest tastes the bowl, and pours out a libation to the gods, when the parents of the parties join hands and declare that the contract shall be completed. All present then partake of the prepared cheer. An entertainment, to which both families contribute equally, is then prepared, either at the dwelling of the bride, or at some convenient place near the house of the bridegroom. To the feast succeed dancing and song. When the night is far spent, the principals in the scene are raised by an uncle of each upon his shoulders and borne through the dance. The burdens are suddenly exchanged, and the uncle of the youth disappears with the bride. The assembly divides into two parties; the friends of the bride endeavour to arrest, those of the bridegroom to cover, her flight; and men, women, and children mingle in mock conflicts, which are often carried to great lengths. Thus the semblance of forcible abduction attends the withdrawal of the bride amongst these Orissan tribes, as it does to a great extent amongst the Hindus, and as it did amongst many nations of ancient Europe, and now does amongst the tribes of the Caucasus.[2] The priest, who had previously bound, after the Hindu fashion, a yellow thread round the necks of the parties,

---

[1] The transaction is virtually betwixt the branches of tribes to which the parties belong.

[2] See 'Primitive Marriage,' by John F. Maclennan, M.A. Edinburgh, 1865.

and sprinkled their faces with turmeric water in the shed used for beating rice, attends them homewards to rehearse a charm wherever a brook crosses their path.

The new wife lives with her husband if a boy, in his father's house, occupying the same couch, and aiding his mother in domestic labours. She leads a life of retirement compared with that of an unmarried girl, abstaining from much dancing, and from the most riotous feasts. When her husband grows up he gets a house of his own, unless he is the youngest son. In the superior age of the bride is seen but a proof of the supremacy of the paternal authority amongst this singular people. The parents obtain in the wives of their sons during the years of their boyhood very valuable domestic servants, and their selections are avowedly made with a view to utility in this character.

Notwithstanding the payment which is made by the father of the bridegroom, the wife is not to be considered the property of the husband.[1]

A Khond wife, if childless, has a right to quit her husband at any time; and even if pregnant, within six months after her marriage; the consideration paid by the husband to her father being in either case returned. And it appears that a wife who chooses to retire to her father's house can in no case be forcibly reclaimed.

Marriage is *ipso facto* dissolved when the husband discovers the wife in adultery ; and generally, when her guilt is indisputably established by other evidence. And a wife who has either voluntarily, or in consequence of such conviction, parted from her husband, cannot again (in some parts of the country) contract marriage. A man may, with the permission of his wife, but not otherwise, contract a second marriage, or retain a concubine during her life, and neither practice is unusual. Concubinage is not reckoned in any degree disgraceful, fathers of respect-

[1] This account refers chiefly to the Khonds of Goomsur and Bond.

able families allowing their daughters to contract this
connexion.   The children of a concubine are in some
districts said to be of inferior rank in the family circle,
and to inherit but a half share of the paternal property.
In others, however, they are in every respect on a footing
of equality with the children of marriage.

The women upon ordinary occasions of festivity only
taste the liquor cup, and habitual intoxication, the great
vice of the other sex, is in them uncommon and held
infamous.   Passing through the districts of Moondagaum
and Hodzoghoro at a season of periodical intoxication, the
blowing of the mhowa flower, of which the favourite
Khond spirit is made, Lieut. Macpherson found the country
covered with frantic or senseless groups of men, but no
women appeared in the least intoxicated.   Upon occasions
of human sacrifice, however, the women mingle freely
and without shame, with the other sex, in the more than
Saturnalian licence by which that rite is accompanied.

The wife and children serve the father of a family while
he eats, then take their meal.   Women for some unknown
cause are never permitted to eat the flesh of the hog.

Khond births are celebrated on the seventh day after
the event by a feast given to the priest and to the whole
village.   To determine the best name for the child, the
priest drops grains of rice into a cup of water, naming with
each grain a deceased ancestor.[1]   He pronounces, from
the movements of the seed in the fluid, and from observations made on the person of the infant, which of his progenitors has reappeared in him, and the child generally, at

---

[1] Captain Burton says (Mission to Gelele, King of Dahomé, 2nd
edition, London, 1864, vol. ii. p. 158), 'The child's name is given on the
eighth day after the Bukono has pronounced what ancestor has sent it.'
From 'The Story of New Zealand,' &c., by Arthur S. Thomson, M.D.,
London, 1859, we learn that 'Before a child was a month old, often before
it was ten days, its head was adorned with feathers, &c. . . . a long list of
names belonging to the child's ancestors was repeated by the Priest, and
when the child sneezed or cried, the name which was then being uttered
was the one selected.'   Vol. i. p. 118.

least among the northern tribes, receives the name of that ancestor.

On the death of the patriarch of a district, the event is everywhere proclaimed by the beating of gongs and drums, where the abbayas and heads of society assemble from every quarter. The body is placed on a high funeral pile. A large bag of grain is laid close by upon the ground, and in it is planted a high staff bearing a flag. Over the grain are heaped up all the personal effects, as the clothes, arms, and eating and drinking vessels of the deceased chief. The funeral pile is then fired, and his family and the people of the hamlet.perform a dance peculiar to this occasion, around the flag-staff until the pile is consumed. The property which is thus exposed, besides much of the live stock of the patriarch, is distributed among the abbayas of branches of the tribe. The priest is usually present, but takes no part in the ceremonial; he may not touch a dead body. The dance around the flag-staff is continued at intervals from the time of firing the pile until the tenth day, when there is a concourse of people from all quarters proportioned to the importance and the fame of the deceased chief. An assembly of the tribe or district is now held, at which the heir of the late patriarch is acknowledged. On the death of a private person his body is burnt on a pile with no ceremony, save a drinking feast, which is given to the inhabitants of the hamlets on the tenth day. Every village has a separate burning ground.

Each tribe possesses a distinct portion of territory, and is presided over by a patriarch, who is the representative of its common ancestor. It is divided into several branches, which are in like manner ruled by their family heads; and finally these subdivisions are composed of a number of villages, each of which is governed by the descendant of a chief chosen by its first founders. Each cluster of tribes is presided over by a federal patriarch. The patriarch of a Khond tribe is aided and controlled in the management of its ordinary affairs by a council composed of the heads of its branches. These again have the patriarchs of villages for their assessors, while the village heads are assisted by the elders of their hamlets. Assemblies of the whole population of the tribe, or of its subdivisions, moreover, are convened, as usage may prescribe, under the directions of the patriarchs of each grade, to deliberate upon general or upon local interests. The federal patriarchs, in like manner, consult with the heads of tribes, and assemble when necessary the entire population of the federal group.

Such is the theory of the social organisation of this portion of the Khond people. But it is nowhere to be seen completely realised. Every conceivable deviation from the model occurs. The tribes are generally much intermingled, although some are said to remain distinct. But each now forms a social body, of which the chief bond is the idea of natural affinity, while a common name, community of interests, of religious rites, of associations, and of traditions render its sense of unity complete.

The patriarchal office, remaining hereditary as to family, has become virtually elective as to person, without having suffered any change in its character; and herein consists a distinguishing peculiarity of the social situation of these tribes. They have, it is believed, attained the first objects of social union, the enjoyment of property, the fruit of fixed industry, in security and freedom, in a greater degree than any people which has been observed living under institutions which are in practice so strictly patriarchal.

The lineal head is most frequently superseded in the case of the federal patriarchs. For example, the late federal head of Goomsur, Dora Bissye, was raised to that office on account of his superior abilities, in the room of his elder brother; while in the case of heads of villages, whose duties nearly all are competent to perform, the regular course of succession is very rarely disturbed.

When a tribe has determined that the chief authority shall devolve, not upon its lineal head, but upon another member of the patriarchal house more competent to rule, nothing takes place in any way resembling either a formal act of exclusion or of deposition. If the patriarch has not yet assumed authority he is passed over, as if by family arrangement. If he should have been recognised, he is gradually and silently superseded, retaining however much of his precedence. In neither case is a successor called to the management of affairs by anything at all resembling election in the form which we associate with that term. The general will is manifested in the form of popular acceptance alone. The chosen patriarch assumes the first place and the chief authority in virtue of the confidence and affection of the community which have rested upon him as the most worthy. The ancient line is restored when a capable son appears.

The patriarch, abbaya, or mullicko of a Khond tribe is simply the head of a family of which every member is of equal rank, the first amongst equals. Unlike the chieftain of a clan, he is in no respect raised above the community whose interests, associations, traditions, and manner of life he shares. None minister to his wants. He has no trace of state however rude; no separate residence or stronghold, no retainers, no property, save his ancestral fields, by the cultivation of which he lives. He receives neither tribute nor aid, save perhaps an occasional harvest offering of good will. The enjoyment of the place of dignity at every public and private festival may be reckoned, as in the case of the Homeric kings, amongst the most valuable, as it is amongst the most agreeable incidents of his situation.

The patriarch of a tribe, whatever may be the degree of his personal authority, undertakes no measures except in emergency, transacts no affairs without the assistance

and sanction of the abbayas, or of the assembled society.
He has charge of the relations of his tribe to the neighbouring tribes and zemindaries.   He leads in war, and
always accompanies the military aids rendered to the
Hindu chiefs.   At home he is the protector of public
order and the arbiter of private wrongs ; conciliating
feuds and dispensing justice, but depending for obedience
to his decisions entirely upon his personal influence and
the authority of his assessors.   He convenes councils of
the abbayas, or of the whole tribe, as usage may prescribe, either for deliberative or for judicial purposes.
He moreover discharges the local duties of patriarch of
his branch and head of his village.

When occasion appears to the heads of a tribe to require a formal expression of the general will, the chief
patriarch sends a summons by the Panwas to every
village to attend upon a particular day, at a central point,
which is selected by him for the assembly.

The nearer hamlets contribute their whole population
to the council, the more distant depute the person or
persons thought best qualified to represent them.   The
place of meeting is generally the open slope of a hill. The
district patriarch and the abbayas of sections first seat
themselves in a circle.   Around them the abbayas of
villages form an outer ring.   The rest of the community
is arranged beyond, and all are armed ; women and
children sit apart, but within hearing distance.

As the day advances, and the assembly begins to fill,
the chief patriarch rises from time to time to demand
whether such an abbaya has taken his place ? whether
such an elder has appeared ? or whether the men of such
a village are prepared for their part ? despatches messengers for some, chides others for delay, and receives
replies, apologies, and explanations loud and various in
return.

The peculiar function of a patriarch of the tribe appears to cease with the completion of the assembly.   He

makes obeisance towards the four quarters of the globe, to the sun, and to the earth, and takes his seat in the circle of abbayas of subdivisions. He convenes the assembly, and is its most distinguished member, but he does not apparently regulate or preside in any way over its proceedings.

In an assembly of a tribe the patriarchs of the inner circle alone usually offer public counsel, and upon its formation one of them immediately rises to address the meeting. He begins generally by touching upon some spirit-stirring theme of the past, the actions of a distinguished man, or the memory of a cherished event, which bear some obvious relation to existing circumstances ; and having by such preface prepared his auditory, he invites from amongst the crowd, within the inner circle, some elder of the people of venerable age and character to bear testimony, as a living record, and as a depositary of the traditions of the past, to the facts upon which the chiefs shall found their respective counsels.

The abbaya then exhibits his view of the matter before the assembly, appealing, as he proceeds, to the reverend witness, who, standing in the centre of the meeting, now vouches, now modifies his statements ; or, taking the part of an interlocutor, maintains a dialogue with the speaker, or interposes episodes in his discourse, while the assembly freely interrupts the patriarch with loud tokens of applause or dissent, but in all cases, it is said, without infringing the natural rules of decorum.

When the heads of the community succeeding each other in debate have fully expressed their views, a plan of action in accordance with the general sense of the assembly is finally determined on and declared by the chief abbaya, when the meeting is dissolved without farther formality.

The councils of villages and those of branches of tribes are similarly held. The jurisdictions of all these councils,

however composed, are, of course, entirely undefined.
Those of each higher grade are simply supplementary to
those below, deciding on matters which the latter have
not sufficient weight to determine. Questions, however,
relating to property in land, or to serious personal
injuries, are referred to the head of the tribe and his
assessors.

Such, then, is the mode in which a Khond tribe is governed; by patriarchs, patriarchal councils, and popular
assemblies; it being carefully remembered that the social
structure and the whole body of usages described, instead
of being characterised by theoretical regularity and uniformity, are eminently local, fluctuating, and partial.

A tribe is called a ' Bengasikia,' as the ' Baska Bengasikia,' or the ' Jakso Bengasikia,' ' Baska ' and ' Jakso ' being the names of the common progenitors. A
branch of a tribe is distinguished by the name of its
first ancestor; thus, *one* branch of the ' Jakso ' tribe is
called ' Kooroo Jaksika.' A village is called ' Nadzoo.'
Khond names seem to be universally taken from natural
objects, never expressing qualities. Thus, there is the
' Meeninga,' or Fish tribe; the Janinga, or Crab tribe; the
Pochangia, or Owl; the Syalinga, or Spotted Deer tribe;
the Grango, or Nilgae.

Each federal patriarch, or hereditary head of a cluster
of Khond tribes, besides mediating in questions between
tribes and in all important disputes to which both Khonds
and Hindus are parties, was usually the sole channel of
intercourse between the tribes and the zemindar in matters of importance, and the adviser of the zemindar in
hill politics, it being obviously the policy of the zemindars
to conciliate the chief people among the mountain tribes.
He is called Bissye in Goomsur, Khonro in Boad, and all
his sons bear the same title, though not the same authority.
But the Bissye or Khonro, from his combination of offices,
possesses unrivalled power of thwarting the zemindar if
he thinks fit.

KHONDS DRESSED FOR BATTLE.

The Khonds are highly distinguished for personal courage, and never ask nor give quarter. They prepare for battle, if with an enemy of a different race, and on some occasions if of a different tribe, by recording a vow of human sacrifice in case of success to the earth god, and by propitiating Loha Pennoo, the god of arms, both in his grove and on the field by the blood of goats and fowls. The priest, who in no case bears arms, gives the signal to engage after the latter offering by flourishing an axe in the air, and shouting encouragement and defiance. They adorn themselves for battle, like most rude nations, as for a feast. They carefully trim their hair, plaiting it in a flat circle on the right side of the head, where it is fastened by an iron pin and adorned with a plume of feathers, and bound with a shred of scarlet cloth when procurable.

An eye-witness gave the following description of a fight which took place betwixt the hostile tribes of Bara Mootah and Bora Des in Goomsur.

At about twelve o'clock in the day the people of Bora Des began to advance in a mass across the Salki river, the boundary between the districts, into the plain of Courmingia, where a much smaller force was arrayed to oppose them. The combatants were protected from the neck to the loins by skins, and cloth was wound round their legs down to the heel, but the arms were quite bare. Round the heads of many, too, cloth was wound, and for distinction the people of Bara Mootah wore peacock's feathers in their hair, while those of Bora Des had cock's tail plumes. They advanced with horns blowing, and gongs beat when they passed a village. The women followed behind carrying pots of water and food for refreshment, and the old men who were past bearing arms were there, giving advice and encouragement. As the adverse parties approached, showers of stones, handed by the women, flew from slings from either side; and when they came within range, arrows came in flights, and

many fell back wounded.   At length single combats
sprung up betwixt individuals who advanced before the
rest, and when the first man fell all rushed to dip their
axes in his blood, and hacked the body to pieces.   The
first man who himself unwounded slew his opponent,
struck off his right arm and rushed with it to the priest
in the rear, who bore it off as an offering to Loha Pennoo
in his grove.[1]   The right arms of the rest who fell were
cut off in like manner and heaped in the rear, beside the
women, and to them the wounded were carried for care,
and the fatigued men constantly retired for water.   The
conflict was at length general.   All were engaged hand
to hand and now fought fiercely, now paused by common
consent for a moment's breathing.   In the end the men
of Bora Des, although superior in numbers, began to give
way, and before four o'clock they were driven across the
Salki, leaving sixty men dead on the field, while the
killed on the side of Bara Mootah did not exceed thirty.
And from the entire ignorance of the Khonds of the
simplest healing processes, at least an equal number of
the wounded died after the battle.   The right hands of
the slain were hung up by both parties on the trees of
the villages, and the dead were carried off to be burned.

The people of Bora Des the next morning flung a piece
of bloody cloth on the field of battle, a challenge to
renew the conflict, which was quickly accepted, and so
the contest was kept up for three days.

The arms of the Khonds are a light, long-handed axe,
with a blade very curiously curved, the bow and arrow,
and the sling; no shields are used.   The axe is used
with both hands, to strike and guard, its handle being for
the latter purpose partly defended by brass plates and
wire.

Their feasts do not bear the exclusively sensual cha-

---

[1] The New Zealanders offered to Tumatauenga (the god of war) the body
of the first person slain in battle.   Thomson's New Zealand, vol. i. p. 100.

racter which distinguishes those of many rude nations.
The women partake in every form of social enjoyment,
but share sparingly in the liquor-cup ; and extemporary
songs or recitations, and dancing, in which the married
and unmarried of both sexes join, are the accompani-
ments of every entertainment. Still every family festival
is a night-long debauch which often leads to gross excess,
and, the guests being armed, to sanguinary brawls.

Finally, the distinguishing qualities of the character of
the Khonds appear to be these : a passionate love of
liberty, devotion to chiefs, and unconquerable resolution.
They are besides faithful to friends, brave, hospitable, and
laborious. Their vices, upon the other hand, are the indulgence of revenge, and occasionally of brutal passion.
Drunkenness is universal ; the habit of plunder exists in
one or two small districts alone.

Amongst savage tribes the state of war is universal.
At a more advanced stage, such as that which the Khonds
have reached, hostility is limited or modified by special
compacts; but war is still the rule, peace the exception.

Hence, while within each tribe order and security prevail, beyond, all is discord and confusion ; everywhere is
seen an incipient or a dying feud, and every tribe has an
unsettled account with the zemindar.

But at the same time the general circumstances of the
situation of most of these tribes, and the ideas and feelings upon which their manners are mainly founded,
determine them powerfully to pacific habits, producing
frequent alliances and tending everywhere to soften
hostility.

Retaliation is, in general, necessarily the sole remedy
for wrongs of whatever order. But each society interposes to prevent the exercise of the natural right of
revenge within its pale by a rude system of compensatory
justice, which has in view exclusively the private satisfaction of individuals, not the vindication of any moral

G

or civil rules of right.   The main provisions of this system are the following.

In cases of murder, the Khonds recognise the right of blood-revenge in the kindred of the deceased; and, like the Bedouins, regard the exercise of this right as a duty; while, unlike them, they consider the acceptance of compensation as in no case disgraceful.   The right to revenge blood appears to extend to relatives within a degree of affinity not strictly determined, and its existence certainly renders murder a rarer crime among the Khonds (as amongst the Arab tribes), than the state of manners would lead us to anticipate.   When the revenge of blood is foregone, the entire personal property of the murderer is awarded in compensation to the representatives of the deceased, and it was uniformly asserted by Lieut. Macpherson's informants, that similar compensation is made in all cases both of excusable homicide and of manslaughter.   In cases of wounding equivalent in property is adjudged if the injury be severe or of a lasting nature, but not otherwise.   In every case, however, the injured party has a right to subsist in luxury at the expense of the offender during the period of convalescence.   For wounds, however serious, given under circumstances of extreme provocation, or in a drunken squabble, slight compensation is awarded.

In cases of theft or of robbery the restitution of the property abstracted or the substitution of an equivalent is alone required by Khond usage upon the first offence; but expulsion from the society follows upon its repetition. This crime is not very common among the Khonds, save in a few particular tracts.   When stolen agricultural produce cannot be recovered, the injured party is put in possession of the land of the plunderer until its produce replaces his loss, one-half of the crop being placed annually to the credit of the offender.   Unjust occupation of the soil, for whatever period, is remedied amongst the Khonds by its simple restoration, without compensation.

A husband in case of adultery, established by his ocular testimony, has a right to put the adulterer to death; and for this offence there is no composition. The adulterous wife (not regarded as the property of the husband) is punishable only by dismissal to her paternal home, and this may be inflicted upon sufficient proof of her guilt by any species of testimony.

Questions of property in land, and of the greater offences against the person, are generally decided with much solemnity by councils of elders convened by heads of sections or of districts, and by the examination of witnesses and of the parties, to both of whom an infinite variety of oaths are administered, while they are occasionally subjected to ordeals.

Of judicial tests the two most sacred are founded on the belief that rice moistened by the blood of a sheep killed in the name of the earth god, will, if eaten by litigants, destroy the perjured, and that a portion of the disputed soil made into clay will, if swallowed by them, have a similar effect. The former test, in which the great Khond deity is adjured, is resorted to only upon the most solemn occasions. The common oaths of the Khonds are upon the skin of a tiger, from which animal destruction to the perjured is invoked; upon a lizard's skin, whose scaliness they pray may be their lot if forsworn; upon the earth of an anthill, like which they desire that, if false, they may be reduced to powder; and upon a peacock's feather: while the universal ordeals of boiling water, oil, and hot iron are constantly resorted to. Boundary lines, when determined by public tribunals, are marked by stones set up with renewed sanctions in presence of the abbayas.

The liberal entertainment of the members of every tribunal with rice, flesh, and liquor, at the conclusion of its proceedings, falls in all cases as costs of suit upon the losing party.

CHAPTER VI.[1]

THE KHOND RELIGION.—HUMAN SACRIFICE AND FEMALE INFANTICIDE.

SECTION I.

THE RELIGIOUS DOCTRINES OF THE KHONDS.

Doctrines common to all the Tribes.

THERE is one Supreme Being, self-existing, the source of good, and creator of the universe, of the inferior gods, and of man.   This divinity is called, in some districts, Boora Pennu, or the God of Light; in others, Bella Pennu, or the Sun God; and the sun and the place from which it rises beyond the sea are the chief seats of his presence.

Boora Pennu, in the beginning, created for himself a consort, who became Tari Pennu, or the earth goddess, and the source of evil.   He afterwards created the earth. As Boora Pennu walked upon it with Tari, he found her wanting in affectionate compliance and ·attention as a wife,[2] and resolved to create from its substance a new

---

. [1] This chapter contains a reprint of the paper above (p. 59) referred to as having been read before the Royal Asiatic Society in 1852, with the exception of the first ten pages—the substance of which has been stated above (pp. 52–58),—and of a preliminary statement of the sources of information, and some details as to the minor deities; which will be found in Appendix A.

[2] There are various accounts given of the nature of Tari's neglect, one of the most generally received being that she refused to scratch the back of Boora's neck when requested to do so.

being, Man, who should render to him the most assiduous and devoted service, and to form from it also every variety of animal and vegetable life necessary to man's existence. Tari was filled with jealousy, and attempted to prevent his purpose, but succeeded only so far as to change the intended order of creation. In the words of a generally received legend :—' Boora Pennu took a handful of earth and threw it behind him to create man ; but Tari caught it ere it fell, and cast it on one side, when trees, herbs, flowers, and every form of vegetable life sprang up. Boora Pennu again threw a handful of earth behind him ; but Tari caught it in like manner, and cast it into the sea, when fish and all things that live in water were generated. Boora threw a third handful of earth behind him, which also Tari intercepted and flung aside, when all the lower animals, wild and tame, were formed. Boora cast a fourth handful behind him, which Tari caught and threw up into the air, when the feathered tribes and all creatures which fly were produced. Boora Pennu, looking round, perceived what Tari had done to frustrate his intentions, and laying his hand upon her head to prevent her further interference, he took up a fifth handful of earth and placed it on the ground behind him ; and from it the human race were created. Tari Pennu then placed her hands over the earth, and said, " Let these beings you have made exist ; you shall create no more !" Whereupon Boora caused an exudation of sweat to proceed from his body, collected it in his hand, and threw it around, saying, " To all that I have created !"—and thence arose love and sex and the continuation of species.'

The creation was perfectly free from moral and physical evil. Men enjoyed free intercourse with the Creator. They lived without labour upon the spontaneous abundance of the earth ; they enjoyed everything in common, and lived in perfect harmony and peace. They went unclothed. They had power to move not only on the earth, but through the air and the sea. The lower animals were all perfectly innocuous.

The earth goddess, highly incensed at the love shown towards man thus created and endowed, broke into open rebellion against Boora, and resolved to blast the lot of his new creature by the introduction into the world of every form of moral and physical evil. She instilled into the heart of man every variety of moral evil, ' sowing the seeds of sin in mankind as into a ploughed field,' and at the same time introduced every species of physical evil into the material creation—diseases, deadly poisons, and every element of disorder. Boora Pennu, by the application of antidotes, arrested and held in abeyance the elements of physical evil; but he left man perfectly free to receive or to reject moral evil.

A few individuals of mankind entirely rejected evil, and remained sinless; the rest all yielded to its power, and fell into a state of universal disobedience to the deity and . fierce strife with one another. Boora immediately deified the sinless few without their suffering death, saying to them, ' Become ye gods, living for ever and seeing my face when ye will, and have power over man, who is no longer my immediate care.' Upon the corrupted mass of mankind Boora Pennu inflicted high moral penalties; and let loose the myriad forms of physical evil by the withdrawal of the antidotes which had arrested them. He entirely withdrew his face and his immediate guardianship from mankind. He made all who had fallen subject to death; and he further ordained that, in future, every one who should commit sin should suffer death as its consequence. Universal discord and war prevailed, so that all social and even family ties were broken up. All nature became thoroughly tainted and disordered. The seasons no longer held their regular course; the earth ceased to bear spontaneously fruit fit for the food of man, and became a wilderness of jungle,

rocks, and mud.   Diseases and death came upon all creatures ; snakes became venomous ; many flowers and fruits
grew poisonous ; and many animals became savage and
destructive.   Man now went clothed, lost the power of
moving through the air and the sea, and sank into a state
of abject suffering and degradation.   Thus the elements
of good and evil were thoroughly commingled in man,
and throughout nature.   Meanwhile, Boora and Tari contended for superiority in fierce conflict : their terrible
strife raging throughout the earth, the sea, and the
sky ; their chief weapons being mountains, meteors, and
whirlwinds.[1]

Up to this point the Khonds hold the same general
belief, but from it they divide into two sects directly
opposed upon the great question of the issue of the contest between Boora and his rebel consort, involving the
whole subject of the practical relation between the two
antagonist powers with reference to man, the source
and subject of their strife.

The sect of Boora believe that he proved triumphant
in the contest, and as an abiding sign of the discomfiture
of Tari imposed the cares of childbirth upon her sex.
Her rebellious will, however, her activity as the source of
evil, and her malignant hostility towards man, remain
unabated, and are ever struggling to break forth ; but she
is so completely subjected to control, that she is employed
as the instrument of Boora's moral rule, being permitted
to strike only where he, as the omnipotent ruler of the
universe, desires to punish.

The sect of Tari hold, upon the other hand, that she
remained unconquered, and still maintains the struggle
with various success.   They fully recognise the general
supremacy of Boora as the creator of the world and the

[1] The comet of 184 was watched by the Khonds with the most intense
interest, each of the opposite parties regarding it as a new and prodigious
weapon in the hand of that deity to which their own worship was chiefly
paid.

sole source of good, invoking him first on every occasion ;
but they hold that his power, exerted both directly and
through the agency of the inferior gods, is insufficient for
the effectual protection of men when Tari resolves to
inflict injury or destruction ; and, moreover, while they
regard Tari as the original source of evil alone, they
nevertheless believe that she has practically power to
confer every form of earthly benefit, both by abstaining
from the prevention of the good which flows from Boora,
and by directly bestowing blessings.

*Doctrines of the Sect of Boora.—The three Classes of inferior Gods.—
Ideas respecting the Soul.—The Judgment of the Dead.*

Boora Pennu, say his sect, resolved that, for his own
honour, his work should not be lost, but that man should
be enabled to attain to a state of moderate enjoyment
upon earth, and to rise after death, through the practice
of virtue, to a state of beatitude and partial restoration
to communion with his Maker. To accomplish these
purposes Boora created a subordinate divine agency in
addition to that of the first sinless men, who, when deified,
were made guardians of man ; and he appointed all the
inferior gods to carry out the first object, one excepted,
to whom was assigned the duty of administering justice
to the dead. It was the office of all these gods to regulate the powers of nature for the use of man, to instruct
him in the arts necessary to life, and to protect him
against every form of evil. It was ordained, however,
that men should obtain earthly blessings, in dispensing
which the inferior gods are vested with a large discretion,
only through seeking their favour by worship with the
offerings which they desire and which are their food ;
while it was specially provided that, as a standing acknowledgment, worship is due of right to Boora and Tari
alone, and is paid to the lower gods only with their express sanction, the names of the two great divinities
should be first invoked at every ceremonial.

The inferior gods are divisible into two classes, distinguished by their origin, their attributes, and the scope of their duties and authority.

The gods of the first class sprang from Boora and Tari. They are unchangeable and not subject to dissolution, and have a general jurisdiction, while the offices of all save the judge of the dead correspond exactly to the primary wants of mankind under their new lot. The first necessity of that lot was that man should live by labour upon the soil, and accordingly the duty assigned to the three first deities is to teach the art of agriculture and to regulate the functions of nature necessary to its practice. It is the office of the first of these gods to send rain, of the second to give new vegetation and the firstfruits, of the third to give the increase and to send grain in every shape. These deities delivered from Boora to man the seeds of all useful plants, taught him to clear the jungle, to make ploughs, to yoke oxen, to know the seasons, and to suit the seeds to various soils. It was necessary also that man should subsist in part by the chase, and a god was provided to instruct him in the arts connected with the pursuit of game, and to lay down rules for its practice. The next condition of man's new lot was that he should live in a state of constant strife, and a god of war was accordingly provided to teach the art of war and to prescribe the laws for carrying it on and for making peace. The establishment of boundaries was necessarily a primary want of a population composed of hostile tribes subsisting by agriculture and the chase, and to meet it a god of boundaries was created.[1]

These six deities, then, were created to meet the primary wants of man on earth after the introduction of evil, namely :—

1. PIDZU PENNU, the god of rain.

---

[1] In some parts of the country the god of boundaries is placed first in the class of minor local deities.

2. BOORBI PENNU, the goddess of new vegetation and firstfruits.

3. PITTERRI PENNU, the god of increase, and of gain in every shape.

4. KLAMBO PENNU, the god of the chase.

5. LOHA PENNU, the god of war (literally the iron god).

6. SUNDI PENNU, the god of boundaries.

To which is to be added, as an inferior god of the first class,

7. DINGA PENNU, the judge of the dead, who will be described hereafter.[1]

The titles of these gods vary in different localities ; and between the three who preside over the functions of nature there is a partial community and interchange of functions. They are invoked next after Boora and Tari at every ceremonial.

Next in rank to this class of inferior gods is the class of deified sinless men of the first age. They are the tutelary gods of tribes and branches of tribes. Like the first class of gods, they are unchangeable and immortal, but they have only a local, or rather tribal jurisdiction.[2] Their aid is supplicated when any common danger threatens a tribe, and they are invoked at every ceremonial after the inferior gods of the first class.

The third class of inferior deities are sprung from the gods of the first two classes. They are the strictly minor and local deities of the Khonds. They are the tutelary gods of every spot on earth, having power over the functions of nature which operate there, and over everything relating to human life in it. Their number is unlimited.

---

[1] The New Zealanders had—' 1. The god and father of men and war; 2. The god and father of the food of man which springs without cultivation ; 3. The god and father of fish and reptiles ; 4. The god of winds and storms ; 5. The god and father of the cultivated food of men ; 6. The god of forests and birds. All these were the children of heaven and earth.'—Thomson's *New Zealand,* vol. i. p. 107.

[2] ' The deified ancestors of one nation never interfered in the affairs of other nations.'—Thomson's *New Zealand,* vol. i. p. 110.

They fill all nature, in which no power or object, from the sea to the clods of the field, is without its deity. They are the guardians of hills, groves, streams, fountains, paths, and hamlets, and are cognisant of every human action, want, and interest in the locality where they preside.

The following are the chief of this class of gods :—

1. NADZU PENNU, the village god.
2. SORO PENNU, the hill god.
3. JORI PENNU, the god of streams.
4. IDZU PENNU, the family or house god.
5. MOONDA PENNU, the tank god.
6. SOOGA PENNU, the god of fountains.
7. GOSSA PENNU, the forest god.
8. KOOTTI PENNU, the god of ravines.
9. BHORA PENNU, the god of new fruits, produced on trees or shrubs.

Such is the subordinate divine agency to which the care of man's temporal interests was intrusted.[1]

Before describing the office and attributes of the god to whom the determination of the destiny of men after death was committed—the god of justice to the dead—it seems necessary to state the ideas of the Khonds respecting the constitution of the soul of man. Men are endowed

---

[1] 'The Fijians have a supreme god to whom is attributed the creation and government of the world, and no images of him are made nor of any of the minor gods. Besides him there is a host of inferior gods, but their rank is not easily ascertained, as each district contends for the superiority of the deity it has adopted and specially worships. As soon as beloved parents expire they take their place among the family gods. Besides their regular gods and deified spirits, the Fijians have idolised objects, such as sacred stones, trees, and groves, and in addition to these certain birds and fishes, and some even are supposed to have deities closely connected with or residing in them.'— *Viti, an Account of a Government Mission to the Vitian or Fijian Islands*, by B. Seeman : Cambridge, 1862, pp. 389–391.

Captain Burton tells us (Mission to Getele, King of Dahomé, 2nd ed., London, 1864, vol. i. p. 139) that in the days of Bosman the little kingdom of Abydah adored three orders of gods, each presiding, like the several officers of a prince, over its peculiar province, and that the list of fetish or worshipped objects is nearly endless.

with four souls.   First, there is a soul which is capable of
beatification and restoration to communion with Boora.
Secondly, there is a soul which is attached to some tribe
upon earth and reborn for ever in that tribe, so that
upon the birth of every child the priest declares, after
inquiry, which of the members of the tribe has returned.[1]
Thirdly, there is a soul which endures the sufferings inflicted as the punishment of sin, and performs the transmigrations imposed on that account.   This soul, moreover,
has the power of temporarily quitting the body at the
will of a god, leaving it weakened, languid, sleepy, and
out of order.   Thus, when a man becomes a priest, this
soul always leaves his body for a time to hold an interview with and receive instructions from the god who has
appointed him his minister; and when, by the aid of a
god, a man becomes a tiger (a subject afterwards adverted
to), this, I believe, is the soul which animates the bestial
form.   Fourthly, there is a soul which dies on the dissolution of the body.

Dinga Pennu, a name of unknown meaning, is the
judge of the dead.   Like the other inferior gods of the
first class, he is sprung from Boora and Tari, is unchangeable and immortal, and has general jurisdiction.

Dinga Pennu resides upon a great rock, or mountain,
called Grippa Valli, or the Leaping Rock, in the region
beyond the sea, from which the sun rises.   The Leaping
Rock is perfectly smooth, and exceedingly slippery, ' like
a floor covered with mustard-seed,' and a black unfathom-
able river flows around it.   To it the souls of men
speed straight after death, and it derives its name from the
desperate leaps which they are compelled to make to
reach and secure a footing upon its surface,[2] which they

---

[1] See p. 72, supra.

[2] 'Bulu, the ultimate abode of bliss, is separated from this world by water,
across which the souls have to be ferried by the charm of Fiji. Before
embarking they have to do battle with Samuyalo, the father of souls,
informed of their approach by the cries of a parroquet. Should they

constantly fail to do, and so break limbs or knock out eyes, contracting deformities which they generally communicate to the next bodies they animate. Upon that rock sits Dinga, engaged day and night in writing on it a history of every man's actions towards gods and towards men, during every life passed upon earth; in receiving the souls of the dead; registering their coming; casting up each man's account of good and evil; passing sentence according to desert, and dispatching the shades by troops to fulfil his perfectly just and inflexible awards. The plan of retributive justice which Dinga administers is, in a word, this. If he judges that a soul has acquired by virtuous conduct a claim to beatification, he permits it at once to pass among the blessed spirits; but if, on the other hand, he judges that it has failed to establish that claim, he recommits it to earth for further probation, after such detention in Grippa Valli as he thinks proper to inflict; sending the soul to be reborn in the tribe to which it belongs, and to suffer in a new life penalties proportioned to its guilt.[1]

The punishments which Dinga Pennu inflicts on souls released from suspense in Grippa Valli include every

conquer, they are allowed to pass on towards the judgment seat of Degei.'—*Viti*, p. 390.

'The Hindu belief is that the passage of the wicked after death to the place of judgment is through dark and dismal paths; sometimes over burning sand, sometimes over stones that cut their feet at every step: they travel naked, parched with thirst, covered with dirt and blood, amidst showers of hot ashes and burning coals; they are terrified with frequent and horrible apparitions, and fill the air with their shrieks and wailing.'—Ward *on the Hindoos*, vol. iii. p. 374, cited in Elphinstone's *History of India*, vol. i. p. 190.

[1] 'The religious belief of the New Zealanders was that which belongs to the infancy of a race. It was a religion dictated by wants and fears. To their gods they prayed for food, to their deified ancestors for the removal or the prevention of evils. They believed in a future state of existence, and that there were spirits within their bodies which never died. There were two distinct abodes for departed spirits: one was in the sky, and called Rangi; the other, denominated the Reinga, was in the midst of the sea, and its entrance was through a cavern in a precipitous rock.'—Thomson's *New Zealand*, vol. i p. 112.

species of earthly suffering, bodily and mental.   Of these
penalties it may be observed, that, amongst diseases,
epilepsy is the most dreaded ;—that poverty is peculiarly
feared by a people among whom reduction to dependence
involves the loss of many social rights and honours, even
tainting the blood so as to exclude descendants from succeeding to the office of chief ;—that the want or the death
of male offspring is regarded as a punishment of the heaviest
kind ; and that the being born with a bodily defect is a
calamity exceedingly felt by people whose first prayer for
their offspring is that they may be brave and beautiful.
But no punishment is considered so terrible as the curse
of base moral qualities, such as cowardice or falsehood,
which bring public infamy upon their possessor and his
tribe.

From the following catalogue of Khond virtues and
vices, the general spirit of the justice administered by the
judge of the dead may be inferred.

The chief sins are—

1. To refuse hospitality, or to abandon a guest.
2. To break an oath or promise, or to deny a gift.
3. To speak falsely, except to save a guest.
4. To break a solemn pledge of friendship.
5. To break an old law or custom.
6. To commit incest.
7. To contract debts, the payment of which is
   ruinous to a man's tribe, which is responsible
   for the engagements of all its members.
8. To skulk in time of war.
9. To betray a public secret.

Whoever commits any of these sins will be born again
afflicted with disease, with poverty, and probably with
mental qualities which will make him infamous.

The chief virtues, on the other hand, are the opposites
of these sins, and amongst them are besides :—

1. To kill a foe in public battle.

2. To fall in public battle.

3. To be a priest.

And, amongst the sacrificing tribes,

4. To be a victim to the earth goddess.

To the soul of any one who shall observe strictly any one of the great virtues, while he shall not be guilty of any one of the great sins, it is considered that the judge of the dead will award a place amongst the beatified.

The beatified souls of men enjoy immediate communion with all the gods; they are in rank little inferior to the minor gods, live with them, and much after their fashion. Every tribe invokes the souls of deceased ancestors in endless array at every ceremonial, after invoking the minor gods; and they especially remember those of men renowned for good or great actions, as for reclaiming waste lands, for extraordinary bravery, for wisdom in council, or for remarkable integrity of life. They believe that beatified souls, although wholly without power, may act as intercessors with some of the gods, as with Dinga Pennu, on the one point of inducing him to restore lost relatives speedily to their homes.

Such are the chief doctrines which are held by the sect which worship Boora Pennu in chief—and are shared, with differences which will be explained, by the followers of Tari. Boora is worshipped, with the ceremonies which will be detailed hereafter, at social festivals held periodically by tribes, branches of tribes, and villages; his followers, while they assign to him the highest precedence as the omnipotent god, never failing to invoke Tari with deep awe and reverence as the second power.

Doctrines of the Sect of Tari.—Origin of Human Sacrifice.

The sect of Tari share, generally, all the doctrines of that of Boora respecting his purpose of providing a partial remedy for the consequences of the introduction of evil, and the creation of an inferior divine agency to effect that purpose. But, whereas the sect of Boora conceive that he perfectly accomplished his intentions, that of Tari hold that her opposition prevented his doing so with respect to the earthly lot of man, while, however, they believe that he carried out his purpose respecting the destiny of his soul after death.

The sect of Tari ascribe to her, exactly as that of Boora do to him, the elevation of man from the state of barbarous degradation into which he fell upon the introduction of evil, by making the disordered earth fit for cultivation, and by teaching the arts of agriculture, the chace, and war; conceiving that she did this through revelations made to mankind directly by herself under a feminine form called Umbally Bylee, and through her priests, while she also permitted men, at her will, to receive instruction and every other form of good which constantly flows from Boora through the inferior gods; and hence, her sect worship all those gods with the ceremonies they require, exactly as that of Boora do, but, with the difference of view and feeling necessarily arising from their opposite opinions on the point of the relative power of the two chief deities. Lastly, the sect of Tari believe that she gave those blessings to mankind, and continues to permit their enjoyment, on the express condition of receiving worship with human sacrifices, which are her food.

A legend, which will be found at length in the description of that worship, gives this account of its origin and of the first benefits that followed upon it. The earth was in a state of soft barren mud, utterly unfit for the use of man. Umbally Bylee, the name of the feminine form which Tari always assumed when she communicated with men, appeared cutting vegetables with a hook. She cut her finger, and as the blood drops fell upon the earth, it became dry and firm. Umbally Bylee said, 'Behold the good change! cut up my body to complete it.' The Khonds declined to do so, ap-

parently believing that Umbally Bylee was one of themselves, and resolving that they would not sacrifice one
another, lest their race should become extinct, but would
obtain victims by purchase from other peoples. They
procured and offered a sacrifice, and, says the legend,
'now society with its relations of father and mother,
and wife and child, and the ties between ruler and subject, arose;' and the knowledge of all that relates to
agriculture was imparted to men.

'Then, also,' says the legend, 'hunting began. A
man brought' (apparently to a priest) 'a rat, a snake,
and a lizard, and inquired if they were fit to eat. Tari
rested on the priest and said to him, "Give names to
all the wild animals, distinguishing those that are fit and
those that are unfit for use, and let men go to the jungles
and the hills, and kill the sambur [1] and all other game
with arrows and with poison."' And men went to hunt.
In like manner, a legend, given at length in the worship of the god of war by the sect of Tari, narrates
how she taught men the art of fighting. 'Boora Pennu,
in the beginning,' it is said, 'created the world and
all that it contains, including the iron of weapons, but
men did not know the use of weapons, fighting in womanish fashion, and wounding one another with sword
grass and spear grass, unable to inflict death.' It then
tells how Tari taught men to make bows and arrows
and axes; and how 'so cruel' was the iron in which
'the terrible goddess,' when she introduced cruelty with
other evils into the world, 'had mingled no drop of pity,'
that none who were wounded lived; but Tari, on the
prayer of her children, taught men how to moderate the
'cruelty of the first iron,' and how to make war.

Thus, say the sect of Tari, did men rise from a state
of degradation, and obtain all the benefits they enjoy,
through worshipping Tari, at her express invitation and

---

[1] A species of deer.

command, with human sacrifices, upon her demonstrating
the efficacy of the pouring out of human blood upon the
earth.   And they believe that the rite and its virtue
were afterwards enlarged by a new revelation and decree.
Men complained to Tari that the benefits she bestowed
on them were insufficient, that there was 'little wealth,
much fear, but few children, deadly snakes and tigers,
and thorns piercing the feet;' whereupon, she expressly
prescribed the extension of her ritual, with new ceremonies and new arrangements for the provision of victims,
and ordained that its efficacy, which was previously limited to those who practised it, should thenceforth embrace all mankind.   And from that time, the sect of Tari
believe that the responsibility for the well-being of the
whole world has rested upon them.

Thus, while they admit the theoretical supremacy of
Boora, her sect make Tari practically the chief object
of their adoration, and believe themselves to enjoy her
special favour.   She is worshipped, like Boora, at great
social festivals held periodically by tribes, branches of
tribes, and villages, while individuals also frequently propitiate her with her great offering.

On the other hand, the opinions and feelings of the
sect of Boora on the subject of human sacrifice are exceedingly strong, and always expressed with great warmth
and force.   They regard it with the utmost abhorrence
as the consummation of human guilt, and believe it to
have been adopted under monstrous delusions devised by
Tari, as the mother of falsehood, with a view solely to the
final destruction of her followers.   From the legends which
will be given at length in describing the worship of Boora,
it appears that they believe that Tari was enabled to induce a portion of mankind to adopt the rite only through
addressing to them a series of temptations and threats,
whilst the remaining portion were preserved from the
great sin through special interpositions by Boora.

One legend narrates, that Umbally Bylee appeared in

the form of a tiger amongst certain tribes which were at
war in the time before the arts of taking life and of public battle were known.   She first killed game daily, to
the delight of all who partook of it.   She then offered to
one of the parties to kill any one of their enemies they
should designate, and having killed him, all regarded her
with unlimited faith, and prayed her to teach them the
art of assuming the forms of beasts (called the art of
Mlcepa) and the art of killing in war.   She consented,
and taught the art of Mleepa to a few persons, upon the
condition that they, in return, would do one thing which
she should require.   This proved to be, that they should
worship her with human sacrifices, the goddess threatening instant destruction if they hesitated.   They brought
out a man for sacrifice, but Boora interposed, as narrated
in the legend, and then taught to men both the art of
Mleepa and that of war.

On another occasion, Umbally Bylee tempted men to
offer the desired sacrifice, by promising to convert the
waste and barren earth into cultivated plains covered
with population and wealth, — 'there being no higher
temptation to hold out.'   They yielded, and a human
victim was prepared, when Boora again interfered, routing
Umbally and her crew.

Tari afterwards made a way through the mountains
for the waters of a lake, and said, 'Behold the power of
my divinity!   Worship me with the blood I require.'
Boora now left men to take their course, and a human
victim was sacrificed ; and thus, say his sect, did the sect
of worshippers of Tari with human blood arise.

General Characteristics of the Khond Divinities. — Legends.

The gods of the Khonds have bodies of human form,
but of ethereal texture.   In size they are generally super-
human,[1] of various colours, and variously attired and

[1] We read in Thomson's New Zealand, vol. i. p. 119, that in some cases the

equipped after the fashion of men ; and the higher are generally larger in stature than the lower gods. They can assume any form at pleasure. They all, with the exception of Boora, Tari, and Dinga Pennu, live exclusively upon the earth, moving at the height of about two cubits above its surface, invisibly to human eyes, but seen by the lower animals. They all have human feelings, passions, and affections ; quarrel, and are reconciled ; fall in love, marry, and have children ; while the minor gods, at least, grow old, and are subject to sickness, and even to a species of dissolution, which a god of superior strength can inflict, and which differs from the death of men in this, that a god on dying is instantly reborn as a child, without loss of consciousness or recollection. The gods live upon flavours and essences drawn from the offerings of their votaries, from the flesh of animals which they kill, generally by disease, for their food, and from corn, the abstraction of which is notified by empty ears in the field, or by a deficiency in the garner. All the gods worship Boora and Tari ; and those of each grade worship those above them with supplications, and with offerings of the lives of victims and the essences of other oblations. They take from men the materials for such offerings ; and the demand on this score is such that the priest has often to reply to inquiries respecting the cause of death of a favourite bullock or pig, that some god or beatified soul required it for a sacrifice to Boora Pennu.

A couple of legends, selected from the endless number current in the country, will give some idea of the mode of life of the gods : —

' A lofty hill, called Bogah-Soro, is a kind of local Olympus on which the gods of a large district hold their councils. The god of the hill, named Bogah Pennu, had,

---

spirits of their deified ancestors became invisible human beings called Patupaiarehe. These spirits, which correspond to our fairies, imps, ghosts and goblins, were supposed to have larger frames and fairer complexions than men, and they amused themselves by singing and playing on flutes.

long ago, a son of strange habits and wayward and sullen mood, who lived entirely apart from his family, and cared for nothing but two pet animals, a horse and an elephant, upon which he lavished his affections, never quitting them day or night, and himself providing for all their wants. The god of the hill was in despair at the unnatural fancies of his son.   He one day managed to persuade him to leave his favourite creatures, in order to carry an invitation to a sister married to a neighbouring god some forty miles off, and, during his absence, transformed the horse and the elephant into two rocks, which are still to be seen on the broad flank of Bogah-Soro.   The youth, on returning home, hastened straight to his beloved animals, and, when he discovered the metamorphosis, fell into a paroxysm of grief and rage.   When, on demanding who had played him the trick, he learned that it was his father, he rushed into his presence frantic with sorrow and indignation, solemnly renounced his family, and prepared to depart for ever.   His father, at length, with infinite difficulty, contrived to pacify him and prevent the execution of his threat, by the solemn promise that he would give him the first horse and elephant that passed that way.   The young god, accordingly, went to the road which winds by the mountain, to watch for travellers ; and there he has ever since sat, sometimes on a clump of bamboos, the top of which is seen flattened and depressed by his weight; sometimes upon the branch of an old Uddah tree, which is bent like a chair.   In the hope of bringing by that road travellers who might be attended by the desired animals, he has, moreover, created around the spot he haunts a most inviting shade, and has converted a clump of common wild mango trees into trees bearing fruit of delicious flavour ; while upon that road travellers are always safe, both from robbers and wild beasts.   A horse and an elephant, however, have never yet appeared in that wild mountain-pass ; but when the Rajah of Purlah Kimedy was, some years ago, flying through the hills in rebellion, attended by both the animals, and meant to go by it, the presence of the young god was opportunely remembered by the Khonds, and the rajah was preserved from destruction by changing his route.'

By the side of the road from Souradah to Guddapore, under a shady mango-tree, is a bright and sparkling fountain which gushes from a basin of golden sand. It is called the ' Brazen fountain,' and this is the accepted story of its origin and name :—

' The daughter of the god of an overhanging hill, one day, when carrying home a brass pitcher of water from a rivulet which runs in the dell close by, chanced to meet the young son of a god of the neighbourhood. A few words of courtesy were first exchanged, and then conversation sprang up between them ; when the goddess relieved herself of the weight of her pitcher by setting it down at the foot of the tree. The conversation passed insensibly into lovemaking, which ended, in the old lyrical way, amid the flowered jungle. There the divine pair have ever since dwelt. The brass vessel of water was naturally forgotten, and became the brazen fountain.'

SECTION II.

THE KHOND WORSHIP.

General Views as to Worship.—The Priesthood.

THE Khonds use neither temples nor images in their worship.[1] They cannot comprehend, and regard as absurd, the idea of building a house in honour of a deity, or in the expectation that he will be peculiarly present in any place resembling a human habitation. Groves kept sacred from the axe, hoar rocks, the tops of hills, foun-

---

[1] ' The gods of the New Zealanders were never worshipped in the shape of images.'—Thomson's *New Zealand,* vol. i. p. 100.

tains, and the banks of streams, are, in their eyes, the fittest places for worship. They regard the making, setting-up, and worshipping of images of the gods, as the most signal proof of conscious removal to a hopeless distance from communion with them ; a confession of utter despair of being permitted to make any direct approach to the deity,—a sense of debarment which they themselves have never felt. The Khonds, however, at one or two places where they are much mixed up with Hindus, preserve with reverence, in a house set apart for the purpose, pieces of stone or iron symbolical of some of their gods.

The Khond priesthood, like every other priesthood, lays claim to divine institution. After the primal intercourse between man and his maker ceased, and the inferior gods were created, these were, for a time, the only mediators between man and Boora and Tari ; but it then became necessary that there should be some men in more intimate communion with the gods, and better instructed in their will and rites than the mass of mankind could be ; and, accordingly, each deity appointed a set of ministers for himself, by calling into his presence the third or moveable souls of the persons selected, and instructing them in their duties. The first priests taught to their sons, or other pupils, the mysteries of the gods they served, and the deities have since kept up their priesthoods by selecting for them either persons so initiated, or others at pleasure. Thus, the priesthood may be assumed by any one who chooses to assert a call to the ministry of any god, such call needing to be authenticated only by the claimant's remaining for a period varying from one night to ten or fourteen days in a languid, dreamy, confused state, the consequence of the absence of his third soul in the divine presence. And the ministry which may be thus assumed, may, with few exceptions, be laid aside at pleasure.

The Khond priests, or Jannis, affect division into two

classes,—one which has given up the world and devotes itself
exclusively to religious offices; and one which may still
engage in every occupation excepting war. The former
class are disposed to hold that they alone are qualified to
perform the rites of the greater deities; but the two
classes pass insensibly into one another, and many of both
are seen who perform every ceremonial, with two exceptions, namely, the rite of human sacrifice—at which a
great and fully instructed priest alone can officiate, and
the worship of the god of war, which his own priesthood
alone can conduct. And this god, it is to be observed,
requires that his priest shall serve him only, while all the
other deities accept divided service from their ministers.

The great Janni who gives up the world does so
absolutely, and after a somewhat striking fashion. He
can possess no property of any kind, nor marry, nor,
according to his rules, even look upon a woman; and he
must generally appear and act as unlike other men as
possible. He must live in a filthy hut, a wonder of
abomination. He must not wash but with spittle; nor
leave his door, save when sent for; except, perhaps,
when he wanders to draw liquor from some neglected
palm-tree in his neighbourhood, at the foot of which he
may be found, if required, lying half drunk. He scarcely
ever wears a decent cloth or blanket. He commonly
carries in his hand a broken axe or bow, and has an excited, sottish, sleepy look; but his ready wit never fails
him in his office. He eats such choice morsels as a piece
of the grilled skin and the feet of the sacrificed buffaloes,
and the heads of the sacrificed fowls; and when a deer is
cut up he gets for his share, perhaps, half the skin of the
head with an ear on, and some of the hairy skimmings of
the pot.

The priest who has not given up the world looks and
lives like other men. He has a wife and family, and
often accumulates wealth. He eats apart from laymen,
but may drink with them. The Khond priesthood have

no endowments of any kind, nor is their land tilled by
public labour. Their only perquisites are some of the
offerings, the vessels used at certain ceremonies, and occasional harvest offerings of good will, when the deity whom
they serve has proved propitious. They have places at
all public and private festivals.

The responsibilities of the public worship are generally
thus divided, between the priest and the secular chief.
The chief, after he and the elders have duly consulted the
priest respecting the will of the god, is held exclusively
responsible for the due performance of the rites indicated,
the test being their result. The chief has, accordingly,
full dictatorial powers in everything relating to the religious ceremonies. He can order any one to perform
any act connected with them, and, in case of disobedience,
the assembly of elders will inflict the instant penalty of
the fine of a goat, a buffalo, or a hog. If any important
ceremonial is not followed by the desired result, the
disappointed people generally demand of the chief the
cause of failure, and he is without an answer. If he
attempts to blame the incompetence of the Janni to
divine the will of the deity, it is replied by the tribe, that
the chief is alone responsible for failing to provide a
competent priest; while the Janni himself casts back the
blame upon the chief with much effect. He will say, for
example, that he is convinced that, at the moment of
sacrificing to the god of the chace, or, as the hunters left
the village, the wife or child of the chief wept—a weakness abhorrent to the hilarious god of hunting when his
favour is invoked, or his bands rush joyously to the
forest; or he may say he conceives the god necessarily
expected a better buffalo than the wretched beast which
the chief provided; or, that he fears the chief must have
grudged even that beast in his heart. If there is to be a
compromise, the priest and chief may declare together
that they see no explanation but that some one who
assisted at the ceremonial must have been wanting in

faith in the gods. The end of such contests, however, very often is the summary decree of a fine by the assembly, when a party immediately proceeds to seize a beast, pig, or sheep from the chief's farmyard, to be forthwith eaten at a common feast.

One of the chief offices of a priest is to discover the cause of sickness, which is held to arise, either from the decree of Dinga, from the especial displeasure of some god, or from the magical arts of an enemy. To ascertain which god is displeased, the inquiring Janni seats himself by the afflicted person, and taking some rice, divides it into small heaps, each of which he dedicates to some deity. He then hangs up a sickle balanced by a silk thread, place a few grains of rice upon each end of it, and calls upon all the gods by name. If the sickle is slightly agitated as a name is pronounced, that is an indication that a god has come and rested upon the heap dedicated to him. The priest, having declared the name of the god, lays down the sickle, and counts the grains in the heap; if the number be odd, the deity is offended; if it be even, he is pleased. In the former case the priest becomes full of the god, shakes his head wildly with dishevelled hair, and pours forth a torrent of incoherent words. The patient humbly inquires the cause of the god's displeasure, learns which of his laws has been broken or rites neglected, and instantly makes the offerings prescribed.[1]

[1] We are told by Mouhot, who passed some time among the Stiêns, the wild mountaineers of Siam, that these people 'have neither priests nor temples, yet they recognise the existence of a supreme being, to whom they refer everything, good or evil; they call him Brâ, and invoke him in all cases. They believe also in an evil genius, and attribute all diseases to him. If any one be suffering from illness they say it is the demon tormenting him, and with this idea make, night and day, an insupportable noise round the patient, which they keep up until one of the party falls in a kind of fit, crying out " He has passed unto my body; he is stifling me." They then question the new patient, asking him, first, what remedies to give the sick man, and how the demon can be made to abandon his prey. Sometimes the sacrifice of a pig or an ox is required, often a human victim; in this latter case they pitilessly seize upon a slave, and offer him up to the evil

Individuals of the Khond priesthood occasionally possess considerable influence, but its power, as a body, is certainly by no means great.

The Worship of Boora Pennu, the God of Light, or Bella Pennu, God of the Sun.

The chief worship paid to Boora Pennu by his sect is at his great yearly festival, called ' salo kallo,' from the Khond word ' salo,' a cattle pen, and ' kallo,' spirituous liquor,—that drunk at this feast being prepared in the cattle pen.   This festival, like that of human sacrifice among the worshippers of Tari, is held about the time of the rice harvest, and is celebrated by every tribe, by each branch of a tribe, and by every village, as a great social rite, in which every one takes a part.   To the tribal feasts representatives are sent from every village to that of the chief of the tribe.   A fully instructed priest alone may conduct the ceremonial, and the festival generally lasts five days.   During that period every one eats freely of fermented rice, called ' kenna,' which has a half intoxicating effect; wild dances, accompanied by bursts of stunning music, are kept up day and night, and every kind of unrestrained and licentious enjoyment is indulged in.

The story of the creation of the world and of man, is recited, as in the legend already given, and with it the narrative of the contest between Boora and his rebel consort; of the acceptance of evil by all mankind save the few who were deified ; the fall into a state of brutish degradation, and the creation of the inferior deities.   In the worship of Boora Pennu alone of the gods, an offering is not absolutely required, although it is never omitted ;

genius.'— *Travels in Indo-China, Cambodia, and Laos,* by M. Mouhot. London, 1864, vol. i. p. 250.

' The revelations of the Fijian priests are made by means of the spirit of the god entering the body of the priest, who having become possessed, begins to tremble most violently, and in this excited state utters disjointed sentences, supposed to be the revelations which the god wishes to make by the mouth of his servants.'—Seeman's *Viti,* p. 394.

and at the salo kallo, a hog, considered the most valuable
victim, is sacrificed.   It is hung up by the hind legs in
the cattle-pen selected for the performance of the worship,
and when stabbed in the neck its blood is scattered widely
around.   The priest then prays to Boora to confer every
kind of benefit, while each individual prays for the good
which he especially desires.

Another great festival of Boora Pennu is called the
feast of 'jakri,' or the 'dragging.'   It is held to com-
memorate the interference of Boora, by the agency of a
minor god, who dragged forth a buffalo to be sacrificed
instead of a man as an oblation to Tari.   The victim at
this festival is a bull buffalo, which has been consecrated
at its birth, and allowed to range at will over all fields
and pastures until five or six years old.   Upon the day
of the ceremonial several ropes are fastened to its neck
and its hind legs, about fifty men seize them, and rush
about with the animal until it is brought up exhausted to
the tree of sacrifice, when the priest declares its submission
to be a miracle.

The priest then recites the following legend of the
origin of the rite, to understand which it is necessary to
observe that natural tigers are believed by these Khonds
to kill game only to benefit men, who generally find it
but partially devoured, and share it; while the tigers
which kill men are either Tari, who has assumed the
form of a tiger for purposes of wrath, or men who, by
the aid of a god, have assumed the form of tigers, and
are called 'Mleepa tigers':—

'The woman, Umbally Bylee, appeared as a tiger, and
killed game every other day, and all ate of it.   There
was at that time a fight between the people of Kotrika
and those of Mundika.   But it was private strife, carried
on in womanish fashion, before the art of taking life, and
that of public battle, were known.   Umbally Bylee said,
" I will kill any one of your enemies you please."   They
said to her, " Kill so and so," and she went as a Mleepa

tiger, and killed him. Then the people placed unbounded faith in her, and said to her, " Teach us this new knowledge, and show us the art of killing." She replied, " I will teach you, but thenceforward you must do one thing." And she accordingly taught the art of Mleepa to a few, so that they practised it; and she then said, " Now you must worship me by the sacrifice of men, or the earth shall sink beneath your feet, and water shall rise in its place, and I will abandon you." The earth heaved terribly, as some think, from the wrath of Boora Pennu ; some, in obedience to the power of the earth goddess. Fear filled the minds of all, and as directed, they set up a pole beyond the village, and brought human victims, and all was prepared for the sacrifice. But now the god of light sent a god bearing a mountain, who straightway buried Umbally Bylee therewith, and dragged forth a buffalo from the jungle, and said, " Liberate the man, and sacrifice the buffalo. I will teach you the art of Mleepa in every form." And he taught that art, and the art of public war.'

The priest at the jakri festival, amongst the numerous recitals in honour of the god of light, gives this account of another interposition of Boora, by the agency of the deified sinless men, gods of tribes : —

' The earth goddess, taking on herself the shape of a woman, and calling to herself a number of attendants of a like nature, came to the hill country, and said to the people, " See what hills and waste lands and jungles are here ; worship me with human blood, and the whole shall become a cultivated plain, and you shall have vast increase of numbers and of wealth." She thus tempted the people, there being no greater temptation to hold out. Then the god of light, beholding her proceedings, sent Mahang Meru and Kopung Meru, Adi Ponga, and Boru Ponga, gods of tribes, to counteract her. We had prepared everything for the sacrifice of a man, when the agents of Boora wounded with the forked axe two of the attendants

of Tari.   The woman Umbally Bylee, seeing the hand of
the god of light, fled instantly with the wounded towards
Kourmingia.   In that tract there was a great lake, and
an island in the midst, where they settled, and there they
fed on greens and other mud produce.   We followed to
attack them, but could not on account of the water, and
returned.'   Then is related the fall into the great sin of
human sacrifice.   ' Now Tari made a way for the waters
of the lake through the hills, and it became dry ; and
Tari said to the people, "See the power of my divinity !
Worship me with the blood I require ; " and the people
believed in her power, and performed the required worship, and they became savage like beasts, until by intercourse with us, as in receiving wives, they became
civilised.'

The priest also generally recites at the feast of 'jakri,'
as at that of 'salo kallo,' the history of the conquest of
the earth goddess by Boora.   He then offers up prayers
for every benefit, and finally slaughters the buffalo at the
sacrificial tree, while every form of wild festivity, eating,
drinking, frantic dancing, and loud music, is kept up for
at least two days.

At the commencement of the ploughing season, the
following worship is performed to Boora.   The representative of the first ancestor of the tribe, whether he
occupies the position of its actual chief or not, goes out
into a field with the priest, who invokes Boora and all
the other gods, offers to Boora a fowl with rice and
arrack, and utters the following prayer :—

' O Boora Pennu ! and O Tari Pennu, and all other
gods ! (naming them).   You, O Boora Pennu ! created us,
giving us the attribute of hunger ; thence corn food was
necessary to us, and thence were necessary producing
fields.   You gave us every seed, and ordered us to use
bullocks, and to make ploughs, and to plough.   Had we
not received this art, we might still indeed have existed
upon the natural fruits of the jungle and the plain, but,

in our destitution, we could not have performed your worship. Do you, remembering this,—the connexion betwixt
our wealth and your honour,—grant the prayers which
we now offer. In the morning, we rise before the light
to our labour, carrying the seed. Save us from the tiger,
and the snake, and from stumbling blocks. Let the seed
appear earth to the eating birds, and stones to the eating
animals of the earth. Let the grain spring up suddenly
like a dry stream that is swelled in a night. Let the
earth yield to our ploughshares as wax melts before hot
iron. Let the baked clods melt like hailstones. Let our
ploughs spring through the furrows with a force like the
recoil of a bent tree. Let there be such a return from our
seed, that so much shall fall and be neglected in the fields,
and so much on the roads in carrying it home, that, when
we shall go out next year to sow, the paths and the fields
shall look like a young cornfield. From the first times
we have lived by your favour. Let us continue to receive
it. Remember that the increase of our produce is the
increase of your worship, and that its diminution must be
the diminution of your rites.'

The following story of a religious war undertaken by
the sect of Boora against that of Tari is a specimen of a
large class of Khond legends recited at the festivals in
honour of Boora :—

'Long ago the people of Boora Pennu resolved, for his
honour, to make war upon the tribes which worship Tari
with human sacrifices. The followers of Boora chose for
their enterprise the month of the year in which human
victims are chiefly offered, and their army moved into
Deegee, in the country of the people of Tari. Difficulties,
however, arose in another quarter, which obliged them
first to break up their force, and eventually to postpone
their undertaking until the corresponding month of the
next year; but they resolved to maintain their ground in
Deegee, by leaving there the two great leaders named
Dorgoma and Kitchima, with a small party. The tribes

which offer human sacrifices then took counsel together, and determined that it was absolutely necessary to destroy that detachment with its leaders; for, said they, "If they shall be permitted to remain, ere the return of the invading army they will have learned all our secret plans, and become perfectly acquainted with our country." The people of the earth goddess accordingly assembled a vast host, every man of which carried a load of ashes, while the women attended with provisions, and they appeared like a swarm of bees upon the hills above the small party of the people of the god of light. The two leaders of that party then said to their men, "We two are here for the glory of the god of light, and by the order of the tribes who are parties to this enterprise, and we must live or die. But no such obligation lies upon you. You are at perfect liberty to save your lives." Of their men a few then returned home, and a part retired to some distance, while the rest declared that they would die with their chiefs. These then prayed thus to their god :—" O god of light! You prevailed in the contest with the earth goddess,—this is our first ground of hope. Again, when the earth goddess and her ministers came to delude us into her worship, you sent the divine four, who drove her from our country; this is our second ground of hope. We have come here to establish your power, and if we shall perish, your authority will be diminished, your past superiority will be forgotten. Oh give us arms!" As they prayed a great wind rushed from a cavern in the side of the hill called Oldura, and scattered to the four quarters of the earth the ashes which the host of the earth goddess had brought to overwhelm the band of Boora Pennu. In evidence of these events the wind roars from that cavern to this day; while the brave chiefs and the brave men who stood by them obtained possession of Deegee, and that rich tract is now divided amongst five or six tribes, their descendants.

'With respect to the projected invasion, it was determined by the triumphant people of the god of light, after mature deliberation, to forego it. It was considered, that no good could possibly arise from attacking the people of the earth goddess, for—they are like the red ants—however much you may cherish them, they will continue to sting you, while, if you kill them, what is gained?'

I may observe here, that the Khond tribes of the sect of Boora Pennu which practise female infanticide allege his permissive sanction for that custom, given on the last occasion on which he communicated directly with mankind. They say that Boora then said to men—'Behold! from making one feminine being, what have I and the whole world suffered! You are at liberty to bring up only as many women as you can manage.'

The Worship of Tari Pennu, or Bera Pennu, the Earth Goddess.

In the worship paid to Tari Pennu by her sect, the chief rite is human sacrifice. It is celebrated as a public oblation by tribes, branches of tribes, or villages, both at social festivals held periodically, and when special occasions demand extraordinary propitiations. And besides these social offerings, the rite is performed by individuals to avert the wrath of Tari from themselves and their families.

The periodical common sacrifices are generally so arranged by tribes and divisions of tribes, that each head of a family is enabled, at least once a year, to procure a shred of flesh for his fields, and usually about the time when his chief crop is laid down. When a tribe is composed of several branches, the victims for the fixed offerings are provided by the branchés in turn, the cost being defrayed by contributions borne by each person according to his means. And such contributions are imperative not only upon members of the tribe, but also upon persons of every

I

race and creed that may be permanently associated with
it, as, through receiving its protection, or by employment
in it, or by possessing land within its boundaries, the express tenure of which is the discharge of a share of the
public religious burdens.

Special common offerings by a tribe are considered
necessary upon the occurrence of an extraordinary number
of deaths by disease, or by tigers; or should very many
die in childbirth; or should the flocks or herds suffer
largely from disease, or from wild beasts; or should the
greater crops threaten to fail: while the occurrence of any
marked calamity to the families of the chiefs, whose
fortunes are regarded as the principal index to the disposition of Tari towards their tribes, is held to be a token
of wrath which cannot be too speedily averted. And that
victims may be readily forthcoming when such special
occasions for sacrifice arise, whoever then gives one for
public use receives its value, and is, besides, exempted
from contribution to the three next public offerings.

Individuals make the great oblation when signal cala-
mities fall upon themselves or their families. Should, for
example, a child, when watching his father's flock, be
carried off by a tiger, supposed to be Tari, the parents fly
to the priest, bring him to their house, dash vessels of
water over him, seat him in his wet garments, and set a
cup of water before him. Into it he dips his fingers thrice,
smells them, sneezes, is filled with the deity, and speaks
wildly in her name. Should he then declare that Tari
had inflicted the blow, offended by her neglected worship,
he will doubtless add that an immediate victim is demanded; and the father of the house will make a vow of
sacrifice, to be redeemed, at whatever cost, within the
year.

Victims are called 'Meriah' by the Oriyas; in the
Khond language, 'Tokki,' or 'Keddi.' Persons of any
race or age, and of either sex, are acceptable victims,
except, I believe, Brahmins, who have been invested with

the thread, and are thence, perhaps, considered already
devoted to the gods.

A victim is acceptable to Tari only if he has been
acquired by the Khonds by purchase; or was born a
victim, that is, the son of a victim father; or if he was
devoted as a child to the gods by his father or natural
guardian.   The principle is, that the victim must be,
either naturally or by purchase, the full property of the
person who devotes him; and thence, should the full
right of that person be interrupted or weakened in any
way—as, for example, by the escape of a victim to an
asylum amongst the sect of Boora, or by his being carried
off by force, or his being delivered up to a British magistrate—his acceptableness is at an end, and it cannot be
renewed unless full property in him be re-acquired, and
he be again dedicated by a Khond.

Victims are generally supplied to the Khonds by men
of the two races called 'Panwa,' or 'Dombango,' and
'Gahinga,' apparently aborigines like themselves, and
attached in small numbers to almost every Khond village
for the discharge of this and other peculiar offices.   The
Panwas purchase the victims without difficulty, or kidnap
them in the low country from the poorer classes of
Hindus, procuring them either to the order of the Khonds,
or on speculation; and they, moreover, constantly sell as
victims their own children, and children of whom, as
relatives, they are the guardians.   Khonds when in
distress, as in times of famine, also frequently sell their
children for victims, considering the beatification of their
souls certain, and their death for the benefit of mankind
the most honourable possible.   An intelligent witness
informed me that he once chanced to see a Panwa load
another with execrations, and finally spit in his face, because
he had sold for a victim his own child, whom the former
wished to have married.   A party of Khonds who saw
the proceeding immediately pressed forward to console
the seller of the child, saying, ' Your child has died that

all the world may live, and the earth goddess herself will wipe that spittle from your face.'

The Meriah is brought blindfolded to the village by the procurer, and is lodged in the house of the mullicko or chief—in fetters if grown up, at liberty if a child. He is regarded during life as a consecrated being, and, if at large, is eagerly welcomed at every threshold. Victims are not unfrequently permitted to attain to years of maturity, and should one then have intercourse with the wife or daughter of a Khond, thankfulness is expressed to the deity for the distinction. To a Meriah youth who has thus grown up, a wife is generally given, herself also usually a victim, and a portion of land and of farm-stock is presented with her. The family which springs from their union is held to be born to the condition of the father; and although the sacrifice of lives so bound to existence is often postponed, and sometimes foregone, yet, should propitiations be required not easy to be afforded, the whole household is immolated without hesitation. And when the victim parents of a family who have been spared happen to belong to different tribes, as soon as they cease to have offspring they are separated and sent to their respective tribes, each accompanied by half of the children.

The escape of victims from their fate is comparatively rare, for several reasons. Except when under distinct apprehensions of death, victims are naturally loth to leave persons who treat them with extreme affection, mingled with deference; moreover, each victim is easily persuaded that where there are so many, and he is so much loved, his turn to die is not at hand. Every victim knows, also, that if he flies and is retaken, he will henceforth be kept in fetters, and will certainly be the first offering; and that his recapture is exceedingly probable, because, while every other person must be received as a sacred guest, a victim is necessarily restored to his owner by all the tribes of the sect of the earth goddess. It is, besides, assiduously impressed upon and believed by victims, that, should they escape from their proper fate, they must perish miserably by disease; while, at the same time, they are convinced that they will be beatified immediately after death by sacrifice.

When a sacrifice is to be celebrated by a tribe, or a portion of one, the following preliminary observances are gone through. Ten or twelve days before the time appointed for the rite the victim is devoted by cutting off his hair, which until then is kept unshorn. When a village receives notice of the day fixed for the sacrifice, all who intend to take part in it immediately perform the following ceremony, called 'Bringa,' by which they vow flesh to Tari. All wash their clothes, and go out of the village with the Janni, who invokes all the deities, and thus addresses Tari Pennu :—

'O Tari Pennu! you may have thought that we forgot your commands after sacrificing such a one (naming the last victim), but we forgot you not. We shall now leave our homes in your service, regardless of our enemies, of the good or the ill will of the gods beyond our boundary, of danger from those who by magical arts become Mleepa tigers, and of danger to our women from other men. We shall go forth on your service. Do you save us from suffering evil while engaged in it. We go to perform your rites; and if anything shall befall us, men will hereafter distrust you, and say you care not for your votaries. We are not satisfied with our wealth; but what we do possess we owe to you, and for the future we hope for the fulfilment of our desires. We intend to go on such a day to such a village, to bring human flesh for you. We trust to attain our desires through this service. Forget not the oblation.'

No one may be excluded from the festivals of human sacrifice, which are declared to be held 'for all mankind.' They are generally attended by a large concourse of people of both sexes, and continue for three days, which are passed

in the indulgence of every form of wild riot, and generally of gross excess.   The first day and night are spent
in drunken feasting and frantic dances, under excitement
which the goddess is believed to inspire, and which it
would be impious to resist.   Upon the second morning,
the victim, who has been kept fasting from the preceding
evening, is carefully washed, dressed in a new garment,
and led forth from the village in solemn procession, with
music and dancing.   The Meriah grove, a clump of deep
and shadowy forest trees, in which the mango, the bur, the
dammar, and the peepul generally prevail, usually stands
at a short distance from the village by a rivulet which is
called the Meriah stream.   It is kept sacred from the
axe, and is avoided by the Khond as haunted ground.
Upon the second day a post is fixed in the centre of the
grove, and in some places between two plants of the san-
kissar shrub.   The victim is seated at the foot of the post,
bound back to it by the priest.   He is then anointed with
oil, ghee, and turmeric, and adorned with flowers ; and a
species of reverence, which it is not easy to distinguish from
adoration, is paid to him throughout the day.   Infinite
contention now arises to obtain the slightest relic of his
person ; a particle of the turmeric paste with which he
is smeared, or a drop of his spittle, being esteemed, especially by the women, of sovereign virtue.   In some districts, instead of being thus bound in a grove, the victim
is exposed in or near the village upon a couch, after
being led in procession round the place of sacrifice.   And
in some parts of Goomsur, where this practice prevails,
small rude images of beasts and birds, in clay and wood,
are made in great numbers for this festival, and stuck on
poles,—a practice the origin or meaning of which is not
at all clear.   Upon the third morning the victim is
refreshed with a little milk and palm-sago, while the licentious feast which has been carried on with little intermission during the night is loudly renewed.   About noon
the orgies terminate, and the assemblage proceeds with

stunning shouts and pealing music to consummate the sacrifice.

As the victim must not suffer bound, nor, on the other hand, make any show of resistance, the bones of his arms, and, if necessary, those of his legs, are sometimes broken; but in every case of which I have heard the details, all such cruelty has been avoided by producing stupefaction with opium.

Instances are related of the escape of the victim at the moment of immolation from the omission of such precautions. About fifty years ago a victim who had been permitted to grow up to manhood in the district of Rodungiah was there led out to sacrifice. The preliminary ceremonies had been gone through, and an intoxicated crowd expected their completion, when the youth said to the chief, ' In suffering this death I become a god, and I do not resist my fate ; let me, then, partake with you in the joy of the festival.' The chief assented, and the young man called for a bowl and drank, when the crowd contended fiercely for the remains of the liquor which his lips had consecrated. He then danced and sang amidst the throng until the sacrifice could be no longer delayed, when he requested the chief to lend him his axe and his bow, that he might once more join his companions armed like a free man in the dance. He received the weapons, and when the chief was busied with the priest in preparing for the last rite, the youth approached him in the dance and clove his skull. He then dashed across the Salki, a deep and foaming torrent, and fled down the ghaut to the keep of Kuli Bissye, of Goomsur. A furious crowd of worshippers followed and demanded his surrender; but the Bissye contrived to parley with them until he could collect a small party of followers, who secretly bore away the fugitive, whose descendants still live.

After the preparations which have been described, the following remarkable invocations, legends, and dialogues are gone through,—the part of the victim in the latter, and occasionally also the parts of the chief and the priest, being sustained in a semi-dramatic way by the best impersonators of the characters that may be found. The form of words in this long ritual, as in all other Khond rituals, it need scarcely be repeated, is not fixed, but admits of endless variation. I give the fullest one in my possession, exactly as it was told to me.

The *Priest*, having called upon the earth goddess, and upon all the other deities by name, first recites this invocation :—

' O Tari Pennu! when we omitted to gratify you with your desired food, you forgot kindness to us. We possess but little and uncertain wealth. Increase it and we shall be able often to repeat this rite. We do not excuse our fault. Do you forgive it and prevent it in future by giving us increased wealth. We here present to you your food. Let our houses be so filled with the noise of children that our voices cannot be heard by those without. Let our cattle be so numerous that neither fish, frog, nor worm may live in the drinking-ponds beneath their trampling feet. Let our cattle so crowd our pastures that no vacant spot shall be visible to those who look at them from afar. Let our folds be so filled with the soil of our sheep that we may dig in them as deep as a man's height without meeting a stone. Let our swine so abound that our home fields shall need no ploughs but their rooting snouts. Let our poultry be so numerous as to hide the thatch of our houses. Let the stones at our fountains be worn hollow by the multitude of our brass vessels. Let our children have it but for a tradition that in the days of their forefathers there were tigers and snakes. Let us have but one care, the yearly enlargement of our houses to store our increasing wealth. Then we shall multiply your rites. We know that this is your desire. Give us increase of wealth, and we will give you increase of worship.'

Now every man and woman asks for what each wishes. One asks for a good husband, another for a good wife, another that his arrows may be made sure, &c. Then the *Janni* says—

' Umbally Bylee went to cut vegetables with a hook. She cut her finger. The earth was then soft mud, but when the blood-drops fell it became firm. She said, "Behold the good change! cut up my body to complete it." The people answered, "If we spill our own blood we shall have no descendants. We will obtain victims elsewhere. Will not the Dombo and the Gahi sell their children when in distress? and shall we not give our wealth for them?" And they prayed thus:—

' " May the gods send the exhausted Dombo, his feet pierced with thorns, to our door! May the gods give us wealth!"

' Their prayer was answered. They procured and sacrificed a victim. The whole earth became firm, and they obtained increase of wealth. The next year many victims came for sale, and the people thanked the gods, saying—" You have sent us victims, and have given us wealth." Thenceforward the world has been happy and rich, both in the portion which belongs to the Khonds, and the portion which belongs to rajahs.

' And society, with its relations of father and mother, and wife and child, and the bonds between ruler and subject, arose. And there came into use cows, bullocks, and buffaloes, sheep, and poultry. Then also came into use the trees and the hills, and the pastures and grass, and irrigated and dry fields, and the seeds suitable to the hills and to the valleys, and iron and ploughshares, and arrows and axes, and the juice of the palm-tree, and love between the sons and daughters of the people, making new households. In this manner did the necessity for the rite of sacrifice arise.

' Then, also, did hunting begin. A man brought in

a rat, a snake, and a lizard, and enquired if they were fit to eat. Then the earth goddess came and rested on the Janni, and said to him, " Give names to all the wild animals, distinguishing those that are fit and those that are unfit for use, and let men go to the jungles and the hills, and kill the sambur and spotted deer, and all other game, with arrows and with poison." And men went to hunt.

' While hunting, they one day found the people of Darungabadi and Laddabarri (tribes of the Souradah zemindary, adjacent to Goomsur, which do not offer human sacrifice) offering sacrifice. Their many-curved axes opened the bowels of the victims, which flowed out. They who went to the hunt said, " This ceremony is ill performed. The goddess will not remain with you." And the goddess left these awkward sacrificers and came with our ancestors. These people now cut trees only. The deity preferred the sacrifice at the hands of our forefathers, and thenceforth the whole burden of the worship of the world has lain upon us, and we now discharge it.

' Tari Pennu in this way came with our ancestors. But they at first knew only the form of worship necessary for themselves, not that necessary for the whole world. And there was still much fear ; and there were but few children, and there were deadly snakes and tigers, and thorns piercing the feet. They then called upon the Janni, to enquire the will of the goddess, by the suspended sickle. He said, " We practise the rite as it was first instituted, worshipping the first gods. What fault, what sin is ours ? " The goddess replied—" In a certain month wash your · garments with ashes or with stones ; make kenna ; purchase a child ; feed him in every house ; pour oil on him and on his garments, and ask for his spittle ; take him into the plain, when the earth goddess demands him ; let the Janni set him up ; call all the world ; let friendship reign ; call upon the names of the first people ; cut the victim in pieces : let each man place a shred of the flesh in his fields, in his grain-store, and in his yard, and then kill a buffalo for food, and give a feast, with drinking and dancing to all. Then see how many children will be born to you, how much game will be yours, what crops, how few shall die. All things will become right."

' We obeyed the goddess, and assembled the people. Then the victim child wept, and reviled, and uttered curses. All the people rejoiced, except those with whom the child had dwelt, and the Janni. They were overwhelmed with grief; their sorrows prevailed entirely over their expectations of benefit, and they did not give either their minds or their faith to the gods. "The world," said they, "rejoices—we are filled with despair;" and they demanded of the deity, "Why have you instituted this miserable heartrending rite?" Then the earth goddess came again and rested upon the Janni, and said, "Away with this grief! Your answer is this: when the victim shall weep, say to him, Blame not us, blame your parents who sold you. What fault is ours? The earth goddess demands a sacrifice. It is necessary to the world. The tiger begins to rage, the snake to poison, fevers and every pain afflict the people—shall you alone be exempt from evil? When you shall have given repose to the world, you will become a god, by the will of the gods."'

Then the *Victim* answers—' Have you no enemies, no vile and useless child, no debtor to another tribe, who compels you for his debts to sell your lands; no coward, who in time of battle skulks with another tribe? Have you none of these to seek out and sacrifice?'

The *Janni* replies—' We have acted upon quite different views. We did not kidnap you on the road, nor while gathering sticks in the jungle, nor when at play. The souls of those whom you would have us sacrifice can never become gods. They are only fit to perish by epilepsy, falling in the fire, or by ulcers, or other dread dis-

eases.   Such sacrifices would be of no avail.   To obtain
you, we cleared the hill and the jungle, fearless of the
tiger and the snake.   We stinted ourselves to fill your
parents, and gave them our brass vessels ; and they gave
to us as freely as one gives light from a fire !   Blame
them !   Blame them !'

The Victim.—'And did I share the price which my
parents received ?   Did I agree to the sale ?   You now
tell me this.   No one remembers his mother's womb,
nor the taste of his mother's milk ; and I considered you
my parents.   Where there was delicate food in the village, I was fed.   When the child of any one suffered,
he grieved ; but if I suffered, the whole village grieved.
When did you conceive this fraud, this wickedness to destroy me ?   You, O my father, and you,—and you,—and
you,—O my fathers !   do not destroy me !'

The *Mullicko*, or chief of the village in which the
victim was kept, or his representative, now says—'This
usage is delivered down to us from the first people of the
first time.   They practised it.   The people of the middle
time omitted it.   The earth became soft.   An order re-
established the rite.   O child !   we must destroy you.
Forgive us.   You will become a god.'

'*The Victim.*—'Of this your intention I knew nothing;
I thought I was to pass my life with you.   I assisted to
build houses, and to clear fields for my children.   See !
there are the palm-trees I planted—there is the mohwa-
tree I planted—there is the public building on which I
laboured—its palings still white in your sight.   I planted
the tobacco which you are now eating.   Look behind
you !   The cows and the sheep which I have tended look
lovingly at me.   All this time you gave me no hint of my
intended fate.   I toiled with you at every work with my
whole mind.   Had I known of this doom, I had still
toiled, but with different feelings.   Let the whole burden
of my soul's grief, as I remember the past, lie upon you.'

The Chief.—' You are about to become a god.   We

shall profit by your fate. We cannot argue with you. Do you not recollect that, when your father came to claim your uncompleted price, you snatched up a shining brass vessel : that we said, " That is your father's," and you threw it at him, and ran away amongst the sheep ? Do you not recollect the day on which we cut your hair, devoting you to sacrifice ? And do you not recollect that when many were sick, and the Janni brought the divining sickle, he declared " The earth demands a victim " ? ' [1]

Then several persons around say—' I should have told you,—and I,—and I; ' and several give answers such as— ' I thought of our hard labour to acquire you, which had been wasted, had you escaped from us;' and,—' You might have known all well.'

The Victim.—' It is true I did observe something of this ; but your aged mothers, and your wives, and your beautiful children, my brothers and sisters, assured me that you were humane, and would never kill one so useful and so beautiful as I. " They will rather," said your mothers and your children, " remembering your acts and your ways, sell these fields, and these trees, and that tobacco, to procure a substitute." This I believed, and I was happy and laboured with you.'

The Chief. —' We cannot satisfy you. Ask your father, who is present. I satisfied him with my favourite cattle, my valuable brass vessels, and my sheep, and with silken and woollen cloths, and axes. A bow and arrows, not four days old, I gave to his fancy. Your parents, forgetting your beauty, forgetting the pleasure of cherishing you, turned their hearts to my cattle, and my brass vessels, and gave you away. Upbraid *them*. Heap imprecations upon them. We will curse them with you, imprecating upon them—that all their children may be similarly sacrificed—that they may lose, within the year, the price for which they sold you—that they may have a miserable and forlorn old age, lingering childless and unfed—that

[1] See above, p. 106.

when they die in their empty house, there may be no one to inform the village for two days, so that, when they are carried out to be burned, all shall hold their nostrils —that their own souls may afterwards animate victims given to hardhearted men, who will not even answer their death-plaints consolingly. Curse them thus, and we will curse them with you.'

The *Victim* will now turn to the Janni, saying—'And why did you conceal my fate? When I dwelt with the Mullicko, like a flower, were you blind, or dumb, or how were you possessed, that you never said, " Why do you cherish, so lovingly, this child—this child who must die for the world ? " Then had I known my doom and leapt from a precipice and died. Your reason for concealment—living as you do apart from men, is—that you thought of yourself, " I am great. The whole world attends on my ministrations." But, world, look upon him ! What miscreant eyes ! What a villanous head, with hair like a sumbully tree ! And see how enraged he is ! What a jabber he makes ! What a body he has got, starved upon worship which depends upon men's griefs ! —A body anointed with spittle for oil ! Look, O world— look, and tell ! See, how he comes at me, leaping like a toad !"

The *Janni* replies—'Child! why speak thus? I am the friend of the gods ; the first in their sight. Listen to me. I did not persuade your father or your mother to sell you. I did not desire the Mullickos to sell their fields to acquire your price. Your parents sold you. These Mullickos bought you. They consulted me, inquiring, " How may this child become blessed ? " The hour is not yet over. When it is past, how grateful will you be to me ! You, as a god, will gratefully approve and honour me.'

The Victim.—' My father begot me ; the Mullickos bought me, my life is devoted, and all will profit by my death. But you, O Janni ! who make nothing of my sufferings, take to yourself all the virtue of my sacrifice. You shall, however, in no respect profit by it.'

The Janni.—' The deity created the world, and everything that lives; and I am his minister and representative. God made you, the Mullicko bought you, and I sacrifice you. The virtue of your death is not yours, but mine; but it will be attributed to you through me.'

The Victim—' My curse be upon the man who, while he did not share in my price, is first at my death. Let the world ever be upon one side while he is on the other. Let him, destitute and without stored food, hope to live only through the distresses of others. Let him be the poorest wretch alive. Let his wife and children think him foul. I am dying. I call upon all—upon those who bought me, on those whose food I have eaten, on those who are strangers here, on all who will now share my flesh—let all curse the Janni to the gods!'

The Janni.—' Dying creature, do you contend with me? I shall not allow you a place among the gods.'

The Victim.—' In dying I shall become a god, then will you know whom you serve. Now do your will on me.'

The acceptable place of sacrifice is discovered the previous night, by persons who are sent to probe the ground about the village with sticks in the dark, and mark the first deep chink as the spot indicated by the earth goddess. There, in the morning, a short post is inserted; around it four larger posts are usually set up, and in the midst of these the victim is placed. The priest, assisted by the chief and one or two of the elders of the village, now takes the branch of a green tree cleft several feet down the centre. They insert the victim between the rift, fitting it, in some districts to his chest, in others to his throat. Cords are then twisted round the open extremity of the stake, which the priest, aided by his assistants, strives with his whole force to close; he

then wounds the victim slightly with his axe, when the
crowd throws itself upon the sacrifice and strips the
flesh from the bones, leaving untouched the head and
intestines.

The most careful precautions are taken lest the offering should suffer desecration by the touch or even the
near approach of any persons save the worshippers of
the earth goddess, or by that of any animal.   During
the night after the sacrifice, strong parties watch over the
remains of the victim ; and next day, the priest and the
Mullickos consume them, together with a whole sheep, on
a funeral pile, when the ashes are scattered over the
fields, or are laid as paste over the houses and granaries.
And then two formalities are observed, which are held
indispensable to the virtue of the sacrifice.   The first is
that of presenting to the father of the victim, or to the
person who sold or made him over to the Khonds for
sacrifice, or the representative of such person, a bullock,
called the ' dhuly,' in final satisfaction of all demands.
The second formality is the sacrifice of a bullock for a
feast, at which the following prayer is offered up.

After invoking all the gods, the priest says :—' O
Tari Pennu ! You have afflicted us greatly ; have brought
death to our children and our bullocks, and failure to our
corn ;—have afflicted us in every way.   But we do not
complain of this.   It is your desire only to compel us to
perform your due rites, and then to raise up and enrich
us.   We were anciently enriched by this rite ; all around
us are great from it ; therefore, by our cattle, our flocks,
our pigs, and our grain we procured a victim and offered
a sacrifice.   Do you now enrich us.   Let our herds be
so numerous that they cannot be housed ; let children so
abound that the care of them shall overcome their parents
—as shall be seen by their burned hands ; let our heads
ever strike against brass pots innumerable hanging from our
roofs ; let the rats form their nests of shreds of scarlet
cloth and silk ; let all the kites in the country be seen in

the trees of our village, from beasts being killed there every day. We are ignorant of what it is good to ask for. You know what is good for us. Give it to us!'

When the victim is cut to pieces, the persons who have been deputed by each village to bring its share of the flesh instantly return home. There the village priest and everyone else who has stayed at home fast rigidly until their arrival. The bearer of the flesh carries it rolled up in leaves of the googlut tree, and when he approaches the village, lays it out on a cushion formed of a handful of grass, and then deposits it in the place of public meeting, to give assurance to all of its arrival. The fasting heads of families then go with their priest to receive the flesh. He takes and divides it into two portions, and subdivides one of these into as many shares as there are heads of families present. He then says to the earth goddess— 'O Tari Pennu! our village offered such a person as a sacrifice, and divided the flesh among all the people in honour of the gods. Now, such a village has offered such a one, and has sent us flesh for you. Be not displeased with the quantity, we could only give them as much. If you will give us wealth, we will repeat the rite.' The Janni then seats himself on the ground, scrapes a hole in it, and taking one of the two portions into which he divided the flesh, places it in the hole, but with his back turned, and without looking. Then each man adds a little earth to bury it, and the Janni pours water on the spot from a hill gourd. Each head of a house now rolls his shred of flesh in leaves, and all raise a shout of exultation at the work done. Then a wild excited battle takes place with stones and mud, in the course of which a considerable number of heads are broken, and all go to the house in which the young men of the village sleep, and there renew the fight and knock down the whole or part of the house. Finally, each man goes and buries his particle of flesh in his favourite field, placing it in the earth behind his back without looking. And here may be noticed the

K

idea which secures the distribution of the flesh of every victim to the greatest possible extent,—that, instead of advantage arising to any one from the possession of a large share of the flesh, all are benefited by a sacrifice in proportion to the number of shares into which the flesh is subdivided. After burying the flesh, all return home and eat and drink, in some places holding a common feast, while in others each family eats apart. For three days thereafter no house is swept, and, in one district, strict silence is observed, while fire may not be given, nor wood cut, nor strangers be received. Upon the fourth day—the people reassemble at the place of sacrifice, slaughter and feast on a buffalo, and leave its inedible portions as a gratification to the spirit of the Meriah.

The ceremonial of human sacrifice is finally completed by the offering of a hog to the earth goddess, a year after its performance, by the village which sacrificed. This offering is called the 'Valka,' and the invocation to Tari is simply this—'O Tari Pennu—up to this time we have been engaged in your worship, which we commenced a year ago. Now the rites are completed. Let us receive the benefit.'

Such are the rites and observances which, in some districts, make up the worship of the earth goddess. But they are subject to many variations. Thus, in one tract the victim is put to death slowly by fire. A low stage is formed, sloping on either side like a roof; upon it the victim is placed, his limbs wound round with cords, so as to confine but not prevent his struggles. Fires are lighted, and hot brands are applied, so as to make the victim roll alternately up and down the slopes of the stage. He is thus tortured as long as he is capable of moving or uttering cries; it being believed that the favour of the earth goddess, especially in respect of the supply of rain, will be in proportion to the quantity of tears which may be extracted. The victim is next day cut to pieces.

The sect of the earth goddess often attempt to introduce secretly fragments of the flesh of human victims into the tracts inhabited by the sect of Boora.   One object in so doing is, to excite the wrath of Boora towards his followers for their failure to prevent the pollution ; but some of the sect of Tari, at least, hoped also by depositing the flesh at the shrines of some of the local deities, to induce in them a taste for the horrid food, and, by its gratification, to seduce them from their rivals. Whatever may be the true theory, both sects are agreed as to the result effected in the following case.   In Cattingia, the people of which are of the sect of Boora, there are spots where certain salts efflorescing upon the soil attract the deer and other wild animals in great numbers, so that they become an easy prey to the huntsman.   The people of the neighbouring tract of Guddapore, who offer human sacrifices, placed in one of the most valuable of those spots a shred of human flesh for the guardian deity.   Since that time, no man of Cattingia has ever seen game there, while no huntsman of Guddapore has ever failed to find it.

The people of Boora Pennu regard with horror the impurity of the country which is polluted with human blood. When they visit it, between the seasons of sowing and reaping, they may not use its fire, but must obtain pure fire by friction ; nor may they use the waters of its pools or fountains until they have first fixed their arrows in them, symbolising their conquest.   In like manner, they may not sleep in a house until they have snatched and burnt a few straws from its thatch, to symbolise its conquest with conflagration.   Death is believed to be often the penalty of the neglect of these precautions.[1]

---

[1] The account of the worship of the inferior gods—the gods of rain, of increase, of the chace, of war, of boundaries, the house god, the village god, the god of fountains, the goddess of smallpox,—has been transferred to the Appendix, as having no direct bearing on the present narrative, although deeply interesting to all who desire to study the natural history of superstition or the mind of this singular people. See Appendix A.

SECTION III.

FEMALE INFANTICIDE.

The practice of female infanticide is, I believe, not wholly unknown amongst any portion of the Khond people, while it exists in some of the tribes of the sect of Boora to such an extent, that no female infant is spared, except when a woman's first child is a female, and that villages containing a hundred houses may be seen without a female child.

The custom has its origin in the ideas and usages which regulate the relations of the sexes, and especially the conditions of marriage amongst these tribes; while, moreover, it is expressly sanctioned and promoted by their religious doctrines.

I can here but very briefly advert to the customs and feelings which the practice of infanticide alternately springs from and produces. The influence and privileges of women are exceedingly great amongst the Khonds, and are, I believe, greatest amongst the tribes which practise infanticide. Their opinions have great weight in all public and private affairs, and their direct agency is often considered essential in the former. Thus, the presence of the sisters and daughters of a tribe is indispensable at its battles, to afford aid and encouragement; and the intervention of its wives, who are neutral between the tribes of their fathers and those of their husbands, is necessary to make peace. The Khond women frequently settle difficult questions between their tribes and the rajahs, through the ladies of these, with whom they are always in communication; while these ladies, it may be observed, are employed on critical occasions as irresistible instruments to sway the Khond chiefs.

But the ascendency of Khond women in these tribes is completed by their extraordinary matrimonial privileges; with respect to which, however, it is to be borne in mind, that intermarriage between persons of the same tribe however large or scattered, is considered incestuous, and punishable by death.

So far is constancy to her husband from being required in a .wife, that her pretensions do not, at least, suffer diminution in the eyes of either sex when fines are levied on her convicted lovers; while, on the other hand, infidelity on the part of a married man is held to be highly dishonourable, and is often punished by deprivation of many social privileges. A wife, moreover, may quit her husband at any time, except within a year of her marriage, or when she expects offspring, or within a year after the birth of a child; and she may then return to her father's house, or contract a new marriage; while no man who is without a wife may, without entailing disgrace on himself and his tribe, refuse to receive any woman who may choose to enter his house and establish herself as its mistress.

Now, a bridegroom gives for a wife of these tribes in which so few women are brought up, a large consideration in cattle and money. The sum is chiefly subscribed by his near relatives and his branch of his tribe, and is paid to his wife's father, who again distributes it amongst the heads of families of his own branch. But, when a wife quits her husband, he has a right to reclaim immediately from her father the whole sum paid for her; while the father, at the same time, becomes entitled to levy a like sum from any new husband to whom she may attach herself. And, it being observed that every man's tribe is at once answerable for all his debts, and bound in honour to enforce his claims, it will be understood that these restitutions and exactions, whether to be made betwixt persons belonging to different tribes or to different branches of the same tribe, must be, even in the simplest cases, productive of infinite difficulty and vexation; while they have given rise to three-fourths of the sanguinary quarrels and hereditary feuds which distract the Khond country. Thence, say the Khonds, ' To any

man but a rich and powerful chief, who desires to form
connexions, and is able to make large and sudden
restitutions, and to his tribe — a married daughter is a
curse.   By the death of our female infants before they
see the light, the lives of men without number are saved,
and we live in comparative peace.'

With respect to the religious sanction of this practice,
these tribes believe, as I have already observed, that
Boora, contemplating the deplorable consequences of the
creation of the first feminine being, his consort, charged
men, or gave them express permission, to bring up only as
many females as they should find consistent with the good
of society.   Now, while they believe that souls condemned
by Dinga to pass successive lives upon earth are ever
reborn in the tribes in which they were first born and
received, they conceive that the reception of a soul into a
tribe, when it is first sent to animate a human form, is
completed only on the performance of the ceremony of
naming the infant on the seventh day after its birth; and
they hold the curious doctrine, moreover, that Boora
sets apart a certain quantity of soul to be distributed
amongst each generation of mankind.   Thence they believe that should an infant die before it is named, its soul
does not enter into the circle of tribal spirits, to be reborn
as often as Dinga wills, but rejoins the mass of spirit set
apart for the generation to which it belongs.   And thus,
by the destruction of a female infant, either the addition
of a new female soul to the number of spirits attached to
a tribe is prevented, and the chance of getting a new
male spirit in its place is gained, or the return of a female
soul by rebirth in that tribe is postponed.

But the exclusion of new female spirits from a tribe
is believed by these Khonds to be of high importance
upon another ground.   They believe that, of the quantity
of soul allotted by Boora to each generation, the less that
is assigned to the women, the more will remain for the
men, whose mental powers will be proportionately im-

proved. And the first prayer of every Khond being for many and highly endowed male children, the belief that the mental qualities of these may be raised by the destruction of the female infants, is no slight incentive to the practice, superadded to the motives afforded by the belief that the number of the males may be increased by it, that it is expressly permitted by Boora, and that it averts much of the strife and bloodshed arising from the capricious dissolution of marriage-ties by women.

The religion of the Khonds, then, is a distinct theism, with a subordinate demonology ; and the sum of its chief doctrines is briefly as follows :—

The supreme being and sole source of good, who is styled the god of light, created for himself a consort who became the earth goddess, and the source of evil; and thereafter he created the earth, with all it contains, and man. The earth goddess, prompted by jealousy of the love borne to man by his creator, rebelled against the god of light, and introduced moral and physical evil into the world. The god of light arrested the action of physical evil while he left man perfectly free to receive or to reject moral evil—defined to be ' disobedience towards God, and strife amongst men.' A few of mankind entirely rejected moral evil, the remainder received it. The former portion were immediately deified ; the latter were condemned to endure every form of physical suffering, with death, deprivation of the immediate care of the creator, and the deepest moral degradation. Meanwhile, the god of light and his rebel consort contended for superiority, until the elements of good and evil became thoroughly commingled in man and throughout nature.

Up to this point the Khonds hold the same general belief, but from it they divide into two sects directly opposed upon the question of the issue of the contest between the two antagonistic powers.

One sect holds, that the god of light completely conquered the earth goddess, and employs her—still the

active principle of evil—as the instrument of his moral
rule : that he resolved to provide a partial remedy for
the consequences of the introduction of evil, by enabling
man to attain to a state of moderate enjoyment upon earth,
and to partial restoration to communion with his creator
after death : and that, to effect this purpose, he created
three classes of subordinate deities, and assigned to them
the office—first, of instructing man in the arts of life, and
regulating the powers of nature for his use, upon the condition of his paying to them due worship ; secondly, of
administering a system of retributive justice, through subjection to which, and through the practice of virtue
during successive lives upon earth, the soul of man might
attain to beatification.

The other sect hold, upon the other hand, that the
earth goddess remains unconquered ; that the god of
light could not, in opposition to her will, carry out his
purpose with respect to man's temporal lot ; and that man,
therefore, owes his elevation from the state of physical
suffering into which he fell through the reception of evil,
to the direct exercise of her power to confer blessings, or
to her permitting him to receive the good which flows from
the god of light, through the inferior gods, to all who
worship them.   With respect to man's destiny after death,
they believe that the god of light carried out his purpose:
and they believe that the worship of the earth goddess
by human sacrifice is the indispensable condition on which
these blessings have been granted, and their continuance
may be hoped for—the virtue of the rite availing not only
for those who practise it, but for all mankind.[1]

---

[1] For some remarks on this chapter, see Appendix B.

CHAPTER VII.

RETURN TO NELLORE AND VISIT TO THE CAPE OF GOOD HOPE.

From January 1838 to January 1841.

ABOUT the end of 1837 Lieutenant Macpherson left
Ganjam and after a short visit to Madras, where Lord
Elphinstone had succeeded Sir Frederick Adam as governor, returned to his duties at Nellore. His health, however, was still very feeble, and in the hope of acquiring a
little vigour he 'broke away,' as he writes on the 28th
April 1838, 'some eighty miles inland to a hill zemindary,
which has been rarely visited, to see all that was to be
seen of the present, and to inquire into the obscure past.
Oodiagherry was the seat of a Hindu principality during
many dynasties, until the Mussulman put his foot on its
neck, when it passed to a family of the Arcot race whose
descendants hold it now. I found a town in which Mahomedan sloth and vice had succeeded to Hindu industry,
and a hill about 1,000 feet in height crested by an ancient
and long-ruined fort. Oppressed by the intolerable heat I
climbed the hill, and discovering a small, well-lighted, half-
ruinous chamber, detached from an old mosque, placed on
the verge of a bastion that overhung the scarped rock ;
finding also my thermometer full 10° lower than on the
plain, and the air cool and light, I there established
myself, and have remained for a fortnight, busy during
the day, in the morning and evening wandering over the
rocky hill and admiring its superb Salvator scenes from
the base to its summit. I told—or should have told
you in my last, that I had not all this time been for eight

days in a fit state to do justice. to the materials for an interesting paper collected with so much hazard and cost in Goomsur, and I really thought the spoil was to escape from my mere inability to stretch out my hand to grasp it. But this little change has set me up so well for these few days that I have completed the topographical part of my report. By the very first ship, probably six weeks or eight at the most from this time, I certainly sail colony-wards. It is a hard but inevitable fate. I have ample and pleasant employment in the statistics of this district, which I have just begun comprehensively to investigate—but all must yield to the grand consideration. I have touched the verge of discretion, says Cadenhead, my oracle. My sole hope, then, is that in this eagle's nest, where I have recovered a trifling amount of nerve for a time, I may manage to live out these weeks in solitude, and complete my picture of Khond nature. The Khond council are in arrangement identical to the letter with that of the shield of Achilles, and the spirit and manner of their public assemblies is that of those portrayed by the old bard ; [1] and when I looked for the passage, was not my Homer gone with all my most valuable books!—plundered in my absence at the wars.

' There is a book expressly " de sacrificiis humanis,"

[1] The following passage is alluded to:—
' Meanwhile a busy throng the forum fill'd :
There between two a fierce contention rose
About a death-fine ; to the public one
Appeal'd, asserting to have paid the whole ;
While one denied that he had aught received.
Both were desirous that before the judge
The issue should be tried ; with noisy shouts
Their several partizans encouraged each.
The heralds still'd the tumult of the crowd :
On polish'd chairs, in solemn circle, sate
The rev'rend elders; in their hands they held
The loud-voic'd heralds' sceptres ; waving these,
They heard th' alternate pleadings; in the midst
Two talents lay of gold, which he should take
Who should before them prove his righteous cause.'
                Iliad, b. xviii. 1 497. Lord Derby's Translation.

quoted in Pashley's Crete—Geusius is I think the name; you might as well ask, in India, for Domesday book; also Voss de Superstitione, &c.

'A little sooner or later the country between the Indus and the Persian frontier will be the stage of important events. Persia is already thrown away, I fear; Russia has acknowledged agents on our frontier, and men's minds are unsettled, to a great extent, throughout the whole of Upper India. Still you are strong enough in Europe and we in Asia, and I foresee no combination of events from which anything is to be dreaded.

'I am constantly thinking whether I could not take my sick-leave up to Egypt and the Black Sea, doing all those countries, and home to Bengal by the Caucasus and some new route from the shore of the Caspian. I am so perfectly orientalised, and get on so easily with wild men, that I am convinced I could go anywhere, and that is the most promising field I know in the present aspect of things.'

'Nellore, 9th January 1839.

'It has been a most interesting and instructive crisis. We have, for the first time, come sensibly in contact with Russia in the East, where, unless new and improbable combinations shall arise, we must continue to be "at war" with her. India was penetrated by the belief that the Shah, supported by the Czar, was advancing with an irresistible host, and, from the Himalaya to Comorin, thrilled with the expectation of change. Mussulman, Mahratta, Rajpoot, Seik, the discontented heads of every nation, rank, and class, laid the foundation of a league to aid in our overthrow. With the retreat from Herat all passed like vapour, and the dream is already half forgotten. Some movements have been made, or are intended on our part, which have told or which promise well. A fine army has been assembled in Bengal, and a small one at Bombay, showing that we are ready. Karak, in the Gulf, has been occupied, and must be maintained as if it were Gibraltar. We render Herat impregnable to Persian engineers; and we put a puppet on the throne of Cabul, on whose conduct much depends. But the real question is, who shall be paramount in Persia? and to me nothing appears to be done while it remains doubtful. I expect bolder action on this side of the isthmus than on yours.'

'Madras, 17th March 1839.

'My tendency to fever not having left me, I am here waiting for a ship to sail away, in the first instance, to the Cape.

'A good deal of anxiety exists throughout Southern India respecting the feelings of the Mussulman population, which, being necessarily hostile to our rule, indulges largely in hopes of change from the contest in which we are engaged in the north-west. The only real ground for uneasiness, however, which I can discern, lies in our ignorance how far their sentiments have extended to the troops. It is not even considered respectable in an officer to be on such terms with any of the men whom he commands, whatever rank or distinction they may have attained, as would make it possible for him to know what they are thinking about; and the temper of the men has been severely tried in this quarter by very unfortunately timed changes in their pay.'

'17th March 1839.

'I take with me a Mussulman lad of fine spirit, who has been the companion of all my wanderings in capacity of valet for several years. Poor boy, he got this vile fever in Goomsur as badly as myself, and though it is very expensive, I cannot but afford him the same means of cure. He will, however, be useful at the Cape, where servants are, I believe, greater and dirtier villains than any in the world. I wish you had seen the battle he had to get away from his newly-married wife, his father-in-law, and all his relations. They look on him as lost for ever. The day of his departure they took him to the mosque, and, I believe, read the funeral service over him, or something like it. I asked him if he knew what the natives of the Cape were like; "yes," he answered, "they have horses' heads!" He also consulted me on the propriety of shaving his black moustaches, which he understood the intense cold of that region would turn red. He has been of infinite use to me by his intelligence and presence of mind, and tact in managing the various races of natives among whom I have been thrown.'

'Madras, 2nd March 1839.

'I have given Lord Elphinstone, at his particular request, my unfinished paper to read; and they say that he has never been seen to take so much interest in anything. It is my intention very strongly to enforce the view that in precipitation lies the sole danger to be apprehended in conducting the people to new habits of life.'

'Cape of Good Hope, 12th June 1839.

'I reached the Cape, after a long and pleasant voyage of nine weeks, some three or four days, ago. The change of climate and of scene has done all for me that could yet be expected, and the complexions of my brother Indians who have preceded me give the best earnest for the future. I can give you no idea of the delight experienced by a half-carbonised animal when he finds himself again in a temperate climate; and though there is here but a town within the arms of a fine mountain, a tract of bare Scotch scenery upon the one hand, and a pretty vine-growing valley upon the other, we are all half distracted with enjoyment. We have cold air and cold water, and a white, good-looking, half-Dutch, half-English population, with complexions of which I had lost even the memory. It were worth while to come but to see the children; the women, compared to our Indian wives and spinsters, are beings of another class. This seems to be a grand place for what I want—animal life.

There is but one drawback, that, having come so much nearer you, and seeing so much that recalls to mind all that is alone really dear to me, I absolutely languish for the better country and you all; yet I must hold by India for a time. Peace soldiering is a poor profession anywhere; in India it is no profession at all.'[1]

'Cape Town, 9th July 1839.

'This is the Cape winter season, when there is rain under and upon Table Mountain, and a sprinkling of snow upon a range of hills of the same height (between 3,000 and 4,000 feet) 60 miles inland. All the trees, save the firs, are leafless; but the heaths are in rich bloom with shrubs of infinite beauty, and, with the exception of a couple of rainy days now and then, the climate is divine. The town is one of the handsomest of its size in the world, built with perfect regularity between the mountain and the bay. The houses are much above the pretensions of the people, and like, I presume, handsome Dutch houses in Europe. In the recently liberated slave population the features of the Malay, Hottentot, and Dutch people are curiously and inextricably blended—a firm, good-humoured, drinking, hard-working race being the result.

'Cape of Good Hope, 20th August 1839.

'Since I last wrote, I have moved out of the pretty Dutch town, the metropolis of the colony, to a lovely village eight miles distant, and three from Constantia, whose vineyards grow that sweet wine. This—Wynberg —is a lovely hamlet, like the most beautiful English village you may have ever seen. It is situated near the base of a long slope of Table Mountain, covered with fir and oak woods, vines, and flowers which enamel the ground like a Turkey carpet. Most of the cottages are inhabited by

---

[1] The rules then in force prevented him from visiting Europe without vacating his staff appointment—a step which might have consigned him to regimental duty and pay for the remainder of his life.

sick Indians ; I am living with half-a-dozen Bengalees in a boarding-house.'

After various wanderings, not devoid of interest, though there is not room here to record them, the traveller writes from

' Worcester, South Africa, 8th July 1840.

'I started in the old fashion which I may have told you of—a stout horse to myself, a second for my servant, and a third for my pack-saddle and baggage, and all alone saving the presence of half-a-dozen volumes, to whose companionship I would have willingly added that of a friend, but that I was to depend entirely upon the hospitality of the country, which is much more readily extended to a party of five than to one of ten. I have been for the last ten days upon the upper mountain, and more gratified, and more improved in health, than I can tell you. It is delicious, clear, cold, mild winter ; I mean in so far as the air is concerned, and the water ; for with the earth it is spring. The scenery is perfectly bare of wood—a few oak-trees, pines, and alders about the farmhouses, but nothing more ; and the whole sur- face is heathy, with bright stripes of greensward mark- ing the course of the streams, and here and there a tract of bushy hillocks sprinkled with your garden mari- gold and anemones, and many heaths even already in bloom. This general surface is grandly divided into basin-shaped valleys by circles of mountains of the most wild, beautiful, and various forms, composed of mingled sandstone, quartz-rock, and hornblende schist, and now running into bare, bleak, blasted ridges, spiry and castel- lated, or toothed like saws, now waving smoothly and green to their summit. But the climate !—I am living at a farm called ' Te Knur '—that is, ' The Chosen '—in a district called 'Freezeland' by the inhabitants, though nearly as well known by the name of 'Scotland.' It freezes every night just enough to coat thickly the standing ponds, and to make the grass crisp under foot. All day it is clear without a cloud, and even my sensitive head feels little or no inconvenience from the sun. I take a glorious run of two hours before breakfast, make a dash on horseback to a neighbouring farm in the middle of the day, and take a long evening stroll in the bracing wind. In a week I have gained a hundred per cent., eyes included ; although everything is against me save the climate and the scene. I should add, save the diet—which is mutton and dry bread, and milkless tea and coffee, and occasionally an ostrich egg ; and of which I have my share from common dishes with mine host the boor and his frow and his dirty children, and relish it infinitely. I had no idea there was a climate in the world like this—although our own is, I believe, what it was, and not much worse—nor that people existed with the complexions or the vigour of those around me ; although cheeks must be red and noses sometimes blue, and farmers like mountain-bulls, and farmers' daughters' faces like peony roses, and farmers' sons like *stirks*, in the old fatherland ; and I may add, that it never occurred to me that India was so far removed in point of climate from what is natural to the pale race which is there dominant. This part of the country being liable to heavy falls of snow, the inhabitants nearly all leave it, with their flocks and herds, in those months, for the vast African plain called the Karoo ; and thither goes my host with his family in a few days, or I would stay longer at Te Knur.

'Since writing the above, I have made a long day's march, mostly on foot, both my riding-horses being dead lame before and behind; but I can now walk almost any distance with pleasure. I, however, happened to light on a quantity of delicious apples as I was leaving Freezeland, and, eating of them, my tongue is slightly furred to-day, and my eyes are as bad as ever. This exactly indicates my state of health. The slightest trifle throws out of tone my whole nervous system.'

' Grahamstown, 3rd September 1840.

'After a ride of some eight hundred miles, I find myself at Grahamstown, the capital of the eastern division of this colony bordering upon Kaffraria. I have gone over a great deal of country, turning my horses' heads wherever there was anything to be looked at—now loitering by the way, now rattling along. Upon the whole, I have been pleased with what I have seen, although it would be very difficult to traverse a like extent of territory presenting so few objects to which interest of any kind can be imagined to attach. With the exception of a few valleys which bear the vine, and a few tracts which produce corn, the country is a vast cattle and sheep walk, and divided amongst Dutch boors in farms of the average extent of 10,000 acres. The surface is either an unbroken heathy waste, or an undiversified expanse covered with low bushes; or it is a bright greensward-covered country, with forests amongst the foldings of the hills, for the most part stiff and formal, but occasionally broken and picturesque.

'I have returned from a delightful ride along the frontier of Kaffirland, under the kind and able guidance of Edward Gordon of the 75th Regiment, who placed his services quite at my disposal. I have been at the kraals of several of the leading chiefs, seen the missionaries and the political agents, and have been infinitely amused and gratified with the glimpse at a new variety of our species. I start from hence to-morrow for Port Elizabeth, where I hope to find a ship going down the coast to Table Bay.'

Lieutenant Macpherson returned to Madras in the steamer ' India,' commanded by Captain Andrew Henderson. He had improved considerably, but he never, to the end of his days, recovered the health he enjoyed before his visit to Goomsur.

CHAPTER VIII.

MEASURES FOR THE ABOLITION OF HUMAN SACRIFICE
AMONG THE KHONDS FROM 1837 TO 1842.

LIEUTENANT MACPHERSON, upon his return to Madras, entered into communication with the Governor, Lord Elphinstone, whose interest in the Khonds continued un- abated, and who required that he should remain at Madras and complete the Report which was to contain the results of his inquiries, along with practical suggestions on the subject of our policy towards the hill-tribes.

It is necessary here to refer to the measures which had been adopted with a view to reclaim the Khonds from the practice of human sacrifice.

The immediate suppression of the rite by main force was of course, from a natural impulse, urged upon the Government by most of those who had any opportunity of addressing it.   But the experience of two campaigns had not been wholly thrown away.

Mr. Russell, in laying before the Madras Government[1] all the information which could be obtained upon this subject, had strongly expressed the opinion that it was vain to attempt to put down by mere coercion a practice which extended into so large a territory, hitherto for the most part independent.

'Setting aside,' he said, 'all considerations of policy and expediency, and regarding the question as one of humanity only, would it be consistent with that principle to pursue a course towards a wild race, ignorant of our manners and character and unable to appreciate our

[1] 11th May 1837.

motives, which would leave them no choice but the immediate abandonment of ceremonies interwoven with their religion, or an appeal to arms against our authority? From all I have seen of them, and know of their country, I feel convinced that no system of coercion can succeed. Our aim should be to improve to the utmost our intercourse with the tribes nearest us, with the view to civilise and enlighten them, and to reclaim them from the savage practice—using our moral influence rather than our power.'

These wise and statesmanlike opinions were fully sanctioned and adopted by the Government of Madras.

After the termination of hostilities in 1837, the dominions of the late Rajah of Goomsur became subject to the authority of a high local officer, known as the 'Collector and Magistrate and Agent to the Governor of Fort St. George in Ganjam,' who was also placed in charge of our relations with the connected tribes.

It was upon this officer, and upon Captain Campbell, his assistant in the discharge of these multifarious functions,—who had also been Mr. Russell's secretary and assistant during the military operations,—that the duty of dealing with human sacrifice naturally devolved.

In order to show what results had been obtained through the measures adopted by these gentlemen for the abolition of the practice, and what was the exact position of the Khonds with reference to their ancient rite when Captain Macpherson approached them with a view to effect its suppression, it is proposed to lay before the reader a few extracts from public documents, and in particular from the Reports which Captain (now General) Campbell officially submitted to the Government.

It appears that about the end of the year 1837 Captain Campbell paid a visit to the Khonds of Goomsur. Having called together the heads of the different Mootahs, he 'informed them that the sacrifice of human victims would no

*L 2

longer be suffered among them, and peremptorily ordered
them to bring to him all persons whom they might have
purchased as Meriahs.'   He likewise ' demanded a declaration that the Meriah Poojah should henceforth be at an
end among them, and that anyone performing it would
subject himself to severe retribution.'[1]

The Khonds submitted to these requisitions ; for (as we
learn from the same officer[2]) 'as the war had not long
terminated, and as the measures then adopted by Mr.
Russell had been most rigorous, the old chief [Sam Bissye,
through whom Captain Campbell explained his wishes]
was able to illustrate and enforce his arguments by the
terrible alternative of another display of the overwhelm-
ing power of the Anglo-Indian Government, should they
obstinately refuse obedience on this important point.'

While Captain Campbell—a year later—was paying a
second visit to the tribes who had given up their victims,
his official superior, Mr. Bannerman, the Agent in Ganjam,
having obtained information that a sacrifice was to take
place at a village to the southward, on the borders of
Goomsur and Purla Kimedy, suddenly made his way to
the appointed spot, supported by a force of upwards of
360 men.   He succeeded in rescuing the intended victim,
a young woman ; but the Khonds made very light of his
exhortations to humanity, replying, ' that they paid no
tribute and owed no allegiance to us; that the Meriah
had always been practised from time immemorial ; that
if the usual ceremonies were omitted, their fields would
be unproductive ; that the victims had been fairly purchased for a price, and, finally, that they had a right to
do what seemed to them fit in the matter.'

Mr. Bannerman deemed it expedient, after his men
had refreshed themselves a little, to retrace his steps ;
bringing along with him several of the elders of the
tribes, as hostages that the Khonds would not obstruct

---

[1] Captain Campbell's Report of 17th January 1838.
[2] 'Personal Narrative,' p. 68.

his return, and with the view of availing himself of 'their influence in obtaining the release of the Meriahs detained in other parts of the Mootah, as well as more fully impressing on them the arguments, which they did not appear to be then in a state of mind duly to appreciate.' Having extorted the surrender of eight other destined victims, he made the best of his way home, 'sanguine that these measures would have a favourable effect throughout the southern parts of the Womunniah Maliahs.'[1]

The actual effect of his interference, as stated two years later,[2] was this :—

'Within three or four days after my departure they sacrificed another victim, at the same place, in lieu of the young woman who was delivered up to me.

'Being impressed, from what I saw of the temper of the Khonds of the southern portion of these Maliahs, with a conviction of the necessity of exercising great discretion in my communications with them, in furtherance of the wishes of the Government, I have been particularly careful to avoid again prematurely agitating the matter, and, in fact, have had no direct communication with the Womunniah Khonds since the time of the visit in January 1839.'

Major Campbell's report of January 1841, telling of a recent visit to the Hills, was most discouraging.

'I could not discover,' he says, 'that any sacrifices had been performed in the Goomsur Maliahs, but I have reason to believe that some of the inhabitants provided victims and sacrificed them in the neighbouring Mootahs,' &c.   *   *   *   *

'*The number of victims purchased within the last year would lead to the conclusion that the intention to continue the sacrifice of human victims exists with undiminished force, and that persuasion and remonstrance have not had the effect anticipated.*   *   *   *   *

---

[1] Maliahs, i. e. hill districts.   [2] 6th February 1841.

'I still continue of opinion, that unless more decided measures are adopted, the Meriah sacrifice will not cease, though it may not be performed openly.

'I most respectfully suggest, for your[1] consideration and recommendation to Government, that the seller and purchaser of a human being for sacrifice should be held equally guilty, and summarily punished with imprisonment and hard labour or stripes—(the latter punishment alone, inflicted with discretion on both parties in the odious traffic, would I think be effectual, more especially if administered at the time and place of detection)—and that a similar punishment, though more severe, should follow conviction in every instance of a human victim having been sacrificed.'[2]

After the perusal of the report just cited, Lord Elphinstone recorded a minute[3] in which he reviewed the whole subject, certainly not in a very hopeful spirit, his experience having been so unsatisfactory. There had been, his Lordship said, various cases of forcible interference, but no good had come of them. 'These examples prove' (he continues) 'that it is not by violent measures that we can hope to succeed. Violent measures must necessarily be partial ones. We cannot coerce the whole of this wide tract of country and the wild tribes that inhabit it at the same moment, and all isolated efforts must end in failure. The delusiveness of partial success, even when obtained by conciliation, is demonstrated in Major Campbell's last report. In the Goomsur Maliahs—which differed essentially from the neighbouring ones, inasmuch

---

[1] The report was addressed to Mr. Bannerman.

[2] The report goes on to say: 'I beg to bring to your notice the great difficulties, delays, and exposure attending a march through the Maliahs with bullock-carriage, owing to which I have on each occasion of visiting the Hills returned with fever; and my followers, less accustomed to cold, have suffered still more severely. With four elephants every Mootah, every village, could be visited, and in a comparatively short space of time; and I need scarcely point out that the more remote and more difficult of access, the more important that they should be visited by the government officers.'

[3] 16th March 1841.

as British power was there acknowledged, and intercourse prevailed to a great extent between the Khonds and their neighbours of the low country—the Moolikoos or priests promised Major Campbell that they would abstain from human sacrifice for ever; but it now appeared that the inhabitants had been in the habit of sacrificing victims in the neighbouring Mootahs, and that since this promise was made not less than twenty-four victims had been purchased in Goomsur, the greater part within the last twelve months. From Lieutenant Hill's[1] rough calculation, in his letter of the 18th December 1840, I estimated the number of victims who are to be put to death in the forty Mootahs of Ganjam alone, at the New Moon feast (Tunkoo) on the 5th of January last, at 240; but these Mootahs are but a small part of the wide region over which we know that this practice prevails.'

After adverting to the intercourse which Major Campbell had, to his great credit, already attempted to promote between the people of the hills and those of the plains, and the establishment of fairs and marts for that purpose,—' We have seen,' Lord Elphinstone proceeded, 'that in Goomsur, which is so differently situated from any other part of the range of country in which it prevails, after a solemn promise given to abstain from the sacrifices, by their Moolikoos and Elders, the Khonds have relapsed into the practice, if indeed they ever discontinued it. However strenuously therefore I would advocate the opening of roads, and the encouragement of intercourse with the hill-tribes, I am not inclined to rely exclusively on these means.'

His Lordship therefore recommended that efforts should be made to acquire influence among the hill-chiefs, to impress their tribes with a just and at the same time a favourable idea of our power, and to raise a semi-military force from among the hillmen. He also desired the appointment

---

[1] An officer in the Survey Department, who wrote several valuable reports on the Khond country.

of an officer who should devote his whole attention to
the management of the hill-tracts, whether connected
with Madras, Bengal, or Nagpore ;[1] and he proposed to
begin with a petty expedition, chiefly intended to obtain
information. The officer who was to be sent should
proceed ostensibly to procure a certain Rajah's assent to
the making of a road to pass through his capital.

The Supreme Government at Calcutta believed with
Lord Elphinstone[2] 'that the best hope of success was
in cautious and gradual measures, by which, without
any direct attack upon national customs or religious prejudices, the natural onward march of civilisation might
be securely facilitated. The deputed officer should cautiously approach any inquisition into human sacrifices,
and confine himself very closely to the immediate purpose
of his mission ;' yet he was to be at liberty to discuss the
subject with friendly chiefs of influence, and declare the
extreme abhorrence with which this custom is regarded
by the British Government, and its right and determination unrelentingly to punish every attempt to entrap or to
steal British subjects for the purpose of immolation.

This policy can only be accounted for by the failure
which, in the opinion both of Lord Elphinstone and of
Lord Auckland, had attended the efforts hitherto made.
Had these statesmen thought that any progress had been
made towards the abolition of the sacrifice, is it conceivable that a new agent would have been instructed so
cautiously to approach any inquisition into the subject?

The subject of human sacrifice having been thus considered by the two Governments, Lieutenant Macpherson
was appointed (as will be more fully stated below) to
carry out their views. Meanwhile Major Campbell continued in charge of the Goomsur Khonds ; and after a
visit to the Hills in December 1841, he submitted a re-

[1] Lord Elphinstone had recommended this measure before, but had been
overruled by the Supreme Government.
[2] 3rd May 1841.

port, dated the 5th January 1842, which possesses much interest as containing his own account of the position of the Khonds in respect of human sacrifice at the close of his first service in Goomsur; for, as it happened, he went to China soon after with his regiment, and did not see the Khonds again for five years.   This report contains the following passage :—

'After the experience of five years, I regret that I have had no cause to change my opinion of the correctness of the principles expressed in my letter of the 16th December 1837,[1] for suppressing the Meriah Poojah,[2] and which were carried [out] by me so successfully, as reported on the 17th January 1838.   To these measures alone are attributable the subsequent cessation of the sacrifice in Goomsur, and the fear and secrecy with which it is still performed in the bordering Mootahs; but the impressions so created are, I regret to say, rapidly fading away, of which I have just had painful proof, having now to report that two children have been sacrificed at the horrid shrine of the Meriah within the past year—one by Jundoo Moleky of Coomeracoopa, and the other by Rama Moleku of Coormingiah.   Of the first there is no doubt, and of the latter there are strong suspicions, amounting to a moral conviction.   Such having occurred in Mootahs so near to us, what may we not apprehend regarding places more distant and less under our observation?   The seller of the first-mentioned murdered child has been apprehended, and shall be forwarded to you as soon as the proceedings are prepared, as well as others who have been apprehended.   I have been fortunate in rescuing eleven victims, male and female, from 13 to 3 years old, making in all 125 rescued by me from the Khonds of Goomsur since 1838;[3] and no efforts shall be spared to discover the persons by whom they were sold.   I used my utmost endeavours, in accordance with the instructions

[1] See below, p. 155.   [2] Sacrifice.
[3] This must include all the victims rescued in 1837 and 1838.

I have received, to impress upon all the horror with which
the Meriah sacrifice is viewed by Government, and to persuade them to discontinue it; but this it is hopeless to
expect they will do, unless to persuasion and conciliation
is joined the power of inflicting punishment, by removal
or otherwise of the purchaser and the sacrificer as well as
of the seller of a child, as already remarked in my letter
of the 22nd January 1841.'

It appears therefore that the utmost that Major Campbell claimed to have effected was not the abolition of
the rite of sacrifice among the people of Goomsur, but
only a cessation of the performance of the sacrifice on
the soil of Goomsur, coupled with secret performance of
the sacrifice by inhabitants of Goomsur on places beyond
their own borders; and that the impressions which he
believed to have been created by his measures were
rapidly fading away, inasmuch as two sacrifices had occurred in districts of Goomsur near to us, and there was
reason to apprehend worse in places more remote—that
is, more distant places within the territory of Goomsur,
for it was only to Goomsur that any measures had been
addressed. He considered it hopeless to expect that the
Khonds of Goomsur would discontinue the sacrifice, unless to persuasion and conciliation were joined the power
—to be stringently exercised—of punishing the purchaser
and the sacrificer as well as the seller.

Major Campbell's Report of 5th January 1842 was
noticed in the following terms in a minute of the Madras
Government (10th December 1842), from which an extract is subjoined :—

'The Agent to the Governor in Ganjam, in forward-
ing the report of his principal assistant, Major Campbell,
expresses his apprehension that the practice [of human
sacrifice] has been revived in the tracts more immediately
under his authority; and this is attributed by both officers
to the stop that has been put to the employment of the
means adopted by Major Campbell in 1837.

'The Most Honorable the Governor in Council[1] is at a loss to understand to what the Agent refers. No prohibition to the prosecution of any general plan for effecting the great object in view has ever been expressed. Major Campbell's plan consisted in " entering the Maliahs with an armed force, calling together the most influential men among the Khonds, and endeavouring to convince them of the barbarity and inutility of the sacrifice—explaining to them our abhorrence and utter detestation of the practice, at the same time ordering them to bring to me all the victims in their possession ; and if I cannot otherwise obtain them, I request permission to purchase them at the prices they cost the Khonds (from 15 to 25 rupees each), and at the same time to use such threats as I may consider advisable to gain the objects in view," [2] &c.—to which are added the gaining over the priests by presents of money.

'The Government observed that experience had shown the employment of an armed force to be impracticable, and that the use of threats which could not be enforced should be avoided. They counselled conciliation, and deprecated whatever might lead to irritation and distrust. The purchase of victims was forbidden, for obvious reasons ; but the other suggestions of Major Campbell were approved. It is doubtful, however, whether the practice ever received a serious check. A passage in Captain Macpherson's last report leads to the belief that it never was discontinued, and Captain Hill has shown that the victims rescued on a former occasion were immediately replaced by others.'

Such, then, was the minute of the Madras Government, recognising the fact of the existence of human sacrifice among the Khonds of Goomsur in January 1842, as shown

---

[1] The Marquis of Tweeddale, who had succeeded Lord Elphinstone as Governor of Madras.

[2] This is an extract from Major Campbell's letter of 16th December 1837, referred to above, p. 153.

by the express official representation which lay before them, though rebutting the attempt of Major Campbell and his superior, the Agent in Ganjam (Mr. Bannerman), to throw upon the Government the responsibility for that admitted fact.[1]

On the other hand, General Campbell now asserts that— 'In January 1842 *the Meriah sacrifice was at an end* among the Khonds of Goomsur, although I did not pretend to have eradicated all inclination for the rite from the minds of these wild people.'[2]

[1] Lord Elphinstone had already remarked, with Major Campbell's Report of 5th January 1842 before him, that 'having constantly acted upon the conviction that we might at any time have done infinitely more harm by taking a step in the wrong direction than by waiting to gain information, and then setting to work systematically upon a carefully and maturely considered plan, and having always felt that it was rather the province of the Government to restrain the misdirected efforts of the local officers than to quicken the natural impulse from which they proceeded, it was not surprising that the intentions of the Government had been sometimes misunderstood, and that its conduct had been frequently arraigned.' His Lordship also observed that, 'Looking back upon all the statements and reports laid before Government, apart from those of Captain Macpherson, he could not find any proposal that amounted to anything like a connected, fixed, or definite plan. Indeed, there was a total lack of such information as might enable the Government or any of its Agents to lay down a settled plan of operations.'—[Minute of 24th September 1842.]

[2] 'Narrative by Major General John Campbell, C.B., of his Operations in the Hill Tracts of Orissa, for the Suppression of Human Sacrifices and Female Infanticide.' Printed for private circulation : London, 1861. P. 47.

'A Personal Narrative of Thirteen Years' Service amongst the Wild Tribes of Khondistan, for the Suppression of Human Sacrifice;' by Major-General John Campbell, C.B. London, 1864. P. 78.

The General adds, in both books, a little further on, that at the period referred to, 'the public performance of the Meriah sacrifice had been entirely suppressed among the hill-tribes of Goomsur'; thus leaving us for the moment in uncertainty whether he means to intimate that the sacrifice itself was at an end, or only that its *public* performance had been suppressed.

These are two very different things (the suppression of the public sacrifice alone being in truth no suppression at all), and the utmost precision is necessary in speaking of them; for this is the cardinal point of General Campbell's whole narrative.

But his real meaning is placed beyond all doubt by a passage at p. 84 of the 'Personal Narrative' of 1864, where he states that it was not necessary for Captain Macpherson to penetrate into the interior of the Khond country, so long as he intended to confine his operations to Goomsur; 'for the Khonds, as I have stated in the previous chapter, *had relinquished sacrifice,*

The reader will judge for himself how far this assertion can be reconciled with the official statement written by General Campbell in that very month of January 1842.[1]

though they clamoured loudly (as they had done when I left them) at the glaring injustice of our tolerating the rite in the adjacent countries of Boad and Chinna-Kimedy, whilst it was not permitted amongst them.'

[1] See above, p. 153.

CHAPTER IX.

APPOINTMENT AS ASSISTANT TO THE AGENT AT GANJAM— RETURN TO GOOMSUR.

1841.

LIEUTENANT MACPHERSON, from the time of his return to India, was engaged in writing his Report on the Khonds. The practical measures which he suggested are explained at great length in the report, and will be mentioned below. It need only be said of them here, that they were intended to apply to all the hill-tribes south of the Mahanuddee, under whatever jurisdiction; that they embraced the establishment of distinct relations with those tribes as subjects, mainly through the administration of justice between independent tribes, and between tribes and the rajahs with whom they were connected; the conciliation of the hill-chiefs and priests, as well as of the rajahs; the rigorous punishment of the Hindu procurers and sellers of victims in the low countries; the investing the agents of Government with large discretionary powers to punish other persons concerned in buying and selling victims, as might be found possible and expedient—the ordinary rules and modes of procedure having been found wholly inapplicable to those wild districts. Subsidiary measures, such as the making of roads, and the encouragement of fairs, were also contemplated; although, in truth, some Khond tracts which enjoyed these advantages had been in no degree improved by them, so far as human sacrifice was concerned. The report proceeds: ' While for the reasons above stated, we are precluded from the use of force as a primary measure, it is to be carefully kept sight of as a secondary means. If we shall gain the mass, the great majority of any tribe, it may be highly advantageous and quite possible to coerce individuals.'

When the report was nearly finished, the writer received (in pursuance of Lord Elphinstone's views, expressed in the minute of 16th March[1]). the civil appointment of ' Assistant to the Agent to the Governor of Fort St. George in Ganjam,' and Instructions were framed for his guidance.

The Instructions directed that, while finding ostensible occupation in surveying a road, he should consider it his first business to inquire into the state of the country and the dispositions of its inhabitants. ' The prevalence of human sacrifice will, of course, be the subject of his early but cautious investigation, and no proper opportunity should be lost of expressing abhorrence of the custom. Care, however, should be taken never to allude to it as a Khond custom, but as a custom prevalent among barbarous tribes in every part of the world, repudiated by all civilised beings, and equally contrary to the law of God and man.'

In the meantime he went to collect further information about the habits of the Khonds from various state-prisoners in the fort of Gooty, about 300 miles to the north of Madras—and in particular from his old acquaintance Dora Bissye.[2]

'Cuddapah, 16th August 1841.

'I left Madras last month for Gooty, the hill-fort wherein the Madras Government is used to afford opportunity for the maturest reflection to such persons as, from patriotic or other motives, happen to take a decided course against it; and having there communicated, with satisfactory results, with various personages whose sphere

---

[1] See above, p. 152.   [2] Ibid. p. 68.

of action formerly lay in the wide region which is about to become mine, I write this nearly halfway on my way back again to the Presidency. It is a strange scene that fortress—the Gibraltar of this part of the world. It encloses a hill with a triple summit. The central eminence is a cone, about 1,200 feet high, picturesquely formed of vast bare masses of grey granite, and encircled with spiral lines of fortification of the most ponderous Hindu forms, mixed with the lightest Moorish architecture, and with additions of the most chaste and beautiful Greco-Addiscombe school. Within the last circle of the spiral, about an acre in extent, the surface is composed of bare undulating granite shields, forming here and there holes, which, slightly aided by art, form reservoirs of excellent water; and here the prisoners (about 50 in number) dwell in comfortable buildings, quite at large, guarded by sepoys. The first thing that strikes you is, that religion is here everything. There is a little temple, which the prisoners have starved themselves to restore and adorn, to say nothing of the maintenance of its heavy-paunched ministers, who, as the song says, " always preach best with a skin full ;" and the hum of Shaster-reading from palm-leaf books, from every doorway or nook at all shaded, quite fills the air. These prisoners are people who either would not, or could not, do our bidding; probably in settling some dynastic quarrel if they are rajahs, or some ministerial quarrel if they are viziers; or, if they are mere men-at-arms, they would not leave their matchlocks on the wall when the chiefs were up; or, perhaps, they are zemindars who kicked from their hall of audience the officer and process of some court wholly unintelligible and inapplicable to them. I have been listening to and consoling them all, poor people, to their infinite gratitude.

' The Government are awake now to the necessity, both here and in Bengal, of making some decided movement in the human-sacrifice business, but do not know what to do, as sufficient information does not exist. One thing neces-

sary to be done is to secure the co-operation of the Orissa
rajahs, whose domains are scattered amongst the territories of the sacrificing tribes, to whom they stand in
various relations; and it is determined to try to do this first.
Our policy has been to leave these rajahs alone — except
sometimes, as *vide* Gooty—but, above all things, to avoid
acquiring any degree of knowledge about them. Now,
I am to go and attempt to bring those chiefs under
influence; to get them in hand, with a view to their
cooperation in some scheme or another unborn, with
reference to the sacrificing superstition; and to obtain
every species of information about them and the country.
I am to negotiate permission to form a road straight
through that unknown mountain region to Nagpore, and
am further, in the first instance at least, to be my own
General Wade.

'The Madras Government speaks of this solitary road
as if it were a mere new evening-drive at Madras.
Now, I would sooner undertake to drive a line of rail-
road through six English counties. I have found in
that country a hundred and fifty allodial estates in a
square mile, and nowhere on the earth's surface are
the lords of the soil better instructed in their rights,
or more resolute in their defence. In this matter,
now that I have received my instructions, I do not know
practically where I am on a single point—what I can or
what I cannot do. It is, I believe, intended that I shall
be virtually independent, *quoad hoc*, of the Agent, to whom
I am in form strictly subordinate; but the lines which
express our relations cross and intersect at every possible
angle. No man can do what is required in that country
with reference to the Khond superstition save in independence, not of any local agency alone, but, except in
respect of general principles, of the Government itself.
I have asked leave to have back my report, that I
may insert a good many new facts ascertained at Gooty.
I am to have sent with me an officer of the Survey

Department, and a draftsman; a scientific medical officer, to be specially looked for with a lantern, but not yet found; a detachment of sappers for the roads, and an escort of infantry—two companies or so if I will allow it, which I won't, nor a great deal besides of the above arrangement if I can help it; but it will, you see, be an imposing expedition. The only account of my sayings and doings and seeings which I shall be able to write will be in my home-letters. This is no doubt a pity: but seeing that my business is to turn Hindus and Khonds, from the Rajah to the savage in the tree—through the use of means merely moral, and without proselytism— from the gods of their fathers, and that I cannot labour as I did in that country once before,—what is to be done?'

Lieutenant Macpherson paid a short visit to Calcutta, and thence proceeded to the Ganjam district, whence his next letter is dated.

'Gopalpore,[1] 16th November 1841.

'When I wrote from Calcutta I did not expect that Lord Auckland would have had time to notice my business, as he was completely taken up with the Burmese affairs; however, by staying two or three days longer than I intended, I got him fully on the subject. He went through my long report very thoroughly, as did his secretary and chief adviser;[2] and I was then sent for. He said that before he had not had the most distant idea of the thing, and that all that he had said had been said in utter ignorance; that he did not see his way in the least; that it was the most difficult subject which he had ever contemplated—not a question of police and pioneers, but a vast social and religious question—a combination of social and religious questions, the most

[1] Gopalpore, or Munsoorcottah, a little station on the Ganjam coast, consisting of a few bungalows built upon low sandhills, close to the sea.

[2] The late Mr. John Russell Colvin, a civil officer of high character and great ability, who held at his death the post of Lieutenant-Governor of the North-West Provinces.

impracticable for a Government to deal with—and that he would take it up as soon as possible. I told him, as I had told the Madras people, that my "instructions" were nonsense, and that, as they were susceptible of any one meaning quite as much as of any other, I meant to do what circumstances might prescribe. He requested me to write everything that I did or thought to his secretary and confidant for his information, and said that he would be always glad to help me in any way.

'I am much stronger and better than I have been, the intensely cold weather having quite set me up. The difficulties which I have to contend with—between two Governments looking opposite ways, an immediate superior looking a third, foolish orders, rascally public servants, and no one but Baba[1] fit for the work—are infinitely greater than I had any conception of before coming here, and in the eyes of the local agents insurmountable. Still, if I shall have health for myself, and for the one instrument whom I have found, I do not fear. The other of them (second to Baba), an able Brahmin, I should tell you, has just died. The Hindus think themselves polluted by conversation with these Khonds (who, on the other hand, look down upon them), and are dreadfully afraid of the climate, so that I can get no one to go with me who can obtain food elsewhere.'

'Ganjam, 14th December 1841.

'Do you remember, in 1837, my writing to you from Aska, a sugar-growing village, where I commanded with my company during part of the Goomsur disturbance? Here am I in it again, all peace. A missionary's wife met me at the door of the commanding-officer's quarters. The civic authorities, undisturbed by requisitions, are as fat as swine. The detachment clerk, unvexed by returns, waddles. The Ursæ Majores, for which the country is celebrated, lie out beyond their thickets. The wild ducks bill the lotuses, fearless of any pot.

[1] Baba Khan, the Mussulman, who had gone with him to the Cape.

The very oranges seem to grow more peacefully golden upon the trees.

'Bannerman [1] was particularly prepared to extend to me the feelings of mingled indignation and contempt with which he regards the Government—and the Government, to do it justice, had made the most admirable arrangements for setting us by the ears; however, I really believe that I have established a decent working understanding with him, if not a good deal more. He has nothing whatever to do with my proceedings further than to be the medium of reports to Government and of its orders; yet, unless I had hold of his mind, I should be able at some points to do nothing. I have now got my party in the field, effective for work, and within the limits of the Khond country, my camp pitched in the loveliest of these subalpine scenes. I have a pleasant little party—George Macdonell, the captain commanding my escort, formed of the light company of his corps, with a party of 20 sappers and miners attached; Dr. ——, a young Scotchman, of the best class of Indian doctors, who shows a decided scientific interest in vegetables having a culinary value, while he directs the attention of his double-barrel to objects of animated nature chiefly upon the same useful principle. I have besides a surveyor, and a sapper roadmaking sergeant.'

[1] The Agent to the Governor of Fort St. George in Ganjam. This gentleman was a civil officer of experience and character, but extremely sensitive and jealous; and his peculiar turn of mind, together with the anomalous and unfair official position in which he was placed towards Captain Macpherson, led to serious embarrassments.

CHAPTER. X.

SECOND VISIT TO THE HILLS.

1841—42.

Captain Macpherson (he had attained this rank by brevet) now[1] visited, for the purpose of observation, a region, about 70 miles in length by 80 in breadth, lying not in but to the south of Goomsur, and inhabited by the Womunniah Khonds, among whom no one had latterly cared to venture. These were not the people whom Captain Macpherson had already visited, nor had any measures been addressed to them for the abolition of human sacrifice since Mr. Bannerman's unlucky expedition, nearly three years before.[2]

Captain Macpherson's route lay nearly along the line of junction of the non-sacrificing and the sacrificing tribes, at the time of the great annual oblation of the latter.

At first, he says, 'all the villages were deserted before me. I therefore halted in the first valley within the hills, until I felt quite satisfied that different ideas were both established there, and had in some degree preceded me. The nearest hamlets soon gained confidence; then a section of a tribe ventured to come out from the forest— not rushing into my camp in wild and fantastic procession, armed, and dancing, with shouts and stunning music, as is the fashion of these Khonds, but approaching without arms, in extreme fear, and requiring much encouragement to come to my tents; while spies from all the tribes around anxiously expected the result of the experiment. The alarm of the first comers having been dispelled, other

---

[1] December 1841.   [2] See above, p. 148.

parties by degrees, but very cautiously, imitated their example, and I then moved on.   Another considerable pause at the next stage brought all the tribes within a circuit of many miles to my tents ; and thenceforward roads were laboriously cut for my passage through the forest, and I had to choose between those offered to me by the rival tribes who daily crowded my camp.' [1]

'Khond Jungles, 23rd December 1841.

'All is going on well.   My subject-matter acquires a new character from fresh and startling facts every day.   I find that there are numerous tribes who not only do not sacrifice but who abhor the rite, and who, if they imagined that I wished to put it down, would be "up and at them" in an hour !   I find too that female infanticide, unknown where I was before, prevails in many tracts to a prodigious extent, and these the non-sacrificing tracts.   I find here every Khond woman changes her husband several times in the course of her life, while where I was before the scriptural rule is decently followed. I have stolen in to scrawl this from a tribe of 400 savages, whose drums, cymbals, and wild yells almost bring down the tent over my head, while they dance frantically round in mad joy.'

Sacrifices were in preparation all before him.   The non-sacrificing tribes expressed, in the strongest language, the grief and indignation with which they contemplated the impious and revolting worship which was in progress.

'Poor uninstructed fools!' said the sacrificers ; 'they cannot understand that through the virtue of this great rite all mankind, and they themselves, live and prosper !' 'Wretched men!' said the others ; 'they destroy life and devour human flesh without the apology of the tiger and the snake, and believe that they conciliate the gods!' The sacrificing tribes retaliate upon the non-sacrificing but infant-destroying Khonds, by telling them 'to take a

[1] Report of 24th April 1842.

lesson from the most savage beasts, and spare their young!'

The fields of the non-sacrificing tribes were strictly guarded, by night and day, lest an enemy should desécrate the soil by introducing a shred of the flesh.[1]

'The Khonds of the village of Mahrigoodi,' writes Captain Macpherson,[2] 'having been accidentally asked to dig some holes for the stakes of a grass-shed in my camp, expressed their readiness to fell wood, or to render any other service, but declined to disturb, in any way, the surface of the earth at that particular time, the days immediately preceding the full moon in December, when it was being broken all around for the reception of the flesh of victims: and it may be observed that a Khond or a Hindu, who has been present at a sacrifice, would here run the risk of being put to death were he to approach a non-sacrificing village within seven days after the ceremony—but after that time he is reckoned pure.

'The sacrificing tribes of Guddapore, upon the other hand, were everywhere in a state of high exultation and excitement, engaged in performing, or in preparing to perform, the great and vital rite upon the observance of which they believed that their own wellbeing and that of all the world besides depended.

'It was fully expected, both by them and by the non-sacrificing population, that I would now declare, and perhaps enforce, the final and absolute determination of the Government respecting the rite. The latter division of the people hoped fervently that I was come to put an end to it, and was anxious that I should understand that it would cooperate with me in the work, at a word. The former held different views, and its tribes had taken counsel, separately and together, to meet the critical occasion.

'Two general impressions prevailed amongst them. The first was, that the Government was indifferent to the

---

[1] See above, p. 131.   [2] Report of 24th April 1842.

sacrifice. This view was founded upon the fact that no
decisive and comprehensive measures had been adopted
with respect to it, while partial interference had taken
place : stress being laid upon the circumstance that Captain Hill had passed (when on survey) the previous year
through the western tracts, with a party of troops, just
before the time of the great offering, but had done nothing
to prevent it, or to mark the reprobation of the Government.

'The second idea was, that although the Government
certainly disapproved and desired the abolition of the practice, it was conscious that it had no just right to interfere
with it; and the following considerations in support of
this view were communicated to me by several persons,
as forming the ground upon which the Khonds stood, and
which they held to be perfectly unassailable in reason and
in justice. They were thus stated :—

1. Because the rite has been practised from the beginning.

2. Because it has been sanctioned by the Rajahs.

3. Because it is essential to the existence of mankind
in health, and to the continuation of the species.

4. Because it is essential to the productive powers of
nature by which men live.

5. Because it is necessary to the gods for food.

6. Because its suppression by the Government would
be as unjust as the abolition of the Hindu worship at
Juggernath ; but that the Khonds are willing to submit
to a decree which shall include, equally with theirs, the
worship of the Hindus and that of the Mussulmans.

7. Because the victims are the property of those who
offer them, being bought with the fruits of their labour
upon the soil.

8. Because the parents of the victims make them over
fully to the Khonds through the procurers.

9. And finally, because the gods have positively ordained
the rite.

'The course which circumstances, and the spirit of my
instructions, appeared to prescribe to me, equally with a
view to immediate and to ulterior objects, was plain, but
difficult in practice.

'It is to be remembered that no distinct relations have
been established with the Khonds as subjects, even in the
few Mootahs of Goomsur : hence the idea of allegiance
to our power has, necessarily, never entered into their
minds. They have no conception of any social relations,
except those which exist betwixt the different groups of
tribes, and betwixt these and the zemindaries. The Government they regard with very various, uncertain, and
inconsistent feelings, amongst which vague apprehension
predominates. In these sections of the population—partly
owing to their character, which is defective in boldness ;
partly owing to their experience in 1837, which was calculated to produce this result—the sentiment of fear prevails in their conceptions of our power to a degree which
I have not seen elsewhere.

'Now it was, in the first place, plainly desirable to
communicate to these tribes the few elementary conceptions
relative to the character and to the general objects of the
Government, which must precede the establishment of
any beneficial relations with them ; and secondly, it was
highly desirable, both to contradict the impression that
the Government regarded the rite of human sacrifice with
indifference, and to repudiate the idea that consciousness
of defective right on our part prevented us from adopting
decisive measures for its suppression.

'I therefore endeavoured to communicate distinctly to
the minds of the persons (whether Khonds, Hindus, or
Panwas) who appeared to be the best media for their
reception and diffusion, the primary ideas upon those
points with which it seemed most important that they
should be imbued.

'When it was asserted that the designs of the Government towards the hill-people were those of paternal

benevolence alone, not (as was presumed) of hostility ; that the existence of the rite of human sacrifice was a subject of the deepest concern to the Government, and of horror to all mankind beyond these hills ; and that the right of the Government to suppress it, as a rite which all mankind concur in condemning, not as erroneous but as impious and unlawful, did not admit of a question: if, when these assertions were made and argued upon, it cannot be said that conviction was produced in the discerning minds of the Khond patriarchs, their previous judgments were certainly modified, or suspended ; and confidence and goodwill, and the inclination to believe that benefit alone was intended towards them, and the disposition to yield obedience in return, were engendered, while the Government was committed to no specific course of procedure.

'It was obvious that, in the existing state of opinion and of feeling, no advantage whatever could have arisen from my temporarily preventing any of the sacrifices which were in progress around me, by abandoning my immediate objects and my line of march to interrupt them. The impressions which prevailed upon the subject of the views held by the Government in reference to this rite were founded upon its proceedings during the last five years—upon the fact that its measures have been hitherto partial, unconnected, and unsustained; and those impressions, it is certain, can be effectually removed by operations of an opposite character alone. The effects of interference on my part, casually and *en passant,* could have been but to make a few sacrifices be deferred until the next full-moon, or to make it necessary to replace one or two liberated victims ; while, in the meantime, confidential intercourse with all—probably all intercourse with the sacrificing population—would have ceased, and my immediate objects would have been defeated.'

Up to the 27th December the party was in good health. By the 1st January a very considerable portion of it, including many of the most valuable people, was attacked by fever. This occurred when they were in a most beautiful country, and in a climate delightful to the feelings, on a plateau elevated about 2,000 feet above the sea. As Captain Macpherson could not of course carry many sick, and could not in that country leave a man behind, he immediately resolved to send all the sick under the doctor to the low country, and to attempt, with a greatly diminished party, to prosecute the work himself in a part of the country which was upon a different level. But on the 5th January between one-third and one-half of his people were upon their backs. He had a very distinct warning himself, and on the 6th the party were on their way down. With infinite difficulty he dragged the poor people over the series of steep and rugged ghauts which lead to the plains. The sick carriages had all gone with the doctor's party; the sick men were too ill to sit upon the elephants, which were nearly unmanageable, from the illness of their proper attendants; but in the end all got through, with but two deaths.

He had a good account to give of what had been done. He had obtained a great deal of the most desired and valuable information, which he embodied in a long and interesting report to the Government. He had made a survey of the best line of road, which was so bad a line that no sum that could be named could convert it into a road for carriages, or indeed could make anything of it but a very trying bullock road. He had so conciliated a population, which evacuated the country on his approach, that all the tribes within reach came in to him and exhibited such unequivocal feelings of goodwill as to give ground for hope that the first foundations of confidence were laid.

The Khonds of this quarter were in many points dissimilar—in all qualities inferior—to those whom he had before visited and described. He ascertained, during this visit, that the northern and the southern Khonds did not understand each other's language, and that the dialect of the middle tribes differed so much from that of the northern population, that they did not understand it without practice; nor were they acquainted with the Oriyah tongue. He consequently came to the conclusion that it would be wise to address himself, in the first instance, to the abolition of human sacrifice among the tribes of Goomsur, where Oriyah was understood to a considerable extent; but he soon found the means of attacking the practice of infanticide among the southern Khonds.

Lord Auckland had done Captain Macpherson the honour to cause his first Report on the Khonds to be printed and published — a course then rarely adopted; and now, on resigning the Government of India, sent to him a kind and complimentary note, which he valued as having been purely voluntary and very unusual. Indeed, he felt but too justly, that Lord Auckland's departure, and the approaching resignation of power by Lord Elphinstone, would be a great loss to the arduous enterprise in which he had engaged.

CHAPTER XI.

FIRST STEPS TOWARDS THE ABOLITION OF HUMAN SACRIFICE.

1842.

DURING the spring of 1842 Major Campbell left Ganjam, and went with his regiment to China on service. Captain Macpherson was appointed to officiate in his place as principal assistant to the Governor's Agent in Ganjam.[1]

In this new office, while his communications with the Khonds daily increased in interest and importance, he was required to discharge, in addition, the functions of collector, judge, and magistrate of a Zillah or District. As collector he had charge of the revenue of certain large tracts, including Goomsur; as a judge, with a separate court, he had civil and criminal jurisdiction over a great extent of country, which reached to nineteen out of twenty of the suits for property and to the same proportion of the crimes of the district; and as magistrate he was entrusted with the care of the police of the whole province. He had to deal with a set of the wildest rajahs on earth—some spending their whole lives in sport—whom it was no easy matter to keep in order. As a specimen of their proceedings— while one was protecting two illegitimate brothers, who had committed a brutal murder,[2] another sent in a dozen of

---

[1] After discharging the duties for two years he was permanently appointed to this office upon the resignation of Colonel Campbell.

[2] Baba Khan, who was now, under the title of moonshee, interpreter to the Khond Agency—a post for which he was admirably fitted—was in the habit of transmitting occasionally, to a member of Captain Macpherson's family, a chronicle composed by himself in the Teloogoo language, and done into English by the joint efforts of the author and of a half-caste writer who held the

his sirdars, accused of conspiring against his life at the in-
stigation of his younger brother, who wished to succeed
him immediately: and the question was whether the rajah
or his brother was the real conspirator.   The hill-rajahs and
the hill-robbers were in such a state in the southern part
of the country, that it was absolutely necessary that the
magistrate should go amongst them with some troops, and
talk to them, frighten them, give them a few distinct and
rational ideas of their situation, and of the views of the
Government with respect to them.   But there were villains nearer home.   The Brahmins—a class who engrossed
subordinate office all over the Madras Presidency, and who
had a great deal of influence in the practical government
of the country—did not like the district to be too tranquil, because when people did not get into difficulties
they did not pay them for getting them out of difficulties.
'The Brahmins,' writes Captain Macpherson, 'would give
anything to get up a row anywhere; they are absolutely

pen.   Baba thus narrates the murder above referred to: 'My master investigated a case of murder in the Zemindary of Daracote.   The circumstances
were as follows : The Rajah's father had two sons and one daughter. The girl
was well skilled in music, &c., taught her by a Putnaik, who makes poetry.
Suspicion arose that this girl and her teacher were loving one another very
much; upon which the teacher, for fear, deserted the place, but after an elapse
of two years returned to it, and carried on private correspondence with her,
by sending her music, &c.   One day the papers sent happened to be discovered
in the thatch of the house by her brothers, who suspected that some mischievous trick was in negotiation between their sister and the teacher; and
they immediately conspired to behead that man, after a grand festival that
was to be celebrated at Daracote, and at which all the females were to assemble.   They dressed a man in female's apparel, and placed him in a retired
place, and sent the female servant of their sister to the teacher, saying that
her mistress would meet him there at night, after the festival.   The teacher
heard the news with joy, and proceeded to the spot, where the brothers of.
the girl were waiting for him, and immediately murdered him with the
sword.   A police-peon informed the Head of the Police of Aska, who reported the case to my master, and himself proceeded to Daracote to trace out
the murderers.   But the Head of the Police only went to the Rajah's house,
and threatened him and his family, until he received a bribe of 400 rupees,
and a few days after 300 rupees, and his peons received about 100 rupees.
My master enquired fully, and punished and dismissed the police officer, but
the murderers have not been found.'

sick of this quiet in the zemindaries; no business—no plunder—no fun.' He continues:—

'I made a lucky hit some time ago in Berhampore. There were never fewer than some twenty reported and perhaps fifty unreported robberies there in a month, all the thieves being of course Dundassies,[1] &c. I obtained information respecting a Mussulman, of the best family, who had dissipated his property by gambling and vice, and now lived by keeping thieves, and paying the police for their protection. I ordered his house to be searched. The police hesitated until the Mussulman could send away the stolen property, and then wrote to me that he was "the most respectable man in Berhampore." I followed up the stolen goods, and, after a month's trial and infinite false-swearing, convicted the man, and sentenced him to imprisonment and stripes. It was an agonising scene—but a most fortunate one. From that hour there has not been a single theft, great or small, in Berhampore. The whole Brahminhood were furious. To convict a man of good family, and under police protection, and pronounced the honestest in Berhampore! Their occupation was gone! Who would pay for protection now? The despair of the Head of the Police may be imagined when I tell you that he has built a new temple to a new god, with a view to destroy his enemies (my instruments) by magical influences; and some of those instruments have in consequence very nearly died, under fear and fever. Luckily, a man has been got from Pooree, endowed with skill sufficient to undo any spells.'

Captain Macpherson had examined the country so thoroughly as a surveyor that he found his revenue business light. His official duty in this department consisted mainly in adjusting every year, according to the value of the land, the amount of revenue which the Government

[1] Men of the robber castes.

was to exact for the year from each cultivator. 'I have been settling,' he writes, 'not only revenue matters, but every affair in the whole system of life of these honest, respectable, laborious ryots.[1] Instead of letting the poor fools bring their disputes into my court (which I am sorry to say is very far indeed from being free from the chief vices of all courts), I settle everything of every conceivable description, or put it in train of settlement at once— to their infinite thankfulness.

'My daily life is this :—I take my gallop early in the morning; from seven to ten o'clock I write my public letters and reports; from ten to half-past eleven bathe and breakfast. Then my revenue servants and magistracy people encircle me on carpets, each putting in a paper upon the slightest pause of the other, and getting an order, till two or three o'clock; when the civil justice people break in with plaint, answer, &c., or criminals (who have the *pas*) are brought forward. At half-past five or six, I with infinite difficulty break through the crowd on my horse, some twenty or thirty supplicants perhaps waiting to throw themselves down at full length on the road to arrest me, as they do in the morning. I get home and dine at seven, having been thinking all my ride of the Khonds. No sooner is the cloth removed than in walk Baba Khan and Soondera Sing, with faces of the deepest import, overladen with thought and late intelligence, they having been Khonding[2] it from daybreak until that blessed moment. I talk with them until very late. I fall asleep when I can—and then the day begins again. If it has been remarked that I have been very tired during the day, Baba and Soondera never come at night. The latter is the son of a rebel rajah [of Souradah], now dead, who used to keep his children amongst the

---

[1] That is, the Hindu cultivators of the plains.

[2] He had now established himself in the low country of Goomsur, near the Khond border, and the mountaineers came down and communicated freely with him.

Khonds while he fought the Government. Thus the boy ✓
learnt the Khond language, and knows the manners of a
part of the Khond people perfectly. He was of great use
in the Goomsur war, and the Government rewarded him
with a village and lands. I dragged him with some difficulty from his farm, but now he is enthusiastically engaged in this work, and he and Baba combined make an
admirable instrument. He is of Rajpoot race, and is a
very handsome and elegant fellow.

'Now for a morning levee of 200 Khonds, who have
come to tell me that they have just offered a human
sacrifice, but under circumstances which they feel assured
will in my sight perfectly justify the proceeding.'

The state in which he found the Khonds, and his views
of the policy which it was desirable to pursue towards
them, are set forth in the following letter :—

'There have been this year very numerous sacrifices, and
victim-children are going up the hills daily ; and sacrifices
are now again performed openly instead of secretly,
which is perhaps an improvement. Everybody has been
engaged in them—Sam Bissye,[1] of course, with the rest ;
in his immediate neighbourhood four have been sacrificed.
The Khonds and hill Panwas all tell me, without the
least thought of concealment, what they have been about.

'But there is plainly a preliminary point to be determined
before this question of religion need be spoken of : it is
whether the authority of the Government is to be established in these Goomsur Maliahs or not ? We have yet,
in point of fact, established no civil authority there ; and
you will I think agree with me that the establishment of
distinct relations with these Khonds as subjects must
precede any attempt to act upon their religious opinions
and practice. A missionary might begin at the other
end—not, I conceive, the Government. We have assumed
a certain degree of vague undefined authority in these
Maliahs, but have provided no efficient means even for

---

[1] See above, p. 47.

the maintenance of that. The Khonds most anxiously
desire of us justice—not betwixt man and man, which
their own institutions can afford, but betwixt tribes and
their divisions, which the authority of those institutions is
too feeble to reach ; particularly since we deprived them
of their chief patriarch (Dora Bissye) and his family, in the
heads of which was vested a sort of general authority by
these Khonds. Campbell passed many decisions affecting
the most important rights of tribes. There existed no
means of carrying those decisions into effect but the employment of Sam Bissye to see them enforced. Sam has
done nothing but plunder every party to every dispute,
which the power and the wealth with which we have
endowed him enable him to do without difficulty. The
Khonds complain, with perfect truth, that we have interfered, so as partly to induce, partly to compel them to
relinquish the securities for their rights which their own
usages afforded, but have substituted no other guarantees
in their stead ; that we have taken from them their chief
patriarchal family ; declared that they shall not, like all
other Khonds, settle their disputes by battle ; and set
over them Sam Bissye, a *Hindu*, the servant of a *single*
tribe.[1] I have now here numbers of wounded and house-
less men, driven from what Campbell awarded to them
and ordered Sam Bissye to put them in possession of. I
have had no two parties before me whom he (Sam) has
not *freely allowed* that he has plundered as they alleged
—generally of all they possessed ; while he has had no
defence, but that such plunder was necessary for his
subsistence and that of his people. Now I, at least, see
no chance of success in the suppression of the sacrifice
unless we can, as a beginning, obtain entire possession of
the minds of some section of this Khond people. And the
chief means which we possess of effecting this is the establishment of a just and benevolent authority amongst them,
in a spirit and in a form intelligible and acceptable to them.

[1] See above, p. 47.

' When the Khonds shall once be perfectly convinced that the intentions of the Government towards them are those of pure benevolence, I believe that it will be possible gradually to do anything with them—even to make them relinquish the sacrifice ; and I am at least perfectly sure that this can be effected in no other way. That sacrifice might be changed from a public into a secret rite ; it may even be prevented in Goomsur, so that the people will have to cross the boundary for the flesh ; in other words, it may be possible for us, by force in these tracts, to transfer the locale of the rite elsewhere, while we break down the truthfulness of the Khond character, which is its leading and its most hopeful feature, without preventing the sacrifice of a single victim. But until the Government shall determine upon some system of proceeding, and authorise me to carry it out, I can plainly do nothing.'

From the middle of April he used his utmost efforts to win the Khonds to his views. He first took in hand the tribes of the district called Bara Mootah. They went and came very much as they pleased for about three weeks, learning wisdom of every conceivable description from the lips of Baba Khan and Soondera Sing, and arguing day and night regarding the propriety and the necessity of the sacrifice.

Captain Macpherson was enabled to write as follows on the 2nd June 1842 :—

' I have had the Khonds in to reason with me, tribe by tribe ; and the change that has come over their minds, although very far yet from being that which I desire to induce, is very remarkable. How long it will last is also a point for time to solve.

' One cluster of tribes [those of the district called Bara Mootah] has promised to forego the sacrifice, demanding on our part justice, as it is to be had in the low country ; the severest punishment by us of the violation of the agreement ; permission to sacrifice buffaloes, monkeys, &c., with all the ceremonies usual on occasions of human

sacrifice ; to be permitted to denounce the Government
to their gods upon all occasions as the cause of this relinquishment of their ancient worship ; and the indication
to those deities of Baba Khan in particular as the chief
persuader—Baba willingly assuming the entire responsibility. Another group [Athara Mootah] has gone away
to bring me in their victims, and I am anxiously expecting the completion of their intention. There would have
been no difficulty had I sent for them ; but their spontaneous delivery is an extraordinary effort, and I am not
at all certain that the poor people are equal to it.'

The chiefs of Athara Mootah, who went off to submit
the question to their people, met with much opposition :
at the end of seven weeks, however, they intimated that
all were finally agreed, with the exception of the people
of two tracts, who declared that they would not abandon
their ancient worship. Those tracts border upon Hodzoghoro, Sam Bissye's country, and they had an agent
of Sam Bissye residing among them. With Chokapaud,
the Khond district below the Ghauts, there had lately been
little communication. They had, according to the report
of their neighbours, sacrificed as usual during the period
of our connection with them. Their minds were unprepared for the discussion of any subject, and Captain
Macpherson did not communicate with them at this time.

Hodzoghoro, Sam Bissye's country, contained fifty
victims, and the people were bent on sacrifice.

In submitting to the Government an account of these
proceedings, Captain Macpherson proposed that a share of
the Sebundies (the local force, commanded by Gopee
Sing, brother of Soondera Sing) should be made available
for the execution of his decrees above the Ghauts ; that
the local authorities should virtually make and administer
their own laws in the hill-country, and towards all child-
stealers elsewhere ; that they should have power to sentence to six years' imprisonment and 195 stripes, and to
remit such sentence without reference ; that they should

submit proceedings only to the Government, not to the legal tribunals; and that they should be joint-magistrates in Cuttack,[1] to act against procurers, and should have power to try Cuttack procurers.

Lord Elphinstone, before resigning his Government, recorded a Minute[2] in which he expressed his entire approbation of what had been done by Captain Macpherson, and of the measures proposed by him.

After Lord Elphinstone's departure from Madras, the Government of that Presidency recorded the Minute of 10th December 1842, from which a citation has already[3] been made.

In the latter Minute the new Governor (the Marquis of Tweeddale) in Council observed that he was fully aware of the importance of Captain Macpherson's recommendation, that special powers should be entrusted to the local Agents, but that this could not be effected without a legislative enactment. His Lordship granted the request that Gopee Sing with fifty of his men should be placed under Captain Macpherson's orders. He repeated the sanction already given by Government for the formation of a road, recommended by Major Campbell. His hopes, however, lay in a system of combined operations on the part of the Bengal and Madras Governments, and of the Rajah of Nagpore, to be conducted by an Agent residing in the midst of the Khond country, and acting immediately under the orders of the Governor of Madras. The enlarged sphere of action embraced by this plan, together with its great importance, required that it should receive the consideration of the Government of India, and his Lordship in Council resolved to lose no time in bringing it to the notice of that authority.

This well-intended Minute gave Captain Macpherson no instructions, and none of the authority so essential to his

---

[1] Cuttack was under the Bengal Government.
[2] Dated 24th September 1842. See above, p. 156.
[3] See above, p. 156.

purposes; while its obvious meaning was that all active measures should be suspended, to abide the issue of a proposal which was to be submitted to the Supreme Government, but which, it is believed, never was so submitted— certainly not till after the Goomsur tribes were reclaimed without it. Moreover, the climate has always rendered the residence of an Agent in any part of the Khond country absolutely impossible; nor would it have been practicable to establish (as was also proposed) a system of guards and passports at all the points of access to that vast tract of mountain and forest, to prevent the kidnappers from carrying up their victims. .

The Government did not, on this or any other occasion, solve the difficulty which Captain Macpherson had anxiously submitted to it — the embarrassment which was liable to arise at any moment out of the divided and unascertained powers and functions of himself and Mr. Bannerman with reference to a work to which absolute unity of design and rapidity of action were essential. Had the Government but thought fit to declare that Captain Macpherson, though formally subordinate to the Agent in Ganjam, was to be in reality responsible for the execution of its plans, there would have been at once an end of this serious difficulty. The latter officer would have been relieved of responsibility, and Sam Bissye, no longer looking to him over Captain Macpherson's head, might have been rendered harmless after a time. Nothing of all this was done, and the inherent difficulties of the task were greatly enhanced by these unfortunate omissions.

'Gopalpore, 16th October 1842.

'Things are going on at least as well as could have been hoped. I have pitted the power of simple justice against that of superstition — not, of course, expecting the former, unaided, to prevail, but the fight is a far better one than anything which I know of human nature would have led me to anticipate. I have had a very anxious time of it, but two of the great months for sacrifice have been got over without an offering, public or secret, in the parts of which I am trying to make conquest. In other respects I have the people entirely with me. The two chiefs whom I confined[1] escaped the other day ; the whole Khond population rose to retake and bring them back to me. This where, a few years ago, we destroyed the land and those that dwelt therein, and where we have never had anything like firm authority! My people have been settling their complaints by the thousand, difficult matters being reserved until I go up the Ghauts. This is the sole source of my power. But to give justice in form and in spirit suited to these people is nearly as difficult a task as could be attempted. If it should please Heaven to let me have a little health, for a little time more, much will, I trust, be done. The weather is now cold, and I shall get stronger, and I think that I may hope for no fever in the hill-country. I go to a place far more healthy than that which I visited last year, and I shall remain but a short time.'

---

[1] This was for a daring outrage and violation of Major Campell's decree. The confinement was of the lightest character, and all possible pains were taken to make these chiefs understand the real objects of the Government; so that when released, a few months later, they were zealous and useful advocates of the abolition of sacrifice.

CHAPTER XII.

THIRD VISIT TO THE HILLS—OPPOSITION AND REMOVAL
OF SAM BISSYE.

1842, 1843.

' Goomsur, 16th December 1842.

'I HAVE now been for nearly three months debarred, by an accident, from the use of my pen, producing I know not how much of injury and inconvenience. The nerve over the funny bone was somehow injured by the use of the " mugdoors," or heavy sticks used in this country instead of dumb-bells. I am much better, but, being compelled to write a little every day, get on but slowly. I am now out in this beautiful country in this delicious season, at my Goomsur headquarters, Now-gaum, by the station of Russelcondah (*Anglicé* Russell's Hill). I am very well and strong, except the hand, and I am preparing to ascend the Ghauts. I of course have all the nearer Khonds down to me first, and when I see exactly what is to be done, and not till then, I go up and do it. The way in which I have been enabled to keep my ground with the Khonds at least equals my moderate expectations. I find that I made no mistake of any kind last year. In the whole district of Bara Mootah there has been no sacrifice, perhaps for the first time since Time began on its present inhabitants. In Athara Mootah there have been five sacrifices, by the sections of the people who, under the influence of Sam Bissye, did not visit me. But they were not performed in the usual way, the victims being buried whole and unbroken,

KONOBAGRI, NEAR COURMINGHIA, IN THE GOOMSUR KHOND COUNTRY.

The little hill on the left is that of the War God. The grove on the right is the Meriah Grove.

without any festivals or assemblies, and by villages, not tribes. One was on account of a sick man, one on account of the ravages of a tiger, and three as general propitiations; but out of the twenty-one branches of tribes in that country, I command already the chiefs of fifteen, while the rest are beginning to waver. Sam Bissye, by whose permission the sacrifices were performed, is our great man, set up by Russell,[1] and hitherto supposed to be engaged in putting them down. Bannerman, who knows nothing of the matter, is afraid to do any-thing, and looks on the whole Khond subject merely as a nuisance of the first magnitude: and what I am to do with Government, him, and this Sam—the Khonds being in this state, the balance quivering upon the knife's edge—is far from an easy question. I have with in-finite difficulty rallied my poor broken people to advance again, most carefully organised and instructed; while things have developed themselves so that I can now see my way, and commence the lines of a system which pro-mises success : and I have no powers to act, not a single monosyllable of any sort whatsoever.[2] It is a part of the only instructions I ever received,—that I am not to speak of the human sacrifice as a Khond rite !'[3]

'January 1843.

'The history of the change is most curious. I took infinite pains to act upon the minds of the leading men, and of all others last year; and did all that was possible to maintain the impression then given by my emissaries—viz., an invaluable Sirdar[4] (Panda Naick) and many Panwa digalos[5] in my service. Abstinence was comparatively easy to all, save the Mootahs of Cour-minghia and Calingia, whose turn it was to make the public offering; and to them I bent the most anxious

---

[1] See above, p. 47.

[2] The Minute of December 10, such as it was, had not at this time been communicated to him.

[3] See above, p. 159.   [4] Chief.   [5] Interpreters.

efforts.   No people could have been nearer falling; but
they stood, although I believe that Sam Bissye sent his
chief man to persuade one of them to sacrifice.   I trust I
may say that they have relinquished the rite for ever.   I
have had them down, and looked into all their minds, and
I think that with right future management they are safe;
but they are in a most extraordinary state of mind.
They have yielded, they say, to the pressure of the
opinion of all wise and good and great men that the
rite is wrong, and the belief that it has been proved by
the experience of all (who had used it, and given it
up) to be unnecessary, and to the pressure of the
authority of the Circar,[1] from which they desire justice.   They say that their eyes are now opened to the
fact that all men, save themselves (a section of the
Khonds, who can neither boast of richer fields nor of
sharper axes than those of the non-sacrificing section),
abhor this rite, and are convinced, after a long period
of experience, that no god requires it.   And as the
Circar offers them the great advantage of protection and
peace, they will give it up, trusting that their gods will
acknowledge the weight of the constraining influences
under which they act.   Their feelings have taken a turn,
the true origin and course of which I am not certain that
I have yet traced.   Having given up the vital point of
their religion—in fact, its sum—they are necessarily utterly lost, bewildered, and confused, turning everywhere
to seek a resting-point, and finding none.   When I told
them how my forefathers sacrificed, and ceased to sacrifice when instructed, and that they have ever since
grown great,[2] they asked, " What gods were adopted

---

[1] The Government.

[2] The efficacy of this argument is frequently mentioned by Captain Macpherson.   General Campbell states, in his Narratives of 1861 and 1864, that
he used the same argument successfully in 1837, and that the people then
also demanded permission to sacrifice monkeys, &c.   These circumstances
are not mentioned in his Report of January 1838, printed at p. 14 of the
Selections from the Records of the Government of India (Home Department), No. 5, Calcutta 1854.

by them upon the relinquishment of the sacrifice?"
Then their idea was to have sacrifices of bullocks, &c.
to Bera[1] Pennoo *vice* human victims, save that the Mootahs whose turn it was to sacrifice publicly should sacrifice
the monkey; and endless modifications of this plan have
been discussed, but in vain: no satisfactory form could
of course be devised when the necessary ineffaced idea
was excluded. The exact spirit of the part which the
priests have taken I do not yet know: no priest has come
down to me. But the latest tendency of the Bara
Mootah people is to throw off the priesthood bodily,
if one difficulty could be got over. "We can ourselves,"
say they, " conduct with perfect efficiency every indispensable ceremony of our religion except the .great rite
which we have given up; but the priests alone can
enable us to cure our diseases and those of our wives
and children, by informing us, when attacked, which god
is offended, and what is the expiation. Now, had we a
doctor who could cure us without reference to the gods,
as we learn that your doctors cure you, all would be well.
If we remain dependent on the priests for cure, they will
refer all our diseases to the Earth God unpropitiated by
human blood, and we must sacrifice or die." " Send us
a doctor," cried all the poor creatures, at a conference of
the whole Bara Mootah, "and we will make him a god."
I have, of course, been most anxiously on the lookout
for a doctor, and I am in hopes that I have secured one in
an Oriyah Brahmin, who Baba tells me once doctored the
Rajah of Chinna-Kimedy with success, and who has read
many doctorial books, which he inherited, with doctorial
wisdom, from his father, and who will, I hope, do in a way.'

Early in January 1843, Captain Macpherson ascended
the Ghauts, accompanied by Captain Mackenzie, of his
own regiment, as an amateur. He had now heard of the
approval of his measures by the Government, and he
was enabled to act with some confidence, though sadly

---

[1] Bera or Tari, the Earth Goddess. See above, p. 113.

hampered by his divided and imperfect powers; and, though beyond the immediate range of his influence, sacrifices were proceeding daily.   Between thirty and forty, out of his party of a hundred people, suffered from fever.   This, indeed, was better than the preceding year, when the sufferers were 90 per cent.

' I settled,' he writes, 'above one hundred disputes which vexed society—everything which their tribunals could not dispose of, from a dubious claim to a bullock to feuds a century old—a long account of abduction, spoliation, and bloodshed; and no single instance occurred of bad faith in the parties, or of falsehood in the witnesses.   So far as I could go, the people are conquered by the sense of practical benefit conferred, and strongly desire to be within our pale.   While I gave justice upon one hand, I of course laboured to confirm and extend the pledge of non-sacrifice upon the other—and I trust successfully. I have brought away 113 victims, all (except one who was rescued from under the knife in Chokapaud) [1] voluntarily surrendered.   Nearly two-thirds of these came from Athara Mootah, about a dozen from Bara Mootah — the rest from Chokapaud and Tentilghor.[2]   Of the four sacrifices which took place this year in Athara Mootah, old Sam had expressly authorised three; it was

---

[1] 'But,' he says, in his Report of 22nd April 1843, ' with very doubtful advantage, as the disappointed god was immediately gratified by flesh brought from Boad.   Many of these victims, instead of being grateful for their deliverance, have to be hunted like monkeys by the Khonds before they can be caught; so that the prospect of sacrifice cannot be so disagreeable a thing as some people imagine, after all.'   In like manner the late Captain Speke tells us, in his ' Journal,' that in a certain African kingdom which he visited, the king's brothers were, according to immemorial constitutional usage, to be burnt alive on a certain day, and the prospect of this event did not appear to affect their spirits.

[2] In another letter, written a little later, he says: ' One hundred and twenty-five victims were voluntarily surrendered to me, and had the collection of victims been my object, I could have brought away three or four times as many as I did.   At a place not far from me, in Kimedy, I knew of seventy under the control of one man, who soon after sold thirty of them for between 100 and 200 rupees apiece.   But it were mere folly to attempt to operate upon a larger field than we can command.'

matter of great difficulty to determine what to do with
the sacrificers in any of the four cases.   It appeared that
they had acted without any connection with their tribes—
that the sacrifices had been purely private and secret
—the body being buried unshared.   I found that I was so
strong, that after evoking a universal expression of
public condemnation of the breaches of faith, hateful
alike to gods and men, and to the Circar, I could add to
my strength by leaving them otherwise unpunished.   So,
although quite prepared to use coercion if expedient, I
have found coercion unnecessary in aid of the powers
derived from justice and from persuasion ; and I am,
thank God, gratified and satisfied with this commencement of my work.   I have proved that the means which
I suggested, and which alone are available here, are
sufficient to the end.   I saw that justice was the master-
key to the minds of this people, and I have applied it so
as to obtain possession of them.   Its application was
indeed a task of the highest difficulty, and my anxiety
has been great.   But I think that I have escaped important error.'

His plan was not so much to introduce new laws as
to aid the working of the existing institutions among the
Khonds ; giving them his counsel and guidance, but
making their tribal heads his assessors, and parties to
every decree.   He turned his influence, as it grew, to the
question of sacrifice, and in the end was able to form
in every branch of these two tribes a strong anti-sacrificing party, which included about two-thirds of the men
of influence.

The following extract from his Report of 22nd April
1843, may serve to show the delicacy of the task in
which he was engaged, and the patience with which he
overcame the many obstacles which it presented :—

' I passed gradually and cautiously from the less to the
more difficult questions, and finally dealt with those
which seriously engaged the passions of the tribes ;

carrying out the change everywhere, and I believe to the satisfaction of the people. I shall state, by way of example, a single case which long resisted settlement. A woman of Athara Mootah who had been some time betrothed, and for whom the consideration agreed on had been paid, eloped with a lover of Bara Mootah. Her branch of a tribe demanded her surrender, but it was indignantly refused. The established course then was to have required her price from the branch of her seducer, when its refusal would have justified war. But, without making that demand, a party of the woman's branch slew treacherously a kinsman of the lover, who had assisted at the elopement. The kindred of the deceased immediately demanded of me permission to revenge their wrong, or a promise that the Government would avenge it. The heads of the hostile branch admitted the facts to be as alleged, and simply said, that " should the Government resolve to avenge the life taken, they submitted—the slayers were in my camp." But the idea of composition, as in the case of a life taken within a tribe, did not enter into any mind ; and when suggested, it was instantly rejected by both parties.

' I may observe, in passing, that our criminal law, even if it had been applicable here, would neither have been thought just, nor could have settled this feud. By it at least six persons were guilty of murder, but the punishment of more than one of those persons would have been held to be iniquitous by the Khonds, and that so clearly, that a claim for compensation, for any punishment by us in excess of the natural equivalent, would have lain, in the opinion of all, against Bara Mootah. Moreover, the law of compensation, combining tribal with individual responsibility, is—to judge from the rarity of murders here, from the apparent effects of capital punishment upon the Khonds in the years 1835 and 1836, and from all the ideas which I now heard expressed—most probably by far the most effectual law that

could be devised for the prevention of murder from
private or from public motives. Through persuasion and
instruction addressed to each branch separately, and to
individuals, during nearly two months, the minds of
almost all were at length gained—a party of the youth
alone being left for retaliation and war. The two hostile
branches finding that they stood alone, that which had
lost the life first agreed to accept compensation; the
other, after a struggle, during which I pitched my tents
amongst its villages, consented to pay it. The burden
was so allotted that the family of the murderers, in the
first instance at least, lost all their property; while two-
thirds of the balance fell upon the branch, and the tribe
made up what remained. All acknowledged that the
precedent established was a triumph for peace. The
hostile feelings of the disputants seemed soon to subside.
The elders of both parties feasted on a portion of the
compensatory buffaloes and swine; while the young
men of the branch which had paid them drove and
carried the remainder good-humouredly over the border,
and several marriages sprang up between the tribes.'

He had now allied himself directly with the chiefs
and men of influence in each tribe, so as to identify
their authority and that of the Government, and confer
the substantial benefits of justice and peace upon the
mass of the people. He was exceedingly anxious to
secure the co-operation of Sam Bissye; but that wily
chief perceived that this was incompatible with the continuance of the peculiar influence and the gains which
he derived from standing completely between the Government and the Khonds. He considered his person
and his office beyond Captain Macpherson's power, and
he assumed decidedly the part, which he had held his
ground with the Khonds chiefly by affecting, of champion
of the sacrifice. While Captain Macpherson was above
the Ghauts, Sam was below, in communication with Mr.
Bannerman, who not only disbelieved the accusations

against him, but showed him that he disbelieved them, after Sam and his eldest son had confessed the whole to Captain Macpherson.   On that officer's return to the plains, Sam Bissye went up to the Hills, and pretending that Mr. Bannerman had given him authority to sacrifice six victims, sacrificed one at his own place, and induced the Khonds of one tribe to sacrifice two more.   Many remained faithful to the pledge; but, in general, the anti-sacrificing party could not prevent the sacrificers from bringing and burying the flesh.

In April 1843 Captain Macpherson duly placed in Mr. Bannerman's hands, for transmission to the Madras Government, his report of what he had done, and of what had occurred from his want of power; and urged the necessity which existed for Sam Bissye's immediate deprivation of office, and his permanent removal, and the temporary removal of his three eldest sons from the country.   To his surprise and disappointment his urgent application elicited no reply from the Government.   The truth was that Mr. Bannerman was piqued at Captain Macpherson's holding this opinion regarding Sam Bissye, which necessarily implied some reflection on his own penetration; and unhappily, too, he conceived the notion that Captain Macpherson desired the restoration of Dora Bissye to power.   A single question would have satisfied him that he was mistaken; but, instead of making the inquiry, he simply kept this despatch in his desk, along with a second official representation, written in September by Captain Macpherson, who was in despair at the silence of the Government at so critical a time, and who, of course, never suspected—until the month of October, when an explanation took place, and Mr. Bannerman, who had been sick in body and in mind, expressed much regret for what had occurred—that his most important official despatches had been suppressed in this unwarrantable manner.   Already, in the spring, when he had exhorted the

Khonds to adhere to their pledge, and had strongly denounced the violators of it, the Khonds had perceived his
defect of power or of judgment with respect to Sam Bissye ;
and a chief had remarked, 'Instead of cutting down the lofty
tamarind tree in his path, he beats the shrubs which bend
before him !' Now, those who had pledged themselves to
him, braving the antipathy of their race, and daring their
gods, in confidence in his opinions and support, were
crushed by their opponents, and by the belief that he had
abandoned them ; but he had still a party left, for the
people of two tribes had had distinct experience of the
practical benefits of the system which he proposed to
establish, and had pledged themselves to relinquish the
sacrifice on the express condition of the maintenance of
that system. There were but two sacrifices in Athara
Mootah—one public and one private—and none in Bara
Mootah. But in the public sacrifice some people of almost
every branch shared.[1]

The following letter may serve to illustrate the extreme
difficulty of maintaining the British authority in the Hills
during the unhealthy season :—

'I sent up Gopee Singh with a party of Sebundies
to Coorminghia in the depth of the rains, and some
forty low-country paiks[2] besides, to make it plain that
my civil decrees were not to be trifled with. Gopee
and his men were obliged to come away in eight days,

[1] An occurrence of this summer is thus chronicled by Baba Khan : 'On
the 2nd June, while my master was examining a case of smuggling arrack,
and at that moment drinking his broth, the prisoner at the bar, a mean female,
had her eyes fixed on the broth and my master. Myself and several
Brahmins who were there suspected that something would happen to my
master, on account of the bad-looking eye of the woman. About one
o'clock next morning he was attacked with illness. I ran instantly over
to my master, where I found Dr. —— and a native dresser were pre-
scribing their remedies. The natives of the town came to me, and insisted
that Dr. —— had killed two gentlemen before, and he would do the
same to my master. I pacified them gradually, saying that these two
gentlemen died of disease, but not by medicines. By the help of Providence
my master got well very soon.'

[2] A sort of militia holding land on condition of military service.

O

overwhelmed by fever; but I keep the paiks in separate
parties up still, relieving them regularly.   But for this
measure the authority of Government in the Hills would
have been at an end.   I am getting up a connection with
the infant-killing tribes, which I trust will prove beneficial, by giving them Meriah girls in marriage.[1]   I am
acquiring quite a volume of Khond songs: I have a very
pretty lament of some widows over husbands slain in
battle, which I wish I had some one more apt at rhyming
than I am to make a ballad of.'

' Berhampore, 14th September 1843.

'You ask what has been done about Dora Bissye?
He is still on the apex of his fort.   His recall was, of
course, to Bannerman, a monstrous idea, and not having been done at first it could not be done now.   His
nephew, a very fine intelligent young man, visited me
the other day from the zemindary in Bengal where the
family took refuge.   I am very sorry to say that I could
do nothing for him or them.   I could not employ him
among the Khonds as anything but *first*, and this would
not suit existing arrangements.   I sent the poor fellow
to Bannerman with his petition for employment and subsistence for the family, amounting to seventy persons, and
living on charity—a disgrace to the Government!   He
was, of course, infinitely disgusted with his reception
and dismissal—a mere cold order to return whence he
came.'[2]

' Goomsur, 13th November 1843.

'I write to you again from my tent in my noble old
grove of Goomsur, by my old stream—the country an
illimitable sea of corn, broken by rich, deep, many-leaved

---

[1] Some time before this letter was written, he had received a sort of
round-robin from his female Meriah wards, to the effect that if he did not
get them husbands forthwith, they would hang themselves from the trees!

[2] The person spoken of was Chokro Bissye, afterwards head of the insurrection of 1846-47.

woods, and by hills of rarest beauty in form and clothing. To-morrow I shall have all the ryots of its teeming villages around me to make the revenue settlement for the year ; and in a few days more the grove of the Khonds will be thronged by them.   The settlement this year is a very heavy business.   From a fall in the price of grain to the extent of two-thirds, not above half the last year's revenue (though much lowered by me) has been realised, and that amid much distress ; and the difficulty of settling accounts, and arranging for the year with 600 or 700 villages, will be great.   It is a melancholy thing, indeed, to deal with a true, honest, hardworking population under such circumstances.'

' Ganjam, 14th December 1843.

'I see that at home you consider me to be engaged wholly or mainly in the Khond work.   People here consider that work a very small matter, incidental, and of little account compared with my revenue, magisterial, and other business.   Mr. Bannerman sailed for the Cape on the 1st instant, leaving me in charge of the district till his successor should come, which he did yesterday. Before Bannerman went we received the resolutions of Government with reference to my last reports.   The resolutions seem to amount to this : 1. That, with reference to my representations, the Agent shall suspend Sam Bissye from his office, the Government thinking that it is certain that he has abetted and engaged in the sacrifice ; but that I should make *fresh researches* for evidence, and report especially upon them ! 2. That I am to proceed immediately to assure the tribes that the Government means to do *everything to induce them* to give up the sacrifice, &c., &c. ; with an instruction to establish fairs, while no notice is taken of my request respecting the most necessary road. 3. The Government declares that it intends to submit to the Supreme Government a plan for the effectual prevention of the sacrifice.   This is the whole.

o 2

'The real state of things you will understand best from this. I told a party of the most friendly of the Khonds the other day, that "I meant immediately to proceed to the Hills and put matters right." They replied, in their simple, just, and fearless way, "What reason have we to believe you now more than before?" And I am told to go and give more *assurances* to such people! While in charge of the district, and expecting every hour to be relieved, I struck at Sam, converting the *fainéant* order of Government into a reality. Sam was called down from the mountains as usual, and approached, as usual, with his fattest sheep, and large following, to laugh and do homage to me in the old way. I had assembled a large number of the people, whose minds I wished to impress. Sam bowed to the ground in the circle, arose, and was told that his authority had ceased. He could not utter a word. I stated the case fully, for the understanding of all present. The Brahmin officials were not less dumb-foundered than Sam, and looked fearfully in one another's faces, wondering who was to be stricken next. I did not allow the opportunity to pass unimproved with respect to *them.* For the present, however, I arrested only Sam's henchman, chief villain, or what you like—a fellow who, from great projecting tusks, bears the name of Tusker; he is chief robber in a hill-pass. There will be a great movement now in the minds of the Khonds; I expect to regain command of them.'

The result was that Sam Bissye's removal from office and from the country demonstrated signally to all the justice of the Government, and its resolution to carry out its measures; while the downfall of the champion of the sacrifice bore a religious significance, the importance of which cannot easily be imagined. The rite ceased in Goomsur, as will be related in the next chapter.

VIEW IN THE GOOMSUR KHOND COUNTRY.

CHAPTER XIII.

FOURTH VISIT TO THE HILLS — ABOLITION OF HUMAN SACRIFICE IN GOOMSUR.

JANUARY to MAY 1844.

'Khondland, 15th January 1844.

' I ARRIVED above the Ghauts on the 7th instant, and have been since engaged in a very trying contest.[1] The Government have permitted only the suspension of Sam as a public officer, from an office the duties of which have long been merely nominal. I have, by pushing him out of Goomsur, given the suspension some degree of significance; but I am left to fight against his five full-grown sons, two old brothers, with grandsons and nephews by the dozen. The old chief of the country, from whom Sam Bissye has wrested all he has got, is strongly on my side, having given me up his victims last year. Had the Government let me turn out Sam and his brood, all the tribes under him would have necessarily returned to their old allegiance to this man, when the sanguinary superstition would have received a blow the value of

[1] In a letter written in this year, Captain Macpherson says: ' I first do all that I can of my Khond work below the hills, at a safe place. I then go up the hills and complete the work. When it is ploughing-time, or sowing-time, or reaping-time, or any other time in particular, I might as well call upon spirits as upon the Khonds to come to me, or even to talk to me if I went to them; so that it requires very nice arrangement indeed to do business with them.'

which cannot be estimated. I could then have said, decisively, that the battle was won. The people would have sought my justice, like the people of my two tribes [Bara Mootah and Athara Mootah], and would have been, like them, subdued by it. These Khonds [*i.e.* the Khonds of the Mootah of Hodzoghor] now say that Sam Bissye is a martyr for their religion; that the Government may remove him, but that his seed remain, and that any one of his family will do for them; that my two tribes having no heads, received justice from me, and thus became my slaves, and then abandoned their gods; that they, on the other hand, will maintain a chief of the stock which has hitherto ruled them; that they decline my justice, and that they will maintain the ancient faith. Thus at present, you see, there is no opening in the surface of society for my wedge. The people are strong in their faith, and true to its champions. These champions have plundered and tormented them to an incredible extent, and if the Government had let me act as I desired, the recollection of their sufferings would have aided our object in a most important degree. But every wrong is forgotten. "We do not want your justice," they say, "and we will maintain our religion, and will have for our chief one of the race of its great defender." This I allow—and I am sure that you will allow—is a very unpromising state of things. All these Khonds.have come and done homage, and have been told our minds; and the people of my two tribes (whom I have brought here *en masse* to show them how justice is given and how it has been received) have told them, in a way which more than rewards me for all my labour: "That the country had been torn to pieces by bloody feuds and private quarrels—was full of violence and confusion; that valleys had become hills, and hills had become valleys, and all were distracted; that I had come and settled every contest, and given every man his right; and that they now followed me wherever I went, to seek more justice, and to show gratitude." But for this testimony, given in a large assembly, these new Khonds would not have been even tolerably well-inclined towards me. But the impression it produced was prodigious, and it will yet bear due fruit. My plans for managing this people, now hard as stone and deaf as adders, are not fully matured. But I do not despair of managing them, if Heaven will let us live here for a little while. My work of the last two years has stood the trial to which it has been subjected for the last two months far better than I could have hoped : I think I can now pronounce my two districts to be safe.'

'Berhampore, 15th February 1844.

'My last letter to you was from Khondland. I returned here from thence about a fortnight ago, having completely accomplished my objects. I had a hard battle of it, but all my labour is now more than rewarded. The whole of the Goomsur Khond country—a region thirty miles long by twelve broad, and including four great tribes, divided into nearly a hundred distinct branches—is completely conquered, and by the use of moral influences alone. Sam Bissye's sons opposed me with deep art, convincing the Khonds that my authority was very small; that I could but require a few victims, and go off when they were given to me; that Sam's influence and money would procure the reversal by the Agent of all my acts; and that they, the sons, were absolutely devoted to the religion and interests of the Khonds. The Khonds and the sons were thus firmly leagued together, and acted as one man. My first plan was to attempt to convince the sons that their and their father's sole hope of ultimate safety lay in devoting themselves, and gaining the devotion of the Khonds, to my objects,—the proof being the delivery of all the victims. This plan failed entirely. The sons brought in just as many victims as they could persuade the Khonds to give up as necessary to my departure, and no more. They would not run

the slightest risk of breaking with the Khonds, or of falsi-
fying any one of their own pretences or delusions.   I then
entirely changed the ground and the order of battle—my
objects being, first to expose the falsehood of the sons as
to the extent of my authority, and to the mode in which
I would exert it ; and secondly, to transfer the religious
authority of the office of high-priest of the tribe from
Sam to the tribe's ancient Hindu civil and religious head,
who was my tried partisan.   But here I must tell you
that Sam's ancestor, four generations ago, was a victim-
child whom the Hindu head of the tribe rescued, and
made his assistant in the ministry of the guardian-deity of
the tribe.   The descendant of that Hindu head having
opposed the late Rajah of Goomsur, the Rajah made
Sam's father Hindu head or Bissye of half the tribe.[1]
Sam saw that he could not hope permanently to supersede
the old family with the Khonds, unless he could become
sacerdos as well as *rex*; and, about six years ago, sensibly
and simply stole the divinity from his ancient shrine, and
made himself his sole minister, and thence acquired a vast
accession of influence.   Now I resolved to restore this
deity—a lump of stone—to the shrine and the keeping of
its ancient minister, my partisan.   The Khonds stood so
determinedly aloof from me that I could not be quite certain of their feelings as to the act.   I had had slight fever
at the foot of the Ghauts, and again above the Ghauts; and
I could not be sure of remaining for an hour to deal with
its possible consequences.   But if the move succeeded, it
was checkmate ; and I had acquired great faith in War-
burg's fever-drops.   My plan was to call the sons and all
the Khonds to a council at my tents ; then to declare my
resolution to the sons only, and to send them in charge of
Baba to make over the god, his sanctum being quietly

---

[1] The manner in which Hindus and Khonds are mixed up together in
the Hills is very difficult to explain. Here were two Hindu families contending for the headship of a Khond tribe. The divinity was the local or
village god.

surrounded by a few men-at-arms ; while I detained the
Khonds in council, and poured into their ears an oration
suited to the occasion.   All was fully prepared : I began
to state my resolution to the sons : a fit of fever came on,
but providentially, as it was to come, before the critical
words passed my lips.   I now indeed began to fear that
I must quit the unwon field.   But my head was up next
day, and I made the move.   It was perfectly successful :
Baba and my other chief instruments acted their parts in
a masterly way.   No difficulty occurred save to Baba,
who found it no easy matter to persuade the sons to make
delivery with anything like a pleasant grace, even under
a torrent of consoling reflections, most logically deduced
from the doctrines of faith and necessity.[1]   After an

[1] Baba's narrative of these proceedings is as follows:—' On the 22nd
of January my master proved better.   We sent again for Borjo and the
brothers of Sam Bissye, and said to them, " We trusted that you would
pursue the counsels of the Government, but you did not; and our purposes are become useless, through you and your perverseness.   What
do you say of the accusation of the Dulbehra against you, that your
father stole his deity ? "   They replied : "It is true the deity belongs
to the Dulbehra, and the Circar may do as they choose."   Then Borjo, son
and heir to Sam Bissye, was ordered to deliver the stolen god to the Dulbehra.   A warrant was issued.   Gopee Singh, the Sirdar of the Sebundies,
proceeded to the village of Sam Bissye, where the deity was deposited, and
surrounded it with his guard, who walked thither quite unsuspiciously and
wanderingly, as if they were only going for water to the river.   I proceeded,
by my master's orders, with some Sebundies, and the Dulbehra with some of
his Khonds, and Borjo, the son of Sam Bissye, together with an elephant
to impart respect and fear, to see the deity restored.   All this while the
Sirdar was on his horse, moving to and fro from the house of Sam Bissye
and the raised shed of the deity.   Borjo walked slowly and crookedly
behind, as a buffalo some one was dragging against his will, he pulling backwards.   Then the Dulbehra, the Sirdar, and myself entered the god's shed,
and asked Borjo, son of Sam Bissye, what deity was placed there.   He
answered : "Bodo Ravallo, the god that was stolen from the Dulbehra."
At that instant Borjo's countenance looked like a cat when it misses its
prey, deeply distracted and angry, and foolish also.   I ordered to excavate
the deity, who was half-buried in the earth   While digging the Dulbehra
said to Borjo, "This god is not mine; you have concealed it somewhere
else, and substituted another stone here, staining it with the blood of
goats."   I told the Dulbehra that " Eight or ten years has expired since the
deity was brought away, and probably you were too young then to be able
to recognise the deity now.   Your grandfather is here—send him to see."   The

hour's explanations with the council, the poor Khonds
were gained; the falsehood of the denial of my authority
was fully established to their minds by its exertion in the
matter of the great god of the land. The old Hindu
head (called the Dulbehra) was exalted to the skies. No
food was eaten in the house of Sam that day. The Khonds
gradually became mine under the application of my justice. They pledged themselves to give up the sacrifice,
and are still sending in their victims through the Dulbehra:
his authority is re-established over the whole tribe. The

old man dug up the deity, and examined it, and said, "It is ours." After
identifying the deity, who was without shape, and weighing about 75 lbs.,
the Dulbehra's servant for worshipping it rolled it round with a new wet
garment, and placed it on the head of his son, a young man. Borjo stood
like a stone, and highly angry, but remembering that his father was in confinement. We all slowly brought the deity to my master, who was then sitting
before his tent, under a large mango-tree, with Soondera Singh and all
the Khonds of Hodzoghor and Tentilghor in a council, relating to them,
"That in former times all nations sacrificed, and lived very poorly; but
gradually, by their own experience or that of others, they relinquished the
practice, and became prosperous. When we came to Bara and Athara
Mootahs, we intended to come to you also; but there existed a barrier
between us (meaning Sam Bissye), which we have, by the determination of
Government, demolished, and our objects are become known to you. The
Khonds of Bara Mootah and Athara Mootah are here, who are well aware
of our views. This restoration of the god to the Dulbehra, is it just or unjust?" They answered, "A very just proceeding!" Since which day
the Khonds turned their minds entirely to ours, and believed our power
to be highest; attended in crowds, gradually growing larger, to our tents,
and not only in the day, but by night also, to hearken to our wise counsels,
and they believed all that we said to be the truth. Before all this
happened—viz., on the 13th of January 1844—the Khond women of the
village of Lennapadra, of Tentilghor in Athara Mootah, came to my master,
who gave beads and looking-glasses, to the young ones especially, and
told them that they must positively prevent their husbands from sacrifices;
and, pleasingly for them, declared their children all beautifullest, and sent
them away to their homes with gladness.'

On this restoration of the deity to its owner, it may be observed that
the proceeding was in the fullest accordance with usage. A suit may be
brought, in the courts of British India, to recover possession of a religious
office, or of a Hindu temple; to establish an exclusive right to conduct
the religious duties of the temple, and to receive the offerings made by any
who may choose to resort to it: nor, in truth, would the functions of
government be adequately discharged if, while effect is given to ordinary
civil rights, claims which the people regard as peculiarly sacred were left to
be enforced by the sword or the war-axe.

other tribes of Goomsur, already partially gained, became entirely mine after this consummation, the conquest of Sam's proper domain.'

As a specimen of the manner in which Captain Macpherson communicated with the Khonds, it may be worth while to insert here his memorandum of the proceedings of a council held at Tentilghor, during this visit to the Hills:—

'Asked the assembled chiefs of Hodzoghor, "Well, have you communicated with all the people, and what is the result?"

'"We have told it to all, and most of the small people are here present: let them hear the proposal from your lips, lest they suspect us of having framed it, in any degree, from the desire to become great with the Government, or the desire for dress, for cloth, and for money."

'Then said I: "Formerly all the world, English, Hindus, Mussulmans, sacrificed men. To some knowledge came, and they taught others, and by degrees the rite has been abolished, save amongst you. Bullocks are one with bullocks, horses with horses, deer with deer—so all men have the same interests. We seek merely to communicate to you a good which we have learnt, and to save you from a sin. We know the history of the world from reading and writing, and the state of it from travelling; you know nothing of this. But we ask you—Look at Bara Mootah and Athara Mootah, which have given up their victims and the sacrifice; look at them, and see whether our acts have not been purely beneficial, and whether they have suffered from giving up the rite?"

'A principal Mullicko then said to the assembly: "All are here present, from the oldest Panwa to his youngest son, from the oldest Sittra to his youngest son, from the oldest Mullicko to his youngest son. This counsel of the Circar appeared good to us. We communicated it to you—you hear it again. Let it not be said in future times, 'Those old men received this advice, and made us act upon it, and we have been ruined.' We are the old and passing—you are the young, who will remain. Do you form your judgment and declare it."

'Ootan Sing Dulbehra: " O Mullickos of all Mootahs, hear ! I have received the counsel of the Circar : I am convinced that it is good ; I am prepared to devote my life to carry it out. Again, Sam Bissye has long concealed this counsel from you, and upheld opposite ideas by every art. You see what the Circar and the gods have wrought on him. On both these considerations this new counsel is embraced by me. In carrying it out, I know neither friend nor enemy, nor great man nor small man. I am for carrying it out, and I will execute all wishes of the Government with respect to it. Now, unless you are at present fully resolved to adopt this counsel, you may hereafter say, ' The injury to our religion has arisen from the Keout[1] whom we established to save and protect us from the Circar.' I declare that I will expend my life to carry out this design. If you object to this course on my part, say it at once, and express your desire for my removal before the Circar."

' Then the most ancient white-headed dim-eyed Mullicko, after consultation, answered : " You have desired me, O Mullickos, to give the answer. My strength is gone, my mind is gone—all my faculties are weakened. But I will answer. Let those who are disposed assist me. A Meriah child is not a buffalo's calf, that in time will plough ; nor a cow's calf, good to eat ; nor a sheep, to drop lambs ; nor a brass pot, of which, when broken, ornaments may be made ; nor the iron of an axe, which, when worn, may yet barb arrows : and after what we have heard, and after our discussions respecting it, what part is there for us to take—what is the use of keeping them ? We have got none."

' At this point murmuring and confusion of face arose

---

[1] The family of the Dulbehra belongs to the caste of Keouts, or river-fishermen.

among the Khonds, and our people immediately said,
" If you really mean to say you have no victims, say
so at once." All the Khonds said, " That was not our
meaning ;" and the old speaker said that he had forgotten. The old man was then neglected, and two old
Mullickos came forward and said, " Our meaning was
this. At present towards our victim-children, whom
we mean to kill, we feel little affection, and do not fear
the sin of their death. When we shall give up the √
sacrifice, we shall regard them with affection, and look
on the sin of their death with fear. Again, in delivering up the children to us Mullickos, people will think,
' As this child was not to be sacrificed, I have lost a
valuable herdsman, or a woodcutter, or a ploughman,
or a child on whom my affections were set,' and he will
feel angry with the Mullicko who informs and takes the
child ; so to prevent informing and taking, let every man
declare at once what victims he has."

' Then a number cried out, " I have one," " I have √
two," &c., and all told their victims except two. We
told them, " Say, if you will, that you have none ; but
should it be proved that you have, you cannot again show
your face in the council." Then they confessed they had
certain victims. Then we said, " We trust that no evil
counsel will hereafter induce you to sacrifice, and that no
ignorant people in the jungle will do so, acting separately,
as has been the case in Athara Mootah." They replied,
" You establish your house here ; the offenders, will they
not be known to you ? " ' [1]

[1] Baba Khan says, that a little later—' We sent for the Khonds of
Athara Mootah and Bara Mootah, who assembled the following day, and
held a public council on the affair of Jeetto Mullicko, Lengo Mullicko,
and Gotta Mullicko, who were Sam Bissye's three chief accomplices in
sacrificing. My master, Soondera Singh, and myself were present. My
master questioned Jeetto Mullicko : " Why did you sacrifice ? " He √
answered : " My f mily were sick ; a barn broke and fell unawares on
my wife, and she died ; a tiger devoured my buffalo ; and another woman
died in childbirth ; and I also was dangerously ill. Then Gunda Mullicko told me, ' What are all these sufferings ? Why not sacrifice a
victim ? I will go and take Sam Bissye's permission to offer one, as I

Captain Macpherson, soon after his return to the plains, was enabled to report as follows :—

'I have the high satisfaction to state that the great season of sacrifice is past, and that there has been no apparent tendency to sacrifice in any part of the Khond country of Goomsur. The stage of progress attained by each tribe in the religious change has, however, been distinctly marked in this period. The tribes of Bara Mootah and Athara Mootah, most advanced, have not received from the festivals held around them a particle of the flesh into their soil. Five men of the latter (of whom one was a priest) attended a sacrifice within the Bengal frontier, brought away flesh, and buried it secretly in their village-fields. When the act was known the people instantly compelled them to dig it up, and sent them with it to my chief agent, demanding their punishment by the Government, as false to it and to them, and deeply criminal in the sight of the gods. I have detained the priest, but hope that it may be possible to release him soon. The Khonds of Hodzoghor, as was to be expected, have brought flesh to many of their villages. The districts of Tentilghor and Chokapaud, as I am at present informed,

have heard that he has got permission from the Circar to sacrifice victims.' Then I told Gunda Mullicko that 'I have no victims to sacrifice, and am unable to go just now; you had better go for me.' Upon which Gunda Mullicko said, 'You have a piece of land in Hodzoghor, and I will procure you a victim for it; then sacrifice, and get better of your sickness.' Then Gunda Mullicko went to Sam Bissye, and related of Jeetto's ailment. Sam Bissye stated to him that—'Although the Circar prevents you from sacrifice, do not you relinquish it; as that is the most precious medicine, and none other medicine is worth. I have got permission from the Circar to sacrifice six victims, and I have already sacrificed three.'" Jeetto and the rest also said : "We believed Sam Bissye's report to be true, for when he returned into this country from Nowgaum, he came publishing most notoriously that he had Government liberty to sacrifice six victims, and we believed it; and as the Circar did not in the least punish him for his former sacrifices, we imagined what he published was the truth; otherwise we should not have committed this sacrifice." Then my master asked the council what was their decision. The principal Khonds answered, that "they are entirely guilty, and the Circar must certainly punish them severely." Then we placed Jeetto Mullicko, Lengo Mullicko, and Gotta Mullicko in arrest, also the negotiator Gunda Mullicko; and my master gave the Khonds their usual presents, and dismissed them.'

have remained almost but not perfectly pure. The whole number of victims rescued this year is 142, and all are Khonds or Panwas, or of the other castes permanently resident on the Hills, except two Hindu children from the low country bordering on the Ghauts. The experience of this and of last year proves that the practice of kidnapping children from the low country has nearly ceased in this part of the district.

'With respect to the future, I conceive that it is established that if the climate of the southern tracts shall be found endurable for one or two months in the year, the abolition of the sacrifice throughout the Khond country may be accomplished. The great difficulty has necessarily been in the first step; in the acquisition of the necessary knowledge—the formation of efficient instruments—the completion of an experimental operation upon a scale sufficiently large to test the principles applied. The great moral and intellectual aptitude of the Khonds to receive the ideas which it is desired to communicate to them sanctions the expectation that their progress in improvement will fully correspond to the opportunities which shall be afforded to them—that they will make a noble return for wise tutelage.'

The following is dated 'Aska, 14th March 1844 ' :—

'Great has been my need all this time of an assistant in this work. I am now out in the district, my tents pitched in a delightful wood, near my old village of Aska. I am drawing in revenue and doing civil justice, besides Bow-street and Lord Mayor's cases without number ; and I have Khonds[1] down daily, and the sacrificers

---

[1] The Khond witnesses who came to give their evidence against certain prisoners were living in 'Lunjapilly, a village of Soondera Sing, granted to him by Government. One morning, on a sunshiny day, while Soondera Sing was coming on his palanquin to see my master with these Khonds, one of them remarked, with astonishment and laughter, "See! that palanquin was made in the low-country; it is very beautiful, painted with colours, fixed with boards, lined with cloth, and iron fixed to it; how well it looks!" Another said: "The senses of the low-country people are not worth a cowry. How many men must have taken how

in my pledged tribes last year, as fixed companions, learning and giving wisdom. I have also Sam and his sons prisoners at large, under a very sharp look-out by Baba and his establishment.'

Captain Macpherson's health had now quite given way, and having provided against the repetition of the obstinate and preposterous resistance offered to the work of abolition, by obtaining the sanction of the Government to the removal of Sam Bissye and three members of his family from the district, he recommended Mr. John Cadenhead as the fittest person to take charge of the Khonds in his absence. That gentleman had attended him in the long and severe illness caused by his first visit to the Hills, and had kindly written for him when the state of his eyes made it impossible for him to use a pen. After removing to a distant part of the country, he had still kept up a close correspondence with Captain Macpherson, and was intimately acquainted with everything that had been done for the abolition of human sacrifice and infanticide. He was not only a man of much skill in his profession, and in the collateral sciences, but one who had a mind capable of dealing with political and social questions, as well as a ready and energetic character, combining great benevolence with a high and independent spirit. Accordingly, Mr. Cadenhead was suddenly—and without even the form of consulting him as to his in-

much trouble in making this palanquin! They felled wood, sawed it into planks, placed them together, and formed them into a palanquin; and then it is only comfortable for one individual, and great wastage of money, while on account of one person many suffer much labour. If that man was to walk and go, he would save his money, and not give trouble to others. Is not this a wise business? If one-quarter part of the money expended by Soondera Sing on that palanquin was spent in purchasing good meat and the marrowbones of buffaloes for himself, and all was so consumed by him, it would give vast strength to his limbs, be palatable to his mouth, and fill his stomach for a long time to his heart's content. The low-country people have, I think, little sense."—*Baba Khan's Letters.*

clinations—ordered to relinquish his medical charge in the pleasant district of Salem, and to undertake the laborious duties of Principal Assistant to the Agent in Ganjam; while Captain Macpherson prepared to visit Calcutta and Madras, with a view to explain the state of Khond affairs, and to obtain authority to act against the sacrifice not only in the Madras territory, but in all the districts round about.

'Goomsur, 3rd June 1844.

' From the whole Khond work not being under me, but partly under me, partly under the Agent, partly under Bengal, the obstacles in the way of its completion are multiplied to the greatest possible extent. It is a great thing that my strength endured just to this point. I really do not think I could have carried on the war much longer, whatever the stake. Had the Government behaved with the least shadow of reason, I should by this time have accomplished at least six times as much.'

'Gopalpore, 4th July 1844.

'The Government has entirely approved of and confirmed all that has been done. They perused my report with " the highest satisfaction;" and "such success having attended the measures employed, they desire to record the sense they entertain of the merits and exertions of the First Assistant Agent, the chief instrument in effecting this important change in the Khond habits and religious principles." But now, it ought to be recollected that the Government has done all it could to prevent this success; that my only instructions have been—first, in 1841, to visit the Khond country, but not to allude to the sacrifice as a Khond rite; secondly, in 1842, to wait for a plan of operation to be framed by the Government; and thirdly, in end of 1843, to suspend Sam and do nothing *more* whatever on my peril—the Government being convinced

P

that I could not succeed, while poor Bannerman was apparently determined that I should not. The Government has ordered everything I have asked for in the fullest and most cordial way, only asking if I wish to have a more condign punishment than perpetual exile inflicted on the old villain Sam. The best thing they have done, an act for which I am thankful indeed, is their most ready decree, according to my desire, of gold medals to Baba and Soonderah, "in testimony of the appreciation by the Government of their meritorious and important services." It will greatly help the service.'

'Gopalpore, 17th July 1844.

'If I had proper assistance and authority, and but a gleam of health—and, if it were possible, but a little use of my arm, which I have thrown back grievously in writing this report,—I could now conquer a great extent of that terrible country in a short space of time, making the conquest of the rest comparatively easy. I now see my way dimly to a beginning of schools amongst the Khonds, and am deeply engaged in getting up an Oriyah Spelling-book, and a First Book of universal religion and morals for them.'

The course of events, then, had been this: A single cluster of the tribes[1] of Goomsur, moved by the promise, and by the experience of practical benefits conferred, and by—to use the expression officially employed at a later period—'the admirable power of individual character'[2] which Captain Macpherson brought to bear upon them, had unanimously agreed upon his requisition to give up its human sacrifice, provided that like terms were imposed upon its neighbours. There was no general sickness or failure of crops during the early and critical period, and that cluster of tribes stood firm and true to its compact.

[1] Those of the district of Bara Mootah.
[2] See the 'Memorandum (prepared at the India House) of the Improvement of the Administration of India during the last Thirty Years:' ordered by the House of Commons to be printed, 12th February 1858.

A second cluster of tribes[1] had entered into a similar convention, not at first unanimously; but all had been won over, by delicate and firm treatment, to a perfect adoption of the new system.

The tribes of the two remaining districts[2] of Goomsur stood out for a time, while the native local agent of the Government was suffered to employ, for the maintenance of the sacrifice, the influence which he derived from that situation.   But upon his removal they gave way, moved by the zealous persuasion of the reclaimed tribes, and by their own experience of Captain Macpherson's administration of justice.   Thus the whole of the Khonds of Goomsur were gained.

[1] Those of Athara Mootah.
[2] Hodzoghor and Chokapaud.

CHAPTER XIV.

RESULTS OF CAPTAIN MACPHERSON'S MANAGEMENT OF THE SACRIFICING KHONDS.

1842-1844.

It has been shown that when Captain Macpherson assumed charge of our relations with the Khonds, early in 1842, the sacrificing tribes, notwithstanding Major Campbell's praiseworthy efforts during upwards of four years, retained undiminished their determination to continue the sacrifice of human victims.

We have now arrived at the summer of 1844. The whole of the tribes of Goomsur had entirely abandoned human sacrifice.[1] The exact religious significance of

---

[1] General Campbell tells us, that when he returned to Goomsur in 1847, after an absence of five years, he learnt with unfeigned pleasure that no public performance of the Meriah rite had taken place since he had left the Khonds, and he could not discover that there had been any private one. He believed they had remained faithful to their pledge, and he marked his approval of their steadfastness by bestowing upon them some pieces of red cloth, a decoration which it seems was in request among these barbarians. ('Personal Narrative,' p. 93.) The statement attributed to the Khond chiefs by General Campbell is not literally true, as we have seen; for many cases of sacrifice occurred, and some were punished, in Goomsur after his departure in March 1842, which are stated in the records of the Agency (a fact which he had probably forgotten when he wrote the passage in question); and he is certainly in error when he attributes to the pledge exacted by himself in December 1837—to which his own reports show that the Khonds paid little regard while he remained in Ganjam — their alleged abstinence from the sacrifice during the five years which succeeded his departure. But as the sacrifice had been given up soon after March 1842 by the tribe of Bara Mootah, and had been

the change, so far as regards the sacrificing Khonds, was not fully developed until a later period. Meanwhile, it may be observed, that though proselytism was forbidden by the policy of the British Government, and by the nature of the instruments employed, yet all events were interpreted by the Khonds in their own way, and translated into their own forms of thought and expression. The supreme purely beneficent Creator, whom the Circar (or Government) was known to worship, was identified by the Khonds with their god of light, the source of all good; and they believed that his power was prevailing over that of the earth-goddess, whose malignity they had hitherto endeavoured to disarm by human sacrifice. 'The Circar' (said they) 'is a present power, and can visibly do more for our good than the earth-goddess can do to our injury: therefore the God which it serves must be more powerful. The pressure of the Government must excuse us to the earth-goddess: it is irresistible, for it is beneficent, but to be irresistible it must be beneficent.'

As a mere coercive power the Khonds had defied the Government to the end. They had laid down their lives cheerfully rather than infringe the duties of hospitality, and they feared the vengeance of their gods more than they feared our severities. But the pressure of the Government, when allied with the tribal authority to which they had always looked up, with the free play of their own institutions, and with measures of practical beneficence, was irresistible; and they rightly referred the abolition to its orders, both as an excuse to the earth-goddess, and as a merit of their own with the Government.

To go into a country and find every man convinced

afterwards entirely abandoned, the Khonds, whose notions of time are very rude, and who had discontinued the rite for a considerable time, might, without intentional falsehood, have somewhat antedated the discontinuance.

of the necessity of human sacrifice—to leave them, in
little more than two years, abhorring human sacrifice,
and eager to cooperate in the prevention of it among
others; to find every man believing firmly in the supremacy of the evil principle—to leave all convinced, and
acting upon the conviction, that the Supreme Being is
purely beneficent; to effect, in a country all but inaccessible, more than had ever been effected in India by those
who were able to take up their residence among the
people, and had full scope for unremitted action; to
effect this without (indeed against) instructions, under
severe and dangerous sickness, paralysing the Agent's own
strength, and causing his followers to fail him continually,
while he was frequently thwarted by his immediate superior, and coldly supported by the Government: all this
was very remarkable service.

It was effected not by accident, nor by knack, nor by
hysterical humanity, rushing in and seizing one victim to
be saved at the expense of another :

> Who overcomes
> By force, hath overcome but half his foe.[1]

The result was obtained by making the abolition a
Khond movement; by sapping the religious conviction
of the necessity of human sacrifice, and showing that
all the material interests of the tribes, and those which
had most weight with the best men, would be promoted
by abolition.   No doubt it would have been easy to pro-
claim—easier than to execute—a crusade against these
devil-worshippers and murderers: but (besides being in-

---

[1] Captain Macpherson wrote from Calcutta, 22nd April 1845 :—'A conquest of force is no conquest at all.   Whenever I heard that any man of
consequence was spreading opinions opposed to mine, I called a council, and
prayed him to state his views there.   He did so; and I could always either
convince him, or make him confess himself silenced,—a great triumph for
my partisans.'

accessible) they were men, and had human reasons and motives for their conduct. The question was, by what inducement could they be led to desist? and to solve this, of course it was necessary, in the first place, to learn what were the reasons and motives which were to be overcome. In the meantime, the rescue, whether by force or by ransom, of any particular victim, or number of victims, could not affect the disposition to sacrifice, any more than the shaking the ripe fruit from a tree prevents it from bearing a similar crop next season.

To discover the real causes of the practice was extremely difficult. But by continued and patient observation of the people—in the forests, in the prisons, under circumstances the most various—some knowledge of their inner life was at length painfully won.

Had their thoughts soared above the idea of temporal good and evil, it might have been difficult indeed to turn them in a new direction. But it was found that they looked upon famine, disease, and worldly misfortune and death as the inevitable and the main consequences of any intermission of the rite.

The object was to hold out to them the absolute denial of this, to prove it by the experience of a season, and to present to them some counterbalancing advantage.

The countervailing benefit was the redress of their chief want—the settlement of feuds and disputes which their institutions could not cope with : and this, not by superseding them in the management of their own affairs, which would have wounded the pride of a free and independent people, but by associating the Government with them in the administration of justice, supplying a moderating and an executive power.

The effect was produced not by introducing any new theory, but by building on the old foundation; by calling into healthy action the principles already recognised among

them, and suited to their character ; by making them feel
that the change was their own experiment for their own
interest—not the experiment of the Government for ends
of its own.

The result was that they looked to the good actually experienced, and they inferred that the evil deity, which they
had braved in strong faith and reliance on the Government, could no longer hurt them ; not merely because
they expected the Government to protect them, but because in the Deity which the Government professed to
serve (the purely beneficent Deity) they recognised a
Being whom they already dimly knew, but had not
regarded as omnipotent. They had themselves always
worshipped the principle of Good, which they called the
god of light, though they had believed its power to be
less than it now appeared. Its real power being now
ascertained, the earth-goddess ceased to be regarded as
the dominant power, and was at last (as we shall see a
little later) renounced as an object of adoration, and
the higher religious belief in a Beneficent Omnipotence
was established ; or, in other words, instead of worshipping
the devil they came to worship God, though their conceptions were still very rude and imperfect.

But unless the acts of the Government were consistent
and systematic, the faith which the Khonds placed in
it could not be maintained. We know how the chosen
people of God—in whose sight He had wrought such
wonders as the earth had never before witnessed, and
whose daily life was a miracle—lapsed into disobedience
and idolatry upon the slightest discouragement ; and it
is not surprising if the poor barbarians of the Orissan
hills were not very firm in their new opinions. While
the Goomsur chiefs, therefore, avowed their conviction of
the needlessness of human sacrifice, they loudly declared
that they could not prevent their people from reverting
to the rite if they saw it continued by the inhabitants
of the adjoining districts : such continuance being in

their eyes a proof that the Government was indifferent on the subject, as they could not understand how the sacrifice could be forbidden on one side, and permitted on the other side, of an imaginary boundary-line, which they had seen the same Government wholly disregard in the Goomsur war.

CHAPTER XV.

MEASURES FOR THE ABOLITION OF INFANTICIDE.

1842–1844.

THE general features of Khond infanticide have been already[1] set forth. Captain Macpherson was the first officer who made any attempt to reclaim the Khonds from this practice; and his efforts in this field were as successful as his other labours, though he said nothing about what he was doing until he had some results to show. Here, as in the other branches of his work, the right principles of operation were discovered, and applied by him on a large scale. The nature of the measures devised and adopted by him will appear from the following statement, submitted to the Government on the 10th July 1844 :—

'The portion of the Khond country in which the practice of female infanticide is known to prevail is included in the zemindaries of Souradah, Coradah, and Chinna-Kimedy, in the Ganjam district. Its area is roughly estimated at 2,400 square miles; its population at 60,000; and the number of infants destroyed annually at from 1,200 to 1,500. It is divided into five districts— viz., Pondacole, Gooldi, Deegee, Boori, and Cundami—and is possessed by a few tribes, which are subdivided into numerous branches. . . .

'These are the chief causes of female infanticide in these tribes—viz., 1st, a belief in its conditional injunction by the Deity; 2ndly, the belief that the practice con-

[1] See above, p. 132.

duces to the birth of male offspring; 3rdly, the opinion
that the distraction and bloodshed which spring from the
capricious dissolution of marriage-ties by women make
the usage the least of two evils.   The extent to which
the practice is carried varies materially in the five districts which I have enumerated.   In Boori I have seen
many villages of above 100 houses in which there was
not a single female child.   In Pondacole, in villages of
that size, one or perhaps two may be found.   In Gooldi
female infants are very rarely reared.   In Deegee the
practice of destroying them is limited to a few tracts on
its border next to Gooldi.   I have no exact information
respecting the usage in Cundami.   I proceed to state the
measures which have been adopted for its abolition, and
their results.

' The main elements in the situation of these two
divisions of the Khonds—that which observes the rite
of human sacrifice, and that which practises female infanticide—being obviously the same, the same general
principles have governed the measures which I have applied to each.   In each division, equally, the peculiar
genius of the people, the form and the spirit of its institutions, and its physical situation, precluding the general
application of the forces by which civilized power can
act directly upon barbarism, have appeared to indicate this
general course of procedure: 1st. To establish the authority of Government over each cluster of tribes, by
supplying their chief social wants beneficially and ac-
ceptably to them—giving them, in the first place, justice
and peace ; and 2ndly. To attempt to obtain the complete
dominion over them, which is necessary to sway them to
the changes desired in their religion and their manners, by
combining, with the direct authority so acquired, every
form of influence which can be created by acting upon
their reason, their feelings, their prejudices, their affections, and on the whole circle of their minor interests.

' I have partially executed this plan in three of the five

districts in which infanticide exists—those of Pondacole, Gooldi, and Deegee, in the zemindaries of Souradah and Coradah : and in effecting its first step—the establishment of authority through the dispensation of justice— I have employed, generally, the same methods of detail, and, in part, the same agency which I used in accomplishing the like work in Goomsur.

' My first objects, necessarily, were the acquisition of exact knowledge of this division of the Khond people, and the formation of fit instruments to act upon it. When these ends were in part attained, and a spirit of confidence had succeeded to the feelings of deep apprehension and distrust which necessarily prevailed in these districts, I proceeded to settle questions of importance in them, where it was quite certain that I could act with distinct and lasting benefit ; it being certain that partial and temporary measures of interference with any portion of the Khond people can produce but unmixed evil, by weakening or breaking down the existing guarantees for order, without establishing others in their stead.   These operations have included, within the last eighteen months, the settlement of a large number of questions of every class, in every part of the nearer tract of Pondacole, and have affected, to a considerable extent, the whole population of Gooldi and of Deegee.   Their general result has been, that the authority of the Government has been completely established in Pondacole and in Deegee, and that the people of these districts anxiously desire the complete extension to them of its justice and protection, as they are afforded to the tribes of Goomsur.

' The tribe of Gooldi is reputed to be superior in courage, in physical strength, and in most Khond virtues, as it is in wealth, in proportion to its numbers and territory, to any other tribe with which we are acquainted. It has never suffered a serious defeat, and not having felt our power in the Goomsur rebellion, it entertains very exaggerated ideas of its prowess and importance.   It is divided into two hostile parties, of unequal strength. The weaker of these has sought and obtained our friendship, and is disposed to obedience, although it is not yet brought under authority. The stronger has availed itself, in some instances, of our mediation; but it is averse to the idea of subordination, and to that of the relinquishment of the practice of infanticide, as its sign. Upon the conduct of this fine tribe, the minds of the whole Khond population in this quarter—both the portion which practises infanticide, and that which sacrifices—is fixed; and upon its complete subjection to the will of the Government very much depends.

'Next in importance to the dispensation of justice, amongst the means employed in this work, has been the use of arguments opposed to the opinions and the reasonings by which the practice of infanticide is supported. With respect to these, I have held—

'1. That the alleged injunction of the Deity, by which the usage is justified, is plainly but a conditional permission, authorising it, at the utmost, only in so far and for so long as the men of any tribe shall find themselves unequal to maintain the peace of society undisturbed through their women—unequal, that is, to the first duties of manhood : the admission of the necessity of the practice by these tribes necessarily placing them in a position of inferiority to all of mankind who are not compelled, by their incapacity to do justice in questions of property arising out of the marriages of their daughters, to destroy them in infancy.

'2. I have simply asserted that enquiry will prove the second alleged cause of the usage—the opinion that male births are increased by the destruction of female infants—to be unfounded.

'3. With respect to the justification, which is laid on the ground that the destruction of infants is a less evil than that which must arise from the contests attendant on the capricious dissolution of their marriages, I have held it to be obvious that the practice of infanticide, and the cause of those contests, react upon each other alternately as cause and effect. Infanticide produces a scarcity of women, which raises marriage-payments so high, that tribes are easily induced to contest their adjustment when dissolutions of the tie occur; while these dissolutions are plainly promoted by that scarcity, which prevents every man from having a wife. On the cessation of infanticide women would become abundant, and the marriage-payment would become small. Every man would have a wife in these districts, as elsewhere; women would have less power to change, and when they did there would be no difficulty in making the requisite adjustment of property.

' But, lastly, the Government is now about to remove entirely this ground for the practice, by preventing contests about property involved in marriage-contracts, by adjudicating all questions respecting it in these districts, as it does in Goomsur. Thus the evil which infanticide is held to avert will finally cease, and with it all pretence of justification founded on the permissive sanction of the Deity.

' These arguments and considerations have been addressed to these Khonds in the same spirit as those which have been adduced to the tribes of Goomsur against the rite of sacrifice. I have invariably appealed directly to the clear reason and the strong affections of this natural and truthful people, avoiding the least offence to their pride, or wound to their self-love—the awakening to hostility of any sentiment or prejudice or passion which I could not control. I have thence, in the first instance, denounced neither of the practices which I have laboured to abolish as a crime : I have but arraigned them as deplorable errors, in which many portions of mankind, including our forefathers, have participated, but from which they have been successively delivered, elevated by their own reason and experience, or by those of others, as we desire to elevate the Khonds.

' It is eagerly admitted by all of this people, that if the usages which we condemn are not founded upon express ordinances of the Deity, or upon necessity, they are deep crimes : and their renunciation follows the complete conviction of the thinking part of it, that they have not those foundations, the Government performing duly its all-important part of tutelage and support.

' The chief of these tribes, a majority of those of Gooldi excepted, have now generaly acknowledged the force of the considerations which I have opposed to their opinions in support of infanticide. They feel deeply the imputation of inferiority with which I have laboured to associate the practice, so grounded upon the alleged permission of the Deity. They admit that the usage, and the evil which it is held to avert, react on each other as cause and effect ; and that when the latter shall be prevented, by the promised extension of the justice of the Government, all necessity, if not every cause that may be alleged, for the former will cease.

' The measure of which I have next to speak has produced effects of great importance. I conceived that between a people organised on the principle of family, and patriarchally governed—amongst whom contracts between individuals are also engagements between tribes, and the important class of marriage-contracts gives rise to the strongest feelings, next to those of religion, which connect society : I conceived that between this people and the Government a new bond of connection, involving influences of the highest value to this work, might be created through the marriage to its chiefs of the female wards of Government saved from sacrifice. I accordingly, about twelve months ago, after careful preparation, bestowed fifty-three of those wards (Khonds and a few Panwas) in marriage upon chiefs and men of influence in Pondacole, half of Gooldi, and Deegee. In the operation I subjected both the principals and their followers, for a long period, to the influences of which I have already 'spoken, settling

the disputes of all, and reasoning with all; while I at the
same time exhausted every art, by which I could hope to
engraft ideas analogous to those of family connection
upon the existing ideas of civil connection with the
Government.

'The degree of influence which has been acquired
through the gradual development of this measure has
surpassed my expectations.   Slight differences in manners,
and feelings respecting persons devoted as victims, rendered
both parties at first averse to marriage, but an entire
change of feeling on this point soon took place.   When it
was found that the bestowal of a ward of the Government ·
denoted its favour and confidence, and was the beginning
of a new and beneficial relationship to it—that the interest of the Government followed its children undiminished into their new families and tribes, giving to these
special claims to consideration,—there arose the strongest
desire to obtain the wards in marriage.   I have since
laboured to strengthen and to multiply the ties between
them, and all connected with them and the Government,
through the maintenance of regular intercourse with them,
and the careful observance, as far as possible, of the forms
and the duties, and the use of the language, of the paternal
relation.   Thus, ideas of connection and of authority,
analogous to those which arise from natural affinity, have
become blended in the minds of these people, to a certain
extent, with their existing ideas of civil connection with
the Government.   Even in Gooldi, where our direct
authority is not yet established, the influence arising from
this quasi-family connection has produced very important
results.   The example of fifty-three heads of families who
have relinquished the usage, forming a close and distinctive
connection with the Government, has necessarily produced
a strong impression upon all; and more authority has
been practically derived from this measure, directly and
indirectly, than I could have hoped to acquire through the

use of all the other means which are available, in a very long period.

'These, then, are the chief measures which have been employed for the abolition of the usage, viz. :—first, the establishment of the authority of Government through the dispensation of justice ; secondly, the use of arguments addressed against the opinions and reasonings by which the practice is supported ; thirdly, the application of influence acquired by the marriage of female wards of the Government to chiefs of the tribes acted upon ; and I may add, as means of high importance, fourthly, the protection of Khond traders from violence on the roads, and from fraud in the markets of the low country ; and fifthly, the use of every art to win the support of the Khond women to our object.[1] . . . .

'I have been at much pains to obtain a correct nominal return of the female children born and preserved in Pondacole, Deegee, and the partly-gained half of Gooldi (showing their tribes, branches, villages, and fathers' names) during the two last years ; and I have the high satisfaction to state, that above 170 female infants have certainly been saved in those tracts in that period—two-thirds of the number within the last fifteen months—through our direct influence.'

---

[1] The manner in which these proceedings were regarded in England appears from the following extract from a letter from the Court of Directors to the Government of Madras, dated 2nd April 1845 : ' We have perused with much interest the further reports submitted by Captain Macpherson of the measures which he has adopted, with so much success, for the suppression of the practices of human sacrifice and female infanticide among the Khond tribes. The judgment and energy which characterise his benevolent efforts warrant us in the confident expectation that he will, at no distant period, succeed in altogether banishing this barbarous rite from the tracts under our control.'

CHAPTER XVI.

MR. CADENHEAD'S MANAGEMENT OF THE KHONDS.

1844-1845.

MR. CADENHEAD, though new to civil office, proved himself fully equal to the charge which the Government had
confided to him.   He first visited the infanticidal tribes,
for the purpose of extending the influence of the Government by bestowing some of its wards in marriage there,
and of endeavouring to compose once more the internecine
feud which had long raged between the people of Grundawady and those of Darungabady, the two branches of
the great tribe of Gooldi.[1]   Some extracts from his letters,
written at this time to Captain Macpherson, are here
subjoined, as illustrative of Khond manners :—

'Souradah, 14th December 1844.

'Two or three days ago about 130 of the chief people
of Pondacole, Deegee, and the Grundawady portion of
Gooldi arrived.   To-day we bestowed on the chief men
twelve of our female wards in marriage.   They were in
great request ; every unmarried man would gladly have
received one.   We have retained eight for the Darungabady portion of Gooldi, whose arrival we are looking
for with deep anxiety.   In the three first-named districts it is alleged that there has been no destruction
of female life since your measures last year.   Many of
the Pondacole people who were not pledged to preserve
their children have nevertheless done so, led by the

[1] See above, p. 221.

example of their neighbours. The marriages went off with great *eclât*, but were attended with an unexpected difficulty. The hussies absolutely pretended to have a right of choice ! One little vixen unconditionally refused to accept the one chosen for her—a fellow of herculean mould, about forty-five years old, and a man of wealth— / and, forsooth, because she said he was too old for her ! We were absolutely obliged to give her to another somewhat younger. Hercules, however, was not disappointed ; we gave him another.

'Their state of mind is highly favourable on every point, except in the case of the continued warfare on the part of the Grundawady portion of Gooldi. They say, "You promised us justice. Give it to us in this case, which is our great, our only grievance. Restore our fields of which we have been forcibly dispossessed, and save our villages from fire and pillage ! You forbade us to combine to wage war on our opponents or to protect ourselves, as Government was to put an end to strife, and to arbitrate between us. Fulfil your promise !"

' We by no means see our way yet. The management of the assemblies is, as yet, difficult to me—especially as I take up your work in the middle, and these people wont bear repetition.

'The delay in the final settlement of the new plan and of your return has been a great blow to us. We confidently anticipated great deeds Boad-wards ; and now, after the completion of our work here—if, by God's blessing, we shall be able to complete it—we shall be reduced to comparative inactivity. Mr. Anstruther[1] restored the revenue supervision of Souradah[2] on my letter. Had he not done so, I think we could have done nothing; we

---

[1] The gentleman officiating for Mr. Bannerman.

[2] Souradah was a zemindary under the Ganjam Agency, and had, owing to local causes, been withdrawn from Mr. Cadenhead's control. But it was only in the character of collector, or representative of the Government in the exercise of rights which in some respects bear analogy to those of an

should have been entirely powerless, and the object of
ridicule to the whole population.   With these difficult
people of Gooldi we cannot afford the loss of an atom
of our status.'

' Souradah, 23rd December 1844.

'In my last I told you that the Darungabadians, 300
in number, were on their way to visit us.   Next day the
300 dwindled to five men of no note, followed next
day by twelve—only one of whom was a chief of any
influence.   We exerted all our energies to produce an
impression on them, and we set them and the Grundawadians a-talking to discover the original cause of quarrel ;
wherein, of course, there was no difficulty.   The minds
of the two parties were at once displayed by their manner
of carrying on the conversation.   It was done with
little animation, and without us to keep it agoing, could
not have been commenced, and would at once have
ceased.   At first the Darungabadians turned their backs
entirely on the others, and addressed their talk solely to
us.   After a time they veered round a little, but never
fairly looked at the others ; and addressed part of their
conversation to them—opposing their statements by
counter-statements.   The Grundawadians, on the other
hand (all except the chief), looked at them fairly, and
had no hesitation in directing their talk to them.   After
doing all we could, we sent the small party back to
their section, with directions to assemble all its members
to ascertain, and to return and report to us in seven days,
their views—whether the branch was inclined to peace,
or was still determined to persist in war with their
brethren of Grundawady ; in which case we should
manifest our intentions with regard to them.

'It is plain that nothing can be done towards suppressing
infanticide till our supremacy is acknowledged, and our

universal landlord [see above, p. 175], that any officer could have that
authority with the people of Souradah which was necessary to influence
them to abstain from infanticide. Mr. Cadenhead therefore urged and obtained its restoration.

mediation in the administration of justice accepted as its type ; and of course also, until this happens, we cannot bestow upon them in marriage the damsels whom we have reserved for them.'

'Souradah, 26th December 1844.

'Old Strikana Bunje[1] is now at Pooree, and has already a vakeel at the Agent's cutcherry. Already people begin to talk. It is highly desirable to have the old villain sent back to his lair at Benares. He is here to create annoyance in some way or other ; at all events, his near neighbourhood unsettles men's minds. Sam Bissye's sons still try to keep up his and their influence. They are already spreading reports that Sam Bissye is forthwith again to present himself and establish old customs.'

'Souradah, 28th December 1844.

'We are now full of hope. From the Darungabadians' report, confirmed by our Panwa spies, it appears that fear is the prevalent mental state at present, and the branch, generally, is therefore disposed to conclude peace at the Circar's desire ; the only dissentient being a very chief man who has lost two brothers in the course of the war, and who declares that he must fight for another season, so as to have two lives equivalent to his brothers, and that then he will be prepared to speak of peace. We had a talk this morning ; the Darungabadians came first, and some soon after the Grundawadians. It was plain at once that the minds of the Darungabadians had undergone a change ; they did not turn their backs on the other party, and soon entered freely into talk. There was a long conversation, of a very satisfactory character ; and we were nearly breaking up to bestow one of our wards on the Darungabadians, when, happily, a Grundawadian proposed that they should drink together and then talk. The chief Darungabadian—a *dour chiel*—

---

[1] Formerly Rajah of Goomsur. He was the father of the deposed rajah, who died in 1836.

at first opposed this proposal, on the ground that the representatives of the whole branch were not present; that he was only the head of one brother's house; that the head of the other was absent.   It was of course immediately retorted that they said they had come in the name of all; whereas now, when a proper plan of conciliation was proposed, they said they were merely the representatives of one sub-branch.   After a few words the drinking plan was agreed to and arranged, the first objection having somewhat the appearance of maiden coyness.   Well, we seated them to their drink, and in a twinkling all were as "thick as thieves:" those who a moment before were ready to break each other's· heads were now sworn brothers.   The *dour chiel* and the Grundawadians had a long and most satisfactory talk; the younger spirits then let off their superabundant steam in a grand conjoint dance, and we solemnised the marriages.   They all danced off the ground, and have now gone to feast on a pig, as happy as possible.   We thus have them entirely in our own hands.   As soon as the ground is dry and supplies ready we start, four days hence or so.   The affair will now occupy us three or four days, at the most; whereas formerly no one could foretell or foresee its end—a most happy change of aspect, and, as you may imagine, it has quite revived our drooping spirits.   We bestowed one of our damsels on the *dour chiel,* and the other three on fine young fellows, all sons of chiefs—one a very excitable spirit, and apparently one of the war-party.   Of course all these must be our firm friends and allies, and we have thus secured an immense diversion even in the midst of the adverse camp, if indeed it can now be called so; as the Darungabady party, long before the termination of the fray, began to bespeak an equal measure of the Circar's affection to that heretofore bestowed on the Grundawadians, and to arrange plans of cooperation for the general good.'

Having thus laid the foundation of confidence and amity

between the contending parties, and between the Government and each party, Mr. Cadenhead proceeded to Gooldi to complete the pacification.　He writes[1] :—

'I first held counsel with each party separately; discussed the circumstances of the feud, and the necessity which had now arisen for a final pacification.　As the people of Grundawady had already done, so now those of Darungabady used every art to excite my feelings against their opponents.　They declared that it was quite impossible for them, while the earth was still moist with the blood of their chief, while his ghost still wandered unappeased, to make peace, to enter into friendly relations with his slayers; who were, moreover, so false, that though, after concluding peace, they might not attempt to injure them by open violence, they would yet unceasingly exert their diabolical magical arts for their destruction.　They then begged for one more year's war, after which they would be prepared to listen to terms of peace.　Finally, they pleaded for one grand pitched battle, to be waged in my presence—a proposition also made by the people of Grundawady.　Those who had been gained at Souradah excused themselves as impotent to alter the tendency of the feelings of the people.　They said they had done their utmost to produce a pacific disposition in their brethren, but had failed, as the warlike propensities of all classes were too strong to be swayed by their individual efforts.　At last, perceiving my purpose fixed, they gradually yielded.

'It is the custom of these tribes when, after being engaged in war, they meet to conclude peace, to allay their feelings of still ungratified animosity by performing a war-dance in each other's presence, during which they mutually defy each other, and vaunt their prowess in war; occasionally, with loud cries, rushing towards each other, flourishing their axes, as if to meet in mortal combat.　Fearful that such a mimic display might end in a terrible

[1] Report of 17th March 1845.

reality—either from excited feelings mastering yet immature better resolves, or through the wilful malice of some
violent favourer of war—I had my small party drawn up in
double line between the factions.   The people of Grundawady did not propose to dance, but, after performing their
salutations, retired to a little distance and quietly seated
themselves.   The people of Darungabady also approached
in perfect quietness, the chiefs unarmed and with smiling
countenances : suddenly a young lad, and a brother of
the slain chief, commenced whooping and dancing ; in a
moment the whole mass was in commotion, pouring forth
the foulest abuse against their opponents.   The chiefs did
their utmost to control the .excitement, without avail.
For a little while the people of Grundawady bore the
abuse with calmness ; at length their patience forsook
them—they rose as one man, and endeavoured to rush on
their foes.   The scene was now one of fearful excitement.

'Happily, the sepoys and sebundies behaved with the
utmost coolness and determination ; and we succeeded,
after a hard struggle, in beating back both parties
without serious injury to anyone.   But a different result
was so imminent, that one Grundawady axe actually took
effect, though, fortunately, the injury was no more than a
scratch.   When the excitement was in some degree allayed,
the chiefs met, and the question of the engagement to be
entered into for the preservation of peace was discussed
with as much calmness and good-humour as if nothing
had occurred.   After much animated discussion, it was
finally agreed that the ceremonial should be the most
binding their religion and customs could furnish.   On
the morning of the second day after, it was completed,
apparently amidst general joy.   I then made arrangements for the maintenance of peace hereafter, through the
settlement of all disputes between tribes and branches as
they should arise ; and I told them that Government
was determined to put an end to, and would certainly
punish those who should hereafter engage in, private

warfare. At this meeting, as well as at a preceding visit from the chiefs of Darungabady, agriculture and commerce formed the chief topics of conversation, whereas formerly war had been the sole engrossing subject.

'In the course of these negotiations I derived most material assistance from the four wards married into the Darungabady tribe, and from their husbands—the paternal bond which now united these to Government having equal if not superior strength to the tribal bond. I determined, therefore, still further to increase this connection, by the bestowal of other five wards who still remained to be disposed of, introducing one into the family of the malcontents. Besides these, I also introduced thirteen others into districts where their influence was most likely to be beneficially exercised.'

Mr. Cadenhead on this occasion remarks as follows:—
'The effects of Captain Macpherson's operations among these tribes have been the establishment of the supremacy and, to some extent, the actual exercise of the authority of Government over the tribes of Pondacole and Deegee ; and a tendency among the surrounding people to regard it as a rightful—certainly irresistible—controlling power, followed in one [of those tribes] by an entire relinquishment, and in the other by a notable decrease, of the practice of infanticide. In like manner the new political relations with the tribes of Darungabady, Grundawady, and their nearer allies, now entered into, may with certainty be expected to effect their entire abandonment of this practice. . . . It is, moreover, to be remarked, that since Captain Macpherson's first visit to these tribes, their ideas with regard to infanticide have undergone important modifications. They have perceived the force and truth of his arguments, admit the inutility of the practice, and deeply feel the imputations on their manhood involved in its continuance under the conditional religious sanction adduced by them, while the rest of mankind do not require to resort to it. So

sensitive were they on this point, that they cut short the conversation on the subject, saying that—" They had already heard and understood the will of the Government ; that they were not beasts, that we should deem it necessary again and again to repeat the same sentiments to convince them of their truth, and to induce them to yield obedience." '

Mr. Cadenhead proceeds :—' In his report, dated 10th July 1844, Captain Macpherson states that, since the commencement of our operations among these tribes, 170 children had been saved chiefly through our efforts. It now affords me the highest gratification to be able to affirm, after the strictest enquiries, that since the date of that report not a single child has been destroyed in the two districts of Pondacole and Deegee, and that many have been saved in Boree and in Gooldi.'

This testimony of Mr. Cadenhead—an officer of great acuteness—shows that Captain Macpherson had not been misled as to the effect of his measures in checking infanticide.

Leaving the infanticidal tribes, Mr. Cadenhead next visited the (late) sacrificing tracts of Goomsur. Hodzoghor he found much distracted by the intrigues of the family of Sam Bissye, who held themselves out as the champions of the restoration of the ancient rite, and had got up a most dangerous conspiracy against the Dulbehra ; and he considered it plain that the Khonds could be led to believe in the stability of the policy of the Government only by the permanent removal of every member of the family to a distance from the Hills. The administration of justice had been satisfactory to the Goomsur people, and very few complaints were brought to him for decision. In conclusion, he reported as follows :—

' The forbearance of the Khonds of all the Goomsur tracts with respect to sacrifice has been greatly tried by the state of affairs in Boad ; where they have seen sacrifices celebrated, the orders of Government with regard

to the delivery of victims set at nought, and the authority
of the Rajah openly resisted.

. . . . 'I conceive that our measures in Goomsur
are not in immediate danger, while it is generally
believed that the Boad, and all other tracts where the
rite is still celebrated, will soon be subjected to the
same system which has proved successful in Goomsur,
and while no event occurs violently to disturb men's
minds. If, however, immediate steps shall not be· taken
to bring all under one uniform system ; if, in spite of the
efforts at present directed towards Boad, the rite shall
still continue to be there celebrated ; if, month after
month, the very shouts of the sacrificers shall be heard
by people who have only relinquished the rite condition-
ally ; or if, while our efforts are still distracted and
diverse, any great calamity—such as famine or desolating
sickness—shall overtake the Goomsur tracts, their fall
would seem to be inevitable. In the one case they would
conceive themselves no longer bound to adhere to their
share of the contract, since we had apparently failed to
perform ours ; and, in the other, the general overwhelm-
ing dread of the wrath of their gods would soon over-
power the individual fear of the anger of Government.

'Besides the woman intended for sacrifice in Hodzoghor, and her infant of two months, I brought down
two boys and a girl from Athara Mootah. These, when
the victims of Athara Mootah were delivered up, had
escaped, and remained hid till Captain Macpherson left
the Hills, when they returned to their former possessors,
with whom, as these gave surety for their safety, they
were allowed to remain. As these parties now declined
to continue answerable for them, I removed them to
Nowgaum and Souradah.'

Some of the occurrences of this summer are worth
noting :—

'Gopalpore, 5th June 1846.

'The result of Baba's and Soondera's last visit to Souradah has been a grand assembly at Darungabady,—not tribal but branch—at which the weak war-party was finally, I hope, suppressed. A flying visit to Boree next season en route to Boad will, I think, render us supreme in Sikko Bodo, and place Khond infanticide in this quarter among the things that were.

'What would Sir H. Hardinge say to his ideas on vaccination having been anticipated many years ago by some imperial Colonel who, by means of the rajah—if I remember rightly—had the whole country side caught and vaccinated at once? Every other man now bears good and laudable marks to this day. And you may further tell him that we did not neglect to take the initiatory step.'

Notwithstanding the continued bad influence of the sacrifices in Boad, which more than once caused the chiefs of Goomsur to declare to Mr. Cadenhead that they must immediately recur to the practice unless it was prevented among their neighbours; yet through Mr. Cadenhead's excellent management, the Goomsur Khonds were preserved from the dreaded lapse into their ancient bloody practices, though those of them who lived near Boad were much in the position of a reclaimed drunkard who is placed in the midst of a drinking party.

It may be convenient to mention in this place what became of the victims rescued by Captain Macpherson. The statement is taken from the latest of the admirable series of articles on the Khonds, contributed to the 'Calcutta Review' by the Rev. Dr. Duff,[1] to whom Lord Hardinge communicated all the official papers for the express purpose; articles remarkable, above all things, for their scrupulous accuracy and impartiality, and to which these Memorials are greatly indebted :—

'The victims of both sexes, who had been stolen from parents that could be discovered, were, in every such in-

---

[1] 'Calcutta Review,' vols. v., vi., viii., x.

stance, restored to their families. Those whom their unnatural parents had sold were not, save in one or two very
special excepted cases, restored to them, because it was
all but certain that they would sell them again.

'The males under age, whose parents or natural
guardians could not be discovered, and who consequently
remained under the sole tutelage of Government, were
variously disposed of in such ways as promised most for
their benefit. In the year 1843, and subsequently, when
Captain Macpherson acted as head assistant to the Governor's Agent, Ganjam, he gave of those children to all the
Christian householders, whether European or East Indian,
who offered and engaged to support and bring them up
usefully until they could maintain themselves. Of the
rest, for reasons unknown to us, he gave a few for *bonâ
fide* adoption by Mussulmans whom he knew to be men of
substance and good character. In this mode of distributing
a portion of them he acted according to the rule which he
found in existence, of giving only one victim to each individual applicant.

'Mr. Sutton, of Cuttack, having applied for a large
number (150) of victims, Captain Macpherson transmitted
his application to his own superior, Mr. Bannerman, who
alone could warrantably deal with it. On Mr. Bannerman's leaving the district, early in 1844, and Captain
Macpherson's assuming temporary charge of his office,
the latter found that nothing had been done in the matter
of Mr. Sutton's application. He then at once addressed
the Madras Government, proposing that it should empower
him to distribute the victims in considerable numbers
amongst the several missionary and charitable institutions
that would engage to support, train, and educate them—
giving to each institution according to its apparent means
of making effectual and permanent provision for them.
Before receiving any reply to this communication, and
under the direct instruction of Mr. Anstruther, who soon
succeeded Mr. Bannerman as acting Agent, he gave some

eight or ten boys into the charge of the military chaplain
at Vizagapatam, who made them over to a missionary
there, from whom they effected their escape back to
Captain Macpherson a few months after, when, with the
chaplain's consent, they were delivered to the Baptist missionaries at Berhampore.

" At last the Madras Government wrote, in reply to the
letter of the beginning of 1844, that its desire was, that
such of the victims as were not otherwise already provided
for should, if possible, be reunited, if not to their families,
at least to their tribes or race; and directed Captain
Macpherson to report if this could be accomplished.   In
reply, he stated that they might be engrafted on the low-
country Khonds by settling them in their villages, and
setting them up, each with a plough and a pair of bullocks
and a year's seed, with a grant of a piece of jungle-land.
The Government adopted this proposal, and sanctioned
the expenditure of fifteen rupees a victim, which its execution would entail.   Before, however, the plan could be
fully carried out, Captain Macpherson was compelled by
ill-health to leave the district.   But it is specially worthy
of note, that throughout the whole time a schoolmaster
was employed by him to teach the boys to read and write
Oriya—the language already spoken by some, and more
or less understood by the majority of them, and the only
one containing any ready-made books; and this the Agent
found, by occasional examination, that they were very
fairly taught.   The females were also employed in spin-
ning thread, but the results of their labours in this department did not amount to anything very considerable.

'As to adults, or those who had reached the age of pu-
berty, they were variously disposed of, under sundry
checks and guarantees for their welfare.   Young men
became servants or apprentices, or were set up as petty
farmers, in the manner already indicated.   Of the rescued
females, all, with a very few exceptions, were of marriage-
able age, or just approaching to it.   Many of them were

married to male victims and to persons of inferior caste
in the low country, receiving small dowries of ten or
twelve rupees from the Government. Of the rest, four-
fifths were married to Khonds of substance and influence
in the infanticidal tribes; and arrangements were made
for a like disposal of the remainder, all under the
strongest securities for proper treatment and adequate
provision—any failure or shortcoming in the stipulated
contracts or engagements being foreordained as sure to
incur the serious displeasure of the Circar, or supreme
Sovereign Power.'

Captain Macpherson's fixed purpose was, as early as
possible, to carry education into the Hills—his great object
being, through the moral and religious advancement of
the Khonds, by educating them, to complete and render
permanent the change in their ancestral faith and usages,
which he had first brought about through personal, social,
and political means. While he was in Calcutta in 1845,
he repeatedly wrote to Mr. Cadenhead, expressing his
great anxiety that some measures should be adopted as
speedily as possible to attempt to establish schools on the
Hills. To effect this, the first thing to be done was to
reduce the Khond language to writing and exactness, in
order that it might be properly taught to the persons who
should be fit to undertake the office of schoolmasters; so
that they, in their turn, might be duly qualified to
communicate with their pupils. Towards the end of 1845,
therefore, Mr. Cadenhead began the acquisition of the
Khond language, but was able to make comparatively slow
progress from the numerous demands upon his time and
attention. The increasing difficulties in the Agency compelled him again and again, temporarily, to suspend his
labours in the matter. Nevertheless he persevered; and
eventually he succeeded in collecting and writing out, in
the Oriya character, an account of the manner in which
the Meriah rite is performed, and of its origin—as nearly
as possible in the words of the religious songs or hymns

which are chaunted at the time of the sacrifice by the
parties engaged in its performance; an account of the
origin of a feud between two tribes, and of the sacrifices
and ceremonies to the god of war on the commencement
of hostilities—of the battles—and of the return to peace;
an account of the Khond view of the creation of man;
an account of the Khond reasons why men, but not animals,
are doomed to labor;. four purely Khond fables, and two
fables translated from the Oriya.[1]

[1] See 'Calcutta Review,' vol. x., p. 336.

CHAPTER XVII.

THE HILL AGENCY—FIFTH VISIT TO THE HILLS.

NOVEMBER 1845—MAY 1846.

ANOTHER and a more gloomy chapter of this little history must now be presented. For fifteen months Mr. Cadenhead (though much embarrassed at times, through the impatience with which the people of Goomsur witnessed the sacrifice going on unchecked in Boad) carried out most successfully the plan of operations devised and acted on by Captain Macpherson for the suppression of the sacrifice, and of female infanticide, through measures essentially conciliatory.

This time was spent by Captain Macpherson in communicating personally with the Supreme Government with reference to the comprehensive Agency which it was proposed to establish for reclaiming the hill-tribes of Orissa from both their sanguinary practices 'by gradual and voluntary operations, without resorting to force or intimidation.' [1]

As the tribes addicted to these customs were scattered through territories subject to different jurisdictions, the new Agency was to be superintended by the Government of India, as the paramount power. Unfortunately, the gentlemen forming the Government of Madras were disposed to make it a point of honour that they should

---

[1] Resolutions of the Government of India, dated 19th July and 6th December 1845.

retain the control of these operations, which, they observed, had prospered in their hands ; although they had
written, for three years together, that they were about to
submit a new general plan to the Supreme Government.
Being overruled, they felt deeply wounded, and they hotly
contested every square mile of territory which it was proposed to assign to the new Agency.

It was intended that the Khond tracts should be separated for a time from the political divisions to which they
belonged—should be placed under the new and special
Agency, which, it was hoped, would reclaim them—and
should be restored, one by one, to the old authorities,
whenever that work had been accomplished.   But not
only were the Khond tracts to be thus separated : the
Hindu Rajahs or Zemindars of the low-country to whom
they were attached, and without whose cooperation it
would have been vain to approach them, were also to be
placed under the Agent.   Thus the neighbouring civil
jurisdictions would be shorn of part of their territory,
and the sphere of influence and profit of the native
establishments[1] would be circumscribed.   The native
employés in Ganjam naturally viewed this change with
jealousy, and being aware that the Government at Madras
was highly adverse to it, thought they should at once
promote their own interests and gratify their superiors
by opposing it in every way.   A similar feeling prevailed
among the officials of the districts of Cuttack and of the
South-west Frontier.

The Government of India—framed chiefly for review,
and at no time happily constituted for direct and original management—was now inexpressibly weakened
by the departure of the Governor-General, Sir Henry
Hardinge, to the North-west, his legal powers in Southern India passing to Sir T. H. Maddock, as President of
the Council.

The organisation of the Agency had been greatly

---

[1] See above, p. 147.

impeded by the grave political questions with which the Governor-General was occupied. Had Sir Henry Hardinge, who entirely adopted the principle of the measure during the autumn of 1844, thought fit at that season to devote but a little time to its details, the constancy of the Goomsur Khonds would have been saved from a long and severe strain; those of Boad must have yielded to the influence of an Agent manifestly supported by the earnest will of the Government, and empowered to assure them of kind treatment; and the abolition movement might soon have been extended to more distant regions. At length, in November 1845, after a delay which had greatly unsettled men's minds in Orissa, Captain Macpherson returned to Ganjam with the title of 'Governor-General's Agent for the Suppression of Meriah Sacrifice and Female Infanticide in the Hill Tracts of Orissa.' The requisite legal powers, however, had not even yet been conferred upon him, though he had urged upon the Government the necessity of immediate action upon the district of Boad before the return of the season for sacrifice.

When, at length, he was empowered to act, the Zemindary of Souradah, the scene of his most successful operations against infanticide, was, by an unhappy accident, omitted from the territory assigned to him. He had formerly influenced the people of Souradah as representative (under the Ganjam Agent) of the Government:[1] he had now lost that derivative authority, and had not received any new authority in his own person, as they had been led to expect; but with the sanction of Mr. Bannerman, who had returned from the Cape, he resumed his operations among them, assuring them that he should soon receive full powers to administer the affairs of their zemindary.[2]

[1] See above, p. 227.

[2] He would have gone at once to Boad, but he could not do so without previous personal communication with the Rajah; and the Rajah had purposely gone out of the way, so that he could not be conferred with till the middle of February.

'I have been dealing,' he wrote in the beginning of 1846, ' with the infanticidal tribes, and have got through the work to a wish. The practice may certainly be considered at an end in the tracts on which I have acted. After communicating very fully with all the infanticidal tribes of Souradah, I am very thankful that I can say that we could not wish them to be in a better state of mind, and that I am now engaged in active aggression upon the neighbouring tribes of Chinna-Kimedy. Our justice, producing order everywhere, and the influence derived from the invaluable device of wiving the chief men with the honoured daughters of the State—our rescued victim-girls—have given us complete mastery over these tribes, considered the most intractable division of the Khond population in this quarter. Cadenhead managed them very well in my absence, under trying circumstances.

' We are, as yet, all well, living in a beautiful mango-grove by a river which springs in the mountain-chain fifteen miles off.'

There was much to render the attempt upon Boad a difficult and doubtful enterprise. The people could only be approached through their head ; and the wretched little Court of the Rajah was agitated by conflicting personal and family pretensions. The Rajah's own title was doubtful; two men of influence contended for the office of premier; two families carried on a hereditary strife for the office of Khonro (equivalent to Bissye, and involving the chief management of the Rajah's relations with the Khonds) ; it was impossible to form connections with any of these chiefs, without throwing his rival into violent opposition.

Moreover, the tribes could not be dealt with singly, like those of Goomsur, because they had been accustomed to act in groups for common objects, and because they were divided into a great number of nearly independent branches, which it was necessary to keep in view at the same time.

The tract over which they were scattered in Boad was about ninety miles long by thirty broad, difficult of access, and very little known ; and the nearest point of it was forty miles from any place where the Agent could permanently reside.

The jealousy of the Rajah opposed a further obstacle to the introduction of the direct authority of Government into the Khond country ; all the Zemindars regarding their tracts of that country as the stronghold—in their language 'the maternal bosom'—to which they had owed, and might still owe, the preservation of their families, and of their qualified independence.

The Boad Khonds having already learnt, from the example of Goomsur, that a community might abandon sacrifice and yet live, had made up their minds to yield, if they found that the 'Circar,' notwithstanding its long delays, was really in earnest ; but they offered to the earth-goddess one immense valedictory sacrifice, comprising 125 victims—which might have been prevented if the Government of India had acted with more alacrity in giving powers to the Agent.

Notwithstanding all these difficulties, the case pressed for action—Boad must be won or Goomsur would be lost; and in March 1846, though the safe season was over, the Agent, with Mr. Cadenhead (who had been appointed to the office of Principal Assistant in the new Agency), went to the Hills of Boad, preceded by the Rajah, who had at length appeared, and had promised his cooperation.

After some very curious preliminary fencing and finesse, the Boad Khonds yielded to the persuasions of the Agent, and of the Goomsur Khonds, who attended him (as the reclaimed tribes had formerly gone with him among the unreclaimed tribes of Goomsur[1]) as the zealous missionaries

---

[1] See above, p. 198.

of abolition.   They came into allegiance to the Government, and brought their victims to him, at a place called Bissipurra, to the number of 172 ; and he commenced the decision of their cases in conjunction with the tribal authorities, one of whom, a chief of importance, observed— 'I now see the magic by which Goomsur has been conquered!' Everything seemed to be in the best train, when suddenly the Khonds grew distant and reserved in their demeanour : they had become possessed with the delusion, that the delivery of their victims was a token of subjection, and that they were forthwith to be subjected to taxation and forced labour.

This absurd notion was produced by the machinations of Kurtivas, the Rajah's uncle, but of illegitimate birth ; who, having once held and abused the chief power in Boad, desired to involve the Khonds in difficulties with the Government, and so to increase his own importance and recover his former position.

Ever since a partial interference with the rite had commenced on the part of the Cuttack authorities, this man had received fees for permitting each sacrifice that took place.   Aided by certain Hindu and freebooting Khond chiefs, who for good reasons did not wish to see Boad brought under obedience to the Government, he set on foot intrigues, in which he contrived to involve the Rajah himself, in order to distract the minds of the Khonds, and engage them in forcible opposition to the Agent ; assuring them that, if they resisted that officer successfully, they would be withdrawn from his jurisdiction, and retransferred to that of the Commissioner of Cuttack.

The Rajah and all his servants naturally desired to remain under the jurisdiction of Cuttack, being already acquainted with the usages and with many of the public officers of that province ; while the Khonds firmly believed that the Cuttack authorities did not require the absolute relinquishment of the sacrifice, but only the annual delivery of a certain number of victims.

Captain Macpherson, on observing this change in the Khonds of Boad, sent for the leading men, and told them that if they repented of having delivered up their Meriahs, they were free to take them back and to go in peace. They refused, saying that they had given them up voluntarily, and that they did not intend to recur to human sacrifice. But they maintained their reserve, and did not open their minds. Next morning they returned, in a state of wild excitement, and demanded the delivery of the Meriahs. They had, they said, abandoned the sacrifice, but they had discovered that their delivery of the victims was a token of servitude, and they were determined to have them back.

The Rajah, seeing that Captain Macpherson had ordered his escort to fire at once if any violence was attempted, felt how deeply he was compromised by this outbreak, which he had fomented; and, trembling for his zemindary and his life, he now interposed, and requested that the victims might be given up to *him*, upon his personal pledge for their safety, and also for their redelivery when he should have had time to disabuse the minds of the Khonds. The Meriahs were given up to the Rajah accordingly. By delivery to the Agent, they had ceased to be acceptable victims.[1] It may be stated in this place,

[1] See above, p. 115: and see also Appendix C. General Campbell makes the following statement ('Personal Narrative,' p. 89):—'I have no wish to dwell upon these deplorable mistakes of judgment, or to bring odium upon any one responsible for them; but I must say, that I have not the faintest doubt that this rapid transition of the Khonds from a spirit of confidence and obedience, as evinced by the delivery of their victims, to one of distrust and revolt, accompanied by demands not unlike threats, was caused exclusively by the exactions and oppressions to which they had been subjected by the native assistants of Captain Macpherson. Money was extorted from them, cooking utensils were forcibly carried away, and even the Rajah himself was mulcted of a pair of gold armlets.' This is the allegation of two noted rebels and supporters of the sacrifice. It was solemnly enquired into, and the following decision pronounced by the Government of India, adopting the Report of Mr. Commissioner Grant (mentioned below, Chap. XXI.):—'It is alleged by Kurtivas Baboo and Bir Khonro, that the native servants abused and ill-treated the Khonds, and insisted on their paying them money. Mr. Grant is satisfied that the

that they were in course of free redelivery to Captain
Macpherson, when he was suddenly removed from office
in March 1847 ; that upwards of sixty of them had been
delivered to him, while not one perished, before that date ;
and that after his removal had taken place, under circumstances which might naturally be expected to expose the
remaining victims to the utmost danger,[1] the rest of them
were recovered by General Campbell in the spring of 1848,
with the exception, as he states, of three, who ' had been
sacrificed to defeat the success of our [i. e., his own and
his assistant's] endeavours ; ' while, on the contrary,
Captain Frye, the General's successor in office, uses
language which can only be understood as a positive
official denial that any one of them was sacrificed.[2]

From the day when the victims were delivered back
to the Rajah, the Meriah question became one of
secondary importance ; and it was on the grand delusion
of the intended taxation and forced labour that the resistance to the Government turned. No doubt, if the
resistance had ultimately proved successful, the Khonds
would have attributed its success to the revived power of

charge is wholly untrue, and that the real cause of the rising was an idea
infused into the minds of the Khonds—not by any person connected with the
Agency, and not by reason of any act of any person connected with the
Agency—that giving up their Meriahs was only the first step to taxation and
servitude.'—Resolution of Government of India, 7th October 1848.

According to General Campbell (' Personal Narrative,' p. 88), the Rajah
of Boad ' was a poor imbecile youth, utterly incapable of influencing Khonds
or others, for good or evil. His guarantee, if ever given, which he himself
stoutly denied, was entirely worthless.' It was not on account of the
personal qualities of the Rajah that his guarantee (which was the very
basis of all his subsequent communications with Captain Macpherson)
was valuable, but on account of his great hereditary influence. General
Campbell says, in his Report of 16th April 1848 :—' The Rajah of Boad
with his Paiks rendered good service, and I invariably supported his
authority with the people of the Maliahs. He very strongly protested
against being made responsible for the redelivery of the Meriahs restored
to the Khonds, and professed his utter inability to accomplish it himself ;
nevertheless, he very creditably exerted himself, and his protracted sojourn
in the Hills has no doubt been a cause of great expense to himself and his
establishment.'

[1] See below, Chapter XX.   [2] See Appendix C.

the earth-goddess, and would have relapsed into human sacrifice; but this was not the point upon which they commenced and continued their opposition.

The only question for Captain Macpherson to consider was—What was the right course for an Agent to pursue, who had been entrusted with power for the express purpose of bringing about the abandonment by these Khonds of their most ancient rites, by convincing them, as he had done in Goomsur, that the sacrifice was unnecessary?

Many will say, 'These men had arms in their hands. True, they were savages; it was their first meeting with the Agent; they were under a delusion which they had not intelligence to resist, propagated as it was by the very men whom they had been accustomed to look to for guidance. Nevertheless, the authority of the Government should have been vindicated—they ought to have been shot down without mercy!' This sounds more vigorous, but Captain Macpherson chose the better part, and he was amply rewarded by the result: for it was the opinion—afterwards fully ascertained—of every man in Boad whose opinion was of any value, that the forbearance shown on this occasion proved only the lenity and kindness of the Government, and ultimately led to the voluntary submission of those who now stood out.

The main and permanent end of the Agency, the substitution of a true for a false belief on the subject of the necessity of the sacrifice, had been attained. This advantage was endangered, without any fault of the Agent, by a movement arising out of a misapprehension of our objects, and it could only be retrieved by a proceeding to which there were serious objections. That proceeding was adopted; the embarrassments connected with it were in due time successfully disposed of, and the great object was secured.

What actually took place in the first instance was (as will be shown) a disturbed state of the hill-country of Boad, one-half of which Captain Macpherson (though grievously hindered by causes over which he had no control) had, at the moment of his removal, reduced to friendly obedience; while he was daily obtaining fresh adhesions in the other half, which must have been completely in his hands in a few days. What would have followed if a different course had been adopted, was the confirmation of the Khonds in all their delusions, and probably a war for their faith, which would have retarded for many years any further attempts at abolition.

Had the policy adopted by Captain Macpherson upon this occasion appeared to the Goomsur Khonds in any light save that of a further proof of the paternal mildness and benevolence with which he had always treated the hill-people, they must inevitably have inferred that the power of the earth-goddess was again in the ascendant, while that of the 'Circar,' which they associated with the god of light, was on the wane. But so far was this from being their impression, that they during this very year voluntarily abandoned the worship of the earth-goddess, and transferred their adoration to the supreme beneficence, which they worshipped under the name of the god of light.[1]

The victims having been given up, there was nothing further to be done at that time in Boad; and the Agent withdrew across the Goomsur border to Kunjeur, a few miles off. The Rajah and Kurtivas (the latter formally disavowing all connection with the rising) thought proper to accompany him thither; but he sent them back the same day to their own country,[2] to undeceive the Khonds, and bring in the victims.

The Rajah of Boad, after an ineffectual attempt to fulfil his promise, returned to the low-country. Kurtivas remained with the excited Khonds at Sangrimendi, a few miles from the camp of Captain Macpherson, who had now been reinforced by three companies of sepoys. Sam

---

[1] See above, p. 216.
[2] General Campbell's assertions on this subject are noticed in Appendix D.

Bissye's sons had been in concert with the conspirators at Bissipurra, where the victims were given up, and they brought the excited mob of Boad to attack the Agent's camp at Kunjeur in Goomsur on the 19th of March. There was no religious question here—it was an act of simple rebellion, and Captain Macpherson ordered a few shots to be fired to disperse them. One man was wounded, when all instantly fled across the Boad frontier; pursuit was prohibited. A week after, the Agent moved into Hodzoghor to put an end to the divisions of that tribe, having all its legitimate heads with him. By their advice he arrested five of the partisans of Sam Bissye's sons, who were providing large supplies for future mobs from Boad, and exciting the Khonds against the Government. One of the sons of Sam Bissye gave himself up.

• On the 1st of April, a mob of about 1,000 men, led by the two sons of Sam Bissye who were still at large, came to demand the release of the prisoners on pain of attack. A small party of the Agent's Sebundies and matchlock Paiks fired; four Khonds fell, and the whole crowd fled. A party of sepoys being added for show and noise, they were chased to a village, their place of rendezvous, about a mile from the camp, in which the sons of Sam Bissye and their friends had stored large supplies of provisions. That village the Khonds who accompanied the Agent plundered and fired. Its destruction was, unfortunately, rendered absolutely necessary by the circumstance that this mob intended not to fight and return home, but to take up its quarters in that and the neighbouring villages, and issue daily to attack the camp, or insult it at a safe distance; to send parties to cut off the dawks (letter-post), to prevent the collection of forage, and to pick off unarmed followers from the jungle.

The Agent now renewed his efforts to induce the partisans of the sons of Sam Bissye to submit to the authority of the Government and of their tribe: a very few came in and were pardoned—the rest held out with

inflexible obstinacy. The question of the reduction to
obedience of this party in Hodzoghor obviously involved
that of the maintenance or abdication of the authority of
the Government in the Khond tracts of Goomsur.

There was, in the judgment of all the Hindu and Khond
chiefs, and of every person with Captain Macpherson who
could form an opinion, but one mode of compelling this
party to submit—viz., the destruction of a few of their
villages. The recusant Khonds had moved from their
villages, according to the universal usage on such occasions, with their families and their property, into the
most inaccessible recesses of the Hills. But the season for
cultivation approached, and if they should not then be
sheltered by habitations, their fields must lie untilled.
Were their huts now destroyed, they must either promptly
make peace with their tribe (for *the tribe* was loyal: it
was only a faction that was in rebellion), so as to obtain
temporary hospitality and aid to construct new dwellings—
or entirely forego the cultivation of their lands for a year.
Thus, should they remain at war, the destruction of their
huts would be an extreme evil; while if they submitted,
as the labour of a very few weeks would suffice to rebuild
them, it would inflict only a moderate hardship—but a
light penalty for their offence. No description of force
can apprehend or kill the Khonds in their mountain fast-
nesses. They can be assailed there only, as was done in
the original Goomsur war, by parties sent expressly to
discover and burn their temporary dwellings and property,
and drive their families into the forests; the fighting men
are quite intangible to troops.

But had it even been possible to devise slower processes for the reduction of these malcontents, such
processes could not have been executed; for the great
and daily-increasing sickness both of Captain Macpherson's civil establishment and of his escort now
compelled his immediate return to the low-country. He
had therefore no course left but to direct the burning of

five villages of the chief recusants, and to authorise a division of the tribe itself to execute a like decree against the hamlets of three most faithless and determined public enemies in it.   The family of Sam Bissye having left their village, carrying away all their property, it was set fire to, either wilfully by their enemies, or by accident, but against the Agent's express orders.

The effects anticipated from this measure were immediately produced.   All both in Goomsur and in Boad were convinced that the authority of the Government was to be maintained ; the partisans of the sons of Sam Bissye immediately submitted ; the ascendency of the legitimate chiefs of the tribe was re-established, and all solemnly abjured the connection with Boad.   The sons of Sam Bissye fled thither with their families, and the Agent left the Goomsur tribes in perfect tranquillity on the 15th of April.   That tranquillity continued as long as he held office, except in one little tract[1] where no village had been burnt.   It has been already mentioned that these wooden villages are of no great value, being abandoned as a matter of course after they have stood about fourteen years, or earlier if they are thought to be haunted.[2]   In point of fact, the burnt villages were all rebuilt and reinhabited within five or six weeks.   To sum up in the words of Captain Macpherson :—

'In Boad my measures towards the Khonds were checked, at an advanced stage of their progress, by a bold and successful intrigue by the uncle of the Rajah, carried on with his privity and with the aid of certain Hindu chiefs, for the attainment mainly of his personal objects.   The Rajah, admitting his participation in that intrigue, sought and obtained an opportunity to atone for his fault by counteracting and remedying the evils produced.

'In Goomsur the uncle of the Boad Rajah attempted— for the same general objects, and through the same means,

---

[1] Lower Bopulmendi.   [2] See above, p. 61.

strengthened by the aid of the sons of Sam Bissye of Hodzoghor—to excite the Khond tribes to opposition to my authority. He succeeded only in a single section of Hodzoghor, devoted to the family of Sam Bissye. That section has been reduced to obedience to the authority of the Government and the tribe, but partly through coercive means, the necessity for the use of which is to be deplored.'

Some have objected to this mode of coercion, although both before and since the events just narrated it has been repeatedly resorted to in various parts of India.[1] The objection has arisen from the erroneous supposition that Captain Macpherson adopted the measure for the suppression of the sacrifice, and that the destruction of the villages involved the destruction of all the property of their inhabitants; from the habit of associating the idea of the burning of villages with the infliction of the worst horrors of war at once upon the innocent and the guilty; and from the notion that he might have pursued a course less repugnant to the general feelings of those who were distant from the scene.

But this measure was resorted to in no respect for the suppression of the sacrifice—for there had been no question of sacrifice in Hodzoghor for the three preceding years—but solely for the restoration of order among a portion of the population which had long been in allegiance to us. To leave that section of Hodzoghor leagued

---

[1] See above, p. 45. We find in the 'Personal Narrative' (p. 212), that General Campbell ordered the village of Bundari to be burnt, as the only means of saving the lives of the victims, whose sacrifice would have assuredly followed that which had been already perpetrated, had it been left unpunished; and (at p. 223) the people of Toopunga having attacked General Campbell, so that he was compelled to fire in self-defence, 'the courage of the men of Toopunga failed; and they fled, leaving their villages (from which all property had been removed some days before) to the mercy of the excited followers of the Oriyáh Chief of Shoobernagery who accompanied me, and who, with the matches of their matchlock guns, set fire to three small clusters of houses.' Indeed, to judge from certain recent notices of Khond affairs, it would seem that no other form of coercion applicable to the hill-country has yet been discovered.

in arms against our authority, and in opposition to the rest of Goomsur, would have been to leave Goomsur to anarchy; while the Government, which had induced the tribes to give up their old security for rights, the appeal to arms, was specially pledged to afford to them the blessings of order and peace. The villages destroyed were empty, and they were far fewer than the number indicated for punishment by the body of chiefs of Goomsur.[1] The measure produced immediate obedience; it was just, necessary, and successful.

[1] The Khonds do not consider themselves distinctly defeated unless their villages are destroyed.

CHAPTER XVIII.

RETURN FROM THE HILLS — RUIN OF THE INFANTICIDE WORK—NEGOTIATIONS WITH THE BOAD RAJAH—GENERAL WORSHIP OF THE GOD OF LIGHT—REFUSAL OF ESCORTS.

APRIL—OCTOBER 1846.

AFTER reaching the plains, Captain Macpherson wrote as follows to a friend : —

'Nowgaum, 20th April 1846.

' I do not think that my difficulties could have been greater than they lately have been. I cannot say one word as to the future, except that I see grounds for hope, and it may, I trust, be God's will that we shall prevail. I am thankful to feel that were the work to be done over again, I would pursue precisely the same course which I have taken. There is, of course, plenty of room for difference of opinion as to my policy, and the mass of men will simply judge by the result when it comes ; but I trust that when fully explained to you, you will approve of it. Although terribly poisoned with malaria and medicine, and worn out by the heavy strain of unintermitting anxiety, I am glad to say I can look forward with some confidence to be able to fight out the battle. Nothing alarms me so much as the idea of devolving the least of my responsibilities upon another person. You cannot, I dare say, understand the tone of malignant exultation in which some of the Madras writers on Khond affairs indulge : [1] I confess it is utterly inconceivable *to me.* I should have thought it impossible that an Agency like mine, working for good ends in the teeth of what all intelligent men know to be all but impossibilities—I should indeed have thought that such an Agency, whether successful or the reverse, would be sure of all men's sympathy. But this is not to be concealed—a portion of the Madras Government, its friends and supporters, have made the question of the creation of my jurisdiction under the Supreme Government a vital question, and would rejoice beyond all measure at my failure.'

While the Supreme Government was surprised and annoyed by the statements regarding Khond affairs contained in some of the Madras papers, it received no report from Captain Macpherson, who had not been in the habit of reporting officially to the Madras Government till some time after the conclusion of his tours in the hill-country, and had never been informed that the Government of India desired that he should communicate with it more frequently.

There can be no doubt that it would have been wise to make an exception upon this occasion ; and, in fact, he did write very fully (though his letters were not in the form of an official record) to Mr. Secretary Bushby immediately upon his return to the plains. But Sir T. H. Maddock administered what Captain Macpherson styled 'a wig of the grandest,' because an official Report had not been made ; and required that for the future very full diaries and other records should be kept, and should be forwarded once a week. Accordingly, from this time

---

[1] About this time he wrote : 'The newspapers have had the most preposterous stories. I believe we have all been killed outright, &c. There have been one or two stories which only the most consummate malice could have devised. I turned out of camp a poor half-caste, delirious with fever, fear, and brandy. A scribbling youth got hold of him, and sent every word of his drunken nonsense to a Madras paper.' In another letter he complains of the public use made of a note written by a very young man upon wholly erroneous information, while the same writer's immediate correction of his own mistakes was not noticed.

to the end of Captain Macpherson's tenure of office, a mass of minute information, such as never probably emanated from any Agency in India in an equal space of time, was duly registered and laid before the Government. When Sir T. H. Maddock received the Report which he had called for, he declared that as the Government had not been duly informed at the time, it could now pronounce no opinion whatever as to the Agent's proceedings.

Before pursuing the history of the sacrifice question, it is right to mention once more, and for the last time, the fate of the infanticidal districts. During the summer Captain Macpherson wrote to a friend as follows :—

' You may recollect how well my plans have worked in Souradah ; not a child-murder in it for about two years. Well, I demanded it of the Government at first; then it was not given by mistake ;[1] but I re-demanded it on the 20th February last. It is not yet given. The people believe it will not be given ; do not at all understand a *to be and not to be* authority ; and have to a great extent broken loose from me, and taken to infanticide again. This is the plain deplorable truth, and I am perfectly helpless.'

Nevertheless, the official delays continued, and in October he was compelled to write thus :—

' I scarcely know what to say respecting the state of Souradah, which you know I had brought to give up infanticide entirely; but for my own justification, I must say all one of these days, when I see precisely how matters stand.

' I gained an ascendency over its tribes, as being master of the Zemindary, as being in the place of the Rajah, and having his sons[2] identified with me in the service of the Government.

' Souradah being considered nearly one with Goomsur, I was placed in great difficulty from its not being put under

---

[1] See above, p. 243.

[2] Soondera Sing and Gopee Sing, mentioned above : the latter was now dead.

me when Goomsur was given; but my assurance that it
would be immediately given, and Bannerman's abstinence
from settling its revenue at my public request, enabled me
to struggle on, though scarcely able to hold my ground
against his cutcherry,[1] who of course declared that,
although the Acting Agent had failed to keep Goomsur,
Bannerman would never yield another hill.   The Madras
Government referred the question of giving me Souradah,
&c., to Bannerman (i.e., invited reasons why it should
not be given).   Bannerman, as I am informed, not only
wrote that no more should be given, but that some
should be taken away ; and, believing that he had settled
the matter, he forthwith proceeded to settle the Souradah
revenue [2] a few weeks ago, and without even giving me
notice, to enable me at least to make an effort to save
my work.   Bannerman's cutcherry now declared that his
day of triumph was come, and the people opposed to
my influence in the Souradah tribes everywhere incited
them to destroy their children, and with very abundant
success.   This is a more heart-breaking thing to me, and
to those who have laboured so long and so admirably
with me, than you can at all imagine.   Its general effect
upon the Khond population, on the Rajahs, and on the
cutcherries, you can now well understand ; knowing that
my main difficulty is the conviction, drawn directly from
the cutcherries of the three Agencies with which I am in
contact, that the Government is in no degree in earnest
against either sacrifice or infanticide.   Bannerman's ec-
centricity is well known.   He has always regarded the
Khond work as a high personal impertinence to himself,
making it impossible for him to listen to one word connected with it.   I was able to keep him tolerably straight
while we were in Ganjam, near the coast, together, but

---

[1] Establishment.

[2] To settle the revenue was to announce that he was, and, consequently,
that Captain Macpherson was not, the person in official charge of the
district.

being bound to this spot for twelve months, I have quite
lost sight of him; and here is our infanticidal work,
known to all to be a complete undeniable success, coming
or come to the ground.'

Souradah was of course given to the Agency, but only
when all the mischief had been done.

Those who are not aware of the very great influence
exercised by the native employés of the Government, will
learn with surprise that such proceedings should be tole-
rated as are disclosed in the following letter :—

'The Tahsildar [1] of Goomsur, who is identified with
the chief man of Bannerman's cutcherry, has during the
last three months laboured indefatigably, as a man like
him labours only for the advancement of a matter nearest
his own heart and the hearts of his superiors, to make
the management of these tracts difficult or impossible to
me.   He some time ago canvassed all the renters of my
villages to petition the Government against their trans-
ference to me, and when the Khonds got their heads
loose the other day, urged them again to do so, on the
assurance that my power must now cease, and that he
would remit them two kists,[2] &c. on their re-transference
to him.   He laboured vehemently at that time to excite a
panic in the country, by announcing that a great religious
Khond war had broken out, and must embrace all the
hill-country — that the district would be immediately
plundered, so that all must bury their goods, and prepare
to take their families to the Hills.   He demanded a
guard of troops over his treasury, and told the officer
commanding Russellcondah to strengthen his guard
and prepare for defence.   His reports and, I am told,
his private letters (at which he is a great hand, being a
poet and that sort of thing) to Madras, and especially to
a person in confidential office, were all of the same com-
plexion, and the effect which for the moment he contrived

---

[1] Receiver of revenue.   The name of this man was Sooriah Narain.
[2] Periodical payments of land revenue.

to produce was not small; this work, moreover, is not ended, but proceeds industriously. The renters had too much sense to petition for re-transference to a man whom they had been petitioning me and every other officer in charge of Goomsur for these eight years to remove, and people soon found out the gross hoax of the Khond war; but I know not what effect the intimations by this Tahsildar to the Board Rajah may produce.

'I shall be in a great difficulty if Bannerman's cutcherry shall act, as it now threatens, with systematic hostility to me, in the belief that such action is pleasing to the Madras Government and to its own head. I plainly could not go on against such hostility. It could be put down, I think, only by the Ganjam Agent's taking a strong course against it—not by my bringing charges (which might or might not be substantiated) judicially against his servants, which would necessarily produce exasperations and recriminations without end. I grieve to say I cannot at present appeal to him to make such an effort with any hope of success.

'I shall state in my Report the effect which has been produced by the Board Rajah's continuing to look to Cuttack, of which looking the Government has evidence from the Cuttack Commissioner, and shall say that if Rajahs under me look anywhere but to me I can certainly effect nothing. On this the Supreme Government might perhaps say something distinct to the Madras Government to repeat to its Ganjam Agent.'

The first object of the Agent was to obtain the zealous and hearty cooperation of the Rajah of Board. He therefore pressed the Rajah to come to him; and accordingly, in the beginning of August, he came in, bringing with him some of his principal people. Kurtivas and another fomenter of rebellion were at the same time brought in under constraint. Captain Macpherson would willingly have used Kurtivas for the attainment of the objects of the Agency, had it been possible to employ him; but his treacherous character rendered this very hazardous in itself, and, moreover, he could not have been employed without making enemies of other chiefs much more powerful, and alienating all loyal and respectable men in Boad. What passed on the occasion of the Rajah's visit is thus narrated :

'I of course set immediately upon the party collectively, and each individual separately, and in ten or twelve days had them in as satisfactory a state as I could possibly have hoped. I found that the Rajah, as I supposed, had all along desired to fulfil his engagement, but had been utterly powerless to do so against Kurtivas and the Proraj. And I found that he and his people were convinced that the Government meant to tax the Khonds when they should be brought to give up the sacrifice, but that it was by no means absolutely determined upon its suppression ; in fact, that the Rajah and his servants held very nearly the ideas of which they were pledged to disabuse the Khonds.

'I therefore first put Kurtivas under close restraint, and then marched him towards the coast to the high satisfaction of all, and put the Proraj into confinement here.[1] Secondly, I gave the Rajah and his people by degrees the convictions I desired them to hold, and gave them a written declaration of the intentions of the Government towards Rajah, Bissyes,[2] and Khonds, which they declared to be all that could be wished for. At this stage of the proceedings a very important event occurred. As I was giving the Rajah his audience of leave, in rushed the Hindu chief and all his Khond chiefs of the great tract of Bulscoopa in Boad, with green branches,[3] to beg for forgiveness, and made their unconditional submission to me. Last spring I pitched my tents in Bulscoopa in Boad, and its principal chiefs were the first to submit, and were always with me in mind, and thence were

---

[1] At Nowgaum in the low country of Goomsur.

[2] There were many Hindu Bissyes resident in the hill-tracts of Boad, and also many Hindu Paiks—a sort of military colonists, planted in the Hills in old times.

[3] i.e. as suppliants.

treated with infinite hostility by Kurtivas and his con-
federates, and now they took the first opportunity to
rejoin me.

' On the 20th I sent off the Rajah to the Khond country,
hoping strongly that he will be able to fulfil his pledge ;
that, in other words, I shall, by God's blessing, be enabled
fully to carry out my original policy.'

It is satisfactory to know that after this meeting the
Rajah and the friendly chiefs acted in such an earnest
spirit that before November their party embraced two-
thirds of the inhabitants of Boad.

In the meantime, however, the Rajah of Ungool upon
the Mahanuddee, a potentate of no small importance in
native estimation, was at variance with the British authorities in Cuttack ; and meditating resistance to them, he
had taken advantage of the state of feeling amongst the
Khonds of Boad which led to the disturbances in the
spring.   Through the agency of Chokro Bissye (the
nephew of the imprisoned chief Dora Bissye[1]), and the
freebooting chief Bir Khonro (son of Nobghon Khonro,
the chief patriarch of Boad, whose family had been
ousted of part of its dignities by a younger branch, and
who was ever at work to recover his ancient standing),
he contrived, by pulling the wires skilfully, to prevent
the restoration of tranquillity in the Hills.

In August and September, when the submission of all
the tribes appeared inevitable, these two Khond chiefs,
and particularly Bir Khonro, induced a portion of the
Khonds of Boad, and those of the one small tract of Lower
Bopulmendi of Hodzoghor in Goomsur, to which no
measure of coercion had been applied, to make an attack
on the tract of Lienpurra, a border district of Goomsur;
and repeated that attack several times during the autumn,
burning about twenty villages.

---

[1] Chokro Bissye, and the other relatives of Dora Bissye, had taken refuge in Ungool after the Goomsur war, and had dwelt there ever since. See
above, p. 104.

It was the rainy season ; the climate rendered it impossible for the Government to afford to its loyal subjects the protection to which they were entitled ; and Captain Macpherson, having put an end to the custom of private war among the Goomsur tribes, did not think it right to permit the Dulbehra of Tentilghor to retaliate these aggressions in the usual Khond fashion, by raising the tribes of Goomsur to sweep Boad. He made, however, the best arrangements he could for defence,[1] by sending up a guard of Sebundies, to repel attacks upon Lienpurra, having it in view to give reparation to its people for their losses, and to punish the aggressors judicially, as might be found expedient, after the rainy season should be over, and when the Boad tribes should be brought, like those of Goomsur, under the general authority of the Government. During this period also he exhausted every means in his power to induce Bir Khonro to submit.

With the trifling exception of Lower Bopulmendi, the whole of the Khond tracts of Goomsur were tranquil ; and so fully did they respect the power and appreciate the benevolent policy of the Government, that the abolition movement now culminated in the solemn transfer of their worship from the evil being, the earth-goddess, to the Supreme Beneficence, which they identified with the god of Light.

On this subject Captain Macpherson writes as follows :—

' Russellcondah, 23rd October 1846.

' You see that all the tribes of Goomsur have at last joined in a sacrifice to the god of Light. I trust that you will understand the all-important significance of this fact. You see that a true religious change has been in progress, and is gradually being consummated—the blessed change from the service of the evil to that of the good principle. I cannot at all tell you how this fact of the general offering to Boora rejoices us. If it means all

---

[1] See above, p. 193.

it appears to mean, it is an infinite reward to me. Then the direction of the change with reference to the hope of the fulness of God's time!—matter of thought more than speech.'[1]

Captain Macpherson's plan for the establishment of the British authority in the hill-tracts of Boad, was that a conciliatory proclamation should be issued, and that he should enter those tracts with an escort of troops sufficient to show that he really had the support of the Government; while an officer similarly escorted should advance to meet him from Cuttack, and another from the South-west Frontier—thus demonstrating to all that the British local authorities were in unison, and not (as the poor Khonds were industriously taught) at variance with each other.

The Government approved of this plan, and ordered the escorts for Captain Macpherson, though not those for the officers who were to join him from the other Agencies.

The Rajah and his chief advisers (as has been already mentioned) had played their part boldly and well; the rebel leader Bir Khonro, finding himself unsupported, told his mob that he would leave them to fight their own battles, and they all dispersed to their homes. It needed but the appearance of the Agent and the other officers on the scene at the promised time to ensure universal submission.

Unhappily, at the last moment Mr. Bannerman wrote something which induced the officer commanding the Northern Division of the Madras Army to withhold the promised escort, and the Madras Government to sanction their being withheld.

What he wrote Captain Macpherson had no means even of guessing, but the long-hoped-for opportunity was lost, and the rebellious party rallied again, being taught

[1] See above, p. 216.

to believe that if they stood firm they would be retransferred to Cuttack, and would remain untaxed.   Bir
Khonro's motives were purely political.   Neither he nor
his father Nowbghon was a sacrificer.

Thus thwarted (and informed by the Madras Government that he could have no escorts before March!), the
Agent insisted upon taking three companies, not as escorts, but as absolutely necessary to keep the peace, and
ascended the Ghauts about the end of November, to repair,
if possible, the mischief caused by this ill-timed interference.   When the Supreme Government were apprised of
his difficulty, they ordered escorts to join him from Cuttack, distant at least twelve days' march.

CHAPTER XIX.

SIXTH VISIT TO THE HILLS—DISTURBANCES—THEIR
SUPPRESSION.

NOVEMBER 1846—MARCH 1847.

CAPTAIN MACPHERSON'S plans for the restoration of order had been frustrated, as has been mentioned in the last preceding chapter, by the denial of his promised escorts in the beginning of November, which prevented him from proceeding at the critical moment to the Khond country, to take advantage, as he had arranged in concert with the Rajah, of the disruption of Bir Khonro's party, produced by the Rajah's appearance in the resisting tracts.

He issued the proclamation of the Supreme Government in the middle of November, offering pardon to all who should submit, but declaring that those who resisted should be punished at the discretion of the Government.

On the 30th of November he dispersed Bir Khonro's mob at the village of Nowgaum of Bengrikia, when it was on the point of moving to attack him, and had actually fired upon him.

He next distributed the grain-stores of Nowgaum. The chief of the tribe of Bengrikia, and all its people— excepting Nagsun Khonro, the devoted partisan of Bir Khonro, and the leader of the parties which had devastated Lienpurra—then submitted, and every other tribe in Boad made overtures of submission. The Agent then destroyed the grain-stores of Nagsun Khonro, after his tribe had declared that he and the people of his village, who were his immediate relatives and dependents, had separated himself from the tribe and its interests for his own ends.

Neither Captain Macpherson nor any person acting under his directions ever ordered or sanctioned the destruction of a single village in the sacrificing tracts of Boad, or in any part of Boad above the Ghauts; and during his operations there were destroyed in all those tracts by hostile Khonds, against his will, only two empty villages, containing together about sixty houses, and three small empty hamlets, containing altogether about twelve houses, only two houses being burnt in one hamlet.[1]

Upon the 8th of December Chokro Bissye, instigated and supported by the Ungool Rajah, and by the intrigues of Sooriah Narain, headed a rising in the low-country of Goomsur, for the restoration of a Rajah of the Bunje family. The insurgents were the Hindoo Paiks or military tenants of the low-country, and they rose simultaneously in those tracts which had remained under the Ganjam Agent, and in those which had recently been made over to the Hill Agency. With them were the Khonds of the adjoining lowland district of Chokapaud. Bir Khonro,

---

[1] The first village destroyed was that of Nowgaum of Bengrikia, at which Bir Khonro's mob had rallied for all its attacks upon Lienpurra. Captain Macpherson, when his camp was pitched there, thrice extinguished the flames in the village, when fired by its Khond enemies. It was burnt when he left it. The second village destroyed was the empty village of Nagsun Khonro; it was fired in spite of the orders of the Agent's two Assistants. The three small empty hamlets which were burnt by the Khonds were all entirely out of the protection of his camp. When the vast amount of loss and suffering savagely inflicted by the Boad tribes upon the people of Tentilghor is remembered, the all but perfect abstinence of the latter from retaliation, and in reliance upon the final justice of the Government, when the whole country was in their power, was a fact in the highest degree creditable to them. Captain Macpherson authorised the use of the materials of the village of Dirbi Pudhan for firewood when the cowardly murder of some of his unarmed camp-followers by that chief made it necessary that the rest should not, if possible, go to the forest for fuel.

similarly instigated and supported, was enabled to renew the resistance in Boad. Captain Macpherson arrested Bir Khonro, finally paralysing his party in the resisting Khond tracts, and frustrating to a great extent the plans of Chokro Bissye.

There were now to be carried out, simultaneously, two sets of measures—for completing the work of the suppression of the sacrifice in Boad, and for quelling the insurrection in Goomsur below the Ghauts.

The Rajah, his family, and all the chiefs of Boad excepting the immediate partisans of Nobghon Khonro on the Mahanuddee, and in the half of the group of resisting tribes which Captain Macpherson did not visit, were one with the Government. The victims, in the tracts under their influence, were restored. That body of chiefs had entire confidence that the measures of the Government would be carried out in the terms of its proclamation, and cooperated so earnestly that nearly all the heads of the tribes which had not submitted were pledged or prepared to submit upon the Agent's visiting them.

That officer considered it to be certain that when Chokro Bissye should be put down in Goomsur, and one of his own Assistants (who had gone to the low-country) should appear above the Ghauts to co-operate with him, all would submit without a blow; and that when the Ungool Rajah, the prime source of mischief, should be compelled by the Cuttack authorities to abandon his support of Nobghon Khonro, every object would be permanently secured. Not doubting that the Agent in Ganjam would cooperate with him by directing the troops at his disposal to act against the insurgents within his jurisdiction, Captain Macpherson felt confident that the disturbances in Goomsur must be very soon put down, and that Chokro Bissye must be expelled; and he resolved, with the full concurrence of the chiefs, to await that event before moving into the tracts of Boad which had not submitted, labouring in the meantime to confirm and extend the growing circle of his connections, and repelling (but not following up by the destruction of the property and villages of their tribes) the feeble attacks of the mobs of Khonds which on several occasions appeared before his camp.

In the end of January Mr. Cadenhead, having put down the insurrection in the Paik tracts of the Hill Agency, and broken it in Chokapaud, returned above the Ghauts to hunt out Chokro Bissye, and to co-operate with Captain Macpherson. The completion of Captain Macpherson's plan was now certain, so far as the success of his measures could secure it; but from the Agent in Ganjam not having thought fit to direct the action of troops against the insurgents in his jurisdiction, Chokro Bissye found there safe rallying-ground, and the insurrection broke out afresh in a portion of the low-country. It was necessary to despatch an Assistant (Lieutenant Pinkney, a young officer of great promise) immediately to meet that outbreak, and, soon after, the attitude which Nobghon Khonro was enabled by the Ungool Rajah to assume on the Mahanuddee made it expedient to send Mr. Cadenhead with a force to deal definitively with him.

Captain Macpherson maintained his course unchanged towards the moiety of the Board tribes which had not submitted, except that he moved into Sangrimendi, and, without a blow, gained that great tribe thoroughly with the exception of a very few recusant individuals in one section. On the 1st of March he left Captain Haughton[1] (the officer who had been deputed from the South-west Frontier, and who rendered most valuable assistance) to bring in those persons, and to maintain his relations with the tribes around.

To return to the insurrection[2] which took place below

---

[1] Now Colonel Haughton, Commissioner of Cooch Behar, and in charge of our political relations with the Bhooteahs.

[2] The insurrection broke out simultaneously in two Mootahs of the Hill Agency and in three Mootahs of the Ganjam Agency. The insurgents (with the exception of the Khonds of Chokapaud, who had fully abandoned

the Ghauts in December. Within ten or twelve days, the insurgents burnt all the villages in four Mootahs, and half of the villages in a fifth Mootah, committing every species of outrage and excess, and the movement and the devastation were rapidly extending to the whole country. Mr. Cadenhead—to whom, aided by Mr. Pinkney, the task of dealing with the insurrection was confided[1]—had at first but about a single company at his disposal, besides

human sacrifice) were Hindoos: such of them as belonged to Captain Macpherson's Agency had passed under his authority about eight months before, and there had never been the slightest question or dispute between them and the Hill Agency. It is a remarkable fact that General Campbell has omitted to mention that any disturbances took place in Mr. Bannerman's Agency.

[1] The following extracts from Mr. Cadenhead's letters to Captain Macpherson will show how matters stood:—

. . . . . '17th December 1846.—There can be no doubt that these disturbances are caused by the Sumasthanum Paiks and their relatives—by, in fact, that part of the population of the country accustomed to bear arms. Their leader is, as we supposed, Chokro Bissye, who is said to be attended by a party of forty Paiks from Ungool. He is also said to have with him a relative of the Rajah of Ungool, whom he passes off as a son of the Rajah of Goomsur, on whom he has bound the sari of Rajah, and he and his partisans call on all those who have ever ate the salt of the Bunjes to join in their movement. . . . . . I do not anticipate that you will be able to make any progress until this business is put down. I shall be glad if you can hold your ground in Boad till then with a company and D.'s and H.'s escorts. I think all the rest of the troops ought to be sent to meet the difficulty here. After it shall be overcome, the Boad work will fall into your hands like a ripe pear. It is hopeless attempting anything against the incendiaries with the force now with me. I shall be very thankful if I can prevent further destruction in this quarter, and in the Mootahs still untouched.'

. . . . . ' Nowgaum, 21st December 1846.—My policy, since I saw how matters really stand, has been to attempt to limit the destruction and confine the outbreak within as narrow limits as possible, until I can obtain the means of acting against it with energy and effect. . . . . . Besides Belgoonta, I think my presence here has certainly saved all the villages in this immediate neighbourhood, if not Nowgaum itself and Kodinda.

. . . . . . '22nd December 1846.—The armed population has never given up hope of seeing the Raj restored to the Bunjes [see above, p. 229], and the Sirdars have longed for this restoration as the means of increasing their importance. The fixed restrictive rule of the Government is necessarily extremely burdensome to a race accustomed to the fast-and-loose administration of a native authority which they themselves swayed, and they have desired the restoration of that authority as the means of regaining their lawless freedom.'

a few guards posted in the principal villages. He re-
pelled a large body of insurgents in a night-attack upon
a rich trading village, dispersed them a few days after
at two jungle retreats, induced a chief of importance
to return to obedience, and to assist him zealously
with all his partisans, and by a series of able and
successful measures he completely quashed the outbreak
within the Paik Mootahs of the Hill Agency before
January 10. Three or four of the insurgents fell in the
night-attack, two fell on either side at one of the jungle
retreats : this was the whole loss of life and of property
inflicted in arresting a movement which, had it not been
then checked, must have immediately involved at least
the whole of Goomsur.

Mr. Cadenhead then proceeded to reduce Chokapaud,
whence Chokro Bissye had been already driven by an
officer deputed from Cuttack. Chokapaud was the connecting link between the Paik or military Mootahs of
both the Hill Agency and the Ganjam Agency, and the
Khond tracts of Goomsur and of Boad above the Ghauts.
The insurgents had just acquired the highest confidence,
from a small portion of them having been enabled with
impunity to strip a company of Sepoys of its whole baggage, inflicting upon it some loss in men.

The attention of all who were still in resistance, or
who tended to resist in either Agency, was riveted upon
the course and the fortunes of this tract, and everything
depended upon its subjection. It was impossible to get
at the insurgents, personally, in the forests of their most
difficult country. The course therefore was adopted
which has been usually adopted under similar circumstances throughout the world—viz., that of acting against
the resources of the insurgents, destroying their grain,
seizing their cattle, and burning their villages, as the
necessity of each case dictated. By the destruction of
five or six villages and eight hamlets, containing about
150 houses in all, and of a quantity of grain, the in-

surrection was completely broken by the 24th of January. Several chiefs came in, and many of the rest made overtures of submission.   During the progress of these aggressive measures full pardon on a return to obedience was offered to all, save a few leaders and murderers.   As soon as the resistance ceased and a distinct tendency to submission was established, those measures ceased; and Mr. Cadenhead moved above the Ghauts into the Khond country of Boad on the 25th of January, in pursuit of Chokro Bissye, and to co-operate, as already mentioned, with Captain Macpherson.

Mr. Bannerman's inaction at that critical moment—when the movement of a single company of the troops at his disposal, in concert with those under the Hill Agency, by removing the prevalent belief of the antagonism of the two authorities in Goomsur, would have sufficed to put an end to the rebellion—enabled Chokro Bissye to find in the Ganjam Agency a safe rallying-ground for his partisans, and the insurrection was partially renewed in the districts under the Hill Agency[1] about the 25th of January.

A strong reinforcement being expected to arrive soon, Mr. Pinkney was deputed, with three companies at his disposal, to repress that outbreak.   About the 10th of February troops were moved into the disturbed tract of the Ganjam Agency, who dispersed the insurgents there in their jungle retreats, and then helped the troops in the Hill Agency to expel them from Goomsur.   A number of jungle retreats and grain-stores were destroyed, and a herd of cattle was captured.

In the beginning of March the troops were enabled to act at the same moment within both Agencies, and the insurgents lost all hope.   Chokro Bissye fled above the Ghauts on or about the 10th or 12th of March. Captain Macpherson directed, on the latter date, the sus-

---

[1] *I. e.* in the lowland Hindu districts; not in Chokapaud.

T

pension of aggressive measures, and on the 16th proclaimed an amnesty to all save the principal leaders of the insurrection and principals in murders. Upon the 18th his action was arrested under circumstances to be mentioned below ; but the result of his measures in the low-country of Goomsur was the return of the whole population of the disturbed Paik tracts in the Hill Agency to their villages—excepting a few families, the devoted partisans of Chokro Bissye.

In the Goomsur hill-country the people of the one tract of Lower Bopulmendi, who had largely partaken with Bir Khonro's mob in the plunder of their own tribe, were punished, upon the express requisition of the chiefs of Goomsur and the friendly chiefs of Boad, by their grain-stores being given to the men of Tentilghor, whose country they had wasted. Their enemies burnt some of their deserted villages. All, with the exception of the principal chief, immediately submitted.

Nobghon Khonro, in January 1847, with aid from Ungool, plundered and burnt one or two villages of the domain-lands of Boad, blockaded the Podentilla Pass, the great highway for traffic and for pilgrims from the west, and besides closed the Mahanuddee river, plundering and murdering merchants and other travellers. The Khonds of the only tribe above the Ghauts which was distinctly in the interest of Nobghon Khonro at the same time blockaded the Ghauts between the low country of Boad and the Khond table-land, murdering several of the Rajah's Paiks.

Captain Macpherson therefore, upon the 9th of February —when the state of things in Boad above the Ghauts first enabled him to dispense with Mr. Cadenhead's services there, and when the expected arrival of the 18th Regiment was about to place the necessary force at his disposal— instructed Mr. Cadenhead to proceed to the scene of disturbances, to endeavour by every peaceful means to re-establish order, and induce Nobghon Khonro and his partisans to return to obedience ; and if peaceful mea·sures should prove ineffectual, to employ force.

The confidence of Nobghon Khonro and his partisans, based on the support of bodies of men from Ungool (for the Cuttack authorities had not succeeded in arresting the ·hostile action of its Rajah) was so distinct and determined, that Mr. Cadenhead found it absolutely essential to the accomplishment of the objects entrusted to him to destroy two hill-fastnesses of Nobghon Khonro, along with seven other villages, and some of the grain of those of his partisans who had been immediately implicated in the outrages perpetrated and in attacks upon the troops.

The result was that a large portion of the population, including several of Nobghon Khonro's personal adherents, immediately submitted ; that Nobghon Khonro and those who still remained with him protested their desire to throw themselves on the mercy of the Government, and sent messengers to arrange for their submission ; while the Ungool Rajah no longer dared to afford them refuge.

Such was the general outline (to state the details would be useless) of the distinct but closely-related sets of measures which the Agency carried out simultaneously for completing the suppression of the sacrifice in Boad, for putting down the insurrection for the restoration of a Rajah in Goomsur, and for putting down the disturbances which the Ungool Rajah enabled Nobghon Khonro to raise on the Mahanuddee—and these the general results of those measures.

Captain Macpherson, it will be observed, continued to employ the mildest means alone where conciliation was possible and permissible ; but he felt also (as he himself expressed it) that 'to trifle with distinct rebellion is to inflict a most cruel and unjustifiable wrong alike

upon the loyal and the rebellious—that it would be the
height of folly and of inhumanity to hesitate to reduce,
by the destruction of their property, intangible bands of
plundering, burning, murdering ruffians, whose lives and
property were forfeited to the law.'

CHAPTER XX.

DISMISSAL AND VINDICATION OF THE HILL AGENCY——RETURN TO GREAT BRITAIN.

CAPTAIN MACPHERSON came down the Ghauts early in March, as has been already mentioned, for the purpose of meeting a Brigadier-General, who had been appointed to the command of the Northern Division of the Madras Army, and who had been instructed to repair to the scene of the disturbances, to co-operate with Captain Macpherson in restoring tranquillity if he should find things tending to pacification, but to assume civil as well as military charge of the Agency if he should find the contrary to be the case.

Since these instructions were issued, reinforcements had arrived; the troops had at length been permitted to act against the rebels in the Mootahs under the Ganjam Agency, at the same time that they were acting against the rebels in Captain Macpherson's Mootahs ; resistance was at an end, and Chokro Bissye was a desperate fugitive in the Khond country, whence a few days' action of a couple of companies would have driven him for ever, and the whole country above and below the Ghauts would have been at peace.

The Brigadier-General, after an interview with Mr. Bannerman, took as his interpreter and active agent that same Sooriah Narain whose mischievous intrigues have been spoken of above, whom the Ganjam Agent himself had dismissed from the office of Tahsildar of Goomsur, and

who had been twice indicated officially by Captain
Macpherson to the Government as one of the chief pro-
moters of the rebellion.   After the lapse of a few days
the Brigadier-General reported to the Government in
the strongest terms against all the measures of the Hill
Agency—declaring (in the words of Captain Macpherson)
' that the war had not been against the Government but
against my Agency, that I could never pacificate the
country, and that he should have full powers to settle
matters in his own way.   The Government let him take
it, without asking me one question.'   He assumed charge :
Captain Macpherson and his assistants were required immediately to withdraw beyond the limits of the Agency,
while his native servants were not only removed beyond
those limits, but were summarily discharged from the
public service in a body.

The Government (i. e. Sir T. H. Maddock) then apprised Captain Macpherson of the General's accusations,
and informed him that his removal being deemed ' a
measure necessary for the restoration of tranquillity,'
Colonel Campbell[1] had been appointed to succeed him,
and that the Government would record its opinion on his
conduct after it had received his explanations.   Captain
Macpherson immediately demanded an inquiry, and the
Government of India, at the close of a protracted investigation, expressed its regret that it had acted in the
manner just mentioned, declaring the accusations unfounded, and adopting the opinion of the officer who had
conducted the inquiry, that ' the general characteristic
of Captain Macpherson's administration was that of mildness,' that ' no reason existed for fancying that the feelings
of the people towards the Agency would have interfered
with the return of the country to permanent tranquillity
under them,' and that some parts of the policy adopted
after their removal had been attended with lamentable

---

[1] The officer who has been already referred to; now Major-General
Campbell.

consequences to life and property.[1]   It would have been, therefore, unnecessary to dwell upon these events, but for the conduct of General Campbell, who thought fit, in the year succeeding that of Major Macpherson's death, to reproduce these accusations and to assert their truth,[2] without even alluding to the inquiry or its results![3]   As these charges in no way concerned General Campbell or his services, their gratuitous revival by him so many years after the Government had pronounced an honourable acquittal, and so immediately after Major Macpherson had been removed by death, bespeaks a feeling which is rare indeed among British officers.

The charges were met on the instant, and have been finally disposed of as regards the officer who originally made them.   But so far as General Campbell has set them forth in his book, they shall be met, as *his* charges, by a statement of the decision pronounced upon them, and also of some remarkable circumstances connected with the inquiry.   The reader will find them in the Appendix.[4]

The Governor-General, Lord Dalhousie (who had arrived in India during the investigation), as soon as the decision of his Government was pronounced,[5] sent for Captain Macpherson; and after saying that he was sensible that nothing could ever compensate for the treatment which he had undergone, assured him, on behalf of every member of the Government, that to mark their undiminished confidence in him he should be appointed to a suitable office in the Political Department as soon as his health (then entirely broken, and requiring his immediate return to Europe) would enable him to accept it.

---

[1] Resolution of October 7th, 1848.

[2] 'Narrative,' &c.   It is true that General Campbell has not reprinted the charges in his 'Personal Narrative' of 1864, but he has not withdrawn nor in any way qualified them.

[3] See Appendix F.   [4] See Appendix E.   [5] In October 1848.

Such had been the scale of Mr. Grant's inquiries that his final reports were not sent in before the autumn of 1848, and the Resolutions of the Governor-General in Council were not passed till October of that year. Captain Macpherson and his Assistants were dismissed in March 1847 : they had therefore consumed a year and a half in attending (so far as they were permitted to attend) an inquiry into charges which ought never to have been made ; and they had endured the vexation of having those charges hanging over them the whole time, to say nothing of the enormous pecuniary loss which they all sustained—for they had not been *suspended* from office, as is usual during inquiry, but had been summarily removed.

In 1846, Captain Macpherson had barely got through the unhealthy season with life. The campaign in the cold weather had been rendered an anxious one by circumstances for which he was not responsible, and which it was quite out of his power to anticipate ; and before the Government at Calcutta pronounced its opinion, in October 1848, his constitution was completely undermined by continued attacks of fever. He therefore repaired to England to recruit his health, and, though even there he suffered from the constant recurrence of fever, yet he gradually became stronger. The relief afforded to mind and body by this happy interval of freedom, which enabled him to revisit his family and the friends of his youth, and to wander over his own and other countries, exercising his faculty of kindly observation—this and the salutary influence of climate slowly and gradually overcame, to a considerable extent, the action of the Goomsur malaria, which had sunk deep into his system, and his nerves were braced for another struggle. But it was not to come yet.

It may be here fitly mentioned that when he was in the hotel at Cairo, on his way home, a gentleman hearing him addressed by his name came up, and, introducing himself as Colonel Outram, desired his acquaintance, 'having long watched his career,' he said, 'with the deepest interest and admiration.' The acquaintance of two such men naturally and rapidly became a close and intimate friendship.

The Court of Directors, on the 25th September, 1850, minutely reviewed the Resolutions of the Indian Government on Mr. Grant's report, and pronounced a decision not less favourable to Captain Macpherson and his Agency than was contained in those Resolutions.

The first hours of returning health were devoted by Captain Macpherson to remodelling his account of the Khond religion, and recording with the greatest precision the results of the inquiries which had so long been prosecuted by himself and by Mr. Cadenhead; for he felt that without a knowledge of the motives which induced the Khonds to sacrifice, it would always be impossible to address to them reasons which they could understand for relinquishing the rite. The paper, when completed, was communicated to the Royal Asiatic Society of London.[1]

During the inquiries and discussions of 1850–53 on Indian affairs, Captain Macpherson's services were mentioned with high commendation in various quarters, and in particular by Mr. Kaye, the eminent historical writer, whose favourable judgment was pronounced, as that of Dr. Duff had been, not from any previous friendship, but simply upon an examination of all that he and others had done in relation to the Khonds. Mr. Kaye, after a spirited outline of the manner in which the great change was effected, adds :—

'The good work is going on, under diminished difficulties, towards a prosperous conclusion. It was obviously, indeed, a work of which the beginning may almost be said to be also the middle and the end.'[2]

---

[1] See above, Chapter VI.
[2] History of the Administration of the East India Company. London, 1853.

And the Court of Directors finally, in enumerating the good deeds of their administration of India, mentioned no other name than Major Macpherson's in connection with the Khond race, as will appear from the following extracts from a 'Memorandum [1] (prepared at the India House) of the Improvement of the Administration of India during the last Thirty Years:' —

'Among the barbarous tribes who occupy the hill-tracts of Orissa, on the south-west frontier of Bengal, human sacrifices prevailed until a very recent period. By a well-devised and judicious series of conciliatory measures, worthy of a more lengthened record than can be given in this place, the extinction of this enormity has been effected.' [2]   *   *   *

'There still remain to be commemorated a set of proceedings, among the most interesting and the most honourable to our Government which have distinguished the present century—the measures for raising and civilising the oppressed races.

'The first person who is known to have tried the effect of justice and conciliation on any of these tribes was Mr. Cleveland.'

[The paper goes on to mention the benevolent exertions of Mr. Cleveland among the people of the Bhaugulpore Hills, those of Colonels Hall and Dixon in Ajmere, and of Sir J. P. Willoughby, Colonel Ovans, and Sir James Outram among the Bheels; after which it proceeds in the following terms :—]

'Another example is that of the Khonds in Orissa, among whom a policy of the same general character was carried into practice by Major Macpherson. This was the tribe who, as mentioned in a previous part of the present paper, have been induced to abolish human sacrifices.

'The mode in which these objects were accomplished

---

[1] Ordered by the House of Commons to be printed, 12th February, 1858.
[2] Page 18.

was in all cases fundamentally the same; they were effected by the admirable power of individual character.'[1]

Nothing could be more true. In the instance before us the effect was produced by bold reasoning and ready action, based on the closest observation; by the hand ever open and liberal, and the heart overflowing with sympathy and kindness—by unflinching perseverance under extraordinary difficulties. Thus it was that the Khonds of Goomsur were reclaimed; and such an impression was produced on those of Boad, that, so far as could be learnt, no sacrifice took place while Captain Macpherson continued in office.

[1] Page 34.

CHAPTER XXI.

MR. CADENHEAD AND MAJOR PINKNEY.

No better illustration of the character of Captain Macpherson's Khond Agency can be given than that which is afforded by the course of his subsequent service, and that of his two colleagues in the Agency, whom he had selected for political employment and had initiated in political business, and who were included with him in those hasty accusations which General Campbell has deliberately revived, in the punishment without inquiry, and also in the ultimate vindication.

The Government of India had pronounced Mr. Cadenhead's services to have been ' valuable and highly meritorious throughout,' and had declared that nothing had been found to say of him or of Mr. Pinkney save in their praise. And it proceeded to mark its sense of the injustice which had been done them, by reappointing them to political office.

Regarding Mr. Cadenhead, Mr. Commissioner Grant had written thus :—

' During the whole of this period of three months and a half, from the first outbreak in Gullery, he was constantly, in good health or in bad health, scouring these unwholesome jungles and hills, accompanying the troops in all their movements, and present with them in every action ; and my opinion of these proceedings is, that they were conducted with rare spirit and energy, and with great skill, and that they reflect great credit on the conductor of them.'

All this was true : and yet the most valuable part of Mr. Cadenhead's services did not come under Mr. Grant's notice—his skill and tact in managing the Khonds during Captain Macpherson's absence, his hearty co-operation with him when they were together, the ability with which he discharged the arduous civil duties which had been suddenly thrust upon him, the candid and enlightened spirit in which he dealt with the strange questions that were ever and anon presenting themselves among those wild people, the industry and scholarlike penetration with which under many distractions he persevered in acquiring their language, and the genuine kindness with which he strove in every way to promote their welfare.

Upon the close of the Commissioner's inquiry, Mr. Cadenhead was appointed one of the Principal Assistants to the Governor-General's Agent for the South-west Frontier. But it is easier to do injustice than to repair it, and his new post was far inferior in emolument though equal in rank to that of which he had been deprived. Here, however, he cheerfully laboured—thinking little of himself and his family—and consumed the three short years that remained to him of life in works of duty and beneficence. He was sent, in the first place, to the station of Chyebassa in Singbhoom. His official superior, the Governor-General's Agent, resided at a great distance ; and Mr. Cadenhead's duties were to administer justice, civil and criminal, to maintain the peace, and to superintend the revenue—in short, to exercise all the functions of Government.

Singbhoom is a range of slightly elevated undulating land lying between the 21st and 23rd degrees of North latitude and the 85th and 86th degrees of East longitude. Of its population of 331,000, at least 90,000 are Lurka Koles, a wild aboriginal race, whose love of ' harrying the loons of the low-country' brought them into collision with the British Government, which finally took them under its protection in 1837. Previous to that time the Koles were practically independent, although nominally subject to the neighbouring Zemindars. Their organisation was purely tribal, and had all the defects incidental to that system. The chiefs were without any direct power, and with little influence except in accordance with the whims and will of their tribes. Each tribe being wholly independent, there was no power to arbitrate between them, except that of the Hindu Zemindars, whose policy usually led them to foster strife. The quarrels of tribes almost necessarily led to bloody contentions, which only terminated when the losses of one or both compelled a temporary cessation of hostilities.

Although the independent Kole tribes could unite so as to resist an open attack on the part of the Hindu chiefs to reduce them to subjection, they were incapable of evading that gradual and imperceptible reduction, which was the certain and indirect result of the policy of the Rajahs, and they were in the course of being entirely superseded by the Hindoos; the number of independent tribes was rapidly diminishing, their chiefs formed an armed class of some estimation in the Zemindaries, holding their lands on something like a feudal tenure, while the mass of the population were reduced to a servile condition. British intervention to some extent stopped this. The policy of the enlightened officer[1] who assumed charge of the country was, to enlarge the influence of the Kole chiefs, to elevate them into distinct and substantive powers by holding out to them the hope of becoming district and village heads of police, whilst he gave the people a chance of maintaining their individuality as peaceful cultivators of the soil. Of course it required long years of patient administration thoroughly to effect such a change.

Although a kindred race to the Khonds, the Koles do not sacrifice human beings; they offer up to their local divinities buffaloes, goats, pigs, fowls, &c., on occasions of

[1] Colonel Wilkinson.

rejoicing and sorrow. They have (like other very back-
ward races) neither idols nor temples. They burn their
dead in the yards of their houses, and, placing the bones
in an earthen pot, bury them with rice, money, ornaments,
clothes, &c., underneath a heavy stone in the village cemetery. A commemorative stone is likewise fixed upright
on the outskirts of the village, or in some old frequented
spot. A specimen of their composition is subjoined :—

INVOCATION TO THE DEAD.[1]

We never scolded you,   never wronged you.   Come to us back.
    We ever loved and cherished you,   and lived long together
under the same roof.   Desert it not now !   The rainy nights,
and the cold-blowing days, are coming on.   Do not wander here.
Do not stand by the burnt ashes.   Come to us again ! You
cannot find shelter under the peepul,   when the rain comes
            down. The soul will not shield you from the cold bitter wind.
Come to your home !   It is swept for you and clean ; and we ·
    are there who loved you ever ;   and there is rice put for you ;
        and water. Come home, come home, come to us again !

The streams,[2] which are rapid, wash down gold, much
of which is lost, owing to the ignorance of the Koles ;
the iron and copper ores are said to be excellent, and coal
has been discovered near the Ebe River. The tusser-
worm is reared in all the jungles spread over the district,
and the cocoons are bartered with the Hindoos for trinkets.
Massive forests of saul cover the western boundary ; bamboos clothe the hills,[3] and rattans grow in the marshes.
Jaspers, green-stone, quartz, and pebbles are found in the
beds of the rivers. Corundum is abundant. Nor are
antiquities wanting. Indeed, on this head there are wonderful stories current—one of them tells of an immense

---

[1] Translated from the Kole by Captain (now Colonel) Tickell, Bengal
Army. Colonel Tickell's interesting sketch of the Koles has, with other
sources of information, been consulted in framing these pages.

[2] The River Bunnye, between Singbhoom and Sonepore, is said to disappear underground, like the Mole in this country, and then to join the
Kolekaro.

[3] The ranges of hills in Singbhoom are not above 1,000 feet high, and
consist mainly of quartz, but some are of granite.

circle of forty temples, standing two miles apart from each other, buried in an impenetrable forest.

The Kole villages are built in open spots, each house in its own garden, in which maize or tobacco is cultivated. Those of the chiefs are large and substantial, formed in the shape of a square, in the centre of which is invariably a pigeon-house. Intoxication is the great foible of the Koles. Their favourite beverage (eely) is manufactured from rice, and from the mowa-berry a strong spirit is distilled. On cool evenings they assemble beneath the shade of the tamarind-trees in the village cemetery, or else before their doors, where they indulge in singing and dancing. The men and musicians are placed in the centre of a circle of girls, and the latter, with their arms locked round each other, glide backwards and forwards in perfect time, going slowly round the men in the middle.

The Koles, like other mountaineers, have a considerable sense of personal dignity. Mr. Cadenhead was amused, on arriving among them, to observe the sort of ' How d'ye do, my good fellow ? ' air with which a naked Kole waved his hand to him by way of salutation.

Among these people Mr. Cadenhead laboured incessantly for a year, clearing off the enormous arrears of business which he found awaiting him, observing the people with a kindly and sagacious eye, and doing what he could for their improvement.

Mr. J. H. Crawford, late of the Bengal Civil Service, the very able officer who presided over the district, has favoured the Editor of these Memorials with his recollection of Mr. Cadenhead's services :—

' My official association with Mr. Cadenhead was in the political districts of the South-west Frontier Agency, one of the wildest quarters of the Bengal Presidency. I was appointed Governor-General's Agent in June 1849, when he was in charge of the Principal Assistant's Office in Singbhoom, a division of the Agency which comprised the country of the Lurka Koles and the estates of a few tributary chiefs. There I found him, when I visited the district in November, actively engaged not only in administering justice and collecting the revenue, but also in encouraging education and other means of civilising the wild people under his care.

'But a wider field of usefulness was opening to him. By the death, without heir, of the old Rajah of Sumbhulpore, that fine rich district, in the southern quarter of the Agency, had lapsed to the British Government in August, and Cadenhead had been selected to fill the office of Principal Assistant there, and substitute for native misrule a regular system of administration, after annexation had been effected.[1] Happily, the difficulties in the establishment of the British rule, anticipated by the Government, had been obviated; and in January I was able to leave Cadenhead, who had marched down with me from Singbhoom to Sumbhulpore, in charge of the latter district, with a fair field for the exercise of those qualities which peculiarly fitted him for the duty with which he was entrusted. His success was complete. In a few weeks conciliatory treatment of them combined with firmness had won over to him those petty chiefs and subordinate adherents of the old Rajah who had threatened to give trouble. At the same time, by patient assiduity and intelligence, he introduced an effective form of civil and criminal judicature, embracing the cherished native system of Punchayets, or courts of arbitration, as well as an organised system of revenue collections, free from the old oppressive transit-dues and other traditionary imposts.[2] Thus, by the breadth of his views, and the liberality of his judgment, were the useful

---

[1] The country had been devastated by the Mahrattas in 1819, and had subsequently been ill governed. The last Rajah, who was a comparatively respectable man, received one-eighth part of the profits which the dacoits or gang-robbers realised by the exercise of their professional skill.

[2] Mr. Cadenhead drew up, amongst other valuable papers, an elaborate account (which, it is to be hoped, still exists) of the gold-washers of the Mahanuddee and their business.

features of native administration adopted, and those of an opposite tendency discarded.   At his instance the establishment of schools followed in due course, together with dispensaries and other institutions contributing to the moral and physical benefit of those. around him ; and within a year and a half, the territory, which had been a point of difficulty to the Government, became, through the energy of one of its servants, a centre of comparative strength. Unhappily, however, the notorious unhealthiness of the locality at certain seasons remained, and he who had done so much for its improvement in other respects was among the first to suffer from that circumstance.   In a short visit to the interior of his district, in October 1851, Mr. Cadenhead contracted an illness which in a few days terminated his valuable life.

' Hurried and imperfect as is this sketch of his career under my observation, I feel sure that it justifies the opinion I have always entertained, that the Indian Government has seldom been served more efficiently, and never more devotedly, than by our lamented friend.'

In truth, under the modest designation of a Principal Assistant, Mr. Cadenhead had discharged a most difficult political duty with distinguished success.   Unfortunately, because he was a medical man, the Government deemed it a piece of justifiable frugality to leave Sumbhulpore without the usual medical aid, or he might, perhaps, have lived for many years, adding largely to his titles to public estimation, and receiving, in the end, advancement suited to his merits. The Government paid a graceful compliment to his memory, by maintaining a school which he had established.[1]

[1] Mr. Kaye states, in his work on the administration of the East India Company, that Mr. Cadenhead, ' by his unceasing devotion to the interests of the people, alike in the laws of public and of private duty, gained in an extraordinary degree their confidence and affection. Amongst his works of private benevolence may be noticed the institution of a school, which opened in April 1850 with seven pupils, who soon increased to sixty, including youths of the highest families in the district. The system of tuition

With regard to Lieutenant, afterwards Major, Pinkney, Mr. Grant had reported 'that his whole conduct displayed intelligence, energy, and zeal, with aptitude and a degree of discretion remarkable in a young officer without previous experience in civil employment; that the operations in which he was concerned were judicious, necessary, and successful, and that his conduct was strongly marked with humanity.'

Mr. Pinkney, after a short service in Arracan, was transferred, in 1849, to the Saugor and Nerbudda Commission, which administered the affairs of a large province of Central India. In this new territory he laboured, as he had done in Goomsur, with great intelligence and with steadfast zeal and singleness of purpose. He gradually rose to the important office of Commissioner of Jhansi, and his abilities were conspicuously displayed, to the great advantage of the public service, in the days of the Revolt. He was among those who received the Companionship of the Bath for their exertions upon that occasion. He has since died, leaving behind him the reputation of a soldier of brilliant courage, an excellent political officer, and an honest and upright man.

was that of Dr. Duff of Calcutta. On Mr. Cadenhead's death the inhabitants of Sumbhulpore petitioned the Government to maintain the school. The Commissioner warmly seconded their petition, "not only for the direct good which would accrue from the permanent establishment of the school under Government patronage, but as a monument of the active and characteristic benevolence of the founder." The Government immediately apportioned the sum of 240*l.* per annum for its effectual maintenance.'

CHAPTER XXII.

IMMEDIATELY upon Captain Macpherson's return to India, in August 1853, Lord Dalhousie bestowed on him the office of Governor-General's Agent at Benares, a post of little importance, but the only one then at his Lordship's disposal which Captain Macpherson would have cared to fill.

Before he had passed many weeks at Benares, Lord Dalhousie wrote :—

' Adverting to your very intelligible desire for more active employment than that which you now hold, I am happy to have it in my power to offer you the Political[1] Agency of Bhopal, which is now vacant. It is a very satisfactory little State, and will give you 1,500 rupees a month, which is an improvement.'

The offer was at once accepted, although it was not entirely without regret that Captain Macpherson prepared to leave the ' holy city ' of the Hindoos, in which he had begun to interest himself, and where he had recently seen a great variety of people, who came to be introduced to Mr. Colvin, the new Lieutenant-Governor of the North-west Provinces.

' These attenuated shadows ' (he writes) ' of the regality of Delhi—these strong, noble, robust, and workmanlike Sikh chiefs,[2] whom my heart takes in straight ; then the

---

[1] i.e. Diplomatic.

[2] A number of chiefs or members of families which had been in rebellion

shroffs, merchant zemindars, and bankers of 400 years' standing, and insurance companies of Benares—the very essence, pride, and heart of Gangetic commerce, or rather half-heart, Mirzapore holding the other ventricle ; then also its Punditdom, in full strength yet :—all this has passed before me most curiously in these eight days ; and it would be matter of infinite interest to me to look into all classes distinctly.'

On his way to Bhopal he paid a visit to Colonel (afterwards Sir William) Sleeman, Resident at Lucknow, an officer who regarded the people of India with the largest sympathy—who was, like Outram, master of the whole science of their social organisation, and had consequently swayed their minds most successfully. Colonel Sleeman, though not personally acquainted with Captain Macpherson, had long been familiar with his work among the Khonds,[1] and had not failed to seize its peculiar traits. 'The Goomsur work,' he said, 'was not like other Indian district works, a work of administration, but one of policy, civil and religious, and there was not anything like it.'

Captain Macpherson's impressions of Bhopal, from first to last, were agreeable :—

' Sehore, Bhopal, 8th February 1854.

' I got here on the 1st of this month, and what I have seen of this country quite comes up to my expectations. First, in the way of people, I think we are lucky. Then I have a capital large bungalow[2] of twelve good rooms, in a pretty little park about a mile in breadth and three-quarters of a mile in length. A small river flows through it, which is caught by a dam and made a very pretty piece

---

lived under surveillance near Benares, and it was part of the duty of the Agent to manage their relations with the Government.

[1] Colonel Sleeman had written thus of him to Colonel Outram: 'I honour his character, and am delighted to find that Lord Dalhousie has sent him to Benares. He, too, was thwarted by those who ought most to have supported him.'

[2] Thatched house.

of water, and the clumps of trees are the very finest.
There is a capital drive round and through it, where most
of our people come.   I wish I had a picture, for it is one
of the prettiest places you ever saw, having been thus ela-
borately prepared for me, by my friend and predecessor
Maddock.   Then I have a capital garden, and an infinity
of produce.   I have not yet been to Bhopal, twenty miles
distant, to see my queen and her court.   This, however,
I expect to do in a few days ; we shall then have a fine
show.   Nothing can exceed the elegance, I am told, of
this little court.   The men whom I have seen are very
gentleman-like and refined-looking.   The country is a
vast open plain, with bare low hills and clumps of wood
containing magnificent trees.   We have scarcely a car-
riage-drive except in my park, and the solitude is rather
awful.   The work is not heavy at all—perfect rest after
Goomsur ; and this is what I want yet awhile, though I
do hope I shall not be forgotten here.'

'Bhopal, 21st February 1854.

'Bhopal is a very pretty and pleasant little country,
and I like all its circumstances quite as much as I expected.   I have just had my first meeting with the very
interesting court; and all the people of the Contingent being my guests has made it very pleasant.   You
must know we have three Begums, all totally dis-pur-
dahed,[1] who do everything but eat with us with the freedom of European women.   There are the grandmother,
the regent-mother, and the minor Begum on the musnud[2]
—a girl of sixteen, whose marriage is the knotty point
in hand.   The grandmother and mother ride, spear, and
shoot grandly, or have been used to do so—they being
now aged fifty-three and thirty-four respectively.   The
regent is a wonderful woman in the way of government;
for years she has worked everything herself.   With but

[1] A lady of rank in the East is said to sit behind the *purdah*—a screen or
curtain—so as to be concealed from the eyes of men.
[2] The musnud, or cushion of state, equivalent to throne.

eleven lacs[1] out of twenty-two lacs of total revenue at her disposal, she has paid off in eight years ten lacs of debt, reformed all her civil establishments, reorganised her army, resettled her revenue, and set up a new police and judicial system. She has been in the way of working ten and twelve hours daily, visiting every district, and seeing to the drill and equipment of almost every soldier. Her energy is quite wonderful, and her administrative ability very great. Two miles from my tents, the Shah Jehan, the girl on the musnud, met me on her elephant with all her chief ministers and nobles and state. I gave notice that I should arrive at 7 A.M., so the army was out at two and the young queen at five of a bitterly cold morning. She is a fat, not stupid-looking little girl, with one of her cheeks incredibly bulged with a lump of betel; and by her side was her Duchess of Sutherland, a very fine old lady, widow of a first-rate Christian minister of the state—a Bourbon long settled in India. Then we have had durbars,[2]—one at her house, and one for the men at my tents, my ladies looking through a purdah. Then, too, we have been to tea-drinking at her garden, and fireworks and music and nautching. The Secunder Begum-regent talks exactly, in her way, like the fastest European woman you may happen to know—for example, mixing politics with her personalities. We talked of the King of Lucknow's four hundred peris, and of Sleeman, passing to the theory and practice of revenue-surveying; the great mystery of my not being married, and that of the disposal of Nagpore; the question of my age, and that of how the present revenue settlement in Scindiah's country may stand five years hence; the comparative value of Cashmerian and English needlework, and the merits of the English and the Arab military exercises; the terrible nonsense of durbar forms and talk, and then (half an hour

---

[1] A lac, or lakh, is 100,000 rupees, or about £10,000 sterling.
[2] State receptions.

during the nautching) about Ryotwar, Goomsurwar,[1] &c.,
as if we had been a Board of Revenue. I happened
to say, somewhat emphatically, of those matters, that
everything depended on the way any system was worked
—on the "*uml*"[2]—that everything, in fact, was "*uml*."
And I wish you had seen how she turned to her
two ministers, sitting dumb some way off, and cried,
"Gentlemen, do you hear? That's *for you*!" "Uml
is *everything*." And I wish you had seen the salaams
which followed. This and much more of the same kind
was when we went to tea and music in her garden.
She shows a fine Elizabethan taste in the choice of her
officers of state. Our ladies think her commander-in-
chief the finest man they ever saw; his dressing of course
perfect; he is like a much-enlarged, robust D'Orsay. Her
Mahomedan minister is also fit for any court, and has a
garden for relaxation, poor man! next to hers; but you
can easily conceive that no breath of scandal floats at
Bhopal. The ladies' dress is capital—brocade tights, so
tight that they look sewed on. Above are drapery—
mainly jackets and shawls, worn as Englishwomen wear
them—and bare heads, except now and then a silver
scarf.'

'Sehore, Bhopal, 24th April 1854.

'I heard from Outram yesterday, full of his Baroda
success. All smooth and merry there.

'The idea that there is nothing to do at Bhopal is
a mistake. There is so much Persian business that
the mere signing is heavy work. There are such a
number of separate statelings and fragments of states
to be looked after, while you have so many neighbours on your boundaries, all having thieves to catch,
or boundary disputes to settle, or something. Then this

---

[1] I.e., about the land tenures in the Madras Presidency, and in Goomsur
in particular.
[2] Mode of administration.

princess to marry is work enough for one man. But I must say that the amount of experience I am gaining here is prodigious. All the peoples of India, with the exception of some thirty or thirty-five, meet here, and I deal with them all in every relation of life.'

'Sehore, Bhopal, 18th May 1854.

'I am rusticating quietly here, answering millions of petitions, and trying to get smoothly through with our princess's marriage arrangements.[1] The selection of a prince rests with the regent and the Government.'

Colonel Outram having, at the request of the Government of India, given up the Residency of Baroda and undertaken a painful and difficult charge at Aden, Colonel Malcolm, the Political Agent at Gwalior, an excellent officer, was appointed Resident at Baroda, and Captain Macpherson (who attained about this time by brevet the army rank of major[2]) was now advanced by Lord Dalhousie to the more important post of Political Agent at Gwalior,[3] whence the following letter was written:[4]—

'Gwalior, 11th July 1854.

'I have got to Gwalior all well, but I give you an incident to make the most of. A man on the road persuaded me to go a night's journey, not in my palanquin, but in his carriage drawn by bullocks. In the middle of the night it upset, and my face and head were much

---

[1] Colonel Sleeman wrote to him from Lucknow on the 22nd March 1854:—'Pray tell the Begum that she had much better get a husband for her daughter from some other place, for it is a hundred to one against her getting an honest man from Oude.'

[2] In his regiment, the good health enjoyed by his seniors prevented him from ever rising above the rank of captain.

[3] Colonel Outram wrote to him as follows, from Aden, on the 14th Aug. 1854:—'I trust you will like your new charge, and, if so, it will be some consolation to me for my self-sacrifice in leaving the fostering wing of the Government of India, as having been the indirect cause of your advancement.'

[4] In bidding farewell to the unrivalled Secunder Begum, it may be well to state that our Queen has acknowledged her friendly conduct during the Mutinies by conferring upon her the Star of the Order of British India.

smashed, my right eye escaping by a miracle, while all round it was cut and bruised. I lay quiet for four days, and am now all right, but with beauty impaired I fear. I am much charmed with Gwalior. The Residency is a very large two-storied house, full of everything I want in the way of furniture,[1] plate, crockery, &c. At this season too it is pretty, with a capital garden, woods, &c., but in hot weather it becomes a furnace. The worst of it is, however, that I must quit it from the 1st August to the 1st November.[2] There is a swamp near it which is kept for the cultivation of water-melons, and during those months fever inevitably appears, an enemy with whom I will hold no parley. I expected to have charge of Bundelcund, besides the Agency, but I am most glad to say I have not had it put on me. Thus I shall have abundant but not killing work.'

It will be remembered that Gwalior was taken under our particular charge by Lord Ellenborough, in 1844, after its rulers had attacked us and had been defeated in the battle of Maharajpore. The country was thenceforth governed by a Regency, under the advice of a British Agent, during the minority of the heir by adoption, the present Maharajah, who bears the hereditary name of Scindia—a Mahratta ruler, surrounded by a dominant class of Mahrattas, in a country the people of which are not Mahrattas, but are akin to the population of the British territories around them. Gwalior is formed of clusters of small principalities or petty chiefships, Rajpoot, Aheer, Goojur, &c., subdued and annexed by the Mahrattas ; the titular and pensioned representatives of the ancient rulers, regal and tribal, still existing and of course longing for an opportunity to reclaim their own. For the purpose of keeping down these principalities and tribes, a regularly disciplined force, commanded by

---

[1] The furniture was the property of his predecessor, from whom he bought it.

[2] During these months he resided in a house which he hired in the cantonments at Morar, several miles off.

FORT OF GWALIOR.

British officers, and forming part of our Bengal army, was
kept up by us, and paid from the revenues of districts
assigned to us for the purpose by the Gwalior Government.
It was called the Gwalior Contingent.

In 1854 the Maharajah was about nineteen years of age.
His education had been nearly confined to the use of his
horse, lance, and gun, whence his tastes were purely and
passionately military. He seemed to enjoy no occupation
save drilling, dressing, ordering, transforming, feasting,
playing with his troops, and the unwearied study of books
of evolutions, and he grudged no expenditure connected
with that amusement. He was not deficient in courage
nor in quickness of apprehension, but was impatient of
public business; and like other Eastern princes, he was
addicted to pleasure, and liable to be led by low favourites,
who were perpetually tempting him to disturb the regular course of administration by acts of personal interference, whence irregular gains might arise, in which they
would necessarily participate.

Important reforms had been initiated since the establishment of British influence at Gwalior.

In earlier days, the revenues of the State—derived, it
need not be said, chiefly from the land—were farmed by
officers who held permanent contracts, and who were
consequently interested in the prosperity of their districts.
But for ten years before our intervention, these officers were
replaced by a multitude of petty Pundit [Brahmin] farmers,
who, instead of holding permanent contracts, were superseded as often as they were outbid. Every man, therefore, wrung from his district all that he could extort. The
ruined peasantry emigrated in masses. The revenue of
some of the richest tracts fell off by two-thirds; and in
1844, when the British Government assumed the guardianship of Scindia's person and interests, the country was
on the verge of ruin.

· The members of the Regency were pressed by us to
give up the farming system, and to cause the revenue to

be assessed and collected by the officers of the State, under a village settlement for a term of years; but their interests were opposed to such a change, for they were themselves farmers of the revenue (though not in their own names); and all the influential classes—the Pundits, the Bankers, the courtiers, and State servants, were strongly arrayed against the proposed alteration, which would tend to prevent their irregular exactions. It happened, however, during the first year of our control—while Sir Richmond Shakespear lived at Gwalior as Political Agent, in subordination to the Governor-General's Agent, Colonel Sleeman, who resided at Jhansi—that two warlike Rajpoot clans, whom Scindia's Government held under a loose subjection, refused, as usual, to pay their revenue until they should see the force that was to take it. British aid was requested in reducing them, Scindia's commandants having always allotted four battalions of infantry, sixteen guns, and a body of horse, for the collection of the revenue from one of the two clans in question. The Political Agent, while he maintained the authority of the Gwalior Government, thought it right to guarantee to those clans a just and fixed settlement of the land revenue to be paid by them. He accordingly caused a five years' village settlement to be made—that is, leases for five years at a fair rent to be granted by the Government—in the district occupied by the two clans; but the Regency could not be induced to extend it to other provinces.

In 1852, however, Colonel Malcolm being then Political Agent, and Mr. Bushby Agent to the Governor-General, the President of the Regency died; and although but ten months of the Maharajah's minority remained,[1] the British Government embraced the opportunity to introduce the measures of reform which were judged necessary to save the State. It dissolved the Council of Regency, introduced the young Rajah at once to a part in affairs, and

---

[1] Eighteen had been fixed by treaty as the age of the Maharajah's majority.

with his consent appointed to the office of Dewan, or
Prime Minister, Dinkur Rao,[1] a young Pundit of Gwalior,
whose fitness had been tested as an instrument of our
initiatory revenue measures, when Sir Richmond Shakespear perceived his talents and brought him forward.
Mr. Bushby saw in him alone any hope of improving the
administration, while Colonel Malcolm at first conceived .
him to be overrated, but soon pronounced him to be the
ablest and best of the living natives of India.

Dinkur Rao, then, having been appointed to office by
the British Government, to carry out the reforms which
it had determined to introduce, adopted, with Colonel
Malcolm's support, the most active measures for that purpose. Scindia, though old enough to enable Colonel
Malcolm to dispense with a Regency, was not yet practically admitted to the exercise of power.

During the two years which succeeded, Dinkur Rao
effected a great revolution. He set up throughout the
country three departments, of revenue, justice, and police.
In the first, he abolished (throughout a considerable part
of the Gwalior territory) the farming system, and gave ten
years' leases to the people of every village. In the second,
he created a large establishment of Mahomedan judges,
mostly drawn from our territories and courts. In the
third, he established police stations, &c. all over the
country, under a separate organization. His rule was to
give high pay, and to abolish all perquisites, and bribes,
and exactions. On finding that the Pundits—his own
class—deliberately refused to co-operate in any sort of
revenue reform, Dinkur Rao fearlessly resorted to our
North-west Provinces for a supply of persons trained to
public business, retaining only about a third of the old
employés. The Brahmins, of course, resented this; but
the minister steadily held on his course.

Between the departure of Colonel Malcolm for Baroda

---

[1] Now Rajah Dinkur Rao.

and Major Macpherson's arrival, a period of about two months intervened, and during this time the young Rajah, wildly grasping at power, which he was unable to wield, had brought public affairs into the utmost confusion. His bad advisers incited him to insist upon governing as well as reigning, and to dismiss Dinkur Rao, whose continuance in power was a deathblow to their hopes of plunder ; and although the Rajah had fully accepted and had pledged himself to the reformed system of administration, they still strove to bring back the old tyranny. Our treaty with Gwalior provided that the Regency, while it subsisted, should be guided by the advice of our Agents, but it did not stipulate that the Rajah should be so guided. He was therefore free to appoint a new minister if he pleased. All believed that the ministry was at an end. Major Macpherson, on his arrival, had a delicate waiting game to play, not knowing a man in the place, and not having had one word with Colonel Malcolm. He thought it best to leave the Gwalior Court absolutely to themselves to fight it out, determined that the first move should come from the Rajah, and that it should never be in his power to say that we had imposed a minister upon him. So the Rajah at last took it on himself to decide, without even asking the Agent's advice, to retain Dinkur Rao in office.

Although the Maharajah had thus declared for Dinkur Rao, his mind was still kept in an unsettled state for many months by the intrigues of various aspirants to office, and the intermeddling of his grandmother by adoption, called the Baiza Baee, the widow of a former ruler of Gwalior, whose great wealth enabled her to influence Scindia, through the hope of becoming her heir. The political arrangements of Central India, which placed the Agent at Gwalior under the superintendence of the Governor-General's Agent, residing at Indore, 350 miles distant, were but too favourable to native trickery. The plan of raising differences between Scindia and his Dewan, and

between the office of the Political Agent at Gwalior and
that of the Governor-General's Agent at Indore, was a
familiar Indian expedient, and great efforts were made
to bring it into play.   But Sir Robert Hamilton, the
Governor-General's Agent, when his attention was called
to these intrigues, at once made it to be felt by all that he
was in perfect accord with Major Macpherson.   The latter
thenceforth pursued his policy at Gwalior, with the full
support of Sir Robert Hamilton, with whom he of course
continued in full communication throughout, but who left
him a large discretion, seeing that minute interference
could only paralyse the action of an officer so distant, and
whose conduct required to be adapted to circumstances
varying from day to day.

The duties of the Political Agent required him to take
part, by suggestion and advice, in securing to a wide
region that peace and good government which had been
partially restored to it by our interference.   Gwalior is
considerably more extensive than Oude,. and stretches
across Central India ; and it is intermixed with, or touches,
the confines of a great variety of states ; so that its good or
bad government is of importance far beyond its own limits.

To consolidate and to advance the new system of government, and to aid the wise and upright minister in
retaining his influence over the fluctuating and inconstant
will of Scindia ; to imbue the minds of prince and minister
with principles familiar to European statesmen, but new
to Orientals, and to suggest fresh measures for improving
the condition of the people—these were the objects of the
incessant endeavours of the Political Agent.

Scindia, as has been already stated, had, after his first dis-
astrous experiment in governing, freely restored the Dewan
to office, with power to carry out the reformed plan of
administration which we had initiated during his minority ;
and the Agent laboured to impart to him and his Durbar
the will and the power to make that plan, in its completion and development, their own ; leaving to Scindia

the utmost freedom of action consistent with political subordination and the stable maintenance of his administration. The Agent therefore took care not to interfere too much or too visibly, but to allow His Highness and the Dewan, in their spheres, themselves to direct and to work out the administration, considering themselves solely responsible for it, and exclusively entitled to the resulting honour or discredit; to allow His Highness, without question, the utmost latitude of action, especially with respect to his troops and his capital; and at the same time to maintain, by influence and advice, the essential conditions of the administration; as befitted the Power by whose protection Scindia's Government was maintained.

The Dewan was in fact the sole author and worker of the administration. His ambition was to save the State through its good government, and he seemed to understand that the time had passed for any affectation by Gwalior of unreal nationality, independence, or separateness of interest, and that the course left to it was that of municipal energy and prosperity through co-operation, approximation, assimilation to the Supreme State.

The event rewarded the Agent's efforts. His support gave free play to the administrative genius of Dinkur Rao; his suggestions fell upon no barren soil; and Gwalior rapidly advanced in every respect.

To touch briefly upon the public measures adopted during the first three years of Major Macpherson's Agency,—Scindia was induced, at a great immediate sacrifice of revenue, to abolish the transit duties on all the main routes in his dominions, and to lay out a very large sum of money on roads and bridges. The Dewan, with the Maharajah's full support, extended and revised the revenue settlement, and promulgated new codes regulating the Revenue and the Civil and Criminal Procedure.

The Revenue settlement worked with entire success. The dues of the Government were collected with facility, and without a balance, save where staple crops had

failed.   Cultivation and population everywhere increased
—especially in the districts earliest settled.   Wherever
the Agent went, he found contentment and distinct
signs of increasing prosperity.   The people asked for
nothing, except water for irrigation, and, where they
had learnt their value, for roads.

The first object of the Gwalior Government being to
maintain the village municipalities in integrity and energy,
the land of zemindars was not made saleable for arrears
of revenue ; other coercive processes being the same as
in our North-west Provinces.   Claims to zemindary land
after the lapse of a period of thirty years were prohibited.
A village boundary survey was instituted.   The little half-
independent principalities within the Gwalior dominions
were treated in a just and conciliatory spirit, and the
usual quarrels and coercion nearly ceased.

The revenue amounted (in round numbers) to about
800,000*l.*   Before 1843 there had been an annual deficit of 60,000*l.* ; during the period of the Regency,
the annual deficit had been 30,000*l.*   The estimate for
1855–56, after making a liberal provision for all the
objects of government, showed a balance in the treasury
of 15,000*l.*

The code of Civil Procedure was modelled after the
rules then in force in the Punjab, or those of the British
possessions in Burmah.   According to it, the first duty of
the judge is to effect the prevention or the compromise
of suits ; the next, to decide summarily, if possible, but to
call a Punchayet or committee of five where necessary :
in that case, however (contrary to the Punjab rule that
the judge still decides), the Punchayet decide as judges.
Professional pleaders are not admitted.   Coercive processes are nearly the same as in the Punjab, but pay or
pension is first sequestrated ; then land—zemindary land,
however, not being liable to sale ; and lastly, and with
great tenderness and precaution, personal property is
sequestrated and sold.   The Criminal code is in close

accordance with the Punjab rules, but it does not authorise capital punishment.

The Dewan adopted in his codes and his practice as much of our revenue, judicial, and educational systems as the intelligence and feelings of the people could bear. He had to contend with administrative difficulties somewhat analogous to our own, in governing, mainly by an alien and unpopular Mahratta agency, a population nearly identical in constitution and circumstances with those of our North-west Provinces.[1]

By the time that the codes were promulgated, a very large and fairly-paid police, organised like that of the North-west Provinces of British India, was spread over the country. For example, along the Agra and Bombay Road there were stations at intervals of a mile, and parties of horse at intervals of six miles. The number of heinous offences accompanied by violence was very small, save in the Malwa districts. The exaction of labour without pay, formerly the curse of the country, was abolished; as was also the provision of supplies without payment. Weights and measures were adjusted; schools were established in the principal towns and in some village districts; some bazaars and many wells of masonry and timber were constructed.

The Political Agent earnestly called the attention of the

---

[1] The following extract from a letter addressed to Major Macpherson by his old friend Mr. Bushby (the Secretary with whom he had corresponded when in charge of Khond affairs, and whose voice had been raised in vain against the unworthy treatment to which he was subjected), will tend to show the estimation in which this work was held :—

'Hyderabad Residency, 23rd August 1855.—I very much want to assist the Nizam's minister to govern the country better. He is willing and intelligent, but without experience, being very young. His experience is great only in the practices of the people in this vile city, where he learned much in the house and the ministry of his uncle the late Suraj-ool-Mulk. Your able Dewan, my esteemed friend Dinkur Rao, and the chief of the Adawlut at Gwalior, prepared a capital code of law and procedure for the administration of Scindia's country, brief and practicable, lucid in its proportions as well as in its provisions. Could you send me copies and let me know how all is working? Dinkur Rao's paper was the best I have ever seen, and would do credit to the Council of India.'

Gwalior Government to the usage of female infanticide, prevailing amongst the Rajpoot and some other races; and the Maharajah and the Dewan showed themselves anxious to do their utmost for its extinction. In 1855, the Dewan summoned a large assembly of Rajpoot chiefs on the Chumbul, and he and the Agent held with them two long discussions. All declared that the poverty, which had been an excuse for the practice, was at an end. 'We sit here,' said they, 'in cotton and silk dresses, who used to wear rags; and every man has two or three horses in his yard, who, in the old time, had not even an ass.' They moreover alleged that the practice was declining, and, although the Agent was opposed to the valueless formality, they insisted on giving a pledge to discontinue this usage, and to punish the perpetrators by expulsion from caste. His chief hope lay, however, in the Dewan's influence with one great tribe.

The Maharajah was, of course, generally, and the Dewan minutely, informed, from their constantly asking the Agent's advice, and from their endless conversations with him, of his impressions upon every point of policy; but, nevertheless, his first object, to lead them to direct and work out the administration by themselves, was fully attained.

It is not to be supposed that the reforms which have been spoken of were carried into effect without labour and anxiety,[1] caused by the nature of the changes

---

[1] At the end of his first six months at Gwalior, he writes :—'This office, with all its difficulties, is child's-play to what I have been accustomed to. I have actually at times a day to myself! Never, in Goomsur, had I one hour waking or sleeping. I really almost begin to think—to dream—that I may have some days of quiet service in India, like other people.'

In another letter, dated Gwalior, 28th March 1855, after noticing the Maharajah's extreme instability of character, he writes: 'On him, however, rests the structure of government. All we can do is to support it, with the aid of the Dewan and Sirdars, making the best of the circumstances of the day. Rajah and all are now wholly with me, through very lucky management, I venture to say, and so for the day we have bread. I have just got Scindia to do a great thing, viz., to abolish transit duties on his two great lines of road—that from Agra to Bombay, and from Saugor

themselves, necessarily interfering with existing interests; and also in a greater degree by the character of the young Maharajah, influenced as he was by worthless courtiers, with whom the Dewan, a man of high and unbending spirit, disdained to contend for his favour.

Scindia himself, on whom the fate of Oude made a deep impression, declared that but for the English counsels and support, the misgovernment in Gwalior must have equalled that of Oude.

Scindia was at all times anxious to obtain the approval of the Governor-General; and during a visit which he, accompanied by the Political Agent, paid to Calcutta in the spring of 1857, he was highly gratified by Lord Canning's attentions, and by his Lordship's assurance that in case of his death without male issue, the Government would not be disposed to assert its right of succession by lapse, but would recognise an adopted son.

The Dewan and several of the Chiefs of Gwalior accompanied their Prince; and the effect of the railway, steam-engine, electric telegraph, shipping, &c., upon all of

to Bombay—and to reform them on all other lines. I trust I shall be able to leave a good mark upon these poor people.'

Later he writes: 'I have the management of a man who should govern a fine kingdom, and I am able to keep things together and to hope decently for the future. I have much sleepless anxiety, but that is in the trade of whoever deals in politics, and in four years now I look to *final* liberation, with the company I desire, after working every day of my working life. I am just going to a Chobham we are getting up here, several Contingent forces, which will amount to 10,000 men.'

Colonel Outram writes from Lucknow, 4th December 1855: 'Your last indicated that you had no easy path before you at Gwalior, beset as it is by the usual amount at least of Mahratta intrigue; but I doubt not your straightforward mode of conducting business with the young Rajah will keep him straight, in spite of all the rascally endeavours of those about him to get him to thwart your measures. You are exactly the man to " confound their politics," and I only hope you may not get disgusted with the work, as I did at Baroda.'

It may be here mentioned that during the spring of 1856 Major Macpherson visited Calcutta. When he thanked Lord Dalhousie (then on the point of delivering up his charge to Lord Canning) for the kindness he had shown him, his Lordship replied, emphatically, 'What I have done for you is *nothing*.'

them was very great.   Scindia remarked, on seeing a spinning-mill at work, ' What a fine contrivance for saving the sweat of the poor!' and determined to have a steam-engine for his mint.   One of his Mahratta chiefs observed of Calcutta, ' Ah, this is a place to take the conceit out of a man!'   But they were all disgusted at seeing the Brahminee bulls, animals sacred in their eyes, employed in drawing dung-carts along the streets; a measure adopted by order of the Chief Magistrate long before, but which they attributed to the Governor-General's personal command.

CHAPTER XXIII.

1857.

THE MUTINY—THE GWALIOR CONTINGENT KEPT OUT OF THE FIELD.

Soon after Scindia's return to Gwalior from Calcutta, the mutinous spirit which had shown itself in the Bengal Army during the spring became more and more manifest, and the Sepoys at length broke out into open rebellion. Early in May, Meerut was sacked, and Delhi was lost to us; and it was plain that, unless the latter city could be instantly reoccupied, the movement would extend to the whole of Hindostan. The main proximate cause of the rebellion was the conjunction in our army, and to a great extent in our people, of the two convictions—that we had desired to overthrow the native religions for the establishment of Christianity,—and that by the will of our army, united chiefly by that belief, our empire could and must be overthrown.

Scindia and his minister, and a few of the best-informed of his Durbar, or court, did not hold these opinions, but considered the religious apprehension groundless, and believed that, through our Indian or our European resources, the British power must eventually triumph. But the Gwalior Contingent (which was a local branch of *our* army), and Scindia's own army of 10,000 men, and almost all Scindia's private companions and friends, with the great mass of his subjects, shared the convictions of our army and our people; and the task of the Political Agent was to induce Scindia to maintain and act on his own

convictions in co-operation with us, in antagonism to
the revolt, and to oppose it mainly by demonstrating
that he considered the religious panic groundless, and
our power immovable. It was quite uncertain whether,
amid the storm of passion, interest, and prejudices raised
by this great convulsion, the Maharajah's wayward
mind could be led to maintain its confidence in us, so
that he might afford to us, not aid according to his engagements merely, but the earnest and demonstrative
co-operation which the juncture demanded. Had Major
Macpherson's influence over him or that of the Dewan
not been exerted to the uttermost, he might at any
time have broken away, his head turned by the idea of
being chief, instead of relying on the eventual success of
our Government, and might have come with the troops
to try how large a share of dominion he could get.

Fortunately, his close intercourse with Major Macpherson for the three preceding years had led him to
regard that officer with confidence and respect; his visit
to Calcutta had enlarged his view of our resources, and
Lord Canning's intimation that adoption would be permitted to him, had reassured him as to the continuance
of his own dynasty, so far as our Government was concerned; while he was easily led by the Agent to see that
if the soldiery gained the ascendant, the Rajpoot, Jat, and
other ancient races whom his own Mahratta government
held in subjection, would in all probability throw off their
allegiance to him: in short, on this, as on former occasions, he adopted as his own the plans suggested by the
Agent, and he adhered to them zealously.

For a month after the seizure of Delhi by the Sepoys
the English held their ground at Gwalior. As the
situation gradually became more dangerous, the Agent's
communications with the Rajah and Dewan were
ceaseless. When he did not visit Scindia, the Dewan
generally came to tell him his mind, to discuss all the
phenomena of the revolt, and every point of the situation

in Gwalior, and to receive the encouragement so much needed under the extraordinary difficulties of his part.

During this time, Scindia had done his utmost to co-operate with us, by despatching his Bodyguard to Agra, to attend upon the Lieutenant-Governor ; by sending his personal Mahratta troop to Etawah ; by warning the Political Agent, on the 26th May, of the impending defection of the Contingent ; by then arranging personally for making the Residency a place of refuge ; by protecting the families of the Contingent officers, who by order of the Brigadier repaired to it for safety when an immediate outbreak was apprehended ; by inviting those families to his Palace for full security,[1] and thus showing that he was entirely with us. But, to neighbouring chiefs, to the soldiery, and to his people alike, by far the most generally appreciated and unequivocal of his acts was—his giving to his Dewan (regarded by all as the prime enemy of the revolt) his full confidence and the highest powers ; while with the Dewan acted his commander-in-chief Mohurghur, and the second in command, Bulwunt Rao, whose earnest co-operation was indispensable to the management of the troops.

To understand the full meaning of the Dewan's ascendancy, it must be remembered that there existed, ever at Scindia's ear, and especially at his revels, a party composed of the remnant of that faction which brought on the fight of Maharajpoor in 1843, and of the corrupt intriguers whose great aim was the overthrow of the Dewan and the restoration of the system of farming the revenue. Scindia listened, as usual, to this party, and it thought its opportunity had come ; but he met all the Agent's views with the utmost heartiness and candour, and acted thoroughly with the Dewan.

At length, on the 14th of June, when the troops at most of our stations in Upper India had mutinied, the

---

[1] They afterwards returned to the cantonment, to Scindia's deep regret.

Contingent rose at Gwalior.[1]   The outbreak was fore-
shadowed by the usual premonitory symptoms, which yet
failed there, as elsewhere, to open the eyes of the brave
but too confiding officers; and Scindia's warnings, conveyed to them by the Political Agent, went for nothing
as against the consummate hypocrisy of the Sepoys; who,
while they were leagued for the immediate destruction of
their officers, protested boundless devotion to the State,
and execration of the murderous traitors of Meerut and
Delhi; and affected to be profoundly distressed by any
sign of want of confidence, such as that the officers or
their families should sleep elsewhere than in the lines, or
that the British treasure or magazine should be given into
any custody save their own.

Upon the afternoon of the 14th the mess-house and a
bungalow in the cantonment were burnt down, one regiment working with good-humoured alacrity to extinguish
the flames.   About 9 P.M. the artillery loaded their guns.
Their officers immediately went to their lines, but brought
back word that it was a false alarm, the men having
imagined that Europeans were upon them.

But the outbreak commenced immediately after, with
loud shouts, tumult, and bugling in the lines; through
which men rushed calling to arms, 'for the Europeans
had come'—the cry of that night.   The Brigadier ordered
the officers who were with him to their lines.   There
firing began, and gradually extended to the whole station,
while bungalows blazed up.   Then ensued a cold-blooded
massacre, such as had already occurred in other places.

Every commanding officer—Major Blake of the 2nd,
and Sherriff of the 4th Regiment, and Captains Hawkins
and Stewart of the batteries—fell.

Blake went to his lines on the first alarm, and was shot at
his main-guard.   His men, amidst whom Doctor Mackellar

---

[1] That is, the bulk of the force, which was stationed at Gwalior.   The
regiments at out-stations also rose, but not all on the same day.

found him dying, wept over him and professed deep sorrow, declaring strongly, but falsely, that the 4th Regiment had killed him. They themselves, at least, gave him burial, savagely denied to all others. How Sherriff fell amidst the volleys which flew everywhere is unknown. Hawkins, who had with him his sick wife on a litter and five children, besides Mrs. Stewart with her two children, was killed in the cavalry lines, it is said by the infantry, while two of his children also perished. When he fell wounded in front of a hut where the ladies were sheltered, Mrs. Stewart went and took his hand, and the volley which killed him killed her also, with a child. Stewart was wounded that night, but nursed through it by two of his men, and deliberately shot the next day. Doctor Kirk, superintending surgeon, was sought out and murdered in an outhouse. The chaplain, Mr. Coopland, wholly unknown to the troops, was pursued with volleys through cantonments and cut down. Lieutenant Proctor, of the 4th, who had in his care the sick wife of an absent brother officer, and did not attempt escape, was searched out, after concealment through the night, and murdered before his wife by infantry and horsemen. Four sergeants and two pensioners also fell, as did Mrs. Burrows, the widow of a conductor, and Mrs. Pike, a sergeant's wife.

There were killed seven officers, six sergeants and pensioners, three women, and three children—nineteen in all; while there escaped of the men of the Contingent (some under showers of bullets, but favoured by a moonless night) seven officers, one sergeant, and two medical sub ordinates. The women and children likewise escaped, with the exceptions which have been mentioned.

The surviving officers made either for the Maharajah's Palace, or for the Residency,[1] where, under the guard of his Highness' troops, they were safe. Two officers rode straight for Dholepore and Agra.

---

[1] The cantonments and the Residency were each of them several miles distant from the Maharajah's Palace.

The cantonment guards favoured, or aided actively, the escape of several officers and families. Thus, of the 2nd Regiment, three men escorted Lieutenant Pearson, and carried his wife in a litter, seven miles to the Residency; and the guard of the 1st Regiment over the family of its absent commandant behaved admirably.

The rearguard of the 4th Regiment protected most faithfully Captains Murray and Meade and their families, while a party of the 2nd came to destroy them.

Against our rule the Contingent apparently acted as one man; but they were so much divided as to the slaughter of their officers, that four out of seven infantry regiments, two out of four batteries of artillery, and the two regiments of cavalry (excepting a party at Gwalior) killed none.

On hearing of the outbreak, Major Macpherson immediately proceeded to join the Maharajah. His carriage, which contained also his sister, Mrs. Innes, who was on a visit to him (and who showed remarkable presence of mind throughout the whole of these events), and an officer just escaped from cantonments, was soon arrested by the levelled muskets of a party of five or six Sepoys. They belonged to a band of Ghazees, bound to Delhi under Jehangeer Khan, once a havildar in the Contingent, then a favourite captain of Scindia's, now a Ghazee leader of the highest pretensions to sanctity. They vehemently demanded the lives of the English party, with which, besides a Mahomedan escort, were some forty Mahratta horsemen. The Mahratta captain of the bodyguard told Major Macpherson at the time that the Ghazees had yielded on his threatening destruction to all who should oppose him, but it afterwards appeared that he had said he was conveying the Agent, by Scindia's express order, a prisoner to him, whereupon the Ghazees expressed satisfaction and drew back, and the carriage passed on.

The party found Scindia at his palace, the Phoolbagh

(Flower Garden), surrounded by his troops under arms. The Brigadier, and several other officers with their families, had already arrived there ; and they believed that all who were left in cantonments had perished.   Patrols of the Maharajah's troops, most likely to save them, were, however, looking for them in all directions.

Major Macpherson, while desiring that his party should be forwarded to Agra, insisted that he should himself remain with Scindia—an offer which, considering the circumstances under which it was made, evinced no ordinary degree of courage and self-devotion.   But the life of the Political Agent was sought above all others by the rebels, and Scindia positively refused to allow him to remain.   Indeed he thought it so clear, from the attitude of the rebels and the feeling of his own troops, that he could not protect the Europeans for an hour, that he had already ordered for them carriages, palanquins, and an escort of the bodyguard.   He expressed infinite anxiety as to his own course.   Of the rebels, he knew generally that they contemplated either his enrolling and leading them against Agra, or his giving them a large mass of treasure, while, if he refused these alternatives, they would bombard his palace and city.   He feared that his troops would coalesce with them, and, as they had powerful artillery and magazines, he was certainly at their mercy.

So far as his mind could be discerned in the confusion of the scene, it seemed plain that Scindia was prepared to purchase the departure of the rebels from his territory.   But Major Macpherson asked of him, at whatever cost, to detain them within Gwalior until we could assemble an European force to crush them, which might, perhaps, not be before the Dusserah, or the 29th September, while he assured him that the Government would consider this most friendly service.

The Dewan enquired—if it should appear that, for the detention of these rebels against both Governments, no course could avail save that of giving them service, would the Governor-General approve of that? The Agent said that the difficulty was obvious, but that, if no other means might avail, Scindia should detain the rebels by service, until we were ready to deal with them. The Maharajah, through the Dewan, promised that the wishes of the Government should be executed if possible.

The risks incurred by the Agent and his party, consisting of thirty men, women, and children, on their march to Kaintree Ghaut on the River Chumbul, were very considerable.

In Hingonah, a village twelve miles from the Chumbul, they found posted Jehangeer Khan with the band already mentioned, consisting of some two hundred Ghazees, mostly from our or Scindia's ranks. After long parley, he protested that he did not wish to injure the Europeans; and came to visit them, arrayed in green, fingering his beads in ceaseless prayer. But in concert with him, a body of plunderers were assembled to attack them in the ravines fringing the river.

The captain of the bodyguard said he was alarmed by the double danger, from which he saw no way of escape; while his men refused to move forward that night. In the hope of avoiding one peril, Major Macpherson resolved to abandon the carriages and start the ladies and children on horseback, after midnight, by a bridle-path towards Rajghât, lower down the Chumbul. But the Dewan had summoned to aid them Thakoor Buldeo Sing, chief of the Dundouteeah Brahmins, a robust and warlike tribe of that quarter; and at midnight the chief most happily appeared, with a strong body of followers. He declared warmly that he had not forgotten that Major Macpherson had interceded with the Dewan for certain tanks and wells for his people, and he said that they would defend the party with their lives. He placed one body of men to watch Jehangeer Khan, and with another he conducted the Europeans towards the river.   At the edge of the ravines, the bodyguard, despite of remonstrances and reproaches, turned their backs upon the party.   With them went the horse and the palanquin-bearers, while the coachmen were forced on.

On the farther bank of the Chumbul, opposite one of two paths which strike it at the ghât, the elephants and escort of the friendly Rana (Prince) of Dholepore were in waiting.   But a party of Jehangeer Khan's band had taken post during the night in the ravines over that path. As the party proceeded along, however, Buldeo Sing learnt their presence in time to change the route, and all crossed in safety.

The Rana of Dholepore treated the Europeans with great kindness, and gave them safe escort along the highly disturbed route to Agra, which they reached on the 17th.   He extended equal care to a large party of the ladies and children, who soon afterwards followed them from Gwalior in the extremity of distress.[1]

From great exposure in passing his party over the Chumbul, Major Macpherson suffered a sunstroke, which, added to the extreme strain of anxiety which he had endured, produced severe and continued illness.

Sir Robert Hamilton had left India, on leave of absence, in April 1857, and did not return till December 16th ; and from this circumstance, or from difficulties of communication, Major Macpherson had, during the first eight months of the revolt, no intercourse with him, or with the officer who officiated for him.   Our relations with the Gwalior State, therefore, remained during those eight months in the sole charge of Major Macpherson, who, under orders

---

[1] It does not appear to have been part of the plan of the Sepoys to mur-der the women and children.   At least, on the day after the massacre they sent off. after very insulting treatment, those who survived to the Maharajah. He forwarded them to the Chumbul in carts.   To have attempted more had been their certain destruction, as he was very hard pressed to save the lives even of the Christian families in his hereditary service, furiously demanded by the fanatics.

from Lord Canning, communicated (so far as communication was possible, which it was only to a most limited extent) with the Supreme Government direct. But from no quarter did he receive any instructions for his guidance, or any sanction for his proceedings : everything was done upon his own responsibility alone.

Gwalior, while it thus continued in his hands, might have been regarded as in one sense the key of India, or rather, perhaps, as one link of a chain, which could not have given way in any part without ruining our power in India. If the Ruler of Gwalior had either played us false, or succumbed to the strong adverse elements with which he had to contend, the Revolt would almost certainly have been national and general instead of being local and mainly military ; and instead of its fate being decided by those operations in the easily traversable Gangetic valley, upon which public attention was concentrated, we should have had to face the warlike races of Upper India combined against us, in a most difficult country ; and, in all probability, those of the South also.

The Europeans being gone, the Contingent, as part of our army which had brought our empire to its last hour, offered their services to Scindia, but only as his masters : he must place himself at their head (when they would enable him to take Agra, and share our dominions), or he must give them the mass of treasure they demanded to enable them to move off. Unless he conceded one or other of these demands, they would bombard and plunder his palace and city, empty his treasury, and carry off his person. To keep such men near him was like holding a wolf by the ears, and he, of course, desired to buy them off at the lowest price. But Major Macpherson had required of him, as high service to our Government, to detain them. This Scindia and Dinkur Rao, through the most wonderful combination of firmness, courage, and skill, effected up to the 15th of October.

But for Major Macpherson's parting demand and adjuration to the Dewan and his Highness, enforced with all the weight which three years of confidential intercourse could give, to keep the Contingent at Gwalior for *our objects*, at any possible cost or risk to Gwalior or to Scindia personally, it is not to be supposed that Scindia or the Dewan would have kept the Contingent there for a day. They naturally wished to get rid of these sepoys out of their territory. All engagements to the British Government would thus have been fulfilled. Indeed, they could not with propriety or safety have attempted to detain the rebels, except on the express requisition of the British Agent; for the sepoys could only be detained by compliances which must (as the event showed) deeply compromise Scindia in the eyes of any of the British authorities who were not aware that such a requisition had been made. But that they should adopt a course of purely British policy, indicated by the Political Agent, strikingly at variance with what the immediate interests of Gwalior seemed to prescribe, and should work out month after month the Agent's requirements as they did, was a proof of the highest ascendancy on his part, sustained even in absence, and under the utmost pressure of ever-changing difficulties. Had that ascendancy failed for one instant, while from his cell in the fort of Agra he sent to them daily words of encouragement and counsel, in reply to their messages of agony or despair; had they ceased to confide implicitly in his knowledge of every circumstance, and his appreciation of every man's conduct, and, above all, in the correctness of his judgment as to their proper course, and in his power to obtain the assent of the Government to his views in the face of opposite ones, expressed in an important quarter (which all but overthrew Scindia),—the Dewan could not possibly have held his ground with Scindia, nor could he and Scindia have persevered in their course.

The Dewan, as Major Macpherson always emphatically

said and wrote, is a man of rare genius and noble mind. His merit was unspeakably great, and to him everything in fact was due; but without ideas, and convictions, and moral support, which Major Macpherson, or some one in his position, alone could have afforded to him through years of intimate converse—and especially during the month that they spent together after the outbreak, discussing it line upon line,—he must necessarily have been quite powerless to face that storm.

No one save an energetic and far-seeing Political Agent could have supported the Dewan through such a struggle; and no Minister not gifted with great sagacity, courage, and constancy, could have conquered in it, whatever assistance had been afforded him. Nor does the credit, whatever it may be, to which the Agent and the Minister are entitled, derogate at all from the merit of Scindia's conduct.

On the 5th of July, a rebellious force coming from Neemuch reached Agra, and fought Brigadier Polwhele's force. The rebels held the field and claimed the victory, while we retired into the fort, and abandoned, without an effort, our capital station in the North-west to be burnt and plundered during two days; the blood of at least twenty Christians being shed — not by the enemy, who withdrew on the night of the action, but by the ruffians of the city and villages, the traitorous police, and the prisoners who had escaped from the broken gaol.

It was believed that we were entirely broken and paralysed. The Neemuch rebels, by a deputation, conjured those of Gwalior to join them for certain victory; and these demanded vehemently of the Maharajah treasure and supplies for their march, while his own troops recruited from our provinces joined in the demand.

Scindia in this dark hour, when he was supported only by the Dewan and the two chiefs of his troops, had undoubtedly many inducements to take part against us. He had always been possessed by a mania for military

Y

pursuits.   He had a name round which Hinduism would
have rallied.   High influence was inseparable from his
territory, touching states or provinces almost numberless
between the Chumbul and the Godavery—between Bundelcund and Guzerat.   He had 10,000 men of his own,
besides the Contingent, which amounted to 6,000 more,
with siege-train and ample magazine.   A party within
the Durbar, strongly opposed to our rule, conjured him to
seize the hour.   The Nana Saheb, with strong claims on
Mahratta feeling, and the wealth of the ex-Peishwa, and
a large host, triumphed at Cawnpoor.   Of Oude we held
but our beleaguered position in Lucknow.   The chiefs of
Bundelcund, at least, hung upon Scindia's example.   The
Bhopal and Malwa Contingents, and most of Holkar's
troops, were on the verge of revolt.   At Delhi we but
held our ground.   No man was sure of Seikh aid, or of
the China force ; but, above all, the Fort of Agra stood
nearly unprepared, and crowded like a beehive.   Had
Scindia then struck against us—nay, had he even done his
best in our behalf, but failed—the character of the rebellion
might have been changed almost beyond the scope of
speculation.   But he believed in our final triumph, and
that it was his true policy to strain his power to contribute
to it ; and that belief was created and kept alive, in the
face of every difficulty, exclusively by the Political Agent.[1]

The rebels, after the outbreak, had called to be their
general a native officer of the 1st Regiment ; but the
most violent sepoys, in fact, commanded.   These troops

---

[1] A civil officer of great experience, who was present at Agra during
this summer, writes as follows :—' Few know how much we, at Agra, are indebted to Major Macpherson for our immunity from attack by the full force
of the Gwalior Contingent, with their powerful siege artillery.   The real
state of the case was this: the Political Agent had full influence over
Scindia's Dewan, or Prime Minister, the celebrated Dinkur Rao ; the Minister in his turn influenced his master ; and thus Major Macpherson, from
the interior of the fort at Agra, ruled the course of events at the Court of
Gwalior.'—' Notes on the Revolt in the N. W. Provinces of India,' by
Charles Raikes, Judge of the Sudder Court at Agra, late Civil Commissioner with Sir Colin Campbell, &c. ch. xvi. London, 1858.

spent their whole time in councils, Punchayets, courts, and deputations; and the Maharajah was compelled to receive daily—'to report'—one of the latter, composed of officers from every corps with privates delegated to watch them —bodies of from thirty or forty to a hundred men. They menaced, beseeched, dictated, wheedled, and insulted Scindia by turns. For four months he confronted, defied, flattered, deceived them; above all, through endless arts, kept them at loggerheads, until he finally baffled and despatched them to rout by our arms, sending them, not to Agra, where they would have done infinite mischief, but to Cawnpoor, where it was known that they were likely to meet with a European force capable of dispersing them.

It were tedious to recount how he sowed dissensions among the rebels; how he ordered the removal of the wheels of all carts that were within their range, and sent all elephants and camels to distant jungles; how, when a formidable body of rebels from Mhow and Indore, which had been detained by him for some time, broke away towards Agra, he by a secret movement, suggested by the Agent, swept the Chumbul of its boats, so that those who remained could not pass on, and those who had passed could not return; how he summoned from the provinces his chiefs or Thakoors and their retainers. The results may be stated, but the dangers and discouragements he encountered from day to day cannot be portrayed. His conduct, however, on one memorable occasion deserves particular notice.

After the departure of the Mhow and Indore men, the Contingent demanded peremptorily of the Maharajah his final plans, and, to hear them, their officers attended on the 7th of September with some 300 men in his palace-garden. Scindia asked what their wishes were. The officers began to reply; but the sepoys thrust them aside, and said that they had resolved immediately to take Agra and destroy the Christians there, when they would carry Scindia's

banner where he pleased.   He replied that, by their own
showing, they did not await his orders; that their movement, until after the rains, would be against his will, and
they should receive from him neither pay nor supplies.
The sepoys declared indignantly that they had been betrayed; and returning to their camp, planted a green flag
for Mahomedans, a white flag for Hindus.   Deputations
invited Scindia's troops to join them, for their common
objects.   They wrote to pray the rebel force at Banda to
come to crush him, and they prepared their batteries.

Scindia was in despair; one of his corps was certainly
with the rebels, and all, save the Mahrattas, seemed about
to join the green and white standards.   Then he would
have no alternative save to become a puppet in their hands,
or to fly to us.   Had but a bugle sounded or an alarm-
gun fired in his lines that night, his troops would have
risen uncontrollably.   He had every bugle brought to his
palace, and every gun watched.   At daybreak he paraded
his whole force.   He appealed to them corps by corps, it
is said very touchingly, against the insulting coercion
which the rebellious Contingent threatened.   His own
army, though in accord with the rebels in their feelings
towards the British power, did not desire that he should
be coerced by the Contingent; and on his addressing
himself to his best-affected regiment of Gwalior men, that
regiment declared enthusiastically for him.   Then another
corps, mainly of Gwalior men, did so.   Of his two corps
from our provinces, one was fully, one far committed to
the rebels.   But both had Mahratta officers, and they
also professed obedience.   Scindia required that, in proof
of it, one of these corps should give up the ringleaders of
the defection to the green and white flags; and they
gave up twenty men, whom he instantly placed in irons
and in gaol.   He promised daily batta to his troops, and
increased his irregular Thakoor levies from 6,000 to
11,000 men.

The rebels at once planted their batteries against Scindia's palace and city. The Maharajah moved out his whole force, and himself placed every battery and picket, and arranged his Thakoor force. His spirit, and the adhesion of his troops, surprised the rebels. A portion of the Contingent cavalry, which had been for some time with him in a sort of neutral attitude, joined his ranks. He cut off the supplies of the rebels, and doubled his guards on the Chumbul to prevent the threatened return of the Mhow and Indore body from Dholepore. His emissaries sowed fresh dissensions. The 5th Regiment, with which the rest had quarrelled on account of its killing some of the native officers who had led it to mutiny, and the men of the 6th Regiment offered to fight for him. The Banda force would not come to Gwalior. The Contingent lost heart ; professed to be satisfied, after examining accounts, that they had received nearly all 'their own' money—deposited in Scindia's treasury by the Political Agent—and within six days withdrew their guns, while Scindia maintained his posts.

The appearance of Vakeels from the Ranee of Jhansi and the Nana Saheb, bidding high for the services of the Contingent and for their magazine, now introduced amongst them fresh distractions, which Scindia turned to instant account. If they would join the Nana Saheb at Cawnpoor, settling Jhansi and Jaloun for him by the way, the Nana's Vakeel promised to all high pay, while he conferred brigadierships and ensigncies by the dozen ; and finally the rebels asked leave of Scindia to go to Bundelcund and Cawnpoor, instead of to Agra—which he could but promise—about the 23rd of September.

They demanded with ceaseless violence the performance of that promise ; and great indeed was Scindia's difficulty in carrying out our desire—at once to guard against the risk of their precipitating themselves from some new impulse upon Agra, and to delay their march upon Cawnpoor.

By the fall of Delhi, about the 20th of September,

Scindia's situation was of course entirely changed. The delusion that he must at length place himself at the head of the revolt was at an end, although many still believed that our empire must fall. Notwithstanding this event, and the rout and dispersion of the Mhow and Indore sepoys by Colonel Greathed at Agra, on the 10th of October, it was not in Scindia's power longer to detain the rebels from moving upon Cawnpoor, save at the immediate risk of their turning against Agra, to which the party whose object was war and the compromising of Scindia with us at all hazards, still urged them.

The rebels, when at length they marched for Cawnpoor under Tantea Topeh, who had been sent by the Nana to obtain their aid, fiercely wasted Scindia's country, denouncing him as the great enemy and betrayer of their cause; and they extorted money from a chief on their march by destroying his son's eyes with boiling oil.

They reached Cawnpoor on the 1st of December, and being reinforced from Banda and from Oude, they pressed General Windham's force into its entrenchments, but were finally routed on the 10th, by the force under the Commander-in-Chief, Sir Colin Campbell.

Thus a force of at least 16,000 men, of whom upwards of 6,000 were good and unbroken troops, with ample artillery and magazines, was kept out of the field for four most critical months, when the fate of Agra or that of Delhi might have been determined by their movements; and a great territory was interposed, as a non-conductor of rebellious influences, between the disturbed districts and the southern and western regions of India.

It needs but a glance at the map to show what the result might have been had Gwalior sided with the rebels. The Nizam's territories, already sufficiently inflammable, would assuredly have caught fire; and it is questionable, whether in that case any part of Southern India could have been saved.

The difficulty of Scindia's task was greatly enhanced by the state of public opinion in his dominions, where the feelings of the population, Hindu and Mahomedan, were generally very much the same with those of the Hindus and Mahomedans of our own provinces.

It was the opinion of the more intelligent chiefs of the Gwalior State, who were but few in number, that the Bengal native army believed our Government to have intended, through the greased cartridges, to strike at the Hindu and Mahomedan religions in favour of Christianity. But they held that the army was predisposed to revolt through the disaffection of the population, and that the chief causes of the popular dissatisfaction with our rule were—the extinction of Native States, and our consequent measures; the depression of chiefs and heads of society; the resumption, or the conversion into life-tenures, of hereditary rent-free tenures of land, or of hereditary interests connected with land or the land revenue; the alienation of zemindary lands for arrears of revenue, or in satisfaction of civil decrees; the non-conferment of estates or honours for eminent services to the State; the want of conciliatory and confidential personal intercourse between our officers and the native chiefs, heads of society and people; our system of administering civil justice.

In the opinion, however, of the wisest of these chiefs, the examples of Malcolm and Elphinstone, and of many others, showed that our rule could be made very acceptable to the people of India, and its unpopularity arose essentially from the incapacity of the people to appreciate its principles and excellences; from their having forgotten the evils suffered under native governments; and from their impatience of small grievances, engendered through their relief and protection by us from great ones. The mercantile class were contented with our rule, and also the lowest agricultural class, save when moved by sympathy with the higher. Our revenue settlement in the North-west

Provinces was lighter, more equitable, and more acceptable to all than any that ever existed in Hindostan. All blessed the goodness and security of our highways. Under native governments, past and present, the dissatisfaction had been, and was, as great as or greater than under our Government, but different in its origin, and grievances were endured in a different spirit, from their being old, while the governors and governed were one, or were socially intimate.

CHAPTER XXIV.

SCINDIA'S OVERTHROW AND RESTORATION.—ILLNESS AND
DEATH OF MAJOR MACPHERSON.

1858–1860.

THE following letter, written at Agra, on the 27th March 1858, may serve to indicate the state of affairs in Upper India at that time :—

'I have had to write a long letter to Lord C., to try and make him station the European troops of the new Contingent *at Gwalior*. Our principle should be to place commanding forces *at the capitals*: the districts will take care of themselves. Then I am at my wits' end for a Gwalior force—I mean one for the Rajah. His force mainly now consists of men from our provinces, who are all, he says, hostile to us, like our own late army. I proposed to supersede them by Mahrattas, not more friendly, but who will wait on Scindia's will ; and Lord Elphinstone objects strongly to this, believing, I presume, that the Mahrattas want only the Nana Saheb—anybody but us : the sign whereof is the offer of a lac of rupees for his capture. I am considerably anxious as to the effect of Nana coming to Gwalior. Till Jhansi and Calpee shall fall, it must be highly disturbed. The people there don't at all believe that Lucknow is fallen, or that we have a big army ; or why do we leave Calpee so long alone ? They believe that we are hard pressed, though victorious, and say it is their own *policy* to fly and renew the fight, so as to wear us out in the hot weather and rains.'

Scindia—influenced solely by his reliance on Major

Macpherson, and disregarding alike the threats and the
flattery of the Contingent, and the desires of his own
troops, of his intimate friends, of nearly all his chiefs and
people—had allowed himself to be guided by the Dewan
and by his two faithful military chiefs, and had himself acted
with much tact and spirit.   He had thus—at the greatest
personal risk, as is proved by the events which are about
to be narrated—succeeded in effecting the object, vital to
British interests, of keeping the most formidable and best-
appointed body of Sepoys in India out of the field till it
had lost its importance, and he had then sent it to its
destruction.   But he was still left to cope with his own
troops, partly composed (as already mentioned) of Poorbeahs—men belonging to our provinces, who sympathised
with the rebels; while the other portion (the Mahrattas
and the men drawn from Gwalior itself) had with difficulty been combined, by the great zeal and steadfastness
of Mohurghur and Bulwunt Rao, to check and baffle both
the Contingent and Scindia's sympathising troops, and to
prevent them from uniting.   Unhappily, when the danger
seemed to be past, Scindia no longer availed himself of
the skilful pilotage of the Dewan.   He withdrew his
confidence and practical support from Mohurghur and
Bulwunt Rao, preferring his own unworthy favourites, and
in this way lost his hold upon the faithful soldiers who
had stood by him.   At the same time, contemplating the
eventual dismissal of his Poorbeahs, he was so unwise as
to make his intention known to them, thus withdrawing
from them any inducement to adhere to his cause.   He
completed the list of mistakes by massing his whole force
at the capital, where the emissaries and the contagion of
the revolt were strongest.

In May 1858, whilst he was thus unconsciously playing
the game of the rebels, the most dangerous of them all,
Tantea Topeh, was secretly at work in Gwalior, cor-
rupting that portion of his troops which had remained
faithful.

Already, in September 1857, when he went there to gain the Contingent to the Nana, and move it upon Cawnpoor, Topeh had become thoroughly acquainted with the ground. He saw (as was stated by one of his chief agents) that the Maharajah, influenced by the Dewan, was the only serious obstacle to the acquisition of Gwalior to the revolt ; and that the sole hope of mastering that obstacle lay in gaining over the Mahratta and Gwalior divisions of Scindia's troops which still looked to him for guidance, in addition to those who already sympathised with the rebels. Then Scindia might be seized, or overborne, or compromised with us, when the Princes of Hindostan would still rise. These ideas he worked out in May 1858, ere yet the rebel leaders relinquished Calpee to Sir Hugh Rose ; and on the 28th of May, shortly after that event, the rebels moved across the Sinde river, Scindia's frontier, to Amaen. The leaders were—the Rao Saheb, connected, by adoption, with the Nana and the late ex-Peishwa ; Tantea Topeh—in foresight, resource and influence with individuals and masses, the soul of the Nana's cause ; the Nawab of Banda ; the Rance of Jhansi, an ardent, daring, licentious woman, under thirty, who rode in military attire, with sword and pistols, followed by forty horse from Kotah, and by a Brahminee concubine of her late husband.

Major Macpherson had remained in Agra up to May, Scindia declaring truly that he could not receive him until he could appear with an escort of Europeans.

Towards the end of April he had been summoned from Agra to meet Sir Robert Hamilton in Sir Hugh Rose's camp, and to take a force to Gwalior after Calpee should have fallen. He made his way accordingly with Colonel Riddell's troops, and arrived at Calpee in time to see that place—which might have made a serious defence—evacuated by the rebels. Sir Hugh Rose, on hearing what the Agent had to say regarding the state of affairs in Gwalior, perceived the necessity of sending troops thither : for although the Maharajah had been able to hold his ground thus far, it was plain that without the assistance he solicited he could not regain his authority over his subjects and his soldiery—hostile to us, though still held in check by him. But our aid did not arrive in time.

The following letter is from Calpee, 1st June (117° to 120° in tents) :—

' The rebels have next invaded Gwalior, while the force to go there in support of Scindia is still *here*, for want of orders from the Governor-General ; but Sir Hugh Rose has ordered it off to-morrow, at our request. I am in deep anxiety. A rebel mass from Bareilly and Calpee is twenty-four miles from Gwalior, and Scindia has sent out two regiments and eighteen guns and a thousand horse to meet them. If they beat that force, Gwalior is theirs, there being infinite treachery within it. We have, it is true, a small pursuing force within five marches of their rear, quite enough, I think, to meet them separately, or to co-operate with Scindia's, but not to command both the enemy and Scindia's men, which we desire to do. . . .

' The monsoon threatens to overtake and paralyse us ; and for want of an order to march a week ago, all my Gwalior work may be ruined.'

About Amaen were posted, when the rebels crossed, 400 of Scindia's foot, 150 horse, and 4 guns. Scindia's civil officer told the Rao Saheb, ' It is the order of the Maharajah and the Dewan that you retire.' ' And who,' replied the Rao Saheb, ' are you ? A ten-rupee underling of a Soobah, drunk with bhang ! And who are the Maharajah and Dinkur Rao ? Christians ! We are the Rao and Peishwa. Scindia is our slipper-bearer.[1] We gave him his kingdom. His army has joined us. We have letters from the Baiza Baee. Scindia himself encourages us. Tantea Topeh has visited Gwalior and ascertained all.

---

[1] The Scindia family was popularly but inaccurately said to have sprung from a menial servant of the Peishwa.

He having completed everything, I am for the Lushkur.[1] Would you fight with us? All is mine.'—Scindia's detachment did not attempt resistance. Advancing with such boastful words, and affecting to send letters to Scindia requiring his submission, the Rao Saheb paraded his troops, under 5,000 in all, and marched to Burragaon, eight miles from Gwalior.

Scindia's whole force had now been brought to sympathise more or less with the rebels; a large portion was fully with them, and the remainder had no sufficient motive to strike heartily against them for Scindia. Still, the Dewan was confident that, as the small force detached by Sir Hugh Rose was advancing behind them, and as the rebels themselves might be divided by bribery, a selected body of Scindia's Gwalior and Mahratta men—if posted in advance, while the mass of his troops was kept back— would check them for a few days, and give time for our force to come up.

On the morning of the 31st, Scindia was led by his bodyguard and household officers, who were in the interest of the rebels, to move 8,000 men and 24 guns to Morar, to disperse the rebels at once. In the evening, however, the Dewan's advice prevailed, and he marched his troops home, save a portion which was left entrenched at Morar. But, after midnight, His Highness was persuaded, in the absence of the Dewan, suddenly to move his whole force back against the rebels. After a short mockfight, Scindia's troops fraternised with them. The Maharajah fled to Dholepore, attended only by the Dewan, one other gentleman, and some troopers. A very few adherents joined him there, and proceeded with him to Agra.

The Ranees, accompanied by the Sirdars of the state and some officers of the household, went to the fort of Nurwur, thirty miles off. One of them, the mother of

---

[1] i.e. the capital—called the Lushkur or camp; a memorial of the military habits of the Mahrattas.

the Maharanee, believing that Scindia was beleaguered at the Phoolbagh, seized a sword, mounted her horse, and rode to the palace, summoning all to his aid, until she found he was certainly gone. She followed the other ladies on the third day.

Of His Highness's pampered favourites and boon-companions not one man followed him, while scarcely one followed the Ranees. Those men, almost without exception, instantly accepted from the rebels pay, gratuities, rank, and office—or became perfectly intimate with them; while, with few exceptions, the whole population sympathised with them.

The Rao Saheb was greatly disconcerted by Scindia's flight. In papers of the new Dewan appointed by the Rao, Scindia was styled 'a deeply-fixed root of the Nazarenes and strong striver in their cause.' The Rao Saheb invited the Baiza Baee to take charge of the State; but she sent his letters to Sir Robert Hamilton. The Rao Saheb prevented plunder; confiscated only the houses of the Dewan, Bulwunt Rao, and Mohurghur; confirmed nearly all Scindia's officials, appointing Topeh commander-in-chief; and disbursed to Scindia's troops and his own, or appropriated, twenty lacs of rupees and a mass of jewellery, Scindia's loss by robbery and fire being in all from forty to fifty lacs. The Fort was surrendered at once. The Palace and the Residency were destroyed.

Sir Hugh Rose immediately put his forces in motion, and marched upon Gwalior, accompanied by Sir Robert Hamilton and, of course, by Major Macpherson, acting under the orders of the last-named officer. Sir Robert, on entering the Gwalior State, issued a proclamation which greatly reassured the people, and they remained perfectly quiet.

The rebels were beaten; Gwalior was occupied on the 19th of June, and next day Scindia was re-established in his capital. Tantea Topeh and the Rao Saheb escaped. The Ranee of Jhansi fell on the 17th. She was seated, drinking sherbet, 400 of the 5th Irregulars near her, when the alarm was given that the Hussars approached. Forty or fifty of them came up, and the rebels fled, save about fifteen. The Rance's horse refused to leap a canal, when she received a shot in the side, and then a sabre-cut on the head, but rode off. She soon after fell dead, and was burnt in a garden close by. At the same time, the Brahmince concubine of her late husband, who never left her side, received a long sabre-cut in front. She rode into the city, was tended by a Fakeer and the Mahomedan head of police there, and, dying in their hands, was reputed and buried as a Mahomedan convert. The rebels were deeply dispirited by the Rance's death.[1]

Major Macpherson remained at Gwalior,[2] whence the next letter is dated :—

[1] A large portion of Scindia's revolted troops joined the rebels near their own homes in Oude and Rohilcund, or went with Topeh and the Rajah of Nurwur, the only chief of note under Scindia's rule who had risen. The remainder, scattered through the country, were kept quiescent, in sight or in hand, during the rains, and were eventually disarmed and discharged, and most of their ringleaders seized.

[2] His conduct during the crisis of Scindia's overthrow and restoration, and during that period alone, is indicated in the following notice :—

'From the Right Hon. the Secretary of State for India to the Right Hon. the Governor-General of India.

'East India House, 30th November 1858.

'My Lord,—Your Lordship's dispatch, No. 36 in the Foreign Department, dated September 14th, respecting the distinguished services of Sir Robert Hamilton, having been considered by me in Council, I have much satisfaction in expressing the gratification which it has afforded me to read the high testimony which you have borne to the "zeal, energy, and ability displayed by that meritorious officer throughout the arduous and protracted campaign which has now been brought to a triumphant conclusion." Sir Robert Hamilton has, as your Lordship observes, "in circumstances of great difficulty, rendered admirable service to the British Government."

' 2. I observe also, with much satisfaction, the commendatory language in which you have spoken of the services of Major Macpherson, "whose management of political affairs with Gwalior throughout the past crisis has been marked by much judgment and tact;" and of Captain Shakespear, Sir Robert Hamilton's assistant, who accompanied him throughout the campaign, and rendered valuable service to his chief.

' 3. You will be pleased to communicate to these officers the gratification

'Gwalior, 4th July 1858.

'Scindia's whole army at Gwalior, with the exception of a few hundred men, *went*—i.e., both ran away at once and received pay from the enemy. His great chiefs went off with the Baiza Baee. Nearly all his officers, military and civil, at the capital, were more or less fully with the rebels; and all, save a very few, like the Dewan, deserted him utterly—all those men who were with him in Calcutta, for example, save Angria and Phalkeah. But the point of the story is to come. Scindia has received every rebel with open arms, while he repels utterly all who have stood by him. The bodyguard rascals, and those who brought Tantea Topeh in the other day to the Lushkur for eight days, to pave the way for the rebels' coming, all dine with him daily in the old way : to none other does he speak a word. We cannot get him to do anything even to *the man*, the prime villain, his treasurer, who brought in the rebels and robbed his treasury ! His sole wish is to get his army restored in full, through new recruits, and replaced under its officers who have just *betrayed* him, as we should say. I fear he may be wholly unmanageable. . . . .

'My line is to treat Scindia as still our ward, and remove from him the villains who are leading him to destruction.'

It were tedious to relate the difficulties with which Major Macpherson had now to contend—between Scindia, who could scarcely be induced to inflict punishment even upon the most signal offenders, and others who were eager to punish those who had in truth deserved best of the British Government.

'Gwalior, 17th August 1858.

'I am writing in His Highness's Phoolbagh Palace—rows of ·pillars in a garden—and who are just come in

which I have derived from the perusal of this record of their services, and that it will afford me much satisfaction to bring the services of Sir R. Hamilton to the notice of Her Majesty.—I have, &c. &c.

'Stanley.'

but the whole family of Tantea Topeh ! A fortnight ago,
the Soubah of Bhind sent us word that he had captured
some suspicious pundits in the house of an ironsmith.
The Dewan's father-in-law, three days ago—an official
thereabouts—told the Dewan that he believed they were
the Topehs. Instantly the Dewan sent for them, and
here they are. I have been out looking at them. They
are all lying in that pavilion in the Phool Bagh garden,
at which we gathered after the murders. There is a
doubled-up thin old man of eighty-two, Topeh's father,
born in the Deccan, who left it a begging priest with the
ex-Peishwa, and has since lived at Bithoor; two sons—one
bull-like, the other thin and haggard—both near forty ;
one of seventeen, and four children down to a year old,
a very fair beautiful child ; three women, wives of those
three, one old—one with a rather fine indignant-eye-
browed expression—one decidedly pretty, but a mere
child.

'I have been ordering sweetmeats for these hungry
children, not reflecting that their fathers' treatment of
ours was not quite in that fashion.

'I don't know if any act of rebellion can be proved
against these men, but I will try to-morrow. They are
all as quiet and collected as if nothing had happened.
To whose custody do you think I entrust them? To a
troop of Meade's Horse, formed of the Dundouteah Brahmins, who, you may recollect, saved us all in our flight
from Gwalior last year. They are moreover my own
sole guard here, while Durbar and all say I should
have Bombay Sepoys or Europeans ; but here I am " trusting natives" again, like any Brigadier of the old school,
though with a difference, and I think L. would trust
them.

'The only paper this Topeh family have brought in
with them is a sloke or ode of contempt or execration of
the English, which I will send when I can translate it.

'You may like to hear that " the English bray like'

z

asses and run away," and "will fly like a kite with a broken string." '

' 6th September 1858.

. . . . . 'Certainly it seems strange that there should be an article in "The Times" on Scindia, taken entirely from my Report, as far as Scindia's conduct goes, without the faintest allusion to me. It is said that a man who has the telling of his own fights is a fool unless he makes his fortune ; and I suppose I am such a fool. . . . .

'The Palace is occupied by the 71st Highlanders.[1] Scindia, unfortunately, has a daughter again.[2] But the people fired so many guns and squibs, that down rushed the Brigadier with a troop of horse and four guns, &c. to our aid.'

Nothing caused Major Macpherson greater embarrassment or greater pain than the feeling towards the natives which now prevailed among military men. He writes, in November 1858 :—

' It is this that makes me almost despair for India ; for until this state of feeling shall be *reversed*, I see no hope. How admirably Lord Stanley spoke at Fishmongers' Hall on that point ! '

' Gwalior, 19th December 1858.

. . . . ' The circumstances have differed ; the man has been the same. He followed my bidding from the outbreak to the 1st June last, because I did not touch his force (his mania) or his favourites, and let him, of course, have his will; only moulded to meet my policy.

' In 1858 he resisted me absolutely, because that policy required him to sacrifice forces and favourites. Then he fell into a succession of "moods," causing delay and vexation unspeakable.'

---

[1] The conduct of this fine regiment during a whole year obtained for them, in an extraordinary degree, the goodwill and the respect of Scindia and of all the inhabitants of Gwalior.

[2] Scindia had no son.

A little later—

'My difficulties since Scindia's restoration have been boundless, solely from his character, and habitual conduct and relations to his servants. . . . . The great difficulty is to keep the rare Dewan and Gwalior together.' . . . .

Major Macpherson had embodied in an elaborate report, dated the 10th February 1858, not only a full narrative of all that had occurred in Gwalior since the outbreak, but also a statement of the causes of the insurrection as they appeared to the native eye; and Lord Canning had thus written to him during the same spring :[1]

' Your report is admirable, and the course which you have followed throughout will receive the warmest public acknowledgments from me.'

Yet all this time, though Major Macpherson's services rendered in subordination to Sir Robert Hamilton during the crisis of Scindia's fall and reinstatement had been publicly recognised,[2] — the course which at an earlier period he had solely devised and pursued, during those eventful months when so much depended on Gwalior, and to which Lord Canning had promised his warmest public acknowledgments, remained entirely unnoticed ;[3] while offices for which he was highly qualified, and to which he might reasonably have expected to be advanced, were bestowed upon gentlemen whose claims were, to say

---

[1] April 23, 1858.

[2] See above, p. 335.

[3] In the debate on the vote of thanks to the Government and the Army in India, April 14th, 1859, Mr. Vernon Smith (now Lord Lyveden) observed, in the course of his speech :—

' . . . Major Macpherson is also entitled to much praise. He contrived, by management of which we have as yet no knowledge, to prevent the Gwalior contingent, after they revolted, from joining the other insurgents during two or three of the most perilous months of the year; and to him was much to be attributed the maintenance of tranquillity in that part of India at a period when insurrection and attack might have proved most injurious.'—Hansard's Parliamentary Debates, vol. 153, p. 1757.

This was the testimony of a gentleman who had long presided over the India Board, and to whom Major Macpherson was personally unknown.

the least, no higher than his.   This produced some natural expressions of disappointment.

Early in 1859 he wrote—

' I have worked my uttermost night and day, and am not ashamed to look back, and am too old for office under juniors or equals wholly undistinguished, and I want deeply rest or encouragement to go on.   It were hard to live without work in England, but I should be unspeakably happy amongst gowans, heather, and friends—fishing-rod, books, pictures, geology—rising to sociology, if anybody could but get at it,—perhaps a ragged school, about the surest work I know, so far as it goes, which is but a short way truly.   Would no small College take me as Professor of Metaphysics?   I was once famous in it, and could teach up to Voltaire's definition of it, at least. . . .

' By the way, I am sorry to say that all my Khond diaries, &c.—my private ones—are burnt by the rebels; so that I can never, as I intended, tell the tale of their religious conquest.' [1]

During this year Sir Robert Hamilton returned to Europe.   He was succeeded in the office of Governor-General's Agent for Central India by Sir Richmond Shakespear, who, soon after assuming the office, addressed the following note to Major Macpherson, with whom he was not then personally acquainted :—

' I have read your Reports, *all of them*, with real enjoyment; they are admirable, and I am so taken with the one on the Mutinies [2] that . . . . I have learnt much from it. . . . .   Your judgment I admire throughout that awful period, and I am surprised that the important

---

[1] He carried with him from India, in December 1848, in one of the Peninsular and Oriental Company's steamers, a collection of about forty portraits of Khond chiefs, drawn by an artist whom he took to the Hills for the purpose, but he lost them on board the steamer.

[2] The Report of February 10, 1858.   One of the first Indian authorities of the day, to whom this report was submitted in the course of his duty, remarked ' how admirably the British representative had steered his course, with breakers ahead on almost every side.   The tone, too, so good; his tools made so much of, his own part touched so modestly.'

services performed by you have not already been promi-
nently rewarded.

'You may make any use you like of this note; and if
you can put me in the way of drawing attention to your
services, I shall be glad to do my utmost—for assuredly
you have fairly won it.'

At length, in the autumn of 1859, the following paragraph appeared in a very long minute[1] of Lord Canning's,
containing a *résumé* of the services of the various civil
officers in India :—

'26. I recommend to the favourable consideration of
Her Majesty's Government the services of Major Macpherson, the Political Agent at Gwalior. Holding a post
of great importance, far removed from his immediate
superior at Indore, and often struggling against sickness,
he has discharged his difficult duties with complete
success.'

This commendation was regarded as very inadequate
by those who were best acquainted with the affairs of
Upper India.

The following is the opinion of one of the most distinguished of them, Mr. Harington (afterwards a member
of the Governor-General's Council), who was with him
in the Fort of Agra, during the year 1857; who heard
from his own lips, at the time, all that was occurring in
Gwalior, and all that he was doing to meet the course of
events there; and to whose advice it was mainly due that
the Agra Government abstained from an interference in
Gwalior affairs which would have been quite ruinous :—

'Macpherson and I saw each other almost daily during
the time that we were together in the Fort at Agra, and
I not only heard from him all that is contained in his
narrative of events, but I had a personal knowledge of the
admirable tact and judgment which he displayed in dealing with Scindia, and in keeping the Gwalior Contingent

---

[1] Dated July 2, 1859.

with its powerful artillery inactive in its cantonments
until after the fall of Delhi.   We owe Macpherson much
—much more than has been supposed, and very much
more than has been acknowledged.'[1]

The remainder of Major Macpherson's life was occupied
with a continual endeavour to preserve to the people of
Gwalior—in spite of difficulties on which it would not
be desirable to dwell in this place, but which were of a
very trying nature—the just and equable system of government which British influence had established.

The opinions which he formed for himself as to the
great events of the period will appear from the following
passages extracted from his letters :—

'Agra, 12th January 1858.

'Nobody here has an idea of the state of feeling in the

---

[1] With reference to this opinion of Mr. Harington's, it is proper to call
attention to the following passage, in the publication entitled 'India under
Dalhousie and Canning,' by the Duke of Argyll, p. 118 :—

'The weakness of the native princes made their fidelity, in some cases, of
comparatively little value. The only one within the limits of British India
who had any considerable military force, the Maharajah of Gwalior, was
unable to restrain his army from joining the mutineers. This, however, it
may be said, was more our fault than his, because his troops were a Contingent under the old subsidiary system, and virtually formed part of the
Army of Bengal. The friendly attitude assumed by the Government of the
Nizam in the South of India, was the most important aid which we derived
from any native state.'

These remarks, proceeding from a statesman of such eminence as the
Duke of Argyll, show that the facts of the case have not been made sufficiently known in this country. It will be apparent to the readers of these
pages that the Gwalior Contingent was in no sense the army of Scindia, nor
subject to his orders; yet that he did prevent it from joining the rebels
for the four critical months during which such junction would have been
of momentous importance, and contrived that the junction should take
place just where we desired ; also that he restrained his own army (more
numerous than the Contingent, though far inferior in discipline) for nearly
twelve months, and would have prevented it from joining the rebels at all,
if our succour had been given in time. It would have been extremely
difficult, if not impossible, for the Nizam's government to maintain a friendly
attitude towards us in 1857, if Scindia had either gone over, or succumbed
to the anti-British party, or if his own Contingent had mutinied, like
Scindia's. Had Scindia gone over, Nagpore, the Nizam's country, and
Southern India must have followed him.

country, I fear.   In relation to this convulsion I have gazed most intensely at the phenomena in Gwalior, and tried to record them.   The difficulty passes belief. . . .

' I don't know what people will say to my view . . . . that the *primary* cause of the revolt was the deep dissatisfaction of the army with our rule, our government, and our manners, shared with the whole population of Hindostan.   I can get at nothing but this, I grieve to say, for a primary cause.   The army was fully predisposed by this cause to revolt.   It made the cartridge grievance a pretext to rise ;   and the foremost malcontents, princes, &c., seized the opportunity to stimulate and head the rebellion.   The soldiery had a true religious panic from a true grievance ; but had they not been ripe for revolt, they had not revolted about the cartridge, but had sought and found satisfactory explanations and assurances.   But they would have no explanations, and made the cartridge the pretext for revolt.   The Mahomedans, who struck for both religious and secular supremacy, desired both our overthrow and our extinction.   The Hindus, who happily did not make a religious contest of it, desired the overthrow of our rule, but protected life.   Had the Hindus made a matter of religion of it, no one had remained to report. But Benares, Gya, &c. gave no sign.   The great point was, that we had given neither by legislation, nor by missionaryism, nor in any other way, religious offence which could serve the turn of the revolutionists.   But people in England had better not think that they can play at proselytism in India at the cost of any army that they ever put on board a fleet.   The army revolted in the belief that, from the paucity of our European troops, from the army's having possession of our magazines, and from the aid of chiefs and people, they must triumph.   They miscalculated (1) the point of the Sikhs, who saved Delhi; (2) the Chinese expedition, which gave Havelock a force to smash the Nana ; (3) Scindia and the other princes, who had their " doots," and would stand by us till they saw further.

Had Scindia gone, not a prince would have stood for a day. I got him to act in antagonism to the revolt until the Contingent mutinied, and then to keep the Contingent quiescent until we were quite ready to crush them. . . . The army revolted in the face of matchless class advantages, because we do not even attempt to carry the mind of the people with us. . . . . . . In the North-Western Provinces, our sales of Zemindary lands for arrears of revenue, and in satisfaction of civil decrees, have arrayed the whole country against us.[1] Instantly on the revolt, all holders of land by our titles given on such sales were expelled. This extended to every hamlet in the country in which there has been a sale. Yet you are told the country is not against us ! Of course, the confusion from this cause alone is prodigious. Shall we vindicate our titles ? Shall we punish those who kicked them aside ? Our Amlah[2] and police as a body have proved as false as our army. Shall we go back to the old men ? or shall we try a new plan to govern the country, through the aid of the men of family, property, and real influence ? . . . Scindia has done admirably ; but he cherishes next his heart our bitterest foes—the men who brought on Maharajpore in 1843, and who have now been urging him night and day to be up and at us. He listens to and pampers them, but follows the counsels of Dinkur Rao. . . .'

'Agra, 11th February 1858.

' What saved us was that the chiefs of all kinds doubted much that we should fall ; thought rather that we should triumph, and resolved to wait till *after the rains*. The people therefore *waited* also, never rising unled. Had Delhi not fallen when it did, all had risen ; be sure of this. The population of the North-Western Provinces is tribal, unlike Bengal ; and tribes are, of course, chief-led. Were

---

[1] See above, p. 305, where it is stated that the Gwalior code does not follow ours in this respect.

[2] The members of the native civil establishments.

the chiefs decently treated,[1] you would have the whole
population; but without the chiefs, not a man. Everybody
says the Sepoys wanted mastery ; but these Asiatics must
have a tyrant, and look only to having one. Seeing we
had no European army, and that they could beard the
Governor-General, what could they do but rise ? If we
do not bring every Sepoy, like every Thug, to justice, we
shall have no safe platform here.'

'Agra, 28th February 1858.

. . . . 'I see that * * * tells " The Times " that if we
had played with landed rights in the Punjaub as in our
North-Western Provinces, Havelock's battles had been
fought at Calcutta ; and you may be sure he is right.   I
pray you not to imagine that I suppose that the army
revolted *only* because it shared the dissatisfaction of the
people with our rule ; but that it was thereby predisposed
to revolt, the cartridge being but the pretext and watch-
word.   But the subject is endless, with a thousand sides.
Every cause assigned for the revolt has tended to produce
it ; but dissatisfaction with our rule, common to the army
and the people, was the preliminary condition *sine quâ
non* ; and the *main* cause of that dissatisfaction was actual
and apprehended disturbance of rights connected with
the soil, of Maafee tenures, Zemindary huqs, &c. &c.'

'3rd March 1858.

'Let Lord Canning's Government answer just this one
question—Why, when they had before them all the warnings which accumulated up to the middle of April, did
they not bring their European regiments down from the
hills and place them over their magazines, and warn all
officers to look out ? Perhaps it is best as it deplorably

---

[1] Major Macpherson does not allude to any personal ill-treatment of
natives by Europeans; indeed he felt strongly the injustice of the statements which were so currently made in England on that subject.

happened, if the Government will but believe that the
Mutiny arose in the villages, not in the cantonments.'[1]

'Agra, 5th March 1858.

'Are we in future to take the influential classes with
us, or to crush them by brute force, and—yet more de-
testable degradation—by Amlah tyranny? I have never
seen an officer, civil or military, of competent knowledge
and manners, attempt to take those classes with him and
fail. They are most ready to be honourably allied with
the Government, but the terms must be those due to the
whole facts of their civilisation.'

'Agra, 25th April 1858.

. . . 'Lord Ellenborough is far nearer right ideas than
most people; sees that *nothing* saved us the other day, except that we had not done *more* against caste and religion;
and that if by going further in that direction we shall
alienate the people more, the country will be wholly unmanageable for good to anyone. India ruled *here* by
bayonet power, and *there* by platform and hustings power,
will be a wretched work to have a hand in. . . . . .

'The people should be predisposed, through acceptable
civil administration, to regard favourably the religious
change proposed to them. Were not all attempts on the
Khond religion vain until that was done? And when it was
effected, did not the religious change follow? This was
the whole meaning and value of the Khond experiment.
That principle is now the one to be enforced. . . . Set
men to manage each people, or division or denomination,

---

[1] About this time Major Macpherson wrote:—

'You see that Lord Ellenborough quite understands that the population
are hostile to us—that the rising has been a revolt of the people, not of the
army. I alone ventured to say this here for a long time.'

'Rawlinson [the allusion is to a speech of Sir H. Rawlinson, the distinguished Oriental diplomatist and scholar, in the House of Commons] is
very near my view of the thing, and will take it in fully. Nearly every
one I meet now admits it.'

and under them let that people or division, if possible, *govern themselves*, municipally, under our high tutelage : at all events, let each officer keep his division assenting to, or at the very lowest fully acquiescing in, our measures.

'From what I have done, and seen done by many, I think all this is perfectly possible ; the principle being localisation, diversity, individuality of rule, as alone suited to the present condition of India. A strong Governor-General would introduce this system gradually and quietly, without any startling changes or great difficulty. The localisation of the officers would effect much. Here and there a district would soon be remarked rejoicing at the feet of its officers. If these were honoured, others would emulate them. A fair standard would be created, and we should have tolerable content over all. But the prefects *must* take with them the men of influence of *every* kind, or the State must know the reason why.'

The heat of Gwalior, and the intense strain upon his mind during the Mutiny and the difficult and anxious times which succeeded, gradually wore out Major Macpherson's health, and this was very apparent in the autumn of 1859, when he visited Calcutta. During the winter he was deputed to conduct an intricate inquiry into the behaviour of the minister of the Rana of Dholepore during the Mutiny, a point on which the Magistrate of Agra was at issue with the Political Agent at Bhurtpore ; the former alleging that the minister had ravaged our territory and ought to be punished, the latter that he had not committed the offences alleged, but had, on the contrary, done good service.

On the 18th of December 1859, Major Macpherson wrote—

'I am settling the Agra and Dholepore case in the only possible way—by going to each plundered village and hearing its case in the presence of the accused. I will do it as rapidly as possible; but the misl[1] is a camel-load.'

While conducting this inquiry in the pleasant cold season of the Upper Provinces, he at first felt invigorated, and somewhat rested,—being relieved for the time from the anxieties of Gwalior politics. He was on the eve of completing the period of service which would entitle him to retire on a Lieutenant-Colonel's pension; and he was looking hopefully to an early return to Great Britain. But in the midst of his investigation he was attacked by illness, and repaired to Agra, where Brigadier Showers received him with kind hospitality. At length in the beginning of April 1860, feeling worse, and believing that change would do him good, he started for Calcutta, intending to proceed immediately to Europe. The journey was long and fatiguing. On the way he rapidly became worse, from exhaustion and the heat of the weather. His admirable friend, the Dewan, now Rajah Dinkur Rao, met him on his way, and thinking him very ill, offered to accompany him to Calcutta; but the proposal was declined, and he continued his journey, while visions of Scotland, of streams and village greens, and children playing, flitted before his eyes, and were a relief to him during the long and weary nights of his painful travel. His brother, Dr. John Macpherson, who went from Calcutta to Raneegunge, then the terminus of the railway, to meet him, found him suffering severe pain and, in fact, hopelessly ill of congestion of the liver.

At Dr. Macpherson's house in Calcutta he lingered for five days, conscious of the approach of death, and evincing the kindness and consideration for others which always characterised him. He was visited by his valued friend, Mr. Harington, and Sir James Outram. He earnestly urged the latter (whose own health had now greatly

---

[1] Record.—N. B. There were 66 cases to inquire into.

failed) to go home, and not to sacrifice his life by remaining too long in India.

His thoughts naturally turned on the great change which was approaching, and by his own desire, some of the beautiful paraphrases appended to the Scotch version of the Psalms were read to him. While he was listening to the 14th chapter of St. John he became unconscious, and on the evening of the 15th April 1860 his spirit passed away.

He was interred in the Scotch burying-ground in Calcutta. Sir James Outram (who was then, in Lord Canning's absence, President of the Council) and all the members of the Council of the Governor-General, with their Secretaries and Staff, attended the funeral.[1]

The Fort St. George Government Gazette soon after contained the following announcement:—

' The following letter from the Secretary to the Government of India with the Governor-General is published for general information :

'No. 1358.

From Cecil Beadon, Esq., Secretary to the Government of India with the Governor-General, to Colonel Sir R. Shakespear, Knight, Agent to the Governor-General for Central India.

'Simla, 18th April 1860 (Foreign Department).

' Sir,—I am directed to state that the Governor-General has received with deep regret the melancholy intelligence of the death of Major S. Charters Macpherson, of the Madras Army, the Political Agent at Gwalior.

' Major Macpherson's services in the Political Department through a long course of years, especially the part

---

[1] It was also attended by his native servants, who were devotedly attached to him, and whom he had asked to come and see him buried.

he took in the suppression of human sacrifices and infanticide among the Khonds, have gained for him a high place in the long list of distinguished officers who have adorned the Indian Service, and entitle him to the lasting gratitude of the Government and the people of India.—I have, &c.,

'CECIL BEADON,
'Secretary to the Government of India with the
'Governor-General.'

After Major Macpherson's death his name appeared in the 'London Gazette' in a list of new Companions of the Bath.

A very gratifying letter was received by Dr. Macpherson from Dinkur Rao, warmly dwelling on his friendship with Major Macpherson,—on the great assistance which Major Macpherson had rendered to the Gwalior State and people,—on 'his abilities in transacting state affairs—his firm, decided, and upright character, and his good nature and kind heart.'

The sentiments with which he was regarded by his countrymen are expressed in the following passage of a letter addressed to the editor of these Memorials by his lamented friend the late Mr. Ritchie, then Advocate-General, and shortly afterwards a member of the Council of the Governor-General :—

'Calcutta, 9th May 1860.

'I know no man whose loss has been felt more deeply in Calcutta, or who has carried with him to the grave more genuine esteem and regard than he has.[1] It will be most difficult to supply his place, and so I know the Government feel keenly, now that he is gone. From what Sir Bartle Frere[2] (a noble fellow, who is full of enthusiasm about your brother's services) told me, I infer that Lord Canning now sees and deeply regrets his mistake in not

---

[1] In these lines Mr. Ritchie unconsciously anticipated what was ere long to be said of himself.

[2] Then a member of the Council of the Governor-General; now Governor of Bombay.

conferring an adequate reward at once on him, for his invaluable services to the State in its hour of greatest need.'[1]

Major Macpherson was eminently a practical man, but his practice was always based on carefully-considered principles, and he used to say that it was from the study of Guizot that he had learnt how to reclaim the Khonds. He certainly possessed the faculty, however acquired, of calling into play the best energies of all the natives of India with whom he came into contact, and of insensibly imparting to them, whether barbarous or civilized, more enlightened sentiments and a higher tone of feeling. It may be stated with confidence that he invariably did what he conceived to be best for the work with which he was charged, without pausing to consider what would be said of any act, or how it would affect his own interests or his official position; that he was ever disposed to advance the claims of others in preference to his own; that he never forgot a kindness, nor omitted an opportunity of conferring one.

If there be truth in the saying of a great man,[2] that it is a loss to mankind when any good action is forgotten, it may be deemed pardonable to have placed on record these scanty Memorials of a Service in which head and heart were alike unsparingly, and not without worthy results, devoted to the cause of humanity and of good government.

---

[1] When Major Macpherson was on his death-bed, a letter arrived from Lord Canning, too late to admit of its contents being communicated to him, which contained the following passage :—

'7th April 1860.

' I desire greatly to offer you promotion, and have long considered (before the troubles of 1857 arose) that the Government is in debt to you in this respect.'

[2] Johnson, in the Life of Savage.

APPENDIX.

—✦—

A.

(REFERRED TO AT PAGES 84 AND 131.)

———

*Preliminary Statement of the Sources of Information, form-
ing part of a Paper on the Religion of the Khonds, read
before the Royal Asiatic Society in 1852.*

THE British Government first came into immediate contact
with the mountain Khonds in 1835, whilst engaged in military
operations for the reduction of the zemindary of Goomsur in
the Ganjam district, whose rajah had rebelled and taken refuge
amongst them. Upon the completion of those operations in
1837, I was employed in surveying a portion of the newly-
acquired district and the unexplored tracts around it. In performing that duty, I was enabled to obtain a considerable
amount of information respecting the language, manners, institutions, and religion of the Khonds, then almost entirely
unknown. That information, professedly very incomplete, was
embodied in a report, written by order of the Madras Government in June 1841, and afterwards printed by the Government
of India. When I returned to the Khond country in that year,
as an assistant to the Agent of the Government in the Ganjam
district, I found that I had previously visited only the tribes
belonging to one of the two great antagonist sects into which
the Khonds are divided, and that I had, thence, erroneously
described the tenets and observances of that sect as constituting
the whole system of Khond religion. My present object is to
correct that error from the information which I have been
enabled to obtain during my long subsequent connexion with

A A

the people as a subordinate, or the chief, Agent of the Government for the suppression amongst them of the practices of human sacrifice and female infanticide.

The Khond religion exists in oral traditions alone, and the priesthood by which these are preserved is neither hereditary nor strictly organised as a profession ; nevertheless, the ceremonials of the gods, composed of rites, invocations, hymns, legends, and recitals, form a repository of materials, doctrinal and ritual, from which the main outlines and spirit of the superstition may be authentically deduced. And, through inquiries systematically addressed to the best-informed priests and laymen whose full confidence has been gained, the doctrines which do not naturally find a place in the ceremonials, and all the details of these, may be ascertained. Still, with respect to every portion of the following account of the Khond superstition, I beg that, in addition to the obvious difficulty, under any circumstances, of ascertaining and describing from oral statements the opinions, feelings, and sentiments which constitute a system of religion, the following special sources of error may be kept in view. Only the leading ideas, the chief formalities, and the most familiar and significant expressions of this religion are distinctly fixed in the minds even of the best informed of its rude professors. The details of doctrines and of rites, of legends and narratives, vary in every district, and even in different parts of the same district, according as the population belongs to one or other of the two great antagonist sects, and according to the fancies of the officiating priests. Upon many subjects, for instance, there are many different legends, all equally current and equally believed, so that the one which I give is to be considered merely as a sample of those that exist. And hence, in the attempt to present in exact language and a systematic form a body of traditional ideas, I fear that I have, perhaps unavoidably, imparted to the subject an appearance of theoretical completeness and consistency which does not strictly belong to it.

I have to add, that these descriptions are drawn exclusively from the Khond country of the zemindary of Goomsur, and from those portions of the zemindaries of Boad, Duspullah, Souradah, and some neighbouring tracts with the usages of which I am best acquainted.

All the principal legends, hymns, and recitals were taken down by me as they were spoken or intoned by well-informed priests or laymen in the Khond language, and, on account of my imperfect knowledge of that language, translated line by line into Oriya and Hindostanee by persons highly qualified for the task. My late very able and deeply-lamented friend Mr. Cadenhead, who was principal assistant in the Orissan Hill Agency, and a perfect master of the Khond language, also obtained these legends in it, in many cases from sources distinct from mine, and collated my versions with his own made directly from the originals. And lastly, to obtain the inestimable advantage of Mr. Cadenhead's mature views upon every part of this attempt to describe the Khond religion, I sent a draft of it to him in India, which I received back enriched with comments upon every point on which he differed from me, or upon which he could add to my information, either from his own sources or by communicating with the late Soonderah Sing Deo, the Hindu gentleman who was principal native assistant to the Agency, and whose services in that capacity cannot be overrated.

Details as to the Minor Deities, also forming part of the Paper read before the Royal Society in 1852.

Pidzu Pennu, the God of Rain.

PIDZU PENNU, the god of rain, being necessarily regarded as the great cause of vegetation, his worship is in practice nearly identified with that of Boorbi Pennu, the goddess of new vegetation; and his rights are generally, if not always, performed at her shrine, a stone or a tree near every village. .

When it is resolved to invoke the god of rain, the elders, having made their arrangements with the priest, proceed through the village calling out, 'Vessels ho! Vessels ho!' when vessels of arrack are immediately brought out from every house. These are carried by parties of ten or twelve to the tree of Boorbi Pennu. Pidzu Pennu then comes upon the Janni, the offerings are deposited under the tree, and all seat themselves. A great Janni, with two smaller priests and some of the principal elders, then perform the following worship apart from the crowd.

The Janni first calls on Boora and Tari, and then on Pidzu Pennu, and on all the other gods—as Samudur Pennu, the god of the sea, Loha Pennu, the god of war, and Sundi Pennu, the god of boundaries—to make up, as it is considered most important to do, a strong assembly of the peers of Pidzu Pennu, in the hope of their exerting the influence of their opinion upon him. The priest then says, 'O Pidzu Pennu! hear us. What have we come short in our service? In what have we diminished ancient usage? We say not that we have not failed towards you; but if we have failed unconsciously, it was your part to have remembered the constant service of our fathers, and to have intimated to us our fault, not to have visited us thus in wrath. Behold your peers, Loha Pennu, &c. We have worshipped them even as we have worshipped you. Their favour. has not diminished towards us.

'O Pidzu Pennu! is it that you have given your daughter in marriage to the son of some god who is hostile to us, or have made his daughter your son's bride, and under his influence injure us? We men cannot comprehend your divine thoughts, but your fellow-gods, Loha Pennu, Pitterri Pennu, Soro Pennu, &c., know them and judge them. We know not, we cannot know your counsels; but we pray you to remember, to reflect that, if you shall not give us water, half our land must remain unploughed; that the seed in the ground will rot; that we and our children must perish for want of food; that our cattle must die for want of pasture; that the sambur, the spotted deer, the wild hog, and all other game will quit our country, seeking other haunts. We pray of you to remember all this; and that, should you hereafter, when it is too late, relent, either from pity towards us, or from desiring your own food and worship, or from doubting of your reception—should you, when we are no more, seek the worship of another village—we pray you to reflect how little any gift of water will then avail, when there shall be left neither man, nor cattle, nor seed. Therefore, we now address to you these entreaties, while we also beseech all of you, ye assembled gods, to aid and enforce our prayer to Pidzu Pennu, taking to your hearts all we have said.

'O Pidzu Pennu! for you we have brought eggs, and arrack, and rice, and a sheep. Be pleased to eat, and to entertain these assembled gods, receiving from them all the credit due for the goodness of the feast. Oh, give us abundant rain, enough to melt the hill-tops. Go and fetch water for us, if need be, by force or fraud, from the stores of your friends the gods of rain. Bring it in brass vessels, and in hollow gourds, and resting on the sky above our land, pour the water down on it through your sieve until the sambur, unable to live in the forests, shall seek shelter in our houses, and till the soil of the mountains shall be washed into our valleys. Strip off all old leaves and bring out new. Let the vegetation be such, that shoots springing from the newly planted melons shall follow our footsteps, and let it be of such strength that our cooking-pots shall burst next year from the force of the swelling rice. Let the bamboo sprouts shoot out rapidly. Let all the neighbouring tribes come to buy rice of us, and let them alone experience the pains of surfeit. Let there be such a gathering of the beasts of the chase in our green and favoured country, that our axes shall be blunt with cutting them up. But do you, moreover, recollect that we cannot go out in the falling floods. Then do you don your hat, and laying your stick over your shoulder, guard our unenclosed fields from both the wild animals and the tame cattle. Let our full fountains gush upwards. Do thus, and we will next year provide eggs, fowls, a sheep, and liquor for a feast at least equal to this, for the maintenance of your character for hospitality with your brother-gods.'

They then kill the sheep, but may not eat it. Its flesh must be given to Sooudies, or Goands, if any be present; if not, it must be left on the field. Those who take part in this cere-mony, however, drink the liquor with wild shouts and dancing, and return home. The Janni and a few of the old men remain a little behind, to reply to and pacify any god who may by accident have been forgotten at the bidding of the gods, and may now demand the cause. Having gone a few steps, those elders and the priests turn back and say, ' If we have uncon-sciously omitted to do honour on this occasion to any god, we pray of the other deities to intercede for us and pacify him.'

Pitterri Pennu, the God of Increase.

Pitterri Pennu, the god of increase, and of gain in every shape, is worshipped at seed-time, and his worship is in each village designated from the tree, rock, or other spot where it is performed, as the ' mowa-tree ' worship, the ' tank-side ' worship.

Upon the first day of the feast, a sort of rude car is made of a basket set upon a few sticks, tied upon bamboo rollers for wheels. The Janni takes this car first to the house of the lineal head of the tribe or branch, to whom it is essential that precedence should be given in all ceremonies connected with agriculture, and obtains from it a little of each kind of some seed and feathers. He then takes the car to every other house in the village, which contributes the same things, and lastly, it is conducted to a field without the village, accompanied by all the young men, who beat each other and strike the air violently with long sticks. The seed which is thus carried out is called the share of the 'evil spirits, spoilers of the seed.' These are considered to be driven out with the car; and when it and its contents are abandoned to them, they are held to have no excuse for interfering with the rest of the seed-corn.

The next day the people of each house kill a hog over the seeds for the year, and address the following invocation to the god of increase:—

'O Pitterri Pennu! this seed we shall sow to-morrow. Some of us, your suppliants, will have a great return, some a small return. Let the least favoured have a full basket, let the most favoured have many baskets. Give not this seed to ant, or rat, or hog. Let the stems which shall spring from it be so stout that the earth shall tremble under them. Let the rain find no hole or outlet whereby to escape from our fields. Make the earth soft like the ashes of cow-dung. To him who has no iron wherewith to shoe his plough, make the wood of the doh-tree like iron. Provide other food than our seed for the parrot, the crow, and all the fowls and beasts of the jungle. Let not the white ant destroy the roots, nor the wild hog crush the stem to get at the fruit; and make our crops of all kinds have a better flavour than that of those of any other country. We are unskilled in adapting our seeds to different soils; give us wisdom to suit them to each other. Thou art a god created by Boora Pennu. O Pitterri Pennu! if pleased, your bounty is boundless. Be gracious to us.'

After this invocation, the elders feast upon the hogs and the mowa spirit. The young men, however, in revenge for their exclusion from the good cheer, enjoy the privilege of waylaying and pelting them with jungle fruit, when returning from the feast.

Upon the third day, the lineal head of the tribe or branch goes out and sows his seed, when all the rest may do so.

Klambo Pennu, or Pilamu Pennu, the God of the Chace.

The following worship is paid to Klambo Pennu, or Pilamu Pennu, the god of the chace.

When the huntsmen fail to find game, the Janni is required to ascertain and declare the cause of their ill success, which he may find to be either that they have violated some law of the chace, or some of the many rules for dividing and eating the game, or that, as the hunters left the village, some one in it wept—an act most offensive to the god of the chace. From some such cause he may say that Klambo Pennu, or some other god, has ordered the jungle to hide the game, or has made the arrows of the hunter pointless, or has ordered the streams to take away weariness from the pursued game; and he will then direct some rice, an egg, and a fowl to be brought from each house for an offering to be placed on the round stones of Klambo Pennu beside the village, upon which all game is deposited when brought in, divided into the proper shares, and often also cooked. The offering required by the priest being collected, he thus invokes the god:—'O Klambo Pennu! you are our god of the chace. You gave game to our fathers, and were used also to make our arrows sure, to give force to our axes, and keenness to the mouths of our dogs; while, at your shrine, the cooking-fire was never extinguished, and the blood never dry! Behold it now! O Klambo Pennu! lay aside your anger. One cannot always stay the tears of children. Who at a feast can restrain a greedy-guts? This you know; and why, therefore, do you record these faults against us upon your knotted strings?[1] We speak thus, but the benefit of the chace is no less yours than ours. Let us again see the sambur and the spotted deer, and the bison, and the wild hog, and the hare, as we leave our thresholds; and when these animals hear our shout, may their limbs become disobedient, and their hearts panic-struck. Give to our arrows and our axes the poison of the first iron against our game. Make the earth preserve its footmarks. Make a cool wind ever blow from the hill and the forest upon us huntsmen. O Klambo Pennu! make your name great.'

The Janni then rubs an arrow or an axe on the stone of Klambo Pennu; all do the same to their weapons, and they go

[1] The Khonds keep all accounts by knots on strings.

out and bring home something, if it be but a small bird, from
the forest. It is usual, moreover, when a hunting-party is
formed, to require the priest to propitiate the god of the chace
by piling the weapons of the huntsmen by a rivulet, sprinkling
water over them with a handful of long grass, and sacrificing a
fowl, when the god, if propitious, enables him to indicate the
direction in which game is to be sought, and occasionally to
devote so many head to fall. Klambo punishes the slightest
infraction of the rules he has laid down for the division
of game; they are such as—that the head and tail of every
animal belong to the person who kills it, those being considered
the most delicate portions, which he will desire to present to the
old men of his family, and that the under portion of every beast
belongs to the person on whose land it falls.

Loha Pennu, the God of War (literally, God of Iron).

Every village or cluster of hamlets has a grove sacred to the
god of war. In it are buried a piece of iron, believed to be a
relic of the iron of the time when the earth-goddess first introduced poison into iron amongst other evils, and an ancient bow
and arrows and a war-drum of iron, or some one of these weapons. They appear a little above the surface of the ground,
and are seen to emerge somewhat farther before a battle, sub-
siding again on its conclusion. The war-god presides over contests between different tribes, or between Khonds and foreign
enemies, but never over the contests of the people of the same
tribe. He becomes highly incensed if war be not forthwith
declared when the maintenance of rights requires it, and then
shows his wrath by the ravages of tigers and disease. When
such signs appear, the elders assemble and deliberate. The
history of the past is gone over, with a view to discover the
breach of the laws of war which may have offended the god;
and if in the end it is determined that there shall be war with
some ' Kassinga,' or enemy beyond the tribe, the following
ceremonies are gone through.

   The fighting men, having first washed and dressed their hair
with the care required by Khond custom, assemble and place
their ornaments of war, feathers, skins, cloths, &c., before the
god of war in his grove. The Janni takes a fowl, with some
rice and arrack, and invokes the god, while he also calls upon all
the other deities to assemble as witnesses of their proceedings.

He then says, 'O god of war! we have doubtless omitted to give battle, it may be through forgetfulness of your laws, or through weakness, or from considering too much the immature age of our youth, or the scantiness of our provisions; but now, from the ravages of tigers, from the fevers, the diseases of the eye, the ulcers, and the pains in every limb from which we suffer, we conceive that you indicate to us that you have given us sufficient strength, provisions, and wisdom for war. We bring to you our weapons. You have made them strong, now make them keen. We go out to fight our enemies. Send home the erring shaft. Send our stones straight to the mark. Let our axes crush cloth and bone as the jaws of the hyena crush its prey. Make the wounds we give to gape. Let our little men slay big men. When the wounds of our enemies heal, let lameness remain. Let their stones and arrows fall on us as softly as the flowers of the mowa-tree fall in the wind. Let our wounds heal as quickly as the blood-drops from them dry upon the ground. Make the weapons of our enemies brittle as the long pods of the karta-tree. You are our war-god; do you thus aid with your strength us and our allies (whom they name). May the weapons of all of us when we return from the fight be changed in hue. May our women be proud and happy to serve food in battle to brave men like us, so that when other tribes shall hear of their happiness and pride, they shall desire to unite their women to us. May we plunder in victory the villages of our foes of bullocks and tobacco and brass vessels, which our women may bear proudly as presents to their parents. O Loha Pennu! we worship you with fowls, and sheep, and hogs, and buffaloes. We only ask for the aid you gave to our fathers in past fights (naming them) and no new thing. We are their children.'

Then all snatch up their arms, when the priest commands silence, and recites the following myth and invocation, the former containing many of the distinctive doctrines of the sect of Tari : —

'In the first time, when the god of light created the hills and the woods, and the streams great and small, and the plains and the rocks and boundaries, and the tame animals, and the game of the forests, and man, then too he made the iron of these weapons, but the hands of our forefathers did not know how to use them.

'There was a mother, Umbally Bylee, with two children, Allonguarra and Patanguarra, warriors. They came to her one day all wounded, and with bleeding breasts. She said, "What has befallen you?" They answered, "We have been fighting outside people with sword-grass." Their mother cured their wounds, and said, "That is an improper way of fighting, do not fight so again." A few days after, the children came again, covered with burs or spikes of grass as sheep are covered with wool, and said, "We have fought the outside people with bur (or spear) grass." Their mother cured them, and said, "This mode of fighting is improper. Bring the iron of the Hindu country, and make blades for axes and for arrows, and take the damun-tree for axe-handles, and make bows of the thornless bamboo, and wind skins and cloth round the body, and adorn the head with feathers, and go forth to fight. Then shall you become awakened and improved, and cloth and salt and sugar will come to you, and you will see men of different nations and different minds." And they made arrows of this form,[1] and went out to battle, and on both sides very many fell. Then the children came, and said to their mother, "O mother! we have obeyed your orders and very many have died, none of the wounded have lived! We cannot endure the deadly keenness of this iron." She answered, "My child, it is not the fault of the weapons that all whom they wound die. The destructive (or terrible) goddess who made the iron what it is mingled in its composition no drop of pity. Heat the iron in the fire and beat it." They did so, and it became changed, and it slew only those who were ready to die. The mother then said, "Make your arrows henceforth in another form. This arrow, with whatever skill you may shoot, will slay those only who are ready to die." And this form has remained, and to this day it has defended every man's boundaries and property and rights.

'O god of war! now give to our arms the qualities of the first merciless iron. Then shall we be rich in every form of wealth, and we will pay to you the richest worship.'

The priest then cries, 'Now arm and march!' He accompanies the host to the enemies' boundary, over which an arrow is shot from the bundle of some one indicated by the divining

---

[1] A drawing would be necessary to explain the difference between the two forms of arrow-heads.

sickle, and then a branch of a tree is cut and carried off from the enemies' land.

The host next go to the village within whose boundary the shrine of the war-god is situated, and the village chief dresses the branch in clothes and armour, sets it up to personate one of the enemy, I believe, and calls upon the god of light and all the other gods, saying, 'Bear witness that in all these proceedings we have conformed to the rules of the god of war, that victory is therefore now due to us, and that our sufferings from tigers, from fevers, and from every pain ought to cease;' when all shout and say, 'To suffer death we do not object, but, O gods! let us not be *mutilated* in battle. We are the children of such and such great ancestors (naming them). Ye gods! raise our name by giving us victory.' They then take the dressed-up branch and throw it down at the shrine of the god of war, and it is to be observed that they must give their enemies full time to complete similar rites before they attack them.

The following worship is paid to the god of war when peace is made.

When parties are tired of a contest and wish for peace, they make known their desire to some friendly tribe, who send three or four old men to act as mediators. These first visit one of the parties and ascertain its feelings, and then proceed to the other to persuade them to peace. These generally reply in this strain, 'Peace and war are not in our hands, but in the hands of the god, and if he requires war, the arrows will fly of their own accord from our bows.' The mediators reply that this is true, but pray of them if the arrows shall not so fly that they will put all hostility out of their minds and worship the gods, and they add a proposal to ascertain the will of these in their presence. The mediators further persuade them to send word to their enemies that they are going to make that inquiry, and that they propose they should do the same, each side sending two old men to witness the ceremony and observe the minds of their opponents.

In the first place a basket of rice is set out in the house of the Janni or of the chief, and the iron arrow of the god of war is placed upright in it. If it remains erect the war must proceed. If it falls, as it is very apt to do, the peace worship may proceed. In this case the whole population go out into the plain, with the priest carrying some rice and two eggs. He calls upon Loha Pennu and invokes the presence of all the other gods, and says, 'O Loha Pennu! you aided us in this fight to prevent our dishonour, or because your will was war, or that our enemies might not rise upon our heads, or you engaged us in this war to prevent us from being occupied with the service of pernicious gods, or your reason is one proceeding from your divine mind which is hid from us, or perhaps you preferred that we should die by war rather than in any other way, or it may be that the smiths, the weavers, and the distillers solicited you apart for their benefit that there should be war, or it may have been that you were angry that our arms hung rusty in our houses, or it may be that the jungle yams complained that they were being extirpated in the forests, where all penetrate fearlessly in time of peace? or did the honey-bees complain that they had no life from persecution in the leisure of the long peace? or the bullocks that they were dying beneath the yoke in clearing new land? or did the beasts and birds of the forest complain that they were suffering extirpation? or is it that the paths to our friends' houses are worn into stream-beds by the feet of passers to and fro, and that they prayed for war? or is it your reason that there have been breaches of solemn engagements? From whatsoever cause, and through whomsoever—whether smith, honey-bee, breach of engagement, &c.—this war arose, all now seek peace. This is the disposition of our minds. Do you make plain to us the meaning of the signs of your will.'

They now fill a dish with hog's fat, and stick a cotton-wick in it. If the flame burns straight, it is for war; if not, for peace. They now also turn upside down the earthen vessel used in worship, put some rice upon the bottom of it, try if an egg will stand in the rice, and say, 'O god of war! explain these signs; but if they are for peace, do not thereupon become inattentive. Give us full strength to the very end, until we and our enemies, to the last man, have laid down our arms; and do you support us in future, through all generations, as you do now. If we shall have peace now, we will provide liberally for your worship, and increase your service. We your servants pray you to make the minds of all consent to this peace. Do you ascertain distinctly the minds of our enemies, and of their gods, and act accordingly. And let there be perfect harmony in our hearts; and may our feet raise such a cloud of dust in the peace-dance, that it shall not settle in three days, even though the skies should flood the earth. O Loha Pennu! upon that day let there be no rain, and no trouble in childbirth.'

No new answer is required from the god, but the negotiations proceed through a long course until both hosts join in the peace-dance, which rages for three or four hours. All are frantic with excitement, conceiving it to be inspired by the god, and that it would be impious to resist it. The joy of the peace-dance is regarded as the very highest attainable on earth, and the ex-haustion which follows it is considered to demand fifteen days' repose.

The following is the conclusion of the ceremonial of peace-making as it was performed by the tribes of Darungabadi and Grundabadi in 1845, after a long period of destructive war. These tribes are of the sect of Boora, and it will be observed that they expressly ascribe to him the introduction of the sanc-tions of peace.

The Janni having prepared a mixture of water and the earth of a white ant's hill, said, 'Let the warriors of both sides attend. Let the assembled multitudes listen. The beginning of our feud was this. Loha Pennu said to himself, " Let there be war;" and he forthwith entered into all weapons, so that from instruments of peace they became weapons of war ; he gave edge to the axe, and point to the arrow ; he entered into all kinds of food and drink, so that men in eating and drink-ing were filled with rage, and women became instruments of discord instead of soothers of anger. Our abundance of the blessings of peace was given to others, and the means of war alone abounded with us. We forsook love and friendship, and were filled with enmities. So great wars arose. Loha Pennu being satisfied with bloodshed, weapons having become blunt with slaughter, and the earth fat with blood, Boora Pennu wills that the solemn obligations which he appointed in past time to allay the wars and animosities produced by Loha Pennu shall now be entered into, and I now therefore administer those obliga-tions. Let the sharpness of weapons cease ; let the wrath which enters into man with food and drink cease ; and let man resume love and friendship. And do thou, O Pitterri Pennu! (goddess of increase) be gracious to us, and increase and mul-tiply our people, and thou —— be thou far from us.'

The Janni then sprinkled the parties making peace with water and earth.

Sundi Pennu, the God of Boundaries.

The following is the common strain of invocation addressed to Sundi Pennu:—'O Sundi Pennu! keep disease from our boundary, the disease epilepsy and disease of the eye, of the arms, of the legs. Let not the hostile gods of other countries cross our boundary, nor allow the tigers nor the snakes to cross our limits. Do you attract the water of higher countries to our boundary, and do not let stray our useful animals or our game, but do you let pass easily all noxious beasts. Permit not our tame cattle to pass our boundary, but make them grow large within it, like the swelling bitter gourd.

'You were always wont to do us these favours; now, for a small reason, your heart is changed. I, your servant, pray you to dismiss that feeling from your breast. I present to you this fowl, this egg, and this arrack. Moreover we pray you to remember, O god of boundaries! that it is your part to meet and conciliate the hearts of all who approach us. I now go. Do you give a propitious answer, so that henceforth I may have to render you worship in pleasure, not in pain.'

The priest then makes the offering of a fowl or a goat at a point upon the boundary fixed by ancient usage, and generally where a path crosses it.

The god of boundaries is necessarily considered a deity common to any two parties whose lands may adjoin. When these parties are at war, each invokes the god to bear witness to the justice of its cause, and to favour its arms; and, as both may not propitiate him on the same day, the battle is postponed, if necessary, to enable them to do so upon successive days. This god, in a fight, sends the arrows of their enemies to the hands of the party whom he may favour, closes their wounds that they may not gape fatally, and saves their battle-food from being lost in the confusion of the field and from turning sour.

The Worship of the Second and Third Classes of Inferior Deities.

The slight and unfrequent worship of the second class of inferior gods—the deified and sinless men of the first age—appears to require no notice beyond what is given in the statement of the tenets of the Khonds. I proceed to describe the worship paid to the third class of inferior gods—the minor deities, who fill nature and preside over the details of human life.

Idzu Pennu, the House-God.

Idzu Pennu, or the house-god, is the god of every household. He is propitiated by the offering of a hog or a fowl, with rice and arrack, on every occasion of general sacrifice by a tribe or village, and also when the master of the household transacts any private business of importance, as the settlement of a marriage, or any considerable sale of property. The household god, if favourable, increases the grain stored in the garner; and he is specially invoked at all domestic ceremonies, as namings, and at marriages, which every minor deity also is prayed to bless with the benefits in his special gift—as the god of boundaries to take care that the bride passes safely from her father's to her husband's house, and the god of streams to provide that water may abound at her new home.

To Jori Pennu, the god of streams, to Soro Pennu, god of hills, and the other minor local gods, the following is the common style of address, while the offerings are fowls, eggs, rice, and arrack :—

'O god of streams! you visit us with evils, withdrawing your favour on account of our sins. We cannot say that we are faultless, but we have been unable to afford to you a large and full supply of food in worship. Were we, O god of streams, constantly to expend our means upon your rites, and upon those of all the other gods, we should lose our lands; and then, we pray you to consider, where would be your worship? Considering this, we are unable to spend much upon your rites. Oh, receive this apology. We now make small offerings of a fowl or an egg, according to our ability; accept of them graciously. Look with favour upon us, on our wives, and our children, on our cattle, our sheep, our pigs, and their offspring. Do not let them be hurt in going to the water (or to the hill, if the hill-god be addressed). Give us increase of wealth. Accept our worship graciously, and give us your blessing.'

Nadzu Pennu, the Village-God.

Nadzu Pennu, the village-god, is the guardian deity of every hamlet. He is the great object of the familiar worship of the Khonds; the prosperity or ruin of villages is in his hands, and his patronage is implored for almost every undertaking. This deity is familiarly approached by all, at his shrine, which is simply a stone placed under the great cotton-tree which stands in or near every village. That tree, it may be observed, is planted at the foundation of each village, and is regarded with feelings of veneration which may be best understood from the following ceremony, which takes place amongst the sect of Boora Pennu at the foundation of every village, or upon changing the site of an old one.

On the day fixed for the ceremony, the village Janni brings from the jungle the stem of a young cotton-tree, six or eight feet long, having its root and top cut off, but with all its twigs carefully preserved, and the long sharp thorns, which the young branches of this tree bear but the old ones lose, unbroken. The priest, upon entering the village, says to the young tree, ' I bring you, by the order of Boora Pennu, who commanded us to build this village, as did also such and such gods '—naming ten or twelve others. The people of the village are now assembled, with dancing and music and fermented rice, and a hole is dug, in which the tree is planted.

A day or two afterwards, the Janni, having ascertained whether the god requires the sacrifice of a hog or a buffalo, and the animal being duly provided, again meets the assembled villagers by the young tree, when the following rude masque is gone through. An old man, of stupid and clownish look, comes out of the village to where the people are assembled, and, with a surprised and puzzled air, asks the Janni, ' What, I pray you, may be the meaning of the planting of this stick?' The priest replies, ' If you don't know, friend, you must assuredly be a great block—a mere jungle-stick, yourself. And how, O friend block, may I ask, did you find legs to bring you hither? You must have acquired them in some wonderful way. But since you are come to us, I will enlighten you, and make a man of you. Know, then, that when Boora Pennu first ordained that villages should exist, he gave us the tree which you now see planted, for a model in all these respects. That our families should spread like the branches of this great tree, strongly and widely. That our women should resemble its lovely and glowing red flowers. That, as the birds are attracted by the love of those sweet flowers, so the youths of neighbouring tribes should come, attracted by our young daughters. That, as of the flowers of this tree not one falls barren, but all unblighted bear fruit, so should it be with our women. That our sons should, in their youth, be rough, sharp, and keen like the young branches of this tree, which are covered with thorns; but that, as those thorns disappear with age, so should they become smooth and cool when youth is past. And lastly, this tree is given us as an example that we should live as long as it, a most long-lived tree. Boora Pennu thus ordained, and gave us this model tree.' The old man then says, ' And for what purpose, I pray, is this hog, or buffalo ?' The priest replies, ' One places things which are of value on a stand. We place flesh upon leaves, rice in vessels of earth or of metal ; a man rests upon a couch; and this animal is an offering upon which the commands of the deity may rest.' Then the victim is killed, and some of its dung mixed with straw is put upon the cut top of the tree.

Sugu Pennu or Sidruja Pennu, the God of Fountains.

The gods of fountains are objects of the most anxious worship. When a spring dries up the priest is instantly sent for, and implored with the most liberal promises of reward to bring back the water. He first attempts to propitiate and move the god of the spring ; and if he fails to do so, tries the following process. He plucks the cocoon of a wild silkworm from a bamboo-tree, and having emptied it, steals in the dead of night to some living fountain, to try by secret invocations to induce its god to transfer a portion of its waters to the deserted spring ; and this he does at the imminent risk of his life, if his errand should be discovered by the proprietors of the waters which are to be wiled away. The priest, after muttering for a long time alone over the spring, fills the cocoon-shell from it, and returns to the dry fountain, repeating prayers as he goes, which, if favourably heard, will make a stream of water follow his footsteps underground. The chief of the village, with a party of its elders, who have fasted the preceding day, await his return at the dry well, the presence of women at which would be fatal, while that of youths is also interdicted. The deserted basin is now cleared out, and the cocoon cup of water is placed in it. The priest sacrifices a sheep or a hog to Sugu Pennu, and he, if become propitious, either restores the spring at once, or gives signs of satisfaction from which its reappearance may be confidently hoped.

Joogah Pennu, Goddess of Smallpox.

Joogah Pennu, the goddess of smallpox, is a dread power, which cannot be appeased by any worship, and for which the Khonds have no distinct place in their mythology. This deity in her wrath 'sows smallpox upon mankind as men sow seed upon the earth.' When this disease appears in a village, all desert it save a few who remain to offer continually the blood of buffaloes, hogs, and sheep to the terrible power. The people of the neighbouring hamlets can but attempt to prevent her approach by barricading the paths with thorns and deep ditches, and boiling upon them cauldrons of stinking oil.

APPENDIX

B.

(REFERRED TO AT PAGE 136.)

Note upon General Campbell's Strictures on the Account of the Khond Religion.

CAPTAIN MACPHERSON's account of the religion of the Khonds is strikingly confirmed in many of its features (as has been shown in the notes appended to it by the Editor of these Memorials) by the statements of those who have subsequently travelled among other barbarous races. Nor does it less correspond with the observations of earlier travellers. It also fulfils the conditions laid down by philosophers who have reflected upon the natural history of religion.

Thus, M. Guizot says, in 'his Meditations on Christianity'—

' In the different pagan religions, whether of character gross or learned, we have deifications of the different forces of nature or of men themselves.'[1]

' All religions have given a prominent place to the problem of [the] existence and the origin of evil; all have attempted its solution. The good and the evil genius, Ormuzd and Ahriman, * * * * all are so many hypotheses to explain the conflict between good and evil, between order and disorder, in the world and in man.'[2]

General Campbell, however, is never tired of sneering at Captain Macpherson's account of the Khond religion. Yet one might suppose that it came before the public sufficiently accredited. The sources from which it is derived (though not the conscientious labour devoted to acquiring the information embodied in it) are carefully and modestly indicated in the Introduction,[3] to which particular attention is solicited. Captain

---

[1] English edition, London, 1864, p. 256.   [2] P. 56.
[3] See above, Appendix A. In letters written in 1843, Captain Macpherson says—'It is very difficult to learn the traditional lore correctly, and to

Macpherson had for many years made the Khonds his constant study, and he justly regarded their religion as precisely that with which the Agent for the abolition of their chief religious rite was mainly concerned. He was well acquainted with the Oriyah language, though General Campbell is pleased to deny this, as he denies to Soondera Sing—with equal injustice—a due acquaintance with Hindustani. Mr. Cadenhead, whose views are likewise represented in this paper, is rightly styled by General Campbell ('Personal Narrative' of 1864, p. 86) a 'most able and talented officer.' He knew not only the Oriyah but also the Khond tongue, with which the General does not apparently claim any acquaintance. Soondera Sing having passed his youth among the mountain Khonds, was thoroughly acquainted with their religion: a man incapable of misleading others or of being deceived himself upon this subject, and certainly not equal to the invention of a system which should so strikingly correspond with those which are found existing among races at a parallel stage of civilisation in other parts of the world. Baba Khan's good faith in the matter is as incontestable as his singular intelligence, though his task was merely to discover the depositaries of this lore, and to bring them to Captain Macpherson.

But it will be seen, on turning to the Introduction, that the information was not adopted at secondhand, but was taken down by Captain Macpherson personally from the speakers, and in many cases was corroborated by information which Mr. Cadenhead obtained from distinct and independent sources.[1]

ascertain its true sense, as the common priests are not well informed, and those of age and repute are nearly intangible.' . . . 'I have greatly extended my knowledge of the Khond people, and the interest of the subject has grown wonderfully at every step. I find that the country is as rich in religious legends as Arcadia in its prime. There is much floating poetry, too—quite as good as that of any rude people, and there are very good bold invocations of the gods.' And again: 'I have at last got materials with which I could make a kind of Khond book if I had a mind at ease at home. My information is still very defective on many points, and totally undigested. The difficulty of getting it you cannot conceive.' Captain Macpherson, therefore, was perfectly aware that he had undertaken no easy task. Having accordingly bestowed much time, labour, and thought upon the subject, he is entitled to be heard in preference to General Campbell, who, as will presently appear, did not persevere in the inquiry.

[1] General Campbell informs us that the late Captain Frye 'gives four short lines in the Khond language as the creed of the people, and describes their ceremonial in half a page.' Captain Frye could not have meant to

The most prominent of General Campbell's own remarks must now be considered.

First, he asserts that in the paper which he is criticising, 'the author represented the Khonds as a refined people overflowing with the most ingenious ideas.'[1].

The paper—with the exception of the Introduction, which is merely geographical and historical—is printed *verbatim* in the present work. The reader may ascertain for himself whether it contains any such representation, or anything that can afford the slightest warrant for General Campbell's statement.

The next objection is, that ' one of its most remarkable features was the number of deities with which the Khonds were said to be provided.'[2]

It has been shown[3] that they have this in common with other very rude nations. Among them, as among the Canaanites of old, who were further advanced in civilisation, ' human sacrifices, licentious orgies, and the worship of a host of divinities were associated.'[4] But what does General Campbell himself say on this subject? He tells us: ' The sacrifice in Chinna Kimedy is not offered to the earth alone, as in Goomsur and Boad, but to *a number of deities, whose favour is essential to life and happiness*; of these Manicksoro god of war, Boro Pennoo the great god, Zaro Pennoo the sun-god, hold the *chief* place.'[5]

' In Jeypore " the blood-red god of battles, Manecksoroo," (thus they style him) is the deity whom they seek to propitiate by human victims.'[6]

intimate that four lines and half a page adequately represented the superstitions of so many wild tribes spread over a territory 300 miles long. General Campbell says in an official report: ' Lieutenant Frye is labouring very zealously in the acquisition of the language. His chief difficulty lies in procuring a Khond, or indeed anyone, who is in the least acquainted with the religion they profess, or can give any tolerable account of their habits and manners.' This was written on the 17th March 1849, when General Campbell had nearly completed the second year of his second term of service among the Khonds—the first having extended over five years. But the reference to Captain Frye proves too much, for the General says a great deal more about the Khond religion than Captain Frye.

[1] ' Personal Narrative,' p. 160.   [2] *Ibid.* p. 161.

[3] Supra, pp. 92-96.

[4] See Dean Stanley's ' Lectures on the Jewish Church,' p. 209.

[5] ' Personal Narrative,' p. 120. General Campbell is speaking only of those deities to whom he believes that *human* sacrifice was offered.

[6] ' Personal Narrative,' p. 52.

‘ They had heard reports, spread by evil-disposed persons,
that I was collecting Meriahs, for the purpose of sacrificing them
on the plains to the water deity, because the water had dis-
appeared from a tank which I had constructed.’ [1]

‘ Whenever a child is born, a priest, or dessawry, as he is called
in that part of the country, is summoned, and consulted by the
parent as to the future prospects of the new-born infant.   The
astrologer,—for such is the pretended avocation of the priest,—
professes in a mysterious manner to consult the horoscope, and
he also produces a kind of book (called punjee) formed of dried
palmyra-leaves, on which are scribbled some sentences in the
Hindu character, intermingled with *rudely drawn figures of
mythical deities, demons, and devils, representing after their
fashion good and evil spirits.*   Certain mumblings and other
ceremonies, calculated to inspire the parents with a deep feeling
of awe and reverence for the astrologer, are then gone through.
An iron or bone style is finally inserted at random between the
leaves of the book, and the fate of the unconscious baby is
determined by the figure and words to which the style points.
If *the deity* or sign thus capriciously selected represents good,
the life of the little one is spared,’ [3] &c. &c.

So that General Campbell likewise must believe that the
Khonds, like other barbarians, have a multitude of deities.   But
then he does not like to see any attempt to classify them.   He
continues:—

‘ The mythology attributed to the Khonds of Orissa must be
considered marvellous when their present state of semi-barbarism
and gross ignorance is borne in mind.   They are furnished with
a pantheon in which there are deities of various degrees of
power, in a kind of railway classification.   The first class consists of gods of rain,’ [4] &c. &c.

If we take General Campbell’s words literally, it might seem
as if he thought that polytheism is a sign of civilisation.   The
real objection, however, involved in this oddly-worded passage
would seem to be, that the Khond system, as represented by Captain Macpherson, is too complicated for a people so uncivilised.
But the examples which have been given, especially that taken
from Captain Burton’s work, [4] abundantly show that a classified
pantheon is not incompatible with barbarism and ignorance.   In-

[1] ‘Personal Narrative,’ p. 129.   [2] *Ibid.* p. 148.   See above, p. 72
[3] *Ibid.*   [4] See above, p. 91.

deed, the marvel would be if all the deities were of equal rank and power. But what has the General told us?—'That certain specified gods hold the "chief place," or in other words *constitute the first class*, among a number of deities, whose power is essential to life and happiness!'[1]

The Introduction to Captain Macpherson's paper distinctly avows that the completeness and system were inevitably greater on paper than in reality; as is the case with every account of the Greek, the Roman, or the Hindu gods—in short, with every attempt to reduce to writing that which previously existed only in oral tradition.

General Campbell's next sneer is directed against the Khond doctrine regarding the soul:—

' These poor and ignorant people, according to the account here furnished, are not only rich in deities, but as marvellously rich in souls, every Khond being gifted with four, and very remarkable souls they are. No. 1 is capable of beatification ; No. 2 is attached to a tribe, and re-born in the tribe in a manner impossible to be explained; No. 3 endures sufferings and transmigrations, sometimes quits its corporeal tenement to hold communion with a god, and sometimes to enter the body of a tiger ; and No. 4 becomes extinct at its owner's dissolution.'[2]

It is not easy to find a parallel for all the vagaries of savage minds, but other wild races besides the Khonds have very complicated and technical systems of doctrine and practice on many subjects, such as Tapu in New Zealand and Fetish in Africa: and with regard to the soul, many of them hold opinions as strange as those which General Campbell deems so inconsistent with the simplicity which he would expect to find in the Khond doctrines. Thus we learn that in the sorcerer's art in New Zealand there was a modification of the Pythagorean doctrine of Metempsychosis, in which two living bodies are supposed to change souls with each other :[3] that the Tonguese restricted the possession of a soul to chiefs and gentry—but the Fijians go further, allowing it not only to all mankind, but to animals, plants, and even houses, canoes, and all mechanical contrivances :[4] that the

---

[1] See App., p. 373.
[2] 'Personal Narrative,' p. 102.   See above, p. 91.
[3] Thomson's ' Story of New Zealand,' vol. i. p. 118.
[4] 'Mission to Viti,' p. 398.

aborigines of the countries bordering on the Straits of Malacca believe in the immortality of the soul, though some of them seem to have doubts as to the preservation of their individual identity, and look upon life as a simple element in creation, distinct from substance, which on death will return to a common source to be distributed as required :[1] and that in the country described by Captain Burton, the departed often returns to earth in the body of a child, and yet remains in Deadland.[2]

General Campbell too has furnished us with a striking proof of the accuracy of one of the statements which he derides. He says that a Khond, whom he had induced to join his corps of Sebundies, joined in repelling an attack, in which two or three of the assailants were shot; that he became strongly imbued with the idea that one of them was possessed of the power of the 'phulto-bag,' and would certainly destroy him and all his family; that subsequently 'this poor fellow was seized by a tiger and cruelly mutilated. He shortly afterwards died from the effect of his wounds; but before he expired he said that he was one of those who had fired and killed a Khond at Oorladoney, and that this Khond had assumed the form of a tiger, and so avenged himself. It would have required a miracle to have persuaded his friends that his fate was but a strange coincidence.'[3]

Another sneer is levelled at the account of the priesthood :—

' It is also asserted . . . that a priesthood exists, which in its organisation and labours corresponds with the elaborate system of idolatry *provided for* this semibarbarous people. According to this narrative the priest much resembles the medicine-man of the North American Indian, seeking to discover, by certain mystic arts, the cause of the malady he may be called upon to cure, which he usually attributes to the displeasure of some god, or the magic of some enemy whom the patient has offended.'[4]

Now, it being admitted that certain practices are carried on among the North American Indians, why should we refuse to believe that anything of a similar kind exists among other semibarbarous tribes? It is not clear whether the General means to deny the existence of a priesthood, or the employment

---

[1] 'Our Tropical Possessions in Malayan India,' by John Cameron, Esq. London, 1865. See above, p. 134.

[2] Burton's ' Mission to the King of Dahomey,' vol. ii. p. 158.

[3] 'Personal Narrative,' p. 242.   [4] *Ibid.* p. 165.

by the priest of mystical arts. The former seems scarcely possible, as priests are mentioned by himself.[1] The account which he gives of the priest or dessawry (cited App., p. 374), speaks of pretensions which are very much the same with those which he refuses to believe; and 'the officiating zani or priest,' mentioned at p. 211 of the 'Personal Narrative,' would seem to be a personage of the same class.

Again, says General Campbell, 'according to this authority, there is a particular form of worship to every god, with particular traditions respecting him or her, all of which are given in detail, as well as ceremonials for the different seasons;'[2] which, we are given to understand, is very absurd. Yet having so said, General Campbell himself gives us in detail the particular ceremonial and form of worship for the god Manicksoro, ending thus :—'The officiating zani, or priest, standing on the right side, repeats the following invocation,'[2] &c. Here follow, in minute detail, the invocation of the god, the address to the victim, and an account of the remainder of the sacrificial ceremonies!—and elsewhere he records sundry particular traditions.

It has been sufficiently shown in the present Note, and in the references appended to the text, that, in almost every one of the points selected for attack, Captain Macpherson is supported either by a close parallel in the religion of some rude people, or by the express testimony of General Campbell. Indeed, after the citations that have been made, one might almost class General Campbell among the believers in the existence of the religious system set forth by Captain Macpherson. But no : although his own work affords ample and (as being involuntary) valuable confirmation, he will have none of it. He never heard anything like it from his Meriahs[3] or destined victims—not, perhaps, exactly the class whom the Khond priesthood would be likely to take into their counsels on this subject. 'He has reason to believe that he possessed the confidence of the chiefs and priests to an extent never before possessed by a European(!); nevertheless *he* is not in a position to publish such a complete system of mythology as that to which he has been *obliged* to draw the reader's attention, *or anything in the slightest degree resembling it.*'[4]

---

[1] 'Personal Narrative,' pp. 163, 168, 211.   [2] *Ibid.* p. 211.
[3] *Ibid.* p. 163.   [4] *Ibid.* p. 168.

The truth is that General Campbell's want of information is completely accounted for by a circumstance recorded in his printed 'Narrative' of 1861, and in that Narrative only.

'I made many efforts,' he says, 'to acquire correct information on this point; but I met with so many contradictions, and such vagueness and variety of opinion, that *I abandoned the attempt, satisfied* that their so-called religion was *probably* a corruption and admixture of Buddhism and Hinduism, or other ancient systems brought from the plains, from whence, as I have already said, the Khonds originally came'![1]

[1] 'Narrative of 1861,' p. 24.

APPENDIX

C.

(REFERRED TO AT PAGES 247, 248.)

Recovery of the Meriahs.

GENERAL CAMPBELL has not been consistent in his statement of numbers. In the anonymous pamphlet published in 1849 [1] (for which the General has now publicly declared himself responsible),[2] it is said that when Captain Macpherson was removed from office, late in March 1847, upwards of 120 of these Meriahs remained in the hands of their rebellious masters;[3] that Captain Macpherson had only obtained the redelivery of from 45 to 50 of the surrendered Meriahs;[4] and that 'when Colonel Campbell assumed charge of the Agency, in May 1847, the victors still rejoiced in the possession of upwards of 120 of the living trophies of their victory.'[5]

In the 'Narrative' of 1861, the General says: 'In February 1848, 140 of the victims unhappily extorted from Captain Macpherson were still in the hands of the Khonds.'[6]

In the 'Personal Narrative' of 1864 the numbers are swelled to 170:—'I crossed over [in 1847] into the Boad country, where peace had not been perfectly restored, and the surrendered victims still remained in the hands of the wild tribes of the district. The great feat to be achieved here was to get back the 170 victims.'[7]

In the 'Narrative' of 1861, he says that in 1847 three of the redelivered Meriahs 'were cruelly sacrificed ere I could save them;'[8] and in the 'Personal Narrative' of 1864, 'As a tangible proof of their sincerity, they delivered up every Meriah in their possession. Three of the victims, out of the 170 formerly surrendered, had been cruelly slaughtered, in the vain hope of

---

[1] See Appendix F. (Correspondence.)   [2] *Ibid.*
[3] P. 116.   [4] P. 117.   [5] P. 131.
[6] P. 67.   [7] 'Personal Narrative,' p. 94.   [8] P. 105.

propitiating their deity, and preventing the success of our efforts. With these exceptions, I got back all who had been redelivered; the total number rescued in Boad during these operations being 235.'[1]   Here we have three several printed statements, for all of which the General is responsible, and each differing from the other—120, 140, 170.

But Captain Macpherson had recovered between 60 and 70 before his removal from office, as appears by a letter addressed by him to Mr. Commissioner Grant:[2] so that the true number could not have been even the smallest of the three mentioned by General Campbell.   Captain Macpherson calls the original number 172 in his official letters; and, considering the General's inconsistent way of stating the numbers, and his evident readiness to believe the story (for he refers to it again and again in his Narratives, conceiving it to tell against Captain Macpherson), the sacrifice of three of these Meriahs could not be regarded as an ascertained fact, even were it not contradicted by the positive official statement of an officer whose authority on Khond subjects General Campbell at least ought not to dispute.

The late Captain Frye is specially commended by General Campbell.   Towards the end of 1849, the General tells us, he handed over the charge of the Agency (on proceeding to the Cape of Good Hope) to Captain Frye, who indeed appears, from other passages in the 'Narrative,' to have owed his appointment to the General's own recommendation. 'This admirable officer,' he adds, 'had always taken the deepest interest in our labours, and, being an Oriental scholar of the highest rank, had occupied himself most zealously in the acquisition of the Khond language;'[3] and at p. 168 he is quoted as an authority on the subject of the Khond religion.

Captain Frye states, in an official report drawn up by him after a very long tour which he made in the Khond country as Agent, and which ended on the 6th April 1850 :—'According to the Khond system of worship, a Meriah once shown to the Government is considered unfit for sacrifice : *there is no instance on record* of a Meriah so shown being regarded otherwise than as the ward of the Government.'[4]

[1] 'Personal Narrative,' p. 111.   [2] Dated 29th January 1848.
[3] 'Personal Narrative,' p. 193.
[4] Selections from the Records of the Government of India, No. V. (Calcutta, 1854), p. 114.   The case of the rescued ward of Government, who

But if three wards of the Government—three of that particular set of wards of the Government who had been redelivered,
and upon whom public attention had been so much fixed—had
been sacrificed in 1847, as General Campbell says,[1] how could
Captain Frye, with the recently published anonymous pamphlet
of 1849 before him, officially state in 1850 that there was no
instance on record of such an event?

was sacrificed by authority of Sam Bissye, is no exception; for that sacrifice
was sanctioned by Sam Bissye, the chief agent of the Government.

[1] 'Personal Narrative,' p. 233.

APPENDIX

D.

(REFERRED TO AT PAGE 250.)

GENERAL CAMPBELL says ('Personal Narrative,' p. 88):—
'Scarcely had this first concession of the surrender of the victims
been made, when, flushed with such a success, the Khonds again
attacked his camp, which was then retiring on Goomsur. They
now demanded that this imbecile Rajah, who was then accompanying Captain Macpherson, and whom the Khonds supposed
to be a prisoner, should be made over to them. To pacify them,
a second concession was made, and the Rajah was sent back
with them to Boad.'

Now, not only has Captain Macpherson minutely recorded, in
the report cited in the text (of May 17, 1841), the whole of the
events of this period, but his relations with the Rajah became
soon after the subject of a searching public investigation. The
whole of them were minutely scrutinised; yet no such occurrence
as the surrender of the Rajah in consequence of an attack, or of
threats, was ever alleged to have taken place.

Captain Macpherson says, in a paper submitted to Mr. Grant,
the Commissioner of Inquiry:—'The Rajah and Kurtivas had
accompanied me to Kunjeur at their own request, and declared
anew there that they certainly could, and would bring in all, or
at least a great portion, of the Khonds and victims within three
days.' It is obvious that the Rajah and Kurtivas could not now
be useful to the Agent, except in bringing the Khonds to a
right state of mind.

But the writer of the anonymous pamphlet published by
General Campbell in 1849, does not assert that 'the Khonds
again attacked the Agent's camp, which was then retiring on
Goomsur.' He says,—'Shortly after the arrival of the Agent and
his camp at this place [Kunjeur, in Goomsur] it was reported
that the exulting mob, armed with bows, arrows, and battle-
axes, was at Sangrimendi, meditating the forcible recovery of
their Rajah, whom they supposed to be a prisoner. Whatever

may have been the circumstances which induced his attendance on the Agent, or of his early dismissal, we were not careful to learn ; suffice it to say that the Boad potentate, with his uncle —*par nobile fratrum!*—for the pacification of a storm raised, as the Agent tells us, by their own intrigues, was hurried back into the Boad Maliahs.'

Here the insinuation is (for nothing is directly stated) that the Agent dismissed the Rajah in consequence of its being reported that the ' exulting mob' was at Sangrimendi, some miles from his camp—a suggestion not consistent with the General's present assertion that they attacked his camp. If the author of the pamphlet, in whom General Campbell reposed so much confidence that he published [1] his production without having read it, and considered himself responsible for it although he ' did not know anything of its contents until after its publication '[2]— if this writer, who may almost be termed the General's *alter ego*, was not careful to learn in 1849, when he tells us that he was employing himself on the spot in a most elaborate self-imposed inquiry into these events, by the testimony of numerous eye-witnesses,—how can it be known now? And why was he not careful to learn this, when he was careful to pick up everything he could think likely to operate to Captain Macpherson's disadvantage ?

Even the 'Narrative' of 1861 scarcely goes so far as to assert that the Khonds actually attacked the camp. It states (page 54) that ' the Khonds pursued the Agent, and, being joined by some of the Goomsur tribes, demanded the freedom of the Boad Rajah, which was yielded them; and the retreat continued till the arrival of reinforcements from the plains, when the Khonds were driven away.'

This is the third version for which General Campbell is responsible. But the redelivery of the victims occurred on the 14th of March; the Agent retired to Kunjeur on the 15th; and it is on record [3] that he was at Kunjeur on the 19th, and there and then repulsed an attack of some of the Boad Khonds— so that the retreat cannot have been ' continued,' as asserted by General Campbell.

---

[1] See below, App. p. 393. [2] See below, App. p. 399.
[3] Official Report, dated 17th May 1846.

APPENDIX

E.

CAPTAIN MACPHERSON, when he was made acquainted with the Brigadier-General's charges, applied for an opportunity of vindicating himself and his assistants and servants, and prayed that the inquiry might extend to every act of his administration.

A very long investigation accordingly took place, before a Commissioner specially appointed for the purpose—Mr. Grant (now Sir John Peter Grant, K.C.B.), a distinguished member of the Civil Service, who subsequently filled the office of Lieutenant-Governor of Bengal.

When the charges, however, had almost been gone through, and Captain Macpherson's measures in the low-country had been inquired into, and when his policy towards the hill-tribes, the ground which promised him the most certain and signal triumph, remained to be inquired into, where he had from the first demanded that it should be examined, and where alone it could be effectively examined—in the Hills, among the Khonds themselves, and in the presence of the persons accused—the inquiry was cut short by Colonel Campbell, to whom after a few weeks the Brigadier-General had given over charge of the Agency.

Colonel Campbell[1] declared that, for political reasons, Captain Macpherson must not appear in the Khond country. Next it turned out that political reasons prevented Colonel Campbell from sending down any one witness from the Hills, ere yet the country had been crushed under the feet of Sam Bissye, whom Colonel Campbell was engaged in restoring.[2]

Captain Macpherson then agreed to take his chance of the

[1] November 1847. The Commissioner was holding his court at Nowgaum, in the low-country of Goomsur, near the foot of the Hills. The ex-Agency had of course attended him.

[2] 'Sam Bissye,' says General Campbell ('Personal Narrative,' p. 92) 'well knew how to govern these people, and how to make himself both feared and respected. His will emphatically was law.'

evidence of such Khonds as could be collected in the low-country, from the fairs and upon the roads. Mr. Grant had about a hundred of them before him, and their evidence was uniformly favourable to the late Agency.

Colonel Campbell next declared that it was politically necessary that Captain Macpherson's two late chief native officers should leave Goomsur. This requisition was obeyed, and they were sent away; the irresistible belief in the minds of the Khonds being that they were sent away in disgrace through the influence of Sam Bissye; although they had not yet had an opportunity of examining their witnesses in answer to the charges made against them, and their assistance was required for the defence of the late Agency. Finally, Colonel Campbell required that Captain Macpherson should himself quit Goomsur —even the low-country: his Assistants were in like manner excluded. Under these circumstances, Colonel Campbell's attitude could only be considered by the people to be one of open antagonism to the late Agency, and it might seem that there could be little chance of the delivery of free and fearless testimony.

Situated as Colonel Campbell was with respect to Captain Macpherson, it is not too much to say that, however necessary he may have deemed these successive demands for the exclusion of those whose conduct was under investigation (Captain Macpherson emphatically declared that there was not the smallest ground for any one of them, nor did they, it is believed, receive any countenance from the Commissioner), they at least imposed it upon him, as an indispensable condition to a favourable estimation of his motives upon this occasion, that he should for ever after abstain from acts indicating personal hostility to Captain Macpherson.

The course which he actually took was so extraordinary that no less authority than his own would suffice to authenticate the statement of it: it is therefore recorded in his own words.[1]

Mr. Grant afterwards visited the Goomsur Hills, being interdicted by Colonel Campbell from entering Boad. He was not attended by a single member or servant of the late Agency, or by any one on their behalf; such attendance being prohibited by Colonel Campbell. In due time he made his Report, which formed the basis of the final decision of the Government

[1] See Appendix F.

C C

upon the case—contained in a Resolution of the Governor-General in Council, dated 7th October 1848, and in a letter of the Court of Directors of the 25th September 1850, in which that Resolution was reviewed, and a judgment not less favourable to the ex-Agency was pronounced.

General Campbell has been pleased to epitomise the charges, in a paragraph which will be cited. They in truth took a larger range than would appear from his statement, extending to every part of the conduct of the late Agency and its servants; and—as might have been expected under the circumstances—Mr. Grant, a very acute man, coming to inquire and to criticise, and conducting his inquiries under the difficulties above referred to—and the Government adopting his reports, did not approve of everything that had been done; but the result was that while high praise was awarded to the conduct of the two Assistants, Mr. Cadenhead and Mr. Pinkney (upon whom necessarily a less degree of responsibility rested than upon their chief), the Government at the same time recorded its opinion, that 'Captain Macpherson had, with a very little exception, cleared himself and his administration of all General ——'s[1] accusations,' and it informed the latter officer (who had reiterated his charges) 'that every allegation of the slightest importance set forth in his letter had been fully disproved in the course of the inquiry conducted by Mr. Grant.'

The Government at the same time declared that it was 'to be regretted, that putting confidence in General ——'s representations, since ascertained to have been unfounded, his measure of removing the Agency officers of his own authority received the approbation of the Government.'

This, seeing that Governments never retract and never are in the wrong, seems a tolerably near approach to a confession of error.

General Campbell's summary runs thus:—'Major-General[2] —— reported, on the 20th March, that he wished to give all the assistance in his power to Captain Macpherson to give effect to his measures for the restoration of tranquillity; but no change had taken place in the aspect of affairs, and he had come to the conclusion, after communicating with many

---

[1] The officer designated as General —— is not General Campbell, but the Brigadier-General who made the charges.

[2] A mistake for Brigadier-General.

influential persons, and from actual observation, that tranquillity would not be restored under the present Agency, owing to the extreme hatred manifested throughout these districts against Captain Macpherson and his establishment—the result, as is generally stated, of the offensive conduct of the Agency towards the inhabitants of these Mootahs, and above all the harsh and cruel measures resorted to whenever it has been necessary to display the power, as it is termed, of the Government against any of these ignorant and deluded people.' [1]

The following extracts from the Resolution of 7th October 1848 show how these matters appeared to the deciding authority :—

'Mr. Grant' (says the Governor-General in Council) 'was led to believe, from what he saw of the Goomsur Khonds, that both Captain Macpherson and his native officers were much liked by them; and there was, he says, the same negative evidence as regards the seven lowland Mootahs attached to the Agency—viz., the absence of all complaint against them.

'The direct evidence of the very good feeling towards the ex-Agency of the respectable and peaceable classes (village-renters and merchants) of the low-country, Mr. Grant describes as most convincing.

'The conclusion of the Commissioner's investigation, embraced in his 13th Report, which the Governor-General in Council has now reviewed, is a testimony emphatically favourable to Captain Macpherson and his establishment [2] :—

'"On the whole subject I must report the result of my inquiry to be a conviction that no hatred was felt in the districts under the Meriah Agency against Captain Macpherson or his establishment, and neither his conduct nor theirs had been oppressive to the inhabitants of those districts; and that no reason existed for fancying that the feelings of the people towards the ex-Agency would have interfered with the return of the country to permanent tranquillity under them. On the other matters in question, my conviction is that a great change for the better in the aspect of affairs was in active progress during the period between the 14th of March, when General ——

[1] 'Narrative' of 1861, p. 58.
[2] Mr. Grant wrote to the effect that he believed that no Agency in India could have come so triumphantly through such an ordeal in respect of these inquiries.

went to Gullery,[1] and the 20th of March, when he wrote his accusatory letter; that before General —— left the village of Gullery, the people who were living there equalled about two-thirds of its original population, of whom the greater number were people just returned ftom the jungles; that when General —— wrote his accusatory letter it was premature to say that there was no prospect of the return of the people in the jungles, notwithstanding Captain Macpherson's proclamation, because of the dispersion and distance of the absentees—and there was a good prospect of the return of the greater part of those still absent, because a large proportion of the original absentees had already returned within the last few days; that there was not a spirit of universal distrust in the minds of the people of the said districts against the locally-constituted authorities, and no wish for their removal; and that at the time in question much progress had been made towards the settlement of the low-country of Goomsur."

' The charges of inhumanity—as affecting Captain Macpherson the ex-Agent, Mr. Cadenhead the Principal Assistant, or Lieutenant Pinkney the Assistant—including the allegation in relation to harsh and cruel measures resorted to by way of coercion, and the general character of the field-operations of the Agency, have been searchingly and comprehensively investigated in the 8th, 9th, and 12th Reports to Mr. Grant. The Governor-General in Council has no hesitation in pronouncing these charges to have been throughout most unmerited. . . . . Even where the burning of villages was resorted to under specific authority from Captain Macpherson, with the explanation which the Government has now received of the transaction, this officer must be relieved from the blame formerly imputed to him;[2] since there was a manifest necessity for the punishment of the rebel party to which these villages belonged, however much any necessity for the adoption of such a mode of punishment may be to be deprecated.'[3]

---

[1] A village in the Goomsur low-country.

[2] No blame had ever been imputed to him.

[3] Another paragraph of the Resolution may be cited :—' The Governor-General in Council has considered Mr. Grant's 13th Report with the close attention which it deserves, not only as a judicial examination of the grounds (alleged and assumed) on which General —— must be held to have founded his opinion that such was the hatred of the people to Captain Macpherson's Meriah Agency that the tranquillity of the country

To advert to the history which General Campbell has taken upon himself to give of the events of 1847.   He says :—

'The policy pursued by General —— was most successful : the removal of Captain Macpherson and his establishment at once put an end to the opposition to Government, tranquillity was restored, and nothing remained but the embers of the disturbance kept alive by Chokro Bissye.'[1]

This is a little modified in the 'Personal Narrative' of 1864 :—

'General —— quickly marched into the disturbed districts, and through his judicious measures tranquillity was so far restored as to render it possible again to renew operations against human sacrifices, which from first to last had been the sole object the Anglo-Indian Government had in view.'[2]

Mr. Grant's report, adopted by the Government of India, gives a very different account of matters :—

'I have pointed out that the result of the course of policy adopted by General —— has been the burning by rebels in the course of a year of a much larger number [than 35] of *loyal* villages, many of them burnt at night, with destruction of property and some loss of life.

could not be restored while the authority was in his hands, but as an instructive narrative of circumstances which indicate what was the real condition of the feelings of the people in the low-country of Goomsur towards the Government and the officers of the ex-Agency at the time of General ——'s assumption of power, the classes (the Paiks and Khonds of the low-country) concerned in the rebellion, the influence of the Paiks, what may be supposed to have been the object which they and the Khonds had in common respecting a restoration of the Rajah of Goomsur, and the movement, not confined to the division of Goomsur under Captain Macpherson—on the contrary (as principally instigated by the disaffected adventurer Chokro Bissye, who had no exclusive design on Captain Macpherson's division of the Goomsur low-country), simultaneously breaking out within Mootahs belonging to the Ganjam Agent's division; and which further establish the misapprehension and deception whereby the General was induced to make his accusatory representations respecting the conduct of the local authorities to the Madras and Bengal Governments.'

[1] 'Narrative' of 1861, p. 59.

[2] Page 91. What this means is not very clear. Captain Macpherson had rendered up Goomsur wholly reclaimed (see above, p. 212); and as to Bond, we are told in the 'Narrative' of 1861, that up to the latter part of February 1848 the Khonds of Bond 'had been triumphant.' Operations against the sacrifice, therefore, according to General Campbell, were at this time unnecessary in Goomsur; and *if* any took place in Bond, they must have been wholly unsuccessful.

'The indiscriminate release without trial of the prisoners in confinement has had deplorable consequences in respect of the peace of the country generally, and the safety of *loyal* individuals especially.

'The people of Chokapaud, who were then [at the time of Captain Macpherson's dismissal] in rebellion, remained in rebellion until the other day; and all, or nearly all, who were not then in rebellion went into rebellion a few days after General —— took charge, and so remained till the other day.' [1]

To return to General Campbell's statements :—

'The corrupt practices of the native establishment of the late Agency *made it impossible to employ any of them.*' [2]

This is very explicit, and relates to another matter on which one might have supposed that General Campbell could not well be mistaken, as the constitution of his native establishment rested entirely with himself. But what says the Government Resolution ?—

'The third man in rank, by name Sookoomaram, and a few others *were reappointed to office by Colonel Campbell*(!) which could not have happened if Colonel Campbell had considered their original removal a just and necessary measure.' [3]

Mr. Grant considered that several members of the native establishment of the Agency, including Baba Khan and in a less degree Soondera Sing, had been guilty of extortion. Such a charge might easily be brought, easily be backed by testimony, and easily be believed, against the members of any native establishment when turned out of office; for the exaction of irregular gains, though not universal, is yet of very frequent occurrence among all classes of the natives of India, from the reigning prince to the messenger upon four rupees a month. The Agency servants, however, complained that, owing to their second expulsion from Goomsur by Colonel Campbell in November 1847, before their witnesses could be examined, they had been precluded from making their defence: and Mr. Grant himself reported that in the Hills they were generally liked and well spoken of, that in the plains there was no complaint against them, and that no Agency in India could have come so

---

[1] This was written on the 15th June 1848.

[2] 'Narrative' of 1861, p. 63. This assertion is not repeated in the 'Personal Narrative,' but, like the rest of the 'Narrative' of 1861, it stands unretracted.

[3] Resolution of 7th October 1848.

triumphantly through such an ordeal as they were subjected to. These findings do not seem consistent with the supposition of any very serious corruption. Without going into detail on this subject, it may be remarked that Soondera Sing and Baba Khan were the leading instruments of an Agency of which 'mildness' was emphatically declared by Mr. Grant to be the 'characteristic'; that they had adhered to it with inflexible constancy, under many dangers and sufferings, and that they had greatly promoted its success by their zeal and their abilities. Even were it possible—as, for the reasons stated, it is not—to arrive at any certain conclusion regarding these charges, and were that conclusion unfavourable to them,—it would be unfair to judge them, as General Campbell has done, by a standard of morals which he well knows to be inapplicable.

Soondera Sing was a high-bred Hindu gentleman of spirit and ability, and of manners befitting his station; and it is unquestionable that he retained in a most remarkable degree to the day of his death the respect and affection of his own countrymen. Baba Khan was associated with Soondera in all things, and though his school-education had, like that of most Mahomedans, been neglected, he spoke many languages, and was very able and intelligent. He filled at the time of his death the respectable office of Tahsildar of Nellore. These men died prematurely, worn out in the public service. Captain Macpherson and Mr. Cadenhead publicly acknowledged the value of their assistance, and would have disclaimed any credit themselves of which an ample share was not awarded to Soondera Sing and Baba Khan, their zealous instruments and coadjutors. The Hindu and the Musulman in their short day served God according to their measure; and General Campbell would have done well, instead of reiterating his harsh and vindictive accusations against them, to dwell less on the alleged frailties and more upon the undoubted merits of two men who contributed so largely to the work of humanity.

APPENDIX

F.

I.—*Mr. Macpherson to General Campbell.*

6 Stanhope Street, Hyde Park Gardens:
March 7, 1863.

Sir,—A work bearing your name as author, and those of Messrs. Hurst & Blackett as publishers, but purporting to be printed for private circulation, was reviewed in the 'Edinburgh Evening Courant' of the 28th ult. The review contains statements professedly founded on the work in question, and reflecting upon the conduct of the late Major Macpherson, although he is not named in the review. The book was noticed some time ago in the London 'Spectator,' in a review of similar purport.

I am the eldest brother of Major Macpherson. Upon the appearance of the review in the 'Spectator' I wrote to Messrs. Hurst & Blackett (being unacquainted with your address), and asked them to submit to you my request to be favoured with a copy of the work. They have since informed me that they forwarded my application, but I make no doubt that it has failed to reach you. Under these circumstances I now renew my request; and I hope that it will be convenient for you to accede to it at an early date, since, independently of the newspaper notices which have put an end to all privacy, I might have fairly claimed to see, even while its circulation was private, a book which appears to contain reflections upon the conduct of my brother, whom you succeeded in office.

I am, Sir, your obedient servant,

WILLIAM MACPHERSON.

P.S.—A copy, if sent to 6 Duke Street, Edinburgh, will reach me.

Major-General John Campbell, C.B.

II.—*General Campbell to Mr. Macpherson.*

120 George Street, Edinburgh :
March 9, 1863.

Sir,—I have this day received yours of the 7th, and, as re-quested, have forwarded a copy of my book to 6 Duke Street. Messrs. Hurst & Blackett made no communication to me respecting your wish to have a copy of the work, which was written solely for private circulation among my friends ; nor had I any knowledge whatsoever of the reviews of the book which you mention until the papers in which they appeared were forwarded to me casually by a friend ; nor do I know who the writers are. Had my permission been asked to review or notice the work in any manner, I should most certainly have refused my consent.

I remain, Sir, your obedient servant,

J. CAMPBELL.

W. Macpherson, Esq., 6 Stanhope Street.

III.—*Mr. Macpherson to General Campbell.*

6 Stanhope Street, Hyde Park Gardens :
March 16, 1863.

Sir,—I have to thank you for the copy of your ' Narrative,' which you were so good as to send to Duke Street in compliance with my request. At page 202 I observe the following pas-sage :—' By the kind permission of Lord Dalhousie, I published an answer to a tissue of gross misrepresentations which appeared in the Calcutta Review.' As I am not aware of the existence of any publication which bears your name besides the ' Nar-rative,' I beg leave to enquire whether the answer to which you refer is an anonymous pamphlet, entitled ' The Khond Agency and the Calcutta Review— being a Reply in Refutation of the Misrepresentations and Distortions of Facts contained in several Articles on Khond Affairs, published in Nos. IX., XI., XV., and XX. of the Calcutta Review (Madras, 1849)'? If this is not your answer, I shall feel obliged if you will afford me such information as may enable me to obtain a copy of the answer. As the manner in which you mention Lord Dalhousie's name might seem to imply that his Lordship in some degree lent his sanction to the contents of your publication, I shall esteem it a favour if you will acquaint me with the exact terms in which his permission was conveyed.

I am, Sir, your obedient servant,
WILLIAM MACPHERSON.

Major-General John Campbell, C.B.

IV.—*General Campbell to Mr. Macpherson.*

120 George Street, Edinburgh:
March 17, 1865.

Sir,—I have to acknowledge the receipt of your letter of yesterday. The passage which you quote from page 202 of my 'Narrative' has reference to the pamphlet entitled 'The Khond Agency and the Calcutta Review,' &c., for the publication of which and the use of official papers I received the permission of the Governor-General of India, Lord Dalhousie, through the usual official channel; but I do not mean to imply that his Lordship approved or otherwise of the contents of the pamphlet, copies of which were at the time sent to the late Major Macpherson, the leading Indian periodicals, the anonymous writer in the 'Calcutta Review,' the several Governments of India, and the Court of Directors; the latter stating in reply that they did not approve of officers noticing anonymous reflections on their official conduct, and that I ought to have rested satisfied with the approval of my superiors, or words to that effect.

I am, Sir, your obedient servant,
J. CAMPBELL.

W. Macpherson, Esq., London.

V.—*Mr. Macpherson to General Campbell.*

6 Stanhope Street, Hyde Park Gardens, W.:
March 31, 1863.

Sir,—I have received your letter of the 17th inst., in which you inform me that the pamphlet entitled 'The Khond Agency and the Calcutta Review,' &c., is the answer to which you referred as having been published by you. As both your works relate to the delicate subject of the comparative merits of yourself and Major Macpherson, and abound in strictures upon his conduct, it is remarkable that the pamphlet which was published does not bear your name; while the 'Narrative,' which does bear your name, has not been published. Although you say that you had the permission of Lord Dalhousie for the publication of the pamphlet, and for the use of official papers, I cannot suppose that you mean to intimate more than that Lord Dalhousie gave you permission to use official documents in replying to the 'Calcutta Review.' The pamphlet in question relates in great part to transactions in respect of which no observations touching your conduct had been made in the 'Calcutta Review;' and not only is it not professedly yours, but it contains passages calculated to impress the reader with the belief that the work, whoever was its author, could not have been written by yourself. Thus at p. 7 it says—'Our immediate business, however, is with the measures pursued by Captain (now Lieutenant-Colonel) Campbell, and their results. And with the mass of evidence before us, to which we would now respectfully direct the attention of our readers, we cannot hesitate to affirm that to *him* belongs the credit of having laid the foundation of successful operations in the Goomsur Maliahs,' &c. And at p. 61—'For a succinct account of Captain (now Lieutenant-Colonel) Campbell's labours among the Khonds of Goomsur, we would refer our readers to the clear and satisfactory statement which he gave in to Mr. Commissioner Grant. This document well deserves a careful perusal.' In each of these passages a judgment professedly coming from a different quarter is delivered in favour of Lieutenant-Colonel Campbell. No reader could feel at liberty to suppose that the object of these commendations was himself the giver. I understand you to intimate that you transmitted your pamphlet to the Court of Directors, and that the Court stated in reply to your communication that it disapproved of officers noticing anonymous reflections on their official conduct, and that you ought to have rested satisfied with the approval of your superiors. I also gather from your letter that the Court expressed these opinions without adverting to the fact that your pamphlet was itself anonymous, and was full of reflections upon the official conduct of others (which conduct was at that moment passing under the review of the Court), and without noticing the delusive passages to which I have referred. That this should have been so does appear to me so extraordinary, that I cannot but suppose that the matter needs some explanation, or some additional statement, to place it with sufficient clearness before the mind of the reader. On the publication of the pamphlet, Mr. Cadenhead, late Principal Assistant in the Hill-Tracts of Orissa, applied to the Government of Bengal for leave to reply to its misstatements. That permission was refused; and the refusal was confirmed, on appeal, by the Government of India, which (according to the recollection of a person who saw the correspondence) assigned as the ground of its decision, that Mr. Cadenhead's re-employment in the Political Department (whence he had, in common with Major Macpherson and the whole Hill Agency, been removed upon charges made by General[1] ——) was itself a sufficient refutation of anonymous accusations.[2] Major Macpherson, in a memorandum which, upon his return to India in 1853, he submitted to Lord Dalhousie, represented that immediately upon his leaving India his character (recently cleared of the charges of General —— by a solemn decision of the Government) had been assailed anew in an anonymous pamphlet (meaning the pamphlet of which you have avowed yourself the author), having the colour of support from official papers, and reproducing against him the exploded accusations of General —— as if they had never been adjudicated upon, mingled with aspersions as groundless as those; and that this pamphlet had been industriously circulated in India and in England. ‘Confiding,’ he added, ‘that the ultimate vindication of my character is safe with the Government which I have served, and believing that I shall best meet their views by abstaining from doing anything to keep alive the controversy on Khond affairs, to which I never contributed a single line, and which, in its origin and spirit, cannot but be regarded as discreditable to humanity, I have

[1] The officer designated as General —— is the Brigadier-General who made the charges against the Agency in 1847.

[2] The Editor of these Memorials has been informed, since the date of this correspondence, that Mr. Cadenhead's application was not for leave to answer the pamphlet, but for protection by the Government against such attacks from a quarter apparently official, and that the reply was that Mr. Cadenhead had not made out a case for the interference of the Government. This probably meant that, the pamphlet being anonymous, the Government could not assume that it emanated from an official source.

remained silent.' The Government justified his confidence by employing him in offices of honour and difficulty in which he was enabled to render eminent service to the State; and the controversy seemed to have passed into oblivion. But since his death you have come forward to assail his memory. For the sake of his reputation, and of the reputation of his colleagues— Mr. Cadenhead and Major Pinkney, C.B.—who have like him descended into the grave, honoured and lamented, I desired to see your 'Narrative.' I find in it a series of statements, to which might well be applied the language used by yourself with reference to articles in the 'Calcutta Review,' well known to have been written by a man of the highest character, the Reverend Dr. Duff. But I will not now examine your assertions in detail, for I observe in the work an omission which, added to the facts already noticed, appears to me to render further comment useless. At p. 58 you cite and adopt a portion of a report written by General ——, whose name I regret to see introduced by you into this controversy, as I have little doubt that his mistakes arose mainly from his being less conversant with civil duties than with those of his own profession. In the passage cited, Major Macpherson and his whole Agency are charged with very serious offences. What will your readers think when they learn the fact which you have withheld from them—that these charges have been refuted—that Major Macpherson and his colleagues demanded an enquiry into their truth—and that after a protracted investigation, conducted by one of the most distinguished public servants in India, Mr. (now Sir John) Grant, every one of the accusations which you have seen fit to reprint as if they stood uncontradicted, was pronounced by Mr. Grant, by the Government of India, and by the Court of Directors, to have been quite undeserved? Having noticed this grave suppression, I hold myself discharged from the duty of remarking further upon your 'Narrative.' But I cannot help adding that if your 'modest appreciation of your own success' is the correct appreciation, it is strange that persons so well acquainted with Indian affairs as Dr. Duff and Mr. Kaye (see Kaye's 'History of the Administration of the East India Company,' second edition, page 493) should have attributed mainly to Major Macpherson's exertions the progress which had been made in the suppression of human sacrifices; and that they should be supported in this opinion by the authority of the

India House, which, long after the close of your service in
Orissa, dealt with the subject, as you will see by the following
extracts from a ' Memorandum (prepared at the India House)
of the Improvement of the Administration of India during the
last Thirty Years ' (ordered by the House of Commons to be
printed 12th February 1858)[1]. . . . .

Lord Canning too, upon Major Macpherson's death, directed
the Secretary to the Government of India to address to the
Governor-General's Agent for Central India a letter, in which
the following passage occurs :—

' Major Macpherson's services in the Political Department
through a long course of years, especially the part he took in the
suppression of human sacrifice and female infanticide among
the Khonds, have gained for him a high place in the long list of
distinguished officers who have adorned the Indian Service, and
entitle him to the lasting gratitude of the Government and
people of India.'

I need not add that I consider myself at liberty to give
publicity to the correspondence which has passed between us.

I am, Sir, your obedient servant,

WILLIAM MACPHERSON.

Major-General John Campbell, C.B.

General Campbell to the Editor of the 'Edinburgh Courant.'

29 Old Burlington Street, London, W. :[2]
April 7, 1863.

Sir,—I observe that you have published in your paper of the
4th inst. a correspondence which has passed between Mr.
Macpherson and myself, and I have to request that you will
favour me with space for a few brief observations.

I most indignantly repel the insinuation contained in the
following passage in Mr. Macpherson's letter :—' As both your
works relate to the delicate subject of the comparative merits
of yourself and Major Macpherson, and abound in strictures

---

[1] The extracts are here omitted, because they have been printed at p. 282
of the present work.

upon his conduct, it is remarkable that the pamphlet which was published does not bear your name, while the "Narrative" which does bear your name has not been published.'

Of the 'pamphlet' commented upon by Mr. Macpherson—apart from the official letters and papers it contains—*I did not write a line,* nor did I *know anything of the contents* of the pamphlet *until after its publication;* but it was well known that I was responsible for it, and that I courted, nay challenged, refutation—if that were possible—of the facts stated therein.

I stand fast by the truth of every statement contained in my 'Narrative;' and although it was only written for my family and friends, I may now think it right to make it public, as has frequently been suggested to me.

It was not necessary to drag the names of Dr. Cadenhead and Major Pinkney into this discussion as has been done. The latter gentleman has not been named by me, and the former only with respect; neither is Major Macpherson's success in another sphere of duty questioned.

This bitter controversy was simply a personal matter between Major Macpherson and myself as to whom belonged the chief merit of the suppression of human sacrifice in Goomsur; for at that period—with the exception of Boad—the other districts afterwards operated upon by me had not been entered, and the origin of the dispute will appear in the following extracts from a letter, quoted from the 'pamphlet,' which in 1847 I addressed to a high official, through whom it passed to Major Macpherson, then not many miles from my camp, in reply, as will be seen, to statements made by him :—

Para. 23. 'I here assert that, aided by the intrepid old chief Sam Bissye Bahadur Bukshi, *I* put an end to the public performance of the Meriah sacrifice among the Khonds of Goomsur, and that up to the end of 1841, when I last visited them, the cruel rite had not been publicly performed.' [See above, p. 156.—Ed. Mem.]

Para. 30. 'If Captain Macpherson had refrained from attempting to exalt his own reputation at the expense of mine, and if he had confined himself to the vindication of his own policy without nullifying my past and present measures, I would have remained silent, and in silence suffered the obloquy that has for years been cast upon my honest endeavours to pave the way for the ultimate extinction of a revolting rite. But

Captain Macpherson has thought good, officially, to announce to you my entire "failure" in the Meriah cause. In public journals I have often read similar statements, but I have passed them by unnoticed; the intimation publicly communicated to you cannot be treated in like manner, and I will hope that in this recorded intimation of my "failure and his success," submitted to you by Captain Macpherson, you will discern both the cause and the apology for whatever of egotism may belong to this paper.'

I may observe that I feel confident the historian whose name is mentioned by Mr. Macpherson will yet be satisfied that he has—unintentionally I doubt not—done me some injustice.

I remain, &c.,

J. CAMPBELL.